Seaforth
WORLDNAVALREVIEW
2023

Seaforth

WORLD NAVAL REVIEW

2023

Editor
CONRAD WATERS

Naval Institute Press
Annapolis, Maryland

Frontispiece: The US Navy's *Nimitz* class carrier *Carl Vinson* (CVN-70) photographed in August 2021 in the course of 'landing on' a F-35C Lightning II strike fighter. She was the first US navy aircraft carrier to deploy with the new aircraft embarked as part of her air wing. *(US Navy)*

First published in Great Britain in 2022 by
Seaforth Publishing
An imprint of Pen & Sword Books Ltd
47 Church Street, Barnsley
S Yorkshire S70 2AS

www.seaforthpublishing.com
Email info@seaforthpublishing.com

Published and distributed in the United States of America and Canada by the Naval Institute Press,
291 Wood Road, Annapolis, Maryland 21402-5043
www.nip.org

ISBN 978 1 68247 872 1

Typeset and designed by Stephen Dent
Printed and bound in India by Replika Press Pvt. Ltd.

CONTENTS

Note on Tables: Tables are provided to give a broad indication of fleet sizes and other key information but should be regarded only as a general guide. For example, many published sources differ significantly on the principal particulars of ships, whilst even governmental information can be subject to contradiction. In general terms, the data contained in these tables is based on official information updated as of June 2022, supplemented by reference to a wide range of secondary and corporate sources, such as shipbuilder websites. The editor has also taken the decision from this edition to reference displacement in metric tonnes as this is increasingly the international standard used. Given that the figures used are rounded, the practical impact has been minimal in most cases.

1.1 OVERVIEW

INTRODUCTION

Author:
Conrad Waters

'I am more afraid of our own mistakes than of our enemies' designs', wrote the Greek statesman Pericles (495–429BC), the leading citizen of Athens through much of its Golden Age. This statement has broad relevance as the European mainland comes to terms with the shock of its first all-out, state-against-state war following the commencement of Russia's 'special military operation' against Ukraine on 24 February 2022. Certainly, initiation of the conflict looks to have been the result of a massive miscalculation on the part of President Vladimir Putin's autocratic regime, underestimating the strength of Ukrainian resistance whilst overestimating the capabilities of Russia's supposedly modernised armed forces. At the time of writing, the likely ultimate conclusion of hostilities is impossible to predict as intense fighting enters its fifth month. Nevertheless, it seems that the Russian military will be significantly weakened for years to come as it attempts to make good the war's huge materiel losses against the backdrop of an economy weakened by 'Western' financial sanctions.

From a naval perspective, the high profile loss of the lead Project 1164 class cruiser *Moskva* – flagship of Russia's Black Sea Fleet – on 13/14 April 2022 has served to highlight limitations in the Russian Navy's operational capabilities. The first major warship to be lost during combat activities since the 1982 Falklands War, lessons learned from her destruction will doubtless be subject to exhaustive analysis by navies around the world. Whilst somewhat secondary to the main land battles, operations in the Black Sea have shed light on many current aspects of maritime thinking. These include the effectiveness of anti-access/area-denial (A2/AD) strategies; the relevance of amphibious warfare; and the utility of unmanned systems, particularly of aerial drones. Some of these aspects are considered in James Bosbotinis' analysis of the early naval stages of the war that follows this introduction.

Whilst the Russo-Ukrainian War has seemingly exposed Russian errors, the West's recent decision-making does not come off scot-free. Last year's *World Naval Review* highlighted the incongruities inherent in the US Biden administration's confirmation of previous plans to withdraw from Afghanistan; a decision taken without full consultation with its partners in the near 20 year-long venture. The result was the rapid collapse of the previously US-supported regime in August 2021 in events that have drawn comparison with the 1975 fall of South Vietnam. The considerable investment of lives and treasure made in sustaining the two decades-long war – that involved significant use of naval aviation and marines despite its land-locked nature – was written off as part of the strategic re-alignment to refocus stretched US capabilities against the growing threats from Russia and, particularly, China. Whilst this prioritisation of resources is certainly logical, it is reasonable to speculate that the Afghan debacle served to embolden the adventurism being displayed by these near-peer competitors. Indeed, some have argued that the cracks in NATO solidarity exposed by the Afghan collapse encouraged President Putin's Ukraine invasion.[1]

The Project 1164 Russian cruiser *Marshal Ustinov*, sister ship of the ill-fated *Moskva*, transits the Bosphorus in January 2020. The performance of Russia's Black Sea Fleet during the current Russo-Ukrainian War has revealed a number of deficiencies. *(Devrim Yaylali)*

DEFENCE PLANS AND BUDGETS
The future direction of US military strategy under

The Royal Australian Navy is looking to acquire nuclear-powered submarines following announcement of the AUKUS pact. Here the existing *Collins* class submarine *Rankin* – one of the boats that the new submarines will replace – is seen exercising with the Indian Navy Project 28 corvette *Kadmatt* in September 2021 during the AUSINDEX 21 serials. *(Royal Australian Navy)*

President Biden heralded by the withdrawal from Afghanistan has been given firmer shape with the conclusion of a Global Posture Review towards the end of November 2021 and the transmission of a new 2022 National Defense Strategy (NDS) to Congress on 28 March 2022. Only edited highlights of these classified documents have been released to date. However, the 'Pivot to the Pacific' initiated by President Obama is a continuing theme, with the NDS calling out China '… as our most consequential strategic competitor and the pacing challenge …' for the US Department of Defense. In spite of the Ukraine invasion, Russia is accorded a secondary role as an 'acute threat', over and above the 'persistent threats' from Iran, North Korea and other extremist organisations.[2] The Global Posture Review provides some limited insights into what this strategy means in practice, including the enhancement of infrastructure in both Australia and the Pacific Islands to deter potential Chinese aggression. More generally, Australia seems to becoming more pivotal to US strategy in the Pacific. This trend was evidenced by the announcement of the AUKUS trilateral security partnership – also encompassing the United Kingdom – in September 2021. This alliance, which was accompanied by an Australian decision to commence a nuclear-powered attack submarine programme, is discussed in more detail in Chapter 2.2.

A major determinant of the American realignment of military priorities will be the availability of sufficient cash to make the necessary force adjustments. These are also challenges faced by the broader alliance of Western democracies as they adjust to new geopolitical realities. The latest data on international defence spending published by the independent Stockholm International Peace Research Institute (SIPRI) in April 2022 covers the year to December 2021. It is thus unable to take account of the most recent developments. Nevertheless, the data contained in Table 1.1.1 largely reflects the recent upward trajectory of defence spending that has reversed the previous sustained decline in the so-called 'world military burden'. The percentage of

Table 1.1.1: COUNTRIES WITH HIGH NATIONAL DEFENCE EXPENDITURES: 2021

RANK 2021 (2020)		COUNTRY	TOTAL US$BN 2021[1]	SHARE OF GDP 2021	WORLD SHARE 2021	TOTAL US$BN 2020[1]	REAL CHANGE 2020–2021[2]	REAL CHANGE 2012–2021[2]
1	(1)	United States	800.6	3.5%	38%	778.4	-1.4%	-6.1%
2	(2)	China	[293.4]	[1.7%]	[14%]	[258.0]	[4.7%]	[72%]
3	(3)	India	76.6	2.7%	3.6%	72.9	0.9%	33%
4	(6)	United Kingdom	68.4	2.2%	3.2%	60.7	3.0%	3.7%
5	(5)	Russia	65.9	4.1%	3.1%	61.7	2.9%	11%
6	(8)	France	56.6	1.9%	2.7%	52.7	1.5%	13%
7	(7)	Germany	56.0	1.3%	2.7%	53.2	-1.4%	24%
8	(4)	Saudi Arabia	[55.6]	[6.6%]	[2.6%]	[64.6]	[-17%]	[-15%]
9	(9)	Japan	54.1	1.1%	2.6%	52.0	7.3%	18%
10	(10)	South Korea	50.2	2.8%	2.4%	45.5	4.7%	43%
-	(-)	**World Total**	**2113**	**2.2%**	**100%**	**1992**	**0.7%**	**12%**

Information from the Stockholm International Peace Research Institute (SIPRI) – https://www.sipri.org/databases/milex
The SIPRI Military Expenditure Database contains data on countries over the period 1949-2021

Notes:
1. US$ totals for 2021 and 2020 are based on then current (i.e. non-inflation adjusted) prices and exchange rates for the years in question. Exchange rate movements, in particular, can therefore result in significant movements in the US$ figures and explain apparent discrepancies in the table. SIPRI also adjusts previous-year calculations when more accurate data becomes available – this has resulted in several material differences from the 2020 total figures contained in last year's *Seaforth World Naval Review*, impacting the prior year rankings of several countries.
2. The 'real' change figure is based on constant (2020-based) US$ figures.
3. Figures in brackets are SIPRI estimates.

TABLE 1.2: MAJOR FLEET STRENGTHS 2021-2022[1]

REGION	THE AMERICAS				EUROPE & RUSSIA										ASIA								IND. OCEAN	
COUNTRY	USA		BRAZIL		UK		FRANCE		ITALY		SPAIN		RUSSIA		CHINA		JAPAN		KOREA(S)		AUSTRALIA		INDIA	
	2021	2022	2021	2022	2021	2022	2021	2022	2021	2022	2021	2022	2021	2022	2021	2022	2021	2022	2021	2022	2021	2022	2021	2022
Carriers & Amphibious																								
CV/CVN	11	11	–	–	2	2	1	1	1	1	–	–	1	1	2	2	–	–	–	–	–	–	1	1
CVS/CVH	–	–	–	–	–	–	–	–	1	1	–	–	–	–	–	–	4	4	–	–	–	–	–	–
LHA/LHD/LPH	9	9	1	1	–	–	3	3	–	–	1	1	–	–	1	2	–	–	2	2	2	2	–	–
LPD/LSD	22	23	1	1	5	5	–	–	3	3	2	2	–	–	8	8	3	3	–	–	1	1	1	1
Submarines																								
SSBN	14	14	–	–	4	4	4	4	–	–	–	–	12	12	7	7	–	–	–	–	–	–	1	1
SSN/SSGN	54	54	–	–	6	5	6	6	–	–	–	–	25	25	9	9	–	–	–	–	–	–	–	–
SSK	–	–	5	5	–	–	–	–	8	8	2	2	20	20	50	50	21	22	18	19	6	6	15	16
Surface Combatants																								
BB/BC	–	–	–	–	–	–	–	–	–	–	–	–	2	2	–	–	–	–	–	–	–	–	–	–
CG/DDG/FFG	93	94	7	6	18	18	15	14	15	16	11	11	35	35	80	90	36	38	24	24	11	11	22	22
DD/FGS/FS	24	24	2	2	–	–	12	12	–	–	–	–	45	45	75	75	6	6	10	7	–	–	12	11
FAC[2]	–	–	–	–	–	–	–	–	–	–	–	–	30	30	75	75	6	6	18	18	–	–	8	7
Other (Selected)																								
MCMV	8	8	3	3	13	11	13	13	10	10	6	6	40	40	25	25	20	20	9	10	4	4	–	–
AO/AOR/AFS	31	31	1	1	7	7	2	2	4	4	2	2	20	20	12	12	5	5	3	3	1	2	4	4

Notes

1 Numbers are based on official sources, where available, supplemented by news reports, published intelligence data and other 'open sources' as appropriate. Given significant variations in available data, numbers should be regarded as indicative, particularly with respect to Russia, China and minor warship categories (which are sometimes rounded). There is also a degree of subjectivity with respect to warship classifications given varying national classifications and this can also lead to inconsistency.

2 FAC numbers relate to ships fitted with or for surface-to-surface missiles.

global GDP allocated to military disbursements actually fell marginally to 2.2 percent due to the impact of the strong rebound from the initial stages of the COVID-19 pandemic on economic output. However, total world defence expenditure exceeded US$2 trillion for the first time. Moreover, real terms spending increased in seven of the ten countries with the highest military budgets, with Japan, China and South Korea heading the charge. China's defence spending is estimated to have expanded by as much as 72 percent in real terms over the last decade, funded largely by its strong economic performance. By contrast, US military expenditure has fallen by six percent over the same period. These simple facts

The *Freedom* (LCS-1) variant Littoral Combat Ship *Milwaukee* (LCS-5) makes her sideways launch into the Menominee River in Marinette, Wisconsin after being christened on 18 December 2013. The US Navy is looking to decommission these almost brand-new vessels as it seemingly loses faith in the Littoral Combat Ship concept. (Lockheed Martin)

reflect the real challenge America faces in maintaining its longstanding Pacific hegemony in the face of the developing Asian nations sustained economic outperformance.

The West's overly-hasty declaration of a peace dividend at the end of the Cold War is another arguable mistake that is now coming home to roost and something of a scramble is developing to make good long-standing military deficiencies. The most notable example of this has been German Chancellor Olaf Scholz's pledge to meet NATO's longstanding target that two percent of national economic output– as measured by gross domestic product (GDP) – should be devoted to defence spending, an aim that will be supported by a special fund of €100bn (c. US$100bn) to be spent on military procurement. The question is whether the industrial capacity exists to support this largesse.[3] The German naval shipbuilding sector is already adjusting its plans to accommodate the likely increase in orders. In early June 2022, ThyssenKrupp Marine Systems (tkMS) announced the purchase of the defunct MV Werften shipyard in Wismar – previously focused on building cruise liners – with a view to expanding its submarine-building facilities.

The Vietnam People's Navy frigate *Lý Thái Tổ* is one of a quartet of Project 11661E 'Gepard' class light frigates acquired from Russia as part of a major programme of fleet modernisation. *(Arjun Sarup)*

FLEET REVIEWS

The long-term impact of changes in the world economic balance continues to be reflected in Table 1.1.2, which summarises the current strengths of the world's major fleets. Although the traditional Western naval powers have generally stabilised numbers after the long period of significant decline that typified the post-Cold War era, any recovery will be slow. Instead, the pendulum of naval might is seemingly shifting decisively to the Asia-Pacific region. Here ongoing quantitative and qualitative improvements appear to be marching hand-in-hand. Notable developments in the last year have included the launch of China's first catapult-equipped aircraft carrier, *Fujian*, on 17 June 2022 and the commencement of sea trials by India's first indigenously-built carrier, *Vikrant*, during the previous August. It also appears that nuclear-powered submarines – until now the preserve of a mere handful of nations – are set to play an increasing part in the Asia-Pacific balance of naval power. In May 2022, South Korea's new president, Yoon Suk-yeol, and President Biden announced that the two countries would collaborate, inter alia, in developing a new generation of

small modular reactors. This agreement will provide the Republic of Korea with a key nuclear-powered submarine capability, holding out the prospect that the country will soon join Australia in seeking membership of this exclusive club.[4]

Although financial factors go far in explaining the relative decline of the traditional Western fleets, some of the damage is seemingly self-inflicted. Nowhere is this more apparent than with the US Navy. Amongst a number of questionable measures, the latest, FY2023, Department of the Navy Presidential Budget Request proposes the accelerated decommissioning of a number of warships; a move seemingly at odds with long term aspirations to grow the fleet. Amongst vessels recommended for early retirement were all the *Freedom* (LCS-1) variant Littoral Combat Ships in service at the time of the announcement, some less than two years old. The plan to retire such modern vessels seems to run counter to the new Distributed Maritime Operations (DMO) concept – that essentially calls for greater numbers of dispersed but digitally-connected vessels to fight the next Pacific War – and reflects a continued US Navy struggle to define an

optimal future fleet structure. In our opening fleet review, Sidney E. Dean explores some of the factors influencing US Navy force development, as well as current fleet composition, as the service attempts to adapt to a changing strategic environment.

A previous adversary of the US Navy – but one now also being forced to adapt to Chinese 'expansionism' – is the Vietnam's People's Navy. In his latest review of Asian fleets, Mrityunjoy Mazumdar examines the substantial progress that the navy has made with its 'march to modernity' over the past decade, most notably the induction of a new submarine flotilla. He also highlights the challenges faced by a force that will have to overcome significant ideological constraints, as well as a longstanding over-reliance on Russian equipment, as it attempts to complete its wholesale transformation.

SIGNIFICANT SHIPS

Although the US Navy's relative power is waning, it continues to deploy balanced blue water capabilities that are globally second-to-none. Despite the shift towards DMO, it is carrier-based airpower that remains at the core of its potency. March 2022 marked the 100th anniversary of the commissioning of the US Navy's first aircraft carrier – *Langley* (CV-1) – after her conversion from a former collier. For nearly half of the following century, it has been the *Nimitz* (CVN-68) design that has been integral to the fleet's carrier force, with the lead vessel of the ten-ship class being launched on 13 May 1972. Norman Friedman's chapter assesses the factors behind the longevity of the design, noting the various incremental improvements incorporated during a construction phase that extended from the initial order for *Nimitz* in March 1967 to the delivery of the final vessel, *George H. W. Bush* (CVN-77), in May 2009. Whilst his analysis focuses on the design of the ships themselves, he makes the important point that the modularity inherent in their evolving air groups has been an important factor in their continued relevance. *World Naval Review* intends to explore this subject further at a later date.

At the other end of the size-scale to the *Nimitz* class carriers are the British Royal Navy's diminutive *Cutlass* class patrol boats. Constructed by Liverpool-based MST Group to a BMT-developed HPB-1900 design, the two high-speed craft have been ordered to undertake constabulary missions in the waters off the British Overseas Territory of Gibraltar. The editor's review highlights the innovative features of a successful design that has brought warship-building back to the banks of the River Mersey. Another, HPB-1500, variant of the series has already been selected for an eighteen-strong flotilla of high-speed patrol craft to support Ministry of Defence maritime policing activities.

Another interesting and innovative design is the Royal New Zealand Navy's Polar sustainment vessel, *Aotearoa*. The largest warship ever commissioned for New Zealand service, she was built by South Korea's Hyundai Heavy Industries to a Rolls-Royce 'Environship' Leadge Bow concept.[5] Guy Toremans' article provides a detailed insight into the new ship, which is also unusual in incorporating a package of 'winterisation' measures to allow her deployment on resupply missions to New Zealand's Antarctic Scott Base. Whilst *Aotearoa* was designed to meet a relatively unique set of operational requirements driven by New Zealand's geographic position, the growing focus on Arctic operations may well make the ship of more than passing interest to a number of fleets in the northern hemisphere.

TECHNOLOGICAL DEVELOPMENTS

As always, our final section – on technological developments – commences with David Hobbs' annual review of world naval aviation. Inevitably, a major area of focus is a review of the Royal Navy's Carrier Strike Group 2021 (CSG 21) deployment to the Asia Pacific region. As well as demonstrating the United Kingdom's renewed ability to deploy naval power at distance, the mission was also noteworthy in the degree of integration it achieved between allied naval assets. This is becoming an increasingly common theme of Western naval activity, going some way to counter the rising 'strategic competitor' challenges already referenced.

One technological area where the West's capabilities seemingly lag those of its rivals is the field of hypersonic missiles, a weapon system that has seen its first significant operational use in the Russo-Ukrainian war. Norman Friedman's second contribution to this edition explains the technology used in these systems, describing both its strengths and weaknesses. He also analyses the main Russian and Chinese hypersonic missile programmes, as well as the increasing efforts being made by the United States in this sphere.

Richard Scott's concluding chapter returns to the Royal Navy to illustrate the various strands of developmental work that are underway across many of the world's leading fleets to create the navies that will serve in a generation or more from now. Some of these technologies – such as the use of unmanned and, increasingly, autonomous vehicles, as well as the emphasis on modular systems – are already making themselves felt. Others, such as a growing focus on exploiting the potential of artificial intelligence, are far less in the public eye.

SUMMARY

The last year has seen the seemingly diminishing impact of the COVID-19 pandemic replaced by the new scourge of major state-on-state conflict. To this editor, events in Ukraine seem to mark a major turning point in the geopolitical backdrop that ultimately drives naval developments. Whilst growing assertiveness by the so-called revisionist powers has previously been seen as a potential threat to the global democratic world order, their activities have previously been largely conducted in the grey area that exists between legitimate behaviour and out-and-out conflict.[6] President Putin's Ukrainian invasion has crossed this line and the consequences will be far-reaching.

From a purely naval perspective, a new period of investment seems likely as 'hard' warfighting capabilities are prioritised over 'soft' lower-intensity

The Royal New Zealand Navy's new Polar replenishment vessel, *Aotearoa,* pictured during the course of replenishment evolutions with the US Navy Littoral Combat Ship *Charleston* (LCS-18) in September 2021. *Aotearoa* is the largest vessel ever commissioned into New Zealand's fleet. *(US Navy)*

policing configurations. Navies – particularly in Europe – are likely to revert to a structure that more closely resembles that abandoned after the Cold War's end. Investments in new technological solutions will likely intensify. The ongoing ability of navies to adapt to changing circumstances will be demonstrated yet again.

ACKNOWLEDGEMENTS

As always, *Seaforth World Naval Review*'s ongoing survival owes much to a production team headed by publisher Rob Gardiner, designer Stephen Dent and proof reader Stephen Chumbley. The annual also continues to benefit from the clear and accurate drawings produced by John Jordan and from the contributions of a first-rate group of authors. Amongst the ongoing support provided by navies and industry, this year's outstanding assistance from Scott Sargentina, Public Affairs Manager, Royal New Zealand Navy warrants special mention. The editor would also like to thank Lorenz Amiet, Derek Fox, Bruno Huriet, Tetsuya Kakitani, Michael Leake, Bernard Prézelin, Arjun Sarup, Chris Sattler and Devrim Yaylali for use of their excellent photographs. The assistance of my wife, Susan, in proof reading the initial drafts of the text continues to exceed the bounds of spousal duty.

The editor continues to value the feedback provided by readers through various channels. Whilst not all suggestions can be implemented, every comment and criticism is carefully considered. The editor can also be contacted by email marked for his attention via: info@seaforthpublishing.com

From left to right, the Royal Fleet Auxiliary replenishment oiler *Fort Victoria*, the Royal Navy aircraft carrier *Queen Elizabeth* and the US Navy destroyer *The Sullivans* (DDG-68) transit the Suez Canal in June 2021 during the course of the CSG 21 deployment. The mission was noteworthy for the level of integration achieved between its various national participants, including US Marine Corps F-35B Lightning II strike fighters embarked aboard the British carrier. *(Crown Copyright 2021)*

Finally, I would like to close by acknowledging the contribution of my late mother, Mary Madeleine Waters (28.02.1926–10.04.2022) to the creation of the *World Naval Review* series. Descended herself from a seafaring family, her encouragement of my childhood interest in ships and shipping was a key factor in my decision to write my own naval articles. *World Naval Review* would never have existed without her influence.

Conrad Waters, Editor
30 June 2022

Notes

1. See for example, 'Afghanistan debacle played role in Putin's Ukraine decision, general says' posted to the conservative-leaning *Washington Examiner* website – washingtonexaminer.com – on 31 March 2022. The article reported comments made by General Tod Wolters, Supreme Allied Commander for Europe, to a hearing of the US House of Representatives' Armed Services Committee.

2. Information on the Global Posture Review and new NDS was provided in two press releases – 'Biden Approves Global Posture Review Recommendations' and 'DoD Transmits 2022 National Defense Strategy', the latter accompanied by a two-page fact sheet – posted to the US Department of Defense website at defense.gov/News/Releases – on 29 November 2021 and 28 March 2022 respectively. In an interesting article, 'The next National Defense Strategy is coming. These seven points are key to

understanding it' posted to the *Atlantic Council* think tank's blog site – atlanticcouncil.org/blogs/ – on 20 April 2022, the NSD was described as adopting a 1 (China) + 1 (Russia) +3 (Iran, North Korea & extremist organisations) construct to prioritise the threats America must deal with. Whilst these threats are unchanged from previous documents, the 2022 NDS makes the ranking more explicit.

3. A good description of some of the pitfalls facing Chancellor Scholz's proposals was provided by Alexandra Marksteiner in 'Explainer: The proposed hike in German military spending' posted to SIPRI's website on 25 March 2022.

4. For further information on the significance of the US-Republic of Korea deal, see Juho Lee's 'U.S. And South

Korean Cooperation On Nuclear Technology Positive Sign For K-SSN' posted to the *Naval News* website – navalnews.com – on 1 June 2022.

5. Following the sale of much of Rolls-Royce's marine business, the Environship portfolio was subsequently transferred to Norway's Kongsberg Maritime business division.

6. A revisionist power is one that seeks to change the current international world order and replace it with a system that, it believes, will work more to its advantage. It has been commonly applied to nations such as China and Russia that wish to replace a post-Second World War construct based on the concept of liberal democracy with a more autocratic world.

NAVAL ASPECTS OF THE RUSSO–UKRAINIAN WAR

An Initial Assessment

Author:
James Bosbotinis

The Russian invasion of Ukraine marks a turning point for the international system and development of global order. At the grand strategic level, it highlights the gulf between Russian ambition and actual capabilities, whilst confirming the emergence of a bipolar order centred on the United States and China. It has also reinvigorated the West, most vividly illustrated by the decisions by Sweden and Finland to apply for NATO membership. As distinguished naval historian Geoffrey Till states, '… the Russians have committed a monumental blunder from which it will take them years to recover, both militarily and politically'.[1]

In naval terms, the war has highlighted the Russian Navy's modernisation efforts, particularly the development of a long-range precision strike capability with the 3M14 'Kalibr' (SS-N-30A 'Sagaris') missile variant. However, it has also dramatically brought to the fore its enduring and deep-seated weaknesses, demonstrated by the sinking of the Black Sea Fleet's flagship *Moskva*. In this context, Ukraine's ability to hold at risk Russian naval forces illustrates the threat posed by coastal defence systems in the littoral. However, the impact of the Russian de facto blockade, both on Ukraine and on the global food supply system, poses substantial dangers.

THE RUSSIAN INVASION OF UKRAINE IN CONTEXT

Russia's invasion of Ukraine constitutes the culmination of Moscow's challenge to international order. President Putin's February 2007 Munich Speech critical of NATO expansion, the invasion of Georgia in 2008, the 2014 occupation of Crimea and initial assault on Ukraine, the 2015 intervention in Syria, the use of chemical weapons for attempted assassinations in the United Kingdom, and calls for a new European security architecture highlight more than 15 years of growing Russian belligerence and neo-imperial ambition. The subjugation of Ukraine is central to Russia's vision of 'greatness'. As political scientist Pavel Baev explained in 2008, 'The unstructured mix of ideas about common history,

The Project 1164 'Slava' class cruiser *Moskva* pictured transiting the Bosphorus in January 2016. The loss of the cruiser – flagship of Russia's Black Sea Fleet – in April 2022 is widely regarded as a defining moment in the naval campaign that has accompanied Russia's 2022 invasion of Ukraine. *(Devrim Yaylali)*

perceptions of cultural closeness, assessments of intensity of multiple ties, and worries about geopolitical risks, has boiled down to a broad consensus in Moscow elites that Russia could only re-establish its "Greatness" by making sure that Ukraine remains in its sphere of prevailing influence'.[2]

The scale of Russian ambition underpinning its invasion of Ukraine was detailed in a leaked 'victory article', proclaiming the 'reunification of Russia, Belarus and Ukraine', and the defeat of 'Western global domination'.[3] Guided by its desire for recognition as a great power, Russia has – over the past decade – sought the comprehensive modernisation of its armed forces and the development of new thinking for their employment. However, as demonstrated in Ukraine, Russian operational performance does not reflect well on this investment and has exposed deep flaws in Russia's armed forces.

For the Russian Navy, it is the policy document, *The Fundamentals of the State Policy of the Russian Federation in the Field of Naval Operations in the Period Until 2030*, promulgated in 2017, that highlights Russia's ambition. It declares that 'The Russian Federation will not allow significant superiority of naval forces of other states over its Navy and will strive to secure its position as the second most combat capable Navy in the world', while describing itself as a 'great land and sea power'.[4] Throughout the course of its military build-up from late 2021 and 'diplomatic efforts' to 'negotiate' new security treaties with the US and NATO, the Russian Navy engaged in a series of high-profile naval exercises and deployments in line with this aspiration. Most notably, on 20 January 2022, the Russian Ministry of Defence announced that 140-plus ships, submarines and support vessels would undertake a series of exercises in January and February in waters around Russia and in the North Atlantic, Mediterranean, Sea of Okhotsk and the Pacific. Whilst demonstrating Russia's naval presence and pretensions of great maritime power status, the exercises also served as cover for the deployment of significant naval forces to the Mediterranean and the Black Sea.

THE ROLE OF THE NAVY IN RUSSIA'S INVASION

Throughout the course of the Russo-Ukrainian War, the Russian Navy has conducted operations that are broadly consistent with its publicly-stated roles.[5] That is, in the event of hostilities, its key tasks are:

The Russian Navy has seen significant investment in the last decade as part of attempts to reassert Russia's role as a great sea power. This picture shows the Project 11356R *Admiral Grigorovich* class frigate *Admiral Makarov* during her voyage to reinforce Russia's Black Sea Fleet in 2018. Her ability to fire 'Kalibr' cruise missiles has been of significant value to Russian forces during the war. *(Crown Copyright 2018)*

- To destroy enemy land-based facilities at long distances.
- To ensure the sustainability of ballistic missile submarines.
- To destroy enemy anti-submarine and other forces as well as its coastal facilities.
- To maintain a favourable operational environment (i.e. sea control).
- To provide maritime support of contact troops during maritime defensive and offensive operations.
- To undertake sea coast defence.

Aside from the defence of ballistic missile submarines – a role not relevant in the Black Sea – the Russian Navy has sought to achieve these tasks, thereby performing important supporting missions in the wider Russian campaign against Ukraine. The Black Sea Fleet has enforced a de facto blockade of Ukraine, prosecuted long-range strikes utilising ship and submarine-launched 'Kalibr' land-attack cruise missiles (including as part of the opening wave of attacks), conducted amphibious operations in support of the assault on Mariupol, and undertaken naval bombardments of shore targets. Beyond the Black Sea, the Russian Navy has also maintained a significant presence in the Eastern Mediterranean to counter any potential intervention and secure Russia's southern flank.

As of 24 February 2022, the Russian Navy's operational forces in the Black Sea are believed to have included, inter alia, the Project 1164 'Atlant' ('Slava') class cruiser *Moskva*, two Project 11356R *Admiral Grigorovich* class and one Project 1135 'Burevestnik' ('Krivak I') class frigates, three Project 21631 'Buyan-M' class corvettes, and three Project 636.3 'Varshavyanka' (Improved 'Kilo') class patrol submarines. Apart from *Moskva* and the 'Krivak' class *Ladny*, all these classes are capable of being 'Kalibr' armed.

The Russian Navy also deployed an amphibious task group drawn from the Baltic and Northern Fleets to the Black Sea via the Mediterranean in February 2022 to augment the Black Sea Fleet's amphibious assets. The ships transferred included five Project 775 'Ropucha' class tank landing ships and the more modern Project 11711 *Ivan Gren* class, *Pyotr Morgunov*. Had the Russian advance from Crimea succeeded in capturing Mykolaiv and closed in on Odesa, an amphibious landing in support of land operations may have taken place, as was the case with the assault on Mariupol. In any event, it warrants noting that the presence of the Russian amphibious task group, comprising around ten landing ships in total, constituted powerful leverage. It effectively fixed in place Ukrainian forces around Odesa that otherwise could have been deployed to counter the Russian ground assault from Crimea.

Looking beyond the Black Sea, both the Northern and Pacific Fleets deployed 'Slava' class cruiser-led surface action groups – headed by the *Marshal Ustinov* and *Varyag* – that encompassed Project 1155 *Udaloy* class destroyers and the new Project 22350 *Admiral Gorshkov* class frigate *Admiral Kasatonov* to the Mediterranean. These were supplemented by a detachment of four Russian Aerospace Forces' (VKS) Tupolev Tu-22M3 'Backfire' long-range bombers and at least one 9-S-7760 'Kinzhal' hypersonic missile-armed MiG-31IK 'Foxhound' interceptor that deployed to the Khmeimim Air Base in Syria on 15 February 2022. The base was already home to Sukhoi Su-24 'Fencer', Su-34 'Fullback', and Su-35 'Flanker M' jets, as well as a battery of K-300P 'Bastion P' (SS-C-5 'Stooge') anti-ship cruise missiles. It is likely that at least one nuclear-powered attack submarine from the Northern Fleet was also dispatched to the Mediterranean.

UKRAINIAN MARITIME STRATEGY

The initial Russian invasion of Ukraine in 2014 – in particular the annexation of Crimea – had decisively shifted the naval balance of power in Moscow's favour before the latest conflict commenced. This was reflected in a recognition that 'The maritime direction has become the most vulnerable for defence of Ukraine'.[6] The impact of the Russian 2014 seizure of Crimea was, indeed, devastating for Ukraine, resulting in the loss of 'most of its Navy, including 75 percent of personnel, 70 percent of ships and key infrastructure'.

In developing maritime strategy to address this reality, Kyiv has had to confront the challenge of defending an economically critical flank – more than a quarter of the national GDP is generated by regions the economies of which are connected to the Black and the Azov Seas – whilst dealing with significant resource constraints. In this context, the *Strategy of the Naval Forces of the Armed Forces of Ukraine 2035*, published in 2019, articulated a three-stage concept for the development of the Ukrainian Navy, underpinned by a vision emphasising a 'modern, agile and innovative Navy … conducting asymmetric and decisive operations, with highly-motivated and professional personnel, who are determined to win'.[7] Moreover, the Strategy highlighted that, 'In order to defeat a stronger aggressor, the physical component should be used proactively, asymmetrically and with agility, first of all against the most vulnerable enemy's sites. This leads to the second component – conceptual. The conceptual component offers a structure of thinking, an intellectual basis for troops, provides commanders with an ability to understand a situation in a difficult environment, through creativity, resourcefulness and initiative.'

While aspiring to a sea control capability in the long term, the immediate focus for the Ukrainian Navy set out in the strategy is on the sea denial role, which 'can be achieved by conducting air defence, anti-boat and anti-submarine defence, mining and counter-mining actions, electronic warfare, missile and artillery strikes, naval landings, and special actions at sea, and on the rivers'. The development of a sea control capability was originally intended for the period 2025–35, albeit with a local capacity encompassing riverine, ports and coastal areas sought in the 2018–25 period. This period covers what the strategy defined as the first stage for naval development, with the second and third stages covering the periods 2025–30 and 2030–5 respectively. Each stage identifies first, second and third priorities for capability development. For the period 2018–25, those three priorities were, in order of importance:

The Russian Navy significantly reinforced the Black Sea Fleet's naval assets in the run-up to the 2022 Russo-Ukrainian War by passing ships drawn from the Baltic and Northern Fleets through the Bosphorus. This picture shows one of the Black Sea Fleet's existing amphibious ships – the Project 775 'Ropucha' class large landing ship *Kaliningrad* – off Istanbul in April 2021. *(Devrim Yaylali)*

■ Developing coastal zone maritime domain awareness (MDA) and associated intelligence, surveillance and reconnaissance (ISR) capabilities.

- Achieving sea denial, through coastal artillery and mining.
- Obtaining local sea control, as previously noted.

The MDA/ISR capability would be extended to Ukraine's exclusive economic zone (EEZ) under the second stage, with a sea control capability for the EEZ also sought alongside the development of a long-range maritime strike capability. Stage three envisaged a more expansive sea control capability and the acquisition of 'cruise missiles for coastal targets engagement … aimed at destruction of the enemy critical infrastructure in the event of its aggression against Ukraine'.

As of February 2022, the Ukrainian Navy operated a single Project 1135.1 'Nerey' ('Krivak III') class frigate, *Hetman Sahaidachny* (reportedly scuttled in early March) together with around twelve patrol and coastal combatants, a mine warfare vessel, an amphibious ship and various logistics vessels. Ukraine also possessed a nascent coastal defence cruise missile capability following the August 2020 adoption of the RK-360MC Neptune; at least one mobile launcher had been deployed as of February 2022 with at least six more potentially available. Ukrainian Naval Aviation operated a small number of Mil M-14 'Haze' and Kamov Ka-27/Ka-29 'Helix' anti-submarine warfare/transport helicopters, as well as the Turkish-made TB2 Bayraktar unmanned combat air vehicle (UCAV). Since the beginning of the invasion, Ukraine has begun receiving various anti-ship missile systems, including the US-manufactured Harpoon, from NATO countries. In addition, the United States has pledged to provide coastal and riverine patrol boats, as well as an unspecified number of unmanned coastal defence vessels.

THE NAVAL WAR TO DATE

From the start of hostilities on 24 February 2022, the Russian Navy has been undertaking an important role supporting Russia's military campaign. The Ukrainian Ministry of Defence reported that over thirty sea-launched 'Kalibr' cruise missiles were involved in the opening wave of attacks. At the same time, the Russian Navy also moved to attain sea control and impose a blockade on Ukraine. This included targeting naval and port facilities in and around Odesa, Ochakiv and Yuzhny, plus bases on the Sea of Azov coast. The Ukrainian Snake Island was also bombarded by the *Moskva* and the Project

The first phase of Ukraine's three-phase naval strategy envisaged, inter alia, achieving sea control of ports and coastal areas through a fleet of small vessels sometimes referred to as a 'mosquito fleet'. The Project 58155 'Gyurza-M' class armoured gunboats – *U174* is seen here – formed part of this approach. In practice, these ships did little to stem the tide of Russia's initial advance, with a number of the class reportedly falling into Russian hands. *(Ministry of Defence of Ukraine)*

The Ukrainian Navy's flagship – the Project 1135.1 'Krivak III' frigate *Hetman Sahaydachniy* – was under refit at Mykolaiv at the start of the Russo-Ukrainian War. The ship was scuttled at the end of February/early March 2022 due to the threat of capture by Russian forces. *(Ministry of Defence of Ukraine)*

Ukraine's adoption of the RK-360MC Neptune surface-to-surface missile system in August 2020 – followed by the standing-up of the first training missile battery in March 2021 – gave it an embryonic coastal missile defence capability at the start of the Russo-Ukrainian War. The system is reportedly based on the Soviet Kh-35 family of anti-ship missiles. Neptune has been credited with the destruction of the cruiser *Moskva* in April 2022. These photos were taken during a test firing of a prototype of the system in April 2019; the configuration of the operational system is different. *(Administration of the President of Ukraine)*

22160 patrol ship *Vasily Bykov*, before being seized. Merchant shipping has been subject to attack, both deliberate and inadvertent, with an Estonian cargo ship sinking off Odesa after reportedly hitting a mine in late February. Russia reportedly seized two Ukrainian merchant ships in the Black Sea, and

foreign merchant vessels have been damaged by missile attack. The Ukrainian Ministry of Foreign Affairs reported on 30 March 2022 that Russia had deliberately released Ukrainian naval mines captured in the annexation of Crimea in 2014 to drift across the Black Sea. In June 2022, the US reported that

the Russian Navy has mined the Dnieper River and been ordered to mine the approaches to the ports of Odesa and Ochakiv as part of its blockade of Ukraine.

Despite Russia's naval superiority, Ukraine has been able to hold at risk Russian naval forces, in particular those operating in close proximity to the Ukrainian coast. On 24 March 2022, this was vividly demonstrated by a Ukrainian attack on the Russian-occupied port of Berdyansk, resulting in the destruction of the Project 1171 'Tapir' ('Alligator') class tank landing ship *Saratov*. Two nearby

The Russian Project 1171 'Alligator' class large landing ship *Saratov* was an early casualty of the Russo-Ukrainian War, being destroyed on 24 March by an attack on the Russian-occupied port of Berdyansk that also damaged two Project 775 landing ships. *(Devrim Yaylali)*

'Ropucha' class landing ships also sustained damage. Ukraine may have employed an OTR-21 Tochka (SS-21 'Scarab') short-range ballistic missile for this strike, although the use of the TB2 Bayraktar drone has also been speculated.

Most notably, on 13 April 2022, Ukraine successfully employed its Neptune anti-ship cruise missile in an operation targeting the flagship of the Black Sea Fleet, the 'Slava' class cruiser *Moskva*. The loss of *Moskva* the following day constituted a significant blow to the Russian Navy and, in symbolic terms, the wider Russian war effort, especially given its role in the attack on Snake Island and Ukraine's response. It also arguably marked a turning point in

These two grainy pictures are all that are currently available in the public domain to show the devastation inflicted on the Russian cruiser *Moskva* after what is widely regarded as a Ukrainian Neptune surface-to-surface missile strike on 13 April 2022. The cruiser sank the following day. *(Russian Navy)*

The Russian Project 22870 rescue vessel *Spasatel Vasily Bekh* seen in January 2022. She was one of a number of casualties inflicted on Russian forces as they attempted to sustain an ultimately doomed presence on the strategically-located Snake Island. *(Devrim Yaylali)*

the war at sea. *Moskva* provided an important long-range air defence capability with its S-300F Fort (SA-N-6 'Grumble') surface-to-air missile system, which served to limit Ukraine's ability to employ airpower against Russian forces in the north-western Black Sea. No other Russian vessel currently in the Black Sea has an equivalent capability.[8]

From late April/early May, Ukraine commenced operations to contest Russian control of Snake Island. These included launching attacks on the island itself, whilst utilising TB2 Bayraktar UCAVs to target Russian vessels operating in the area. On 2 May 2022, TB2s successfully engaged and destroyed two Russian Project 03160 'Raptor' patrol boats. Subsequently, on 7 May, a Project 11710 'Serna' class landing craft with a 9K330 Tor (SA-15 'Gauntlet') surface-to-air missile system onboard waiting to be offloaded onto Snake Island was also attacked and destroyed.[9]

Ukraine continued to launch attacks on Snake Island into June. On 17 June 2022, the Russian Project 22870 rescue vessel *Spasatel Vasily Bekh*, which was transporting personnel and supplies to the island, was sunk, reportedly by Harpoon surface-to-surface missiles. Ukraine also successfully attacked Russian-occupied oil and gas rigs in the north-western Black Sea on 20 June 2022. The deteriorating situation confronting Russia in the north-western Black Sea was such that on 21 June 2022, the British Ministry of Defence stated that 'Ukrainian coastal defence capability has largely neutralised Russia's ability to establish sea control and project maritime force in the north-western Black Sea'. On 30 June 2022, the Russian Ministry of Defence announced that it was withdrawing Russian forces from Snake Island following continued Ukrainian strikes against the garrison there.[10]

The delivery of 'Western' weapons will likely continue to enhance Ukraine's ability to deny Russia the use of the north-western Black Sea. Moreover, due to the constraints of the Montreux Convention governing transit rights via the Bosphorus, Russia's ability to replace naval losses in the Black Sea is difficult. However, Russia's often overlooked system of internal waterways – The Unified Deep Water System of European Russia – should permit the movement of small surface combatants and even non-nuclear submarines to the Black Sea Fleet as the war approaches its sixth month.[11]

IMPLICATIONS

As of 30 June 2022, Russia controls the Ukrainian Sea of Azov coast, and the Black Sea coast of Kherson oblast. Russian attempts to advance on Mykolaiv, with a view to moving on Odesa, have not been successful. The Russian failure to secure a landward advance on Odesa likely derailed plans for an amphibious landing, either in support of operations against that city or to link up with the breakaway 'state' of Transnistria. Given Ukraine's current ability to deny Russia control of the north-west Black Sea and ongoing deliveries of Western military aid – in particular anti-ship missiles – a renewed Russian amphibious threat is unlikely. The core maritime threat is that of blockade. This poses significant risks; both to the Ukrainian economy and globally.

Although Ukraine may develop an enhanced ability to hold Russian naval surface forces at risk, countering the Black Sea Fleet's submarine force, mine threat and land-based missile forces – especially those deployed on Crimea – will pose a substantially greater challenge. The provision of systems such as the Lockheed Martin MGM-140 Army Tactical Missile System, compatible with the M140 High Mobility Artillery Rocket System and M270 Multiple-Launch Rocket Systems delivered to Ukraine, would, however, enable targets in Crimea – such as the Sevastopol naval base – and Russia itself

Although the Dardanelles and Bosphorus are currently closed to Russian warships under the terms of the Montreux Convention, the network of waterways that forms the Unified Deep Water System of European Russia provides another means by which Russia can reinforce its Black Sea Fleet. *(Pacharus under CC-BY-SA-4.0)*

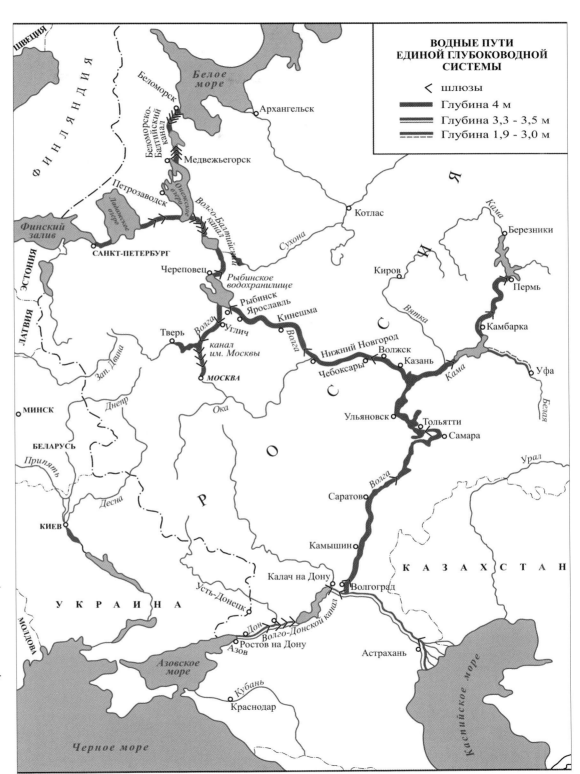

The Project 58155 'Gyurza-M' class gunboat *U175* pictured off Odesa in 2016. Although the strategic Ukrainian port appears secure from Russian occupation for the time being, Russia is still able to undertake an effective blockade of the ports that remain in Ukrainian hands. *(Ministry of Defence of Ukraine)*

A Baykar Bayraktar TB2 UAV pictured in front of its control station. The success of the Turkish drone in the maritime strike role has been a notable naval aspect of the 2022 Russo-Ukrainian War. *(Baykar)*

to be targeted. Given that the deployment of anti-access and area denial (A2/AD) capabilities in Crimea post-2014 has done so much to tilt the regional balance of power in Russia's favour, an ability to put this capacity into question would be most damaging to Russia's position.

The war also raises questions with respect to the Russian Navy's future development. The combination of economic sanctions, combat losses, the likely prioritisation of rebuilding land power, and the Black Sea Fleet's questionable performance – as highlighted by *Moskva*'s sinking – may well not prove promising for future procurement. There could be particular problems if the war extends to Crimea or supply chains are disrupted. The two new Project 23900 *Ivan Rogov* class amphibious assault ships are, for example, under construction at the Zaliv shipyard on the peninsula.

More broadly, the naval aspects of the Russo-Ukrainian War highlight the enduring importance of the human component. Well-trained, competent personnel are a prerequisite for success, a point emphasised in Ukrainian maritime strategy. Equally, the consequences of personnel shortcomings have been vividly demonstrated by the loss of the *Moskva*. Trained, competent personnel are also critical to the effectiveness of advanced weapon systems that underpin A2/AD approaches. Ukraine's use of ground-launched anti-ship missiles highlights the threat posed by such systems, whilst the use of the TB2 in the maritime strike role has been especially noteworthy and points to the opportunities provided by UCAVs for navies large and small.

Similarly, Russia's use of 'Kalibr' cruise missiles, including from ships as small as corvettes, again demonstrates the ability of navies to prosecute strategic strikes. The Russian blockade of Ukraine, and its impact on global supply chains, critically highlights the central role of the maritime trading system to global prosperity, and the multi-faceted means by which an adversary can place this system in danger. Whilst Russia's armed forces have been shown to suffer deep flaws, the threat posed by Moscow's militarist, neo-imperial ambitions cannot be dismissed. In short, the importance of the global maritime system, and the increasingly contested, complex strategic environment, serve to highlight the importance of well-trained and equipped navies that can credibly deter and if necessary, defeat threats to peace.

The Russian Project 636.6 'Improved Kilo' class submarine *Rostov-on-Don* pictured off the Turkish coast. Whilst the current war has demonstrated that Russia's armed forces suffer deep flaws, the performance of its 'Kalibr'-armed units has been one exception. The threat posed by Moscow's ambitions certainly cannot be dismissed. *(Devrim Yaylali)*

Notes

1. See Geoffrey Till, 'Invasion of Ukraine – The Coming War of Logistics' posted to the *RSiS* website – rsis.edu.org – on 10 March 2022.

2. Pavel Baev, *Russian Energy Policy and Military Power: Putin's Quest for Greatness* (Abingdon: Routledge, 2008), p.149.

3. See Alistair Coleman, 'Ukraine crisis: Russian news agency deletes victory editorial' posted to the *BBC News* website – bbc.co.uk/news – on 28 February 2022.

4. A translation of this document by Anna Davis of the Russia Maritime Studies Institute, US Naval War College can be accessed by searching the internet.

5. Ministry of Defence of the Russian Federation, 'Navy: Mission', which is accessible at: eng.mil.ru/en/structure/forces/navy/mission.htm

6. *Strategy of the Naval Forces of the Armed Forces of Ukraine 2035* (Kyiv: Ukrainian Navy, 2019). This is set out in English at: navy.mil.gov.ua/en/strategiya-vijskovo-morskyh-syl-zbrojnyh-syl-ukrayiny-2035

7. Ibid.

8. The precise causes for *Moskva*'s loss have been subject to claim and counter-claim, with the Russian Ministry of Defence initially claiming the ship was lost in heavy seas whilst being towed back to port following a magazine explosion. A detailed assessment of the sinking is provided by Hans Uwe Mergener in 'The Sinking of the Moskva – an Attempt at an Analysis', *Maritime Defence Monitor* – June 3/2022 (Bonn: Mittler Report, 2022), pp.9–14. The edition is available for download at: msd-mag.com/profile/print-issues

9. There has been speculation that two additional 'Raptors'

were destroyed on the same day.

10. UK Ministry of Defence, 'Latest Defence Intelligence Update on the Situation in Ukraine, 21 June 2022'. The Russian Ministry of Defence claimed their subsequent withdrawal was for humanitarian reasons in order to facilitate the transport of grain from Odesa; a claim that has been treated with scepticism.

11. The Unified Deep Water System of European Russia traces its origins to Tsarist times but was created in its current form as a series of combined transportation and hydro-electric schemes during the Soviet era, finally achieving full functionality in 1975. It is able to accommodate traffic of up to 4m in depth along much of its 6,500km length and links the White, Baltic, Caspian and – via the Sea of Azov – Black Seas.

2.1 REGIONAL REVIEW

Author:
Conrad Waters

NORTH AND SOUTH AMERICA

The Biden administration's second, FY2023 National Defense Budget Request essentially highlights the financial challenges faced by the US Navy as it adapts to the growing challenge posed by China's maritime expansion. The budget seeks an increase in headline Department of Defense expenditure to US$773bn. This represents a modest 2.2 percent uplift on the US$756.6bn enacted for FY2022. The relevant figure for the US Department of the Navy is US$230.8bn, a somewhat higher 4.1 percent advance on the prior year's figure. Although these are large numbers by any standards, the fact that America's rate of inflation is now greater than eight percent means that there is actually less money to spend in real terms. The administration's claim that, 'The FY 2023 Budget fully aligns and robustly resources defense priorities' looks more than a little questionable in these circumstances.[1]

The US Navy is currently embarking on a major process of reconfiguration as it attempts to build a fleet that is better suited to high intensity operations compared with the stabilisation activities of the immediate past. Creating a new type of navy needs substantially increased investment in research and development; up over nine percent to US$21bn. It also requires greater procurement of new equipment; raised 5.4 percent to US$54bn. The inevitable result is that there are fewer resources than otherwise would be the case both to crew and to sustain the current fleet. When set against the backdrop of the real-terms financial squeeze, the navy is being forced to make increasingly difficult choices in these areas.

It is this hard logic that has driven the navy's decision to seek the retirement of twenty-four vessels in the course of FY2023. This was eleven more than previously planned, with total withdrawals now calculated as saving US$3.6bn over future years. Some of these warships have reached the end of their effective lives. However, the list of vessels heading for retirement includes relatively newly-built Littoral Combat Ships and expeditionary transport docks that would otherwise have decades of operational life remaining.[2] The proposal has two significant consequences. One is that plans to grow the fleet – a prerequisite of the new Distributed Maritime Operations (DMO) concept – will be pushed far into the future. On the basis of official estimates, it will be another decade before 'battle force' numbers return even to current levels. The US Navy's ongoing failure to expand its fleet stands in stark contrast to the achievement of China's People's Liberation Army Navy. It is not a good sign for the future balance of power.

The other consequence – previously referenced in last year's *World Naval Review* – is ongoing uncertainty about the effectiveness of the navy's warship procurement process. The Littoral Combat Ship, with its flexible, modular design and minimal core crewing requirements, was not so long ago lauded by US Navy leadership as '… having the right capabilities for the times … a ship ready for many different missions …'.[3] Now it is deemed appropriate to toss many of the *Freedom* (LCS-1) variant of the type into the trash-can on the basis they lack the 'lethality' to provide the capability and capacity needed to face down China. It is noteworthy that the original modular concept that initially drove Littoral Combat Ship acquisition has never really been given the opportunity to work before enthusiasm for the type waned. A pertinent question – given that the final three Littoral Combat Ships were authorised as recently as FY2019 at a cost of c. US$525m each – is whether the current navy leadership's procurement decisions will be better adapted to standing the test of time. Amongst others, the editor believes that there are good grounds to be sceptical.[4]

In addition to the huge challenges created by fleet reconfiguration, events of the last year suggest that the US Navy is also dealing with a mounting number of people-related problems. 'Uninhabitable' accommodation allocated to sailors aboard the carrier *George Washington* (CVN-73) – completing an extended refuelling and overhaul at Newport News – has been blamed for a string of deaths. These included three suicides within the course of a week in the first half of April 2022. Some sailors had reportedly even resorted to sleeping in their cars to escape conditions onboard. Press reports have also noted a marked uptick in the number of commanding officers and other senior personnel being relieved of their assignments; at least fifteen during the first half of 2022 or around double the recent average. Clearly, US Navy leadership has much to do on both materiel and personnel fronts as it seeks to maintain the fleet's edge against rising threats.[5]

The *Arleigh Burke* class destroyers *Gridley* (DDG-101), *Chafee* (DDG-90) and *Spruance* (DDG-111) make an impressive sight as they sail in formation through the Philippine Sea on 22 January 2022. However, the US Navy is struggling to maintain overall fleet numbers as it seeks to speed up investment in the next generation of technologies to retain its competitive edge in high-intensity operations. *(US Navy)*

Table 2.1.1: FLEET STRENGTHS IN THE AMERICAS – LARGER NAVIES (MID 2022)

COUNTRY	ARGENTINA	BRAZIL	CANADA	CHILE	COLOMBIA	ECUADOR	PERU	USA
Aircraft Carrier (CVN/CV)	–	–	–	–	–	–	–	11
Strategic Missile Submarine (SSBN)	–	–	–	–	–	–	–	14
Attack Submarine (SSN/SSGN)	–	–	–	–	–	–	–	54
Patrol Submarine (SSK)	–[1]	5	4	4	4	2	6	–
Fleet Escort (CG/DDG/FFG)	4	6	12	8	4	2	7	94[2]
Patrol Escort/Corvette (FFG/FSG/FS)	9	2	–	–	2	6	3	24
Missile Armed Attack Craft (PGG/PTG)	2	–	–	3	–	3	6	–
Mine Countermeasures Vessel (MCMV)	–	3	12	–	–	–	–	8
Major Amphibious Units (LHD/LPD/LPH/LSD)	–	2	–	1	–	–	1	32

Note:

1. Argentina's two remaining submarines are non-operational and unlikely to be returned to service. A number of other Argentinian and Brazilian vessels are of uncertain operational status.

2. Includes one *Zumwalt* class destroyer that is not fully operational.

MAJOR NORTH AMERICAN NAVIES – CANADA

The Canadian National Shipbuilding Strategy (NSS) first announced in 2010 is now gaining traction as implementation of the first naval elements of the programme continues to make progress. August 2021 saw *Harry DeWolf* – the first of six Arctic and offshore patrol vessels – depart Halifax for a four-month circumnavigation of the North American Continent via the Northwest Passage and Panama Canal. It was reported as the first such voyage by a Royal Canadian Navy warship since the icebreaker *Labrador* made a similar maiden deployment in 1954, thereby demonstrating the new design's flexibility. The second-of-class, *Margaret Brooke*, had been delivered to the Royal Canadian Navy for post-acceptance trials the previous month whilst the third ship, *Max Bernays*, was launched in October. Both

these ships were subsequently formally named in a joint ceremony that took place on 29 May 2022 at Irving Shipbuilding's Halifax Shipyard. Assembly of two of the remaining three ships is also underway after the keel of the fifth ship, *Frédérick Rolette*, was laid on 30 June 2022. They will be followed by a pair of modified variants for the Canadian Coast Guard. Latest costs for these unarmed coast guard vessels are estimated at c. C$750m (US$580m) per hull, providing more ammunition for the critics of the costs that have plagued NSS implementation.[6]

These criticisms have also been levied at construction of the navy's two new *Protecteur* class joint support ships. They are being built on the west coast at Seaspan's Vancouver yard to the German Type 702 *Berlin* class design. Total programme costs for the ships are currently estimated at a massive C$4.1bn (US$3.2bn), of which C$3.1bn (US$2.4bn) is allo-

cated to actual construction. More positively, block assembly of the lead ship was reported as being close to completion at the end of 2021. Her launch is expected to take place before the end of 2022 prior to a scheduled, if optimistic 2023 delivery date. Work on sister-ship *Preserver* has yet to start due to priority being given to a coast guard research vessel. This suggests her planned 2026 completion could be a challenge.

The costs of these current programmes pale into insignificance compared with official estimates of C$56–60bn (c. US$43–47bn) for the Canadian Surface Combatant (CSC) programme. This will follow the Arctic and offshore patrol vessels into production at Irving's Halifax yard. Detailed design definition for the planned fifteen frigates – replacements for the existing *Halifax* and now-retired *Iroquois* classes – is now drawing towards its conclusion. It should be followed by approval for project implementation and award of a construction contract for an initial batch of ships in the course of 2022/23. Whilst there has been much criticism of the selection of a heavily-customised variant of the British Type 26 Global Combat Ship design as a basis for the new ships, it is difficult to envisage a different option that would meet Canadian requirements.[7]

In July 2021, reports in the local press revealed that a team had been set up to manage the navy's next major acquisition programme. This envisages replacement of the four existing *Victoria* (former British Royal Navy *Upholder*) class submarines towards the end of the 2030s. The Canadian patrol submarine project's initial aims will be to inform government about potential replacement options so that decisions can be taken to avoid the capability gaps that have impacted previous fleet renewal programmes. In the meantime, the existing boats are due to go through a *Victoria* class modernisation (VCM) programme. The relevant contract is expected to be awarded in the first half of 2023. It will include upgrades to the boats' flank sonar arrays and periscopes with a view to keeping them operationally effective until the new submarines arrive.

The Royal Canadian Navy's Arctic and offshore patrol vessels *Margaret Brooke* (left) and *Max Bernays* (right) pictured at an unusual joint naming ceremony at Irving Shipbuilding's Halifax Shipyard on 29 May 2022. *Margaret Brooke* had been delivered in July 2021 but *Max Bernays* was still in the shipbuilder's hands at the time of the ceremony. *(Irving Shipbuilding)*

Table 2.1.2: CANADIAN NAVY: PRINCIPAL UNITS AS AT MID 2022

TYPE	CLASS	NUMBER	TONNAGE	DIMENSIONS	PROPULSION	CREW	DATE
Principal Surface Escorts							
Frigate – FFG	HALIFAX	12	4,800 tonnes	134m x 16m x 5m	CODOG, 29 knots	225	1992
Submarines							
Submarine – SSK	VICTORIA (UPHOLDER)	4	2,500 tonnes	70m x 8m x 6m	Diesel-electric, 20+ knots	50	1990

The veteran *Halifax* class frigate *Vancouver* – now approaching her 20th birthday – makes an impressive sight as she cuts through the waters of the Pacific in June 2022. Detailed design work on the replacement Canadian Surface Combatant is drawing to a close. *(US Navy)*

The previously troubled CH-148 Cyclone helicopter programme now seems to be drawing to a satisfactory conclusion despite the discovery of cracks in the tail boom of most of the fleet towards the end of 2021. The damage – attributed to a design flaw – was seemingly quickly repaired. Twenty-four of a total order of twenty-eight of the rotorcraft had been delivered by the end of 2021 and good progress has been made in upgrading the fleet to the final, Capability Release 2.1 configuration. Achievement of full operational capability for the programme is targeted for December 2022.

Current fleet strength, unchanged year-to-year, is set out in Table 2.1.2.

MAJOR NORTH AMERICAN NAVIES – UNITED STATES

The US Navy had a total battle force of 298 warships as of mid-2022, a net increase of just one ship over the past 12 months. As previously mentioned, accelerated ship withdrawals mean that this is likely to represent the fleet's peak strength for the foreseeable future. Numbers are scheduled to dip to 285 in FY2023 and reach a low of 280 in FY2027. The US Navy continues to struggle to develop a new, longer-term Force Structure Assessment (FSA). This assessment – informed by the new National Defense Strategy – should now be completed by the time of the FY2024 budget request. In the interim, the Annual Long-Range Plan for Naval Vessel Construction for FY2023 includes three different scenarios; two based on current funding levels and one that requires material additional resources to fund increased procurement. All envisage growth in the numbers of attack submarines, small surface combatants, smaller amphibious vessels and the combat logistics force at the expense of some other categories. However, unsurprisingly, only the last-mentioned achieves meaningful expansion. Under this scenario the naval force inventory would reach 350 ships by FY2040 and grow further to a total of 367 vessels in FY2052; the end of the current planning period.[8]

Table 2.1.3 summarises planned acquisitions over the life of the five-year, Future Years Defense

Table 2.1.3: USN FY2023 FIVE-YEAR SHIPBUILDING PLAN (FY2023–FY2027)

SHIP TYPE	FY2022 Request	FY2022 Funded	FY2023 Request[1]	FY2024 Plan[1]	FY2025 Plan[1]	FY2026 Plan[1]	FY2027 Plan[1]	FY2023-27 Total FYDP[1]
Aircraft Carrier (CVN-78)	0	0	0	0	0	0	0	0
Strategic Submarine (SSBN-826)	0	0	0	1	0	1	1	3
Attack Submarine (SSN-774)	2	2	2	2	2	2	2	10
Destroyer (DDG-51)	1	2	2	2	2	2	2	10
Frigate (FFG-62)	1	1	1	2	1	2	1	7
Amphibious Assault Ship (LHA-6)[2]	0	0	1[2]	0	0	0	0	1
Amphibious Ship (LPD-17 F II)	0	0	1	0	0	0	0	1
Light Amphibious Warship (LSM(X))	0	0	0	0	1	1	2	4
Expeditionary Fast Transport (T-EPF-1)	1	2	0	0	0	0	0	0
Expeditionary Sea Base (T-ESB-3)	0	1	0	0	0	0	0	0
Replenishment Oiler (T-AO-205)	1	2	1	2	1	1	1	6
Next Gen Logistics Ship (T-AOL(X))	0	0	0	0	0	1	1	2
Submarine Tender (AS(X))	0	0	0	0	1	1	0	2
Fleet Tug (T-ATS-6)	2	2	1	0	0	0	0	1
Surveillance Ship (T-AGOS-25)	0	1	0	0	1	2	1	4
Total	8	13	9	9	9	13	11	51

Notes:
1. FY2023 numbers relate to those contained in the relevant Presidential Budget request and are subject to approval by Congress. FY2024–27 numbers are those in the indicative Future Years Defense Program..
2. There is a dispute between the US Navy and Congress as to when this ship, LHA-9, was actually authorised. Consistent with past Congressional action, Congress believes that it was actually approved in the FY2021 programme year.

The US Navy's Future Years Defense Program accords a high priority to maintaining production of attack submarines at the rate of two p.a. Here the latest member of the *Virginia* class – *Montana* (SSN-794) – is seen on initial trials from Huntington Ingalls Industries' Newport News yard in February 2022. She was commissioned on 25 June 2022. *(Huntington Ingalls Industries)*

Program (FYDP). They provide a good indication of the navy's short-term direction of travel whilst the debate referenced above is resolved. A two-unit p.a. 'drumbeat' of *Arleigh Burke* (DDG-51) destroyer and *Virginia* (SSN-774) attack submarine construction is maintained throughout the period. This accounts for US$61bn of a total planned US$133bn, 51-ship procurement programme. The *Columbia* (SSBN-826) strategic submarine project is the other major financial commitment. It costs over US$36bn during the FYDP in a demonstration of just how much renewal of the seaborne nuclear deterrent is impacting overall US Navy capital resources. The inability to move to the previously planned two-ship p.a. acquisition of *Constellation* (FFG-62) class frigates might be one consequence of the strategic submarine programme's financial demands, although shipyard capacity might be another potential consideration. Other notable aspects of the FYDP include the truncation of LPD-17 Flight II amphibious transport dock construction at just three ships and deferral of the start of acquisition of the new LSM light amphibious warship by two years from FY2023 to FY2025. Congress has previously demonstrated a willingness to increase warship procurement above requested levels – five ships were added to the initial eight-ship FY2022 budget request – and it seems likely that additional purchases will be approved for the coming year.[9]

A more detailed status report on the current strategic priorities driving the US Navy's force structure and an overview of current fleet composition is provided in Chapter 2.1A. In addition, Table 2.1.4 provides an inventory of principal warship classes as of mid-2022. These should be used in conjunction with the summaries of developments with respect to specific warship types set out below.

Aircraft Carriers: The US Navy's most recent aircraft carrier, *Gerald R. Ford* (CVN-78), achieved initial operational capability on 22 December 2021 after acceptance of the eleventh and last of the ship's previously troubled advanced weapons elevators. She

Table 2.1.4: UNITED STATES NAVY: PRINCIPAL UNITS AS AT MID 2022

TYPE	CLASS	NUMBER	TONNAGE	DIMENSIONS	PROPULSION	CREW	DATE
Aircraft Carriers							
Aircraft Carrier – CVN	FORD (CVN-78)	1	100,000 tonnes+	333m x 41/78m x 12m	Nuclear, 30+ knots	4,600	2017
Aircraft Carrier – CVN	NIMITZ (CVN-68)	10	100,000 tonnes+	333m x 41/78m x 12m	Nuclear, 30+ knots	5,200	1975
Principal Surface Escorts							
Cruiser – CG	TICONDEROGA (CG-47)	22	9,900 tonnes	173m x 17m x 7m	COGAG, 30+ knots	365	1983
Destroyer – DDG	ZUMWALT (DDG-1000)	2[1]	15,800 tonnes	186m x 25m x 8m	IEP, 30+ knots	175	2016
Destroyer – DDG	ARLEIGH BURKE (DDG-51) – Flight II-A	42	9,400 tonnes	155m x 20m x 7m	COGAG, 30 knots[1]	320	2000
Destroyer – DDG	ARLEIGH BURKE (DDG-51) – Flights I/II	28	8,900 tonnes	154m x 20m x 7m	COGAG, 30+ knots	305	1991
Littoral Combat Ship – FS	FREEDOM (LCS-1)	10	3,500 tonnes	115m x 17m x 4m	CODAG, 45+ knots	<50[2]	2008
Littoral Combat Ship – FS	INDEPENDENCE (LCS-2)	14	3,000 tonnes	127m x 32m x 5m	CODAG, 45+ knots	<50[2]	2010
Submarines							
Submarine – SSBN	OHIO (SSBN-726)	14	18,800 tonnes	171m x 13m x 12m	Nuclear, 20+ knots	155	1981
Submarine – SSGN	OHIO (SSGN-726)	4	18,800 tonnes	171m x 13m x 12m	Nuclear, 20+ knots	160	1981
Submarine – SSN	VIRGINIA (SSN-774)	21	8,000 tonnes	115m x 10m x 9m	Nuclear, 25+ knots	135	2004
Submarine – SSN	SEAWOLF (SSN-21)	3[3]	9,000 tonnes	108m x 12m x 11m	Nuclear, 25+ knots	140	1997
Submarine – SSN	LOS ANGELES (SSN-688)	26	7,000 tonnes	110m x 10m x 9m	Nuclear, 25+ knots	145	1976
Major Amphibious Units							
Amph. Assault Ship – LHD	AMERICA (LHA-6)	2	45,000 tonnes	257m x 32/42m x 9m	COGAG, 22+ knots	1,050	2014
Amph Assault Ship – LHD	WASP (LHD-1)	7[4]	41,000 tonnes	253m x 32/42m x 9m	Steam, 20+ knots	1,100	1989
Landing Platform Dock – LPD	SAN ANTONIO (LPD-17)	12	25,000 tonnes	209m x 32m x 7m	Diesel, 22+ knots	360	2005
Landing Ship Dock – LSD	WHIDBEY ISLAND (LSD-41)	11[5]	16,000 tonnes	186m x 26m x 6m	Diesel, 20 knots	420	1985

Notes:

1 Includes one ship commissioned but not fully operational pending completion of combat systems installation.

2 Plus mission-related crew.

3 Third of class, SSN-23 is longer and heavier.

4 LHD-8 has many differences.

5 Includes four LSD-49 HARPERS FERRY variants.

is, therefore, now clear to embark on her maiden operational deployment, which is scheduled for the autumn of 2022. Three other members of the class are currently under construction at Huntington Ingalls Industries' (HII's) Newport News shipyard. The facility laid the keel for *Enterprise* (CVN-80) on 5 April 2022. A debate continues on the future direction of US Navy carrier construction, including the wisdom of focusing all construction of large, nuclear-powered designs. However, existing plans remain focused on this type of ship and envisage a decision being taken no later than FY2025 as to whether the potential future CVN-82 and CVN-83 should be subject to a moneysaving, combined two-ship buy similar to that used for *Enterprise* and her sister-ship *Doris Miller* (CVN-81).

Surface Combatants: Construction of major surface combatants continues to be driven by the *Arleigh Burke* class. Class numbers have increased by just one to seventy over the past year with the commissioning of the HII Ingalls-built *Frank E. Petersen Jr.* (DDG-121) on 14 May 2022. The pace of deliveries has been slowed by well-publicised delays at General Dynamics' Bath Iron Works facility, with which production is shared. The yard's longstanding President, Dirk Lesko, resigned unexpectedly in April 2022 in another sign that all is not yet well in a facility that experienced a 63 day-long strike in 2020.[10] A total of eighty-nine *Burke*s in various design iterations or flights had been authorised up to FY2022. This will be increased by a further ten ships if the FY2023 FYDP is implemented in its entirety. However, not all these destroyers will be in commission at the same time; *Arleigh Burke* is scheduled to begin the retirement process for older members of

the class in the course of FY2027 when she will have finished 36 years of service.

Bath Iron Works did complete its share of work on *Lyndon B. Johnson* (DDG-1002) – the third and final *Zumwalt* (DDG-1000) class destroyer – in the course of the year. However, she will not be accepted until a second tranche of work relating to combat systems installation is completed. This will be undertaken by Ingalls, who expect to deliver the ship in the course of 2024. Similar work on *Michael Monsoor* (DDG-1001) that is being carried out at San Diego has also yet to be completed. All three ships are to be fitted with launchers for the US Navy's new hypersonic weapon – the Conventional Prompt Strike missile – in replacement for their two 155mm Advanced Gun System mountings, which have never received their intended guided munitions. Work is expected to commence on *Zumwalt* in the course of 2023. This should permit the new capability to enter service during 2025.

Twenty-two *Ticonderoga* (CG-47) class cruisers also remain in commission, although five are slated for withdrawal before the end of 2022. The FY2023 budget proposals envisage another five departing the fleet in FY2023 and all of the remainder by FY2027. Whilst all have reached the approximate end of their planned 35-year service lives, the plan is still controversial. Considerable efforts had previously been made towards implementing a life extension programme for eleven of the ships to retain the air defence command capabilities they provide for carrier strike groups. This investment – and some of the capability it provided – will now be written off.

The *Ticonderoga* class guided-missile cruiser *Mobile Bay* (CG-53) pictured whilst serving with the *Abraham Lincoln* (CVN-72) carrier strike group in the Sea of Japan in April 2022. Under current plans, she will be withdrawn from service in the course of FY2023 as part of an accelerated rundown of the US Navy's cruiser force. *(US Navy)*

Turning to small surface combatants, a total of twenty-four Littoral Combat Ships were in service as of mid-2022. This number was unchanged year-on-year. Deliveries of the *Freedom* class variant *Minneapolis-Saint Paul* (LCS-21) in November 2021 and the *Independence* (LCS-2) type *Canberra* (LCS-30) the following month have counterbalanced the previously-planned retirements of the two classes' prototypes. The more radical retirement plans announced in the FY2023 budget are seemingly driven by the abandonment of the type's anti-submarine module. This will leave the remaining ships of the class focused on either surface warfare or mine warfare missions. The premature withdrawals are largely focused on earlier members of the *Freedom* class, which have suffered from a systemic design defect with their gearing. Only six of the sixteen-strong class will be retained in service, all focused on surface warfare. They will be supplemented by fifteen out of the nineteen *Independence* variants that have previously been ordered, many of which will be dedicated to the mine countermeasures role. Completion of deliveries will allow retirement of the navy's last traditional, *Avenger* (MCM-1) class minehunters, which will all be gone by the end of FY2027.

Meanwhile, detailed design work continues on the *Constellation* class frigates that will form the basis of future US Navy small surface combatant construction. Twenty are eventually planned. Although derived from the Italian FREMM frigate variant, the design's physical size is being expanded to take account of specific US Navy requirements and includes:

A graphic of the new US Navy frigate *Constellation* (FFG-62). Although based on the Italian variant of the FREMM multi-mission frigate, the basic design is being made longer and broader to meet US Navy equipment requirements. This is taking time and physical work had yet to commence on the lead ship as of mid-2022. *(Fincantieri)*

- Lengthening the hull by 7.3m to accommodate larger generators and allow for future growth.
- Increasing waterline beam by 1.3m to maintain stability.
- Revising the bow design to remove the forward sonar dome.
- Changing topside arrangements in line with US Navy requirements.
- A c. 500-tonne growth in full load displacement to c. 7,400 tonnes.

These revisions will support incorporation of a US-specific combat suite that will include an Aegis combat system, the three-faced, AN/SPY-6(V)3 variant of the Enterprise Air Surveillance Radar (EASR) and a 32-cell MK 41 vertical launch system (VLS).[11] Perhaps unsurprisingly, the detailed design work to accommodate these changes is taking time. Accordingly, previous plans to commence construction of the lead ship firstly late in 2021 and then by April 2022 have not been met. However, the navy seemingly remains confident in overall progress with the project and the class's third ship, *Chesapeake* (FFG-64), was ordered in June 2023.

Amphibious and Support Shipping: The US Navy's front-line amphibious fleet has been bolstered by the arrival of the twelfth *San Antonio* (LPD-17) class amphibious transport dock, *Fort Lauderdale* (LPD-26). She was accepted into service from HII's Ingalls facility in March 2022 but has yet to be commissioned. Regarded as a transitional ship to the *San Antonio* Flight II variant, she incorporates a number of improvements and simplifications, most notably abandonment of the previous vessels' distinctive composite stealth masts. However, the expansion to the current iteration of the amphibious flotilla will be short-lived. In similar fashion to the substantial Littoral Combat Ship deletions, the FY2023 budget envisages significant reductions to the US Navy's previously planned force of large amphibious warfare vessels.

The most notable development heralded by the new budget is termination of procurement of *San Antonio* (LPD-17) Flight II amphibious transport docks at just three ships. Already referenced above, this will eventually result in just sixteen of both flights in commission when all have been delivered. This is ten fewer ships than envisaged in the most recent FSA and a seven unit reduction on the combined number of twenty-three amphibious

transport docks and LSD-type dock landing ships that are currently in service. The intention to transition to a smaller fleet of these types is confirmed by plans to accelerate withdrawal of the *Whidbey Island* (LSD-41) and *Harpers Ferry* (LSD-49) classes over the next five years. Four are scheduled to leave service in FY2023. Their effective replacements from around the end of the current decade will be the new light amphibious warship (LAW), which is considered as being better suited to DMO and Expeditionary Advanced Base Operations (EABO) concepts than the current fleet. Conceptual design contracts for the new vessels were awarded to five companies – Austal USA, Bollinger, Fincantieri, TAI Engineers and Halter Marine – in June 2021 but it will be the end of the decade before they start to enter service. Just as is the case for the now discredited Littoral Combat Ships, they will inevitably be less capable and survivable than the warships that they are intended to replace.

The US Navy has previously supplemented its front-line amphibious fleet with a number of secondary types such as the *Spearhead* (T-EPF-1) class expeditionary fast transports and *Lewis B. Puller* (ESB-3) class expeditionary mobile bases. Both have proved to be successful designs subject to extended production, partly through Congressional 'mark-ups' of additional vessels in support of local shipbuilding interests. An additional two *Spearhead* class transports and one expeditionary mobile base were added to the FY2022 shipbuilding programme. Further acquisitions cannot be discounted. Interestingly, however, the current budget request envisages immediate retirement of the two *Montford Point* class (T-ESD-1) expeditionary transfer docks, from which the *Lewis B. Puller* type was derived. It appears that these have been much less successful in service than their successors, being limited by an inability to conduct skin-to-skin moorings with military sealift vessels to transfer equipment in wave swells above 3ft and restricted cargo and accommodation capacity.[12]

The last year has seen considerable progress with

Current US Navy budget proposals envisage the immediate, FY2023 retirement of the two *Montford Point* (T-ESD-1) class expeditionary transfer docks – the lead ship is pictured here – as they have been less successful than envisaged. Both are already being held at reduced operating status. However, work continues constructing the revised *Lewis B. Puller* (ESB-3) expeditionary mobile base variant, which has been better received. *(General Dynamics NASSCO)*

the previously delayed construction of the new *John Lewis* (T-AO-205) fleet replenishment oilers. The lead ship of the six vessels firmly contracted to date commenced builders' trials from General Dynamics NASSCO facility in San Diego in February 2022 and her delivery is now imminent. The second ship *Harvey Milk* (T-AO-206) had previously been christened and launched on 6 November 2021 whilst construction of two of the other four contracted vessels is currently underway. A further pair of the tankers was authorised in the FY2022 programme and six more are planned during the life of the current FYDP. This will take the programme significantly closer to existing plans for twenty of the type. This number was set before the DMO concept had become firmly embedded in US Navy thinking and the high support requirements of a distributed fleet is only likely to increase the requirement for logistic vessels. This could be met by extended construction of the *John Lewis* class. However, orders for a new, smaller T-AOL next-generation logistics ship costing roughly a fifth of the existing design's c. US$750m price-tag are anticipated from FY2026 onwards. It is these vessels that are likely to meet much of the expanded requirement.

Progress also is being achieved with a number of other programmes for smaller auxiliary vessels which seldom enter the public limelight. In October 2021, Austal USA was awarded a contract to build two *Navajo* (T-ATS-6) towing, salvage and rescue ships – the as yet unnamed T-ATS-11 and T-ATS-12 – alongside options for three further members of the class. The contract was notable in being the first steel ship construction programme awarded by the navy to the company, which will be delivered from new steel shipbuilding facilities being completed at its Mobile, Alabama yard. The US Navy is also soon to decide on competing proposals to build the first of its new class of T-AGOS-25 ocean surveillance vessels. These will be larger, faster and more numerous than the ships now in service. Four firms – BMT, Bollinger Shipyards, Thoma-Sea Marine Constructors and Halter Marine – were awarded design studies for the programme in mid-2020 and these have subsequently been used to inform the construction award process that is currently reaching its conclusion.

Submarines: On 4 June 2022, a keel-laying ceremony was held at the General Dynamics Electric Boat Facility at Quonset Point, Rhode Island to mark the formal start of construction on the first of the US Navy's new flotilla of twelve strategic submarines. In practice, some advanced construction work on the new boat – which will be named *District of Columbia* (SSBN-826) – had begun as early as 2016, with major fabrication commencing in 2020.[13] However, concerns remain as to whether or not the significant expansion of nuclear-powered submarine infrastructure that is required to support assembly of the new class has been sufficiently well implemented to meet a planned 2027 delivery date. This is crucial to allow sufficient testing and training before SSBN-826 is scheduled to enter the US Navy's strategic nuclear deterrent operating cycle in 2031. Current plans for the class envisage the second boat in the class – *Wisconsin* (SSBN-827) – being formally authorised in FY2024. Approvals should then accelerate to one submarine p.a. from FY2027 onwards.

Some of the concerns over *District of Columbia*'s timely delivery have been driven by recent delays to production of *Virginia* class attack submarines. These have been held back by bottlenecks in the supply chain, exacerbated further by the impact of the COVID-19 pandemic. There was a 22-month hiatus in deliveries between the handing-over of the Electric Boat-built *Vermont* (SSN-792) in April 2020 and the same yard's *Oregon* (SSN-793) in February 2022. This represents a lag of over a year in the planned schedule. Perhaps ironically it appears much of the setback was due to the need to prioritise production of the more crucial strategic submarine. HII's Newport News – that shares assembly of the *Virginia* class and constructs sections of the *Columbia* class – has also been experiencing difficulties. The acceptance of *Montana* (SSN-794) in March 2022 was reportedly nearly two years behind initial plans. Both yards have invested in expanding production capacity and there is some optimism that combined deliveries can return to a two p.a. drumbeat after recent disruption. In the meantime, some of the pressure on the US Navy's submarine force will be relieved by life-extension work on a number of the remaining elderly *Los Angeles* (SSN-688) class. However, this is not a universal panacea, as overruns with respect to maintenance and repair periods is impacting the availability of operational boats.[14]

Unmanned Vessels: The US Navy remains committed to a dramatic expansion in the use of unmanned vessels as an effective means of imple-

The lead *John Lewis* (T-AO-205) class oiler pictured running initial sea trials from General Dynamics NASSCO, San Diego on 1 February 2022. Her delivery is now believed to be imminent. *(General Dynamics NASSCO)*

The Unmanned Surface Vessel Squadron One's *Ranger* and *Sea Hunter* pictured on the way to participate in the RIMPAC 2022 exercises in June 2022. These ships are essentially forerunners of the missile-armed large unmanned surface vehicles (LUSVs) and sensor-carrying medium unmanned surface vehicles (MUSVs) that the US Navy had envisaged would fill out its ranks of manned vessels as part of the DMO concept. However, the US Navy's thinking on unmanned vessels continues to evolve as technologies are evaluated and it is by no means clear that these types will ever enter service. *(US Navy)*

menting the DMO concept. However, its thinking continues to evolve as new technologies are subject to operational evaluation. Previous plans involved the surface fleet being bolstered by both missile-armed large unmanned surface vehicles (LUSVs) and sensor-carrying medium unmanned surface vehicles (MUSVs). A team led by L3Harris was awarded a US$35m contract for the design and construction of an MUSV prototype in July 2020. However, US Chief of Naval Operations Admiral Mike Gilday has recently been reported as saying the plan is under reconsideration following good results from smaller, even more expendable unmanned vehicles that can be deployed off virtually any manned platform. For the time being, the LUSV remains in future plans, albeit an order for an initial production (i.e. non-prototype) vessel has been pushed back to FY2025 as the navy continues to evaluate its options.

Much of this work is being driven by the US Navy's new Unmanned Surface Vessel Squadron One. This stood up in San Diego on 13 May 2022 to assume responsibility for the USVs previously under Surface Development Squadron One's control. Its developmental work has been bolstered by transfer of unmanned vessels from the US Department of Defense's Strategic Capabilities

Office following completion of their experimental Ghost Fleet Overlord Program. A key test of the new squadron's capabilities is scheduled for mid-2022, when its quartet of existing USVs will participate in the biennial RIMPAC exercises held off Hawaii. These will doubtless further inform the direction of future LUSV and MUSV procurement.

Another element planned for the future unmanned force is the extra-large unmanned undersea vehicle (XLUUV). This is defined by the US Navy as a vehicle of greater than 84in in diameter and therefore unable to be launched from existing manned submarines. Contracts for five prototype, developmental XLUUVs were awarded to Boeing in 2019 and the christening and first in-water testing of the lead vessel took place in late April 2022. The US Navy seems to be more committed to this type and acquisitions of six additional units are planned from FY2024 onwards. The current vessel is based on Boeing's 'Orca' design and will initially be trialled in the minelaying role.[15]

Operational Highlights: A degree of overstretch to meet operational commitments has been a continuing reality of US Navy activities. This has remained the case over the past year. As many as 128 ships or 43 percent of the 298-strong battle force were

deployed in March 2022, a figure that represented a recent high. Whilst this might well have reflected a temporary response to events in Ukraine, it was the Pacific that remained the focus of activity. A total of sixty-nine warships – including two carrier strike groups and an amphibious expeditionary strike group – were forward deployed in the Western Pacific at this time. A further ninety-four vessels were based in the Eastern Pacific and Continental US west coast. Whilst the Global Posture Review released in November 2021 provided few firm details, it is clear that the trend of concentrating resources on, first, the Pacific and, next, Europe will continue. The counter-terrorism and stabilisation missions of the post-Cold War era are clearly being accorded a much lower priority in the new era of great power competition. Notably, the press release that accompanied the review confirmed '… the reallocation of certain maritime assets back to Europe and the Indo-Pacific'.[16]

The level of stress inherent in US Navy operations referenced above may have played a part in the severe damage suffered by the *Seawolf* (SSN-21) class submarine *Connecticut* (SSN-22) when it was involved in a high-speed collision with an unchartered seamount during operations in the South China Sea on 2 October 2021. The official report into the incident blamed an accumulation of errors and omissions in navigation planning, watch-team execution and risk management for the collision. However, it is, perhaps, significant that a very high tempo of operations and the presence of defective equipment were also noted. This has some resonance with concerns referenced with US Navy operating culture after the separate collisions involving the destroyers *Fitzgerald* (DDG-62) and *John S. McCain* (DDG-56) in mid-2017. Interestingly, a Government Accountability Office report issued in May 2021 suggested that a fatigue management strategy adopted after these collisions was not being effectively implemented in the surface fleet. It appears that further action might be necessary.[17]

Two key themes of the past 12 months have been the implementation of a series of exercises aimed at proving DMO concepts and increased emphasis on interaction with allied naval forces as part of a renewed focus on building strategic partnerships. Exercise Noble Fusion, which took place early in February 2022, was an example of both these themes. Various elements of the US and Japanese Self Defence forces combined to undertake missions across the Western Pacific's First Island Chain in the sort of high intensity operations that would be necessary should a new Pacific War ever break out. An exercise of a very different nature was held towards the end of June 2022 to assess the potential effects of climate change on a future conflict. The table-top exercise – involving participants from the US Navy, Defense Department and other branches of government, as well as representatives from industry, academia and think tanks – was flagged as an opportunity for participants to evaluate how operations might need to change in a climate-impacted environment. It followed on from the publication of a new Department of the Navy strategy – Climate Action 2030 – setting goals to build climate resilience whilst reducing its own greenhouse gas emissions.[18]

US Coast Guard: The last year has seen the US Coast Guard make steady progress with the recapitalisation of its fleet of cutters of various sizes. The programme of record for this plan dates back to 2004 and envisaged existing assets being replaced by the following three new cutter types:

■ **National Security Cutter (WMSL-750 Class):** Also known as the 'Legend' class, eight of these were to replace twelve *Hamilton* (WHEC-715) class high security cutters. In practice, Congressional action has meant that eleven have been ordered. Nine had been delivered by the end of 2020. Although an order for a twelfth vessel has been mooted, it appears that the programme will conclude when the two remaining vessels under construction at HII's Ingalls yard are completed. The tenth vessel, *Calhoun* (WMSL-759) was launched at the start of April 2022. Average programme cost is estimated at c. US$670m per ship.

■ **Offshore Patrol Cutter (WMSM-915 Class):** Also referred to as the 'Heritage' class, twenty-five of these ships are to replace twenty-nine older medium endurance cutters. Displacing c. 4,500 tonnes, they are only slightly smaller than the more sophisticated national security cutters. Four of the class have been ordered to date from Eastern Shipbuilding Group of Florida and procurement of a fifth has been requested in the Coast Guard's FY2023 budget request. The

The *Seawolf* class submarine *Connecticut* (SSN-22) suffered significant damage in October 2021 when she hit an unchartered seamount in the South China Sea in another incident that raised questions about the US Navy's standards of seamanship. Here the submarine is seen returning to her home base at Bremerton after the incident in December 2021. *(US Navy)*

construction contract for this ship – and potentially for the following ten vessels – has been awarded to Austal. This followed on from an open competition after original contractual arrangements were revised when Eastern Shipbuilding's yard was devastated by a hurricane in 2018. The facility has now recovered from this setback but had been an unsuccessful bidder for the new contract. The lead ship, *Argus* (WMSM-195), will be christened before the end of 2022. Average programme cost is expected to be c. US$410m per ship.

- **Fast Response Cutter (WPC-1101 Class):** Also known as the 'Sentinel' class, sixty-four of these much smaller, c. 360-tonne cutters based on the Damen Stan Patrol 4708 design were projected to replace forty-nine 'Island' class patrol boats. A total of sixty-six of the type have now been authorised following approval of an additional, unrequested pair in FY2022, of which forty-eight have been delivered to date. All have been constructed by Bollinger Shipyards of Louisiana. Average programme cost is c. US$65m per ship.

The Coast Guard is also moving forward with a programme to acquire three new heavy icebreakers, officially referred to as polar security cutters. These will be built by Halter Marine in Pascagoula, Mississippi under a programme estimated to cost US$2.7bn. A contract option for the second vessel was exercised at the end of 2021. However, delivery of the lead ship – to be named *Polar Sentinel* – has been delayed by around a year to 2025 due to the impact of the pandemic and other factors. The Coast Guard's FY2023 budget request proposes acquisition of a commercial vessel to augment its existing operational icebreaker fleet – the heavy icebreaker *Polar Star* (WAGB-10) and the medium icebreaker *Healy* (WAGB-20) – until the new vessels come on line. At least three new medium, Arctic security cutters are also envisaged in the medium term as the strategic importance of the 'high north' continues to grow in importance.

OTHER NORTH AND CENTRAL AMERICAN NAVIES

There is little new to report with respect to naval developments in Mexico, Central America and the Caribbean. In **Mexico,** the current Obrador administration has effectively put a halt to the planned 2019–24 naval procurement programme. Instead, the navy is increasingly focused on its secondary, internal security role. The only major surface combatant of recent vintage – the Damen SIGMA10514 oceanic patrol vessel *Benito Juárez* (the former *Reformador*) – is therefore likely to remain one of a kind for the time being, although she has been extremely active. Her latest deployment is to the US-led RIMPAC 22 exercises, where she will be accompanied by the veteran landing ship *Usumacinta*, the former US Navy *Frederick* (LST-1184).

In the Caribbean, **Trinidad and Tobago's** new Austal-built 'Cape' class patrol vessels *Port of Spain* and *Scarborough* completed the long journey from Australia by heavy lift ship in July 2021. They were subsequently commissioned at a ceremony held at the Trinidad and Tobago Coast Guard base in Chaguaramas on 28 November 2021. In February 2022, *Scarborough* was involved in a tragic incident when her crew fired on a migrant ship that was attempting to ram the patrol ship, resulting in death of a baby boy who was hiding aboard the vessel.

Other naval forces in the Caribbean and Central America continue to benefit from the United States' programme to donate 'Near Coastal Patrol Vessels' to assist the constabulary efforts of friendly nations across the region. Metal Shark is contracted to construct up to thirteen of the new patrol craft, which are based on the 55-tonne Damen Stan Patrol 2606 design. **El Salvador** and **Guatemala** each received a single vessel – named respectively *Río Aguán* and *PM-15* – in July 2021, with **Panama** subsequently commissioning its *General Omar Torrijos* on 2 December. In March 2022, Metal Shark received a contract modification to build vessels seven through to ten of the series under an award valued at US$36m.[19]

MAJOR SOUTH AMERICAN NAVIES - BRAZIL

It has been a mixed year for the Brazilian Navy. As indicated by Table 2.1.5, the flotilla of major surface combatants continues to shrink as a result of the retirement of the Type 22 frigate *Greenhalgh* (the

Many Caribbean and Central American navies are being reinforced with constabulary assets. The patrol vessel *Scarborough* is one of two Austal-built 'Cape' class ships commissioned by the Trinidad and Tobago Coast Guard in November 2021. *(Austal)*

former HMS *Broadsword*). She was decommissioned at a ceremony at Rio de Janeiro on 10 August 2021. This leaves only *Rademaker* (previously HMS *Battleaxe*) in service from the quartet of ships acquired from the British Royal Navy in the mid-1990s. The *Niteroi* class frigate *Constituição* was also due to be decommissioned early in 2022 as the navy consolidates on the three modernised members of the class. However, she has been retained in service until mid-2023 in order to support trials of the new *Riachuelo* class submarines.[20]

The great hope for surface fleet revitalisation is the order for four new *Tamandaré* class MEKO type frigates from the TKMS/Embraer-controlled Águas Azuis consortium. In June 2022 a ceremony was held to mark the successful completion of a test section of one of the design's engine room blocks, thereby paving the way for the commencement of actual production later in the year. For the time being, it remains the intention to deliver the quartet at annual intervals between 2025 and 2029. This schedule appears to be aggressive on the basis of previous Brazilian Navy projects.

In the meantime work continues at Rio de Janeiro Navy Arsenal on the long-delayed *Macaé* class offshore patrol vessels *Maracanã* and *Mangaratiba*. Progress with the former is now well advanced and she should be delivered in the second half of 2022, allowing attention to be turned to her sister. Somewhat further into the future is the completion of a new Antarctic support ship. She will be built at the Sembcorp Marine of Singapore-owned Estaleiro Jurong Aracruz shipyard under a US$150m contract signed on 13 June 2022. Delivery is scheduled for the third quarter of 2025.

The Brazilian Navy's surface fleet continues to shrink as life-expired warships are retired before their replacements arrive. The Type 22 frigate *Rademaker* – formerly the British Royal Navy's *Battleaxe* – is now the only one of an original quartet of the class remaining in Brazil's service. *(Brazilian Navy)*

The last 12 months have seen Brazil's lead 'Scorpène' type submarine *Riachuelo* continue to undergo a lengthy series of sea trials that have now extended for more than 18 months. Given that delivery was anticipated for October 2020 at the time of the boat's launch in December 2018, it would appear that commissioning *Riachuelo's* systems has been more complex than first envisaged. This demonstrates the inevitable challenges of rebuilding a submarine construction industry from scratch. At the time of writing, delivery is now believed to be imminent. It is, however, unclear to what extent the delays will impact the remaining three members of the class or the country's planned nuclear attack submarine.

OTHER SOUTH AMERICAN NAVIES

The last year has seen **Argentina** complete its programme to acquire four 'Gowind' type offshore patrol vessels from France's Naval Group.

Table 2.1.5: BRAZILIAN NAVY: PRINCIPAL UNITS AS AT MID 2022

TYPE	CLASS	NUMBER	TONNAGE	DIMENSIONS	PROPULSION	CREW	DATE
Principal Surface Escorts							
Frigate – FFG	**GREENHALGH** (Batch I Type 22)	1	4,700 tonnes	131m x 15m x 4m	COGOG, 30 knots	270	1979
Frigate – FFG	**NITERÓI**	5	3,700 tonnes	129m x 14m x 4m	CODOG, 30 knots	220	1976
Corvette – FSG	**BARROSO**	1	2,400 tonnes	103m x 11m x 4m	CODOG, 30 knots	145	2008
Corvette – FSG	**INHAÚMA**	1	2,100 tonnes	96m x 11m x 4m	CODOG, 27 knots	120	1989
Submarines							
Submarine – SSK	**TIKUNA** (Type 209 – modified)	1	1,600 tonnes	62m x 6m x 6m	Diesel-electric, 22 knots	40	2005
Submarine – SSK	**TUPI** (Type 209)	4	1,500 tonnes	61m x 6m x 6m	Diesel-electric, 22+ knots	30	1989
Major Amphibious Units							
Helicopter Carrier – LPH	**ATLÂNTICO** (OCEAN)	1	22,500 tonnes	203m x 35m x 7m	Diesel, 18 knots	490	1998
Landing Ship Dock – LSD	**BAHIA** (FOUDRE)	1	12,000 tonnes	168m x 24m x 5m	Diesel, 20 knots	160	1998

Acceptance of the third ship *Storni* on 13 October 2021 was followed by that of the fourth and final vessel, *Contraalmirante Cordero*, on 13 April 2022. A modest revival in local construction has also seen the launch of two 36m naval cadet training vessels from the Río Santiago Shipyard after an extended construction process. Fellow local shipbuilder Tandanor has been authorised to build twelve of its TND 26-40 tugboat series for shipyard service. It will also lead a project to build a new polar icebreaker in replacement for the existing *Almirante Irízar*. This programme is currently at its basic engineering design stage, which will be carried out with the assistance of Finnish consultancy Aker Arctic. The consultancy had developed a concept design for the new 132m Polar Class 4 vessel in 2014. They will now upgrade this in line with evolving regulatory and mission requirements.

Reports continue to circulate about submarine acquisition to revive the Argentine Navy's moribund underwater arm. However, these would require funding of a different order of magnitude to the programmes referenced above and have to be regarded with some scepticism. The navy's ageing existing surface assets also require renewal, amongst ongoing reports of low availability. In mid-2021, it was reported that the MEKO 360 destroyer *Heroína* has been forced to remain in extended layup due to non-payment of storage fees related to refurbishment of a gearbox component that was sent to the United Kingdom over a decade ago for repair.

Neighbouring **Chile's** navy remains in a far stronger operational state, with its eight-strong flotilla of major surface combatants arguably making it the continent's leading naval power. Modernisation of the three Type 23 frigates by local shipbuilder ASMAR's Talcahuano facility that form the core of this fleet was completed in the autumn of 2021 with the return of *Almirante Condell* (formerly HMS *Marlborough*) to the navy's hands. The complex programme – encompassing combat management system, sensor and armament upgrades – will have developed skills that can eventually be employed in the local construction of replacements for the entire flotilla. The country's National Continuous Shipbuilding Plan envisages this will take place from around 2030 onwards.

In the interim, ASMAR is focused on completing the new 'VARD 9-203' type icebreaker *Antártica 1*. She is now around two-thirds complete and will be launched around the turn of the year to meet a

Argentina is making progress with its plans for a new icebreaker to replace the existing *Almirante Irízar*. This programme is currently at its basic engineering design stage, which will be carried out with the assistance of Finnish consultancy Aker Arctic, which produced the original concept – illustrated here – for the project. *(Aker Arctic)*

scheduled 2023 delivery. She is being followed into construction by four LSD-like amphibious and military transport vessels based on the VARD 7 series concept that will replace existing amphibious and transport units. Displacing around 8,000 tonnes, the 110m vessels will be able to transport a c. 250-strong marine infantry force and deploy a medium helicopter and a landing craft. A ceremonial first steel cutting for the lead ship was held at Talcahuano on 27 February 2022 but it will not be until *Antártica 1* is launched that construction will get fully underway.

The election of former guerrilla Gustavo Petro in June 2022 to become **Colombia's** first left-wing president might well impact implementation of the country's current Naval Development Plan 2042 given his stated preference to focus on social programmes. The flagship *Plataforma Estratégica de Superficie* project to build up to five new frigates in replacement of the existing quartet of FS-1500 *Almirante Padilla* class light frigates that form the core of the surface fleet looks particularly vulnerable to further delay or even cancellation. Given previous delays to the new ships, work was already underway

before the election to define the scope of a life extension plan for the existing frigates. These were subject to major midlife modernisation a decade or so ago under the Thales-led Orion programme and are considered to have significant life remaining. Another high priority naval programme under potential threat is acquisition of two amphibious logistic support ships similar to the South Korean-designed *Pisco* built by Peru's SIMA. However, a likely desire to maintain employment at Colombia's state-owned shipbuilder COTECMAR suggests some new construction will continue.

In April 2022, COTECMAR signed a technological collaboration agreement with **Ecuador's** ASTINAVE to share technical know-how. The latter's Planta Centro yard is being upgraded to support construction of the Fassmer MPV70 Mk III multi-role vessel ordered in 2020. However, progress with the ship's construction has reportedly been delayed by the impact of the pandemic.

The most significant development to benefit **Peru's** Navy over the last year has been the arrival of the former Republic of Korea Navy *Po Hang* class corvette *Guise* (previously *Suncheon*) in January

2022. The second of the class to be commissioned by the Peruvian Navy, her transfer reflects the substantial involvement of the South Korean maritime sector in new construction programmes being implemented by Peru's national shipbuilding group, SIMA. The most important of these that is currently underway is assembly of the second *Pisco* class amphibious transport dock *Paita*. She is expected to be launched from SIMA's Callao yard before the end of 2022. This should allow the shipbuilder to commence work on a series of three planned offshore patrol vessels, the navy's next priority programme. Progress is also being made with modernisation of the country's Type 209/1200 submarines. *Chipana* – the first to go through the upgrade project – is expected to return to operational service shortly.

In February 2022, it was reported that the veteran cruiser *Almirante Grau* – formerly the Dutch *De Ruyter* – had been put up for sale for scrap after the failure of attempts to secure her local preservation. Originally laid down as long ago as September 1939, she was the world's last all-gun armed cruiser in commission when finally withdrawn from service in September 2017.

Uruguay's long-delayed plans to acquire new offshore patrol vessels appear to be moving forward following receipt of bids from three shipyards for the two-unit programme. It has been reported that China Shipbuilding Trading Company (CSTC), the Dutch Damen and France's Kership joint venture between Naval Group and Kership are in the running for a contract that could amount to as much as US$200m when logistic support is taken into account. Germany's NVL (formerly Lürssen) were previously in the frame for a three-ship contract but appear to have decided to refrain from participating in the current tender.[21] It appears that the CSTC bid is the most likely to win the contract as China seeks to expand its regional influence. However, the United States also remains active in supporting local naval activity, finalising an agreement to transfer three former Coast Guard 'Marine Protector' class patrol boats to the Uruguay Navy in December 2021.

The political isolation and economic weakness of **Venezuela** means that its fleet remains in a low state of readiness in spite of highly-publicised local initiatives to complete often overdue maintenance of existing vessels. This state of affairs is likely to persist whilst the Maduro regime remains in power.

The Colombian Navy's Type 209/1200 submarine *Tayrona* pictured arriving at the US Navy's Naval Station in Mayport, Florida in May 2022. Like many of the fleet's front-line warships she is now an elderly vessel. However, prospects for fleet renewal have received a setback in the shape of a new, left-wing political administration. *(US Navy)*

Guise – previously the South Korean *Po Hang* class corvette *Suncheon* – is the second of the class transferred to the Peruvian Navy as part of the Asian country's efforts to foster industrial ties in the shipbuilding sector. *(US Navy)*

Notes

1. The US Department of Defense budget materials are available at: comptroller.defense.gov/Budget-Materials/ and the Department of the Navy materials at: secnav.navy.mil/fmc/fmb/Pages/Fiscal-Year-2023.aspx. Comparisons are somewhat distorted by the fact that there were a number of supplementary and Congressional adjustments to the administration's original FY2022 proposal, which initially amounted to US$715bn. Nevertheless there is a broad consensus that the budget is not keeping pace with inflation. A good explanation of the situation is provided in an article by Peter Bacon, Eric Chewning, Chris Daehnick, Jess Harrington, and Nikola Popovic, 'The $773 billion question: Inflation's impact on defense spending' posted to the McKinsey & Company website – mckinsey.com – on 28 March 2022.

2. The *Freedom* (LCS-1) and *Independence* (LCS-2) class Littoral Combat Ship variants, as well as the *Montford Point* (T-ESD-1) expeditionary transport docks, have all been described in chapters written for previous editions of *World Naval Review* that contain lavish official praise for what were then seen as innovative and inspirational concepts.

3. These remarks were made by Admiral Gary Roughead, the then US Chief of Naval Operations, in remarks to the Surface Navy Association's annual symposium in January 2009.

4. The US Navy's tendency to change its mind with respect to smaller warship programmes was highlighted in an article focused on another example of a new class – the Mark VI patrol boats – being prematurely abandoned that was also referenced in last year's *World Naval Review* but is worth revisiting. See Chris Cavas, 'A Problem of Commitment' posted to the *Defense & Aerospace Report* site – defaeroreport.com – on 11 April 2021.

5. The problems aboard *George Washington* have been widely reported, for example by Oren Liebermann and Henry Klapper in 'Sailors say aircraft carrier that had multiple suicides occur among crew was uninhabitable' posted to the *CNN* website – edition.cnn.com – on 7 May 2022. Amongst articles publicising the uptick in commanding officers being dismissed is Konstantin Toropin's 'The Navy Fires Fourth Commander in Seven Days' uploaded to the *Military.com* website on 15 June 2022.

6. An ongoing critic of NSS costs has been *The Ottawa Citizen*'s David Pugliese, who posted an article on the coast guard patrol vessels' price tag – 'Two coast guard Arctic ships to cost $1.5 billion, double the price of same

vessels for navy' – to the newspaper's ottawacitizen.com website on 23 May 2022. It is not, however, clear that the criticism is entirely fair without a breakdown of precisely what the amount covers. The current programme cost for the six navy vessels is estimated at C$4.3bn or around C$715m per vessel but this includes design, infrastructure and other supporting elements.

7. A comprehensive assessment of the history of the CSC programme that largely validates the decisions taken by the Canadian government is provided Richard Shimooka in *No Other Option: Politics, policy and industrial considerations in the Canadian Surface Combatant Program* (Ottawa: Macdonald-Laurier Institute, 2021). This can be found on the institute's website at: macdonaldlaurier.ca/mli-library/papers/

8. This information is contained in *Report to Congress on the Annual Long-Range Plan for Construction of Naval Vessels for Fiscal Year 2023* (Washington DC: Office of the Chief of Naval Operations, 2022), which is available by searching the web. In addition to likely funding restrictions, another constraint is the extent to which industry can eliminate excessive construction backlogs and produce future ships on time and within budget.

9. A good analysis of the US Navy's procurement plans is provided by Ronald O'Rourke, the Congressional Research Service's longstanding Specialist in Naval Affairs, in the regularly updated *Navy Force Structure and Shipbuilding Plans: Background and Issues for Congress RL32665* (Washington DC: Congressional Research Service, 2022). Like the other CRS reports referenced in this annual, these can now be found by searching crsreports.congress.gov

10. Perhaps ironically, Lesko's departure was announced on the same day local union leadership announced an agreement had been reached on interim wage adjustments. A number of journalists speculated about the abrupt parting of ways, including the *Portland Press Herald*'s Hannah LaClaire in 'Bath Iron Works president resigns abruptly without explanation' posted to the pressherald.com site on 8 April 2022.

11. The differences between the Italian FREMMs and their *Constellation* (FFG-62) class frigate progeny are described by Sidney E. Dean in 'Evolving the FREMM', *Maritime Security & Defence* – December 5/2021 (Bonn: Mittler Report, 2021), pp.22–6 and available for download at: msd-mag.com/profile/print-issues

12. See Hope Hodge Seck, 'Marines still have big plans for seabasing ships as 2 head for mothballs' posted to the

Marine Corps Times news website – marinecorpstimes.com – on 20 June 2022.

13. The lead submarine was previously to have been named *Columbia* but this was changed to *District of Columbia* in June 2022. This is reportedly because the life of the existing *Columbia* (SSN-771), a *Los Angeles* class submarine, is likely to be extended and the navy therefore needed to avoid having two boats with the same name in service at the same time. A broader view of the *Columbia* programme is contained in Ronald O' Rourke's *Navy Columbia (SSBN-826) Class Ballistic Missile Submarine Program: Background and Issues for Congress R41129* (Washington DC: Congressional Research Service, 2022).

14. See Megan Eckstein, 'Submarine maintenance backlogs and delays take toll on fleet's development work at sea' posted to the *Defense News* site on 17 February 2022.

15. Another periodically updated Ronald O' Rourke report, *Navy Large Unmanned Surface and Undersea Vehicles: Background and Issues for Congress R45757* provides essential reading on the development of the US Navy's efforts in this area.

16. 'Biden Approves Global Posture Review Recommendations' posted to defense.gov/News/Releases on 29 November 2021.

17. See *Navy Readiness: Additional Efforts Are Needed to Manage Fatigue, Reduce Crewing Shortfalls, and Implement Training GAO-21-366* (Washington DC; United States Government Accountability Office, 2021), available at gao.gov/assets/gao-21-366.pdf

18. See *Department of the Navy Climate Action 2030* (Washington DC: Department of the Navy, 2022).

19. Along with official navy websites, the Spanish-language infodefensa.com and its rival defensa.com remain invaluable sources of additional information on naval developments in Central and South America.

20. The plan to retire *Constituição* was reported on the Poder Naval site – naval.com.br/blog – on 30 January 2022. The site remains an essential source for detailed information on Brazilian Navy developments.

21. The bids were reported by Gabriel Porfillo in 'Three shipyards submit bids for new Uruguayan OPV', *Jane's Defence Weekly* – 20 April 2022 (Coulsdon: Jane's, 2022), p.9.

THE UNITED STATES NAVY

Adapting to the Return to Great Power Competition

Author:
Sidney E. Dean

The United States is the only major power with truly global security commitments. The US Navy (USN) and US Marine Corps (USMC) are a major resource for meeting these commitments. In many regions they maintain a constant presence, geared toward reassuring allies, deterring adversaries, and constituting a potent combat force should a conflict arise. Additionally, they constitute a flexible resource which can be quickly deployed in response to rising tensions in areas with no or minimal US military presence; an important aspect of this is the capability to dial the size and composition of the deployed forces up or down as the situation requires.

Another major peacetime mission of the US Navy is pursuit of maritime security and freedom of navigation on the high seas and in international straits. Threats to civilian shipping – including piracy, terrorism, and smuggling of weapons, drugs or migrants – directly endanger economic interests of the United States and its partner nations, and contribute to regional instability. Attempts by some nations – such as China – to claim sovereignty over international maritime straits must be consistently challenged by sailing USN vessels through these waterways in freedom of navigation operations.

THE RENEWED FOCUS ON GREAT POWER THREATS

During the post-Cold War era the United States' sea services, like the US military as a whole, became increasingly focussed on containing regional actors

F/A-18 series Super Hornet jets from the Blue Angels Flight Demonstration Squadron fly over the aircraft carrier *Carl Vinson* (CVN-70) as the ship returns to San Diego from a six-month deployment across the Pacific in February 2022. The US Navy – along with its sister services – is a major resource for meeting the United States' unique global security commitments but it is being forced to evolve to meet a new era of great-power competition. *(US Navy)*

and combatting terrorism. This focus became even more intense during the military commitments in Afghanistan and Iraq, during which the sea services contributed significant forces to enforce embargos, provide air support to ground forces, and provide large numbers of personnel for inland missions. This focus began to shift during the administration of President Barack Obama, and has become most marked over the past two years. While regional actors such as Iran and North Korea remain a concern, the sea services now emphasise China and Russia as the most serious threats to US and allied interests.

Russia: Following the 2014 Russian annexation of the Crimea, and intensification of Russian naval activities in the North Atlantic, the USN began a slow pivot to improve readiness in an area which had been de-prioritised since the 1990s. The Russian submarine fleet was recognised as a particular threat, given the vulnerability of sea lines of communication as well as sea-floor based data cables connecting North America and Europe. As a result, the USN reactivated the Second Fleet in August 2018. The unit has operational and administrative control over USN and USMC forces along the east coast of the United States and in North Atlantic waters. It plans and conducts maritime, joint and combined exercises in the stated area of responsibility. Additionally, the USN stepped up cooperative training with allies for operations in the GIUK Gap, a maritime chokepoint between Greenland, Iceland and the UK. The US sea services have also stepped up general Arctic readiness training along the entire stretch from northern Norway through to Alaska; this reflects both concerns about potential Russian aggression as well as the realities of climate change, which will make the region more accessible for military operations by multiple parties.[1]

China: Over the past two decades China has become increasingly bellicose in dealing with its neighbours – including many security partners of the United States – and has staked claims to sovereignty over the South China Sea. It has asserted the right to control foreign access to these waters and constructed military infrastructure on uninhabited islands and reefs at the eastern perimeter of both the East and South China Seas. The latter are part of a concerted effort to create Anti-Access/Area-Denial (A2/AD) zones where US forces are unable to operate,

The USN destroyer *Stockdale* (DDG-106) undertakes a training exercise with warships from Pacific partners Australia and Japan in the Philippine Sea during November 2021. The USN is a focal point of the 'Pivot to the Pacific' that commenced during the Obama administration in response to perceptions of a growing Chinese threat to American and allied interests. *(Royal Australian Navy)*

or can only operate under threat of significant losses.

Simultaneously the Chinese armed forces are expanding rapidly. The People's Liberation Army Navy (PLAN) already exceeds the USN numerically and the US Office of Naval Intelligence only forecast Chinese platforms – including coast guard and maritime militia assets – to continue to grow. Moreover, numbers are only one aspect. The Chinese military is rapidly modernising, introducing – among other things – long-range combat aircraft, hypersonic weapons, and so-called 'carrier killer' ballistic missiles. Taken together, these developments enable the Chinese armed forces to pose a serious threat to US aircraft carrier groups and other major surface combatants, as well as regional bases such as Guam and US allies and partners, including Taiwan.

These moves have prompted US strategists to elevate Beijing to the primary long-term threat to US security interests. A resultant 'pivot to the Pacific' was initiated by President Barack Obama with publication of the 2012 defence strategy, and

has subsequently been confirmed by both the Trump and Biden administrations.[2] During a hearing before the House of Representatives Appropriations Committee on 11 May 2022, US Defense Secretary Lloyd Austin assured legislators that – the Ukraine conflict notwithstanding – 'the department's pacing challenge remains countering aggression from China'. Joint Chiefs of Staff Chairman General Mark Milley supported this statement. 'The strategic main effort for the United States military; that is clearly in the Pacific', Milley said during the same hearing. 'Even though we are incurring additional capabilities and investments in what we're doing with Ukraine, it is not having a significant negative effect on our ability to keep pace with China.'

DISTRIBUTED MARITIME OPERATIONS

Given the physical characteristics of the Pacific region – which has now been melded with the Indian Ocean region into a joint Indo-Pac theatre of operations – the primary operational burden in

Although carrier strike groups will remain an important component of future US Navy force structure, the Distributed Maritime Operations (DMO) concept is placing increased emphasis on a construct based on large numbers of dispersed – but networked – assets. Here the Littoral Combat Ship *Tulsa* (LCS-16) operates with the aircraft carrier *Carl Vinson* (CVN-70) in the South China Sea in September 2021. *(US Navy)*

A US Marine Corps M142 High Mobility Artillery Rocket System (HIMARS) fires a rocket while conducting a HIMARS rapid insertion training event in April 2022. The establishment of transient missile-launching sites is a key part of the USMC's new Expeditionary Advanced Base Operations (EABO) concept. *(US Marine Corps)*

responding to Chinese expansionism falls onto the US sea services and the US Air Force. The sea services, in particular, are favouring a move towards Distributed Military Operations (DMO). While USN carrier groups will continue to operate jointly to provide a defensive belt around aircraft carriers, other fleet assets are intended to disperse across the operational theatre. Two tactical advantages are ascribed to this concept of operations. Defensively, dispersal of vessels will make it more difficult for an enemy to track and attack US forces, minimising US losses when attacks occur. Offensively, the concept permits US forces to carry out coordinated and synchronised attacks from various directions simultaneously using long-range precision weapons. This is expected to strain – or even overwhelm – the adversary's air and missile defence systems.

Realisation of the DMO concept depends on maximising development and employment of secure long-range communications systems that enable seamless sharing of sensor data and target tracking among various vessels and aircraft. This is Cooperative Engagement Capability or CEC. The USN also plans to equip as many manned and unmanned vessels as possible with precision stand-off weapons to bolster combat capability across large theatres of operations. These steps will require significant investment in suitably armed and equipped platforms, both manned and unmanned. While the optimal size and composition of the fleet is the subject of intense debate – as will be discussed later in this article – the current CNO, Admiral Michael Gilday, has made it very clear that 'to fight in a distributed fashion you need volume. We do need a bigger Navy, and you can't just talk about capabilities without talking about size.' Realistically, it will take years before the USN is postured to implement DMO fully, although incremental transition to this concept of operations is already underway.

The US Marine Corps' distributed operations transition is considered further along than that of the navy, in part because the associated technology is lighter and can be procured more quickly. The USMC's DMO philosophy and the closely related Expeditionary Advanced Base Operations (EABO) concept centre on forward presence and high mobility in and around contested areas, including within the enemy's A2/AD cordon. The corps plans to deploy small, dispersed land and sea detachments to threaten the ability of adversary forces to concentrate from within their anti-access/area denial umbrella. A key goal is to deny the opponent's freedom of movement along key sea and air lines of communication, and buy time to assemble a larger, high-power fleet or combined-arms force. The mobile units – composed of circa 100 marines each – will switch positions every few hours to every few days. Missions and capabilities will include: reconnaissance and surveillance in support of fleet and air operations; direct-action strikes against enemy air defences, missile launching sites or airfields; establishment of transient missile-launching sites (including deployment of anti-ship and even anti-submarine missiles); and refuelling/rearming stations for F-35B short take off and vertical landing (STOVL) aircraft. Some mission systems – such as vehicle-mounted Naval Strike Missiles – are already being procured in support of the EABO concept. Another crucial element – acquisition of up to thirty-five smaller, shallow-draught transport vessels to be designated as Light Amphibious Warships (LAWs) – is expected to begin in 2025, with delivery of the first vessel in 2028.

BALLISTIC MISSILE DEFENCE

Over the past two decades the USN has added sea-based ballistic missile defence (BMD) to its portfolio. The Aegis Ballistic Missile Defense (Aegis BMD) programme is co-managed by the joint-service Missile Defense Agency (MDA) and the USN. The Aegis BMD system provides selected Aegis-equipped warships with the capability to intercept short- to intermediate-range ballistic missiles. This capability serves both in the force protection role – the defence of major surface ship formations – and also the regional defence of large land areas. Forward-deployed Aegis BMD-capable ships defend European and East Asian allies from potential attacks emanating from such states as Iran and North Korea.

BMD capability is achieved through modifications to the computers and software of the baseline Aegis Weapon System and by arming the ships with BMD interceptor missiles. The current configuration is designated Aegis BMD 5.1 and was introduced in 2019. It is keyed to the Aegis Weapon System Baseline (BL) 9.2C, and utilises the SM-3 Block IIA interceptor missile. Other extant variants include the BMD 5.0 – which entered service in 2015 and which utilises the SM-3 Block 1B interceptor – as well as BMD 4.1 which was introduced

The Aegis Ashore ballistic missile defence facility at Deveselu in Romania is a good example of the breadth of the US Navy's commitments. (US Navy)

in 2020 as a means to upgrade older Aegis warships to the BMD 5.0 capability standard. BMD 6.0 is planned to enter service in 2023, utilising the new SPY-6 radar featuring enhanced capacity and discrimination; this is expected to improve performance against additional threats and against a larger number of targets simultaneously.[3]

The MDA expects forty-eight USN cruisers and destroyers to be Aegis BMD capable by the end of FY2022. Additionally, a land-based Aegis BMD capability – designated as AEGIS Ashore – has been developed. Each facility includes a structure housing an Aegis BMD system and twenty-four SM-3 missiles in a vertical launch system (VLS). The structure, which is staffed by USN personnel, is based on the deckhouse of an Aegis-equipped warship and incorporates a SPY-1 radar. One facility, located in Romania, became operational in 2016 and was upgraded to Aegis BMD 5.1 standard in 2019. Construction of a second installation located in Poland is behind schedule; according to the MDA, the facility may become active by the end of FY2022.

ORGANISATIONAL STRUCTURE AND BASING/PRESENCE

The USN has approximately 345,000 active-duty members, plus around 50,000 ready reserves and nearly 200,000 civilian employees. The Chief of Naval Operations (CNO), a four-star admiral, is directly subordinate to the civilian Secretary of the Navy. The CNO is responsible for the command, utilisation of resources, and operational readiness of the Navy, and is assisted by an extensive staff.

The USN's operational forces are assigned to seven numbered fleets, each of which is responsible for operations in a particular geographic or functional area of responsibility (AOR). These are:

■ **Second Fleet:** Headquartered at Norfolk, Virginia – US East Coast and North Atlantic AOR.
■ **Third Fleet:** San Diego, California – US West Coast and (primarily) the Eastern Pacific.
■ **Fourth Fleet:** Mayport, Florida – South Atlantic AOR (including the Caribbean & Latin America).
■ **Fifth Fleet:** Manama Naval Base, Bahrain –

The command ship *Blue Ridge* (ACC-19) pictured alongside at US Fleet Activities Yokosuka in June 2022. Yokosuka, near Tokyo, is headquarters for the US Navy's Seventh Fleet. *(US Navy)*

Middle East and Northwest Indian Ocean.
- **Sixth Fleet:** Naples, Italy – European & African waters.
- **Seventh Fleet:** Yokosuka, Japan – Western Pacific.
- **Tenth Fleet:** Maritime Operations Centre, Fort Mead, Maryland – The only non-geographic numbered fleet, established in 2010 as the operational force for Fleet Cyber Command. It supports national strategy and the maritime fleet by conducting offensive and defensive cyber operations, space operations and signals intelligence. The headquarters has control of over 100 globally distributed subordinate units.

In addition to numerous large, medium-sized and small installations along the Atlantic, Gulf, and Pacific coasts – as well as inland training, logistics and naval air stations and the facilities focused on Pearl Harbor in Hawaii – the US Navy maintains permanent overseas bases for forward-deployed units. These are primarily in Europe – at Rota, Spain; Gaeta and Naples, Italy; and Souda Bay, Greece – and in Asia: at Apra Harbor, Guam; and Sasebo and Yokosuka in Japan. These permanent bases are augmented by bilateral agreements permitting replenishment or maintenance of deployed ships at military and commercial facilities overseas, including in Australia, Chile and Singapore. The ability to maintain a significant forward presence in all regions of the globe maximises the US military's ability to conduct peacetime maritime security operations and to enhance interoperability and cohesion with partner forces.[4]

US NAVY BATTLE FORCE

The USN's current battle force consisted of 298 ships as of June 2022, of which an average of around a quarter are deployed at any given time. The term Battle Force refers to commissioned United States warships (USS) that are capable of directly engaging in combat operations, as well as to United States Navy Ships (USNS) that contribute to USN warfighting, combat support or service support missions. The term thus encompasses armed combatants as well as Military Sealift Command (MSC) and Naval Fleet Auxiliary Force vessels.

Table 2.1A.1: US NAVY BATTLE FORCE: AS OF JUNE 2022

TYPE	NUMBER
Aircraft Carriers	**11**
Nimitz (CVN-68) Class	10
Ford (CVN-78) Class	1
Large Surface Combatants	**93**
Ticonderoga (CG-57) Class	22
Burke (DDG-51) Class	70
Zumwalt (DDG-1000) Class	1[1]
Small Surface Combatants	**32**
Freedom (LCS-1) Class	10
Independence (LCS-2) Class	14
Avenger (MCM-1) Class	8
Amphibious Ships	**32**
Wasp (LHD-1) Class	7
America (LHA-6) Class	2
San Antonio (LPD-17 Class)	12
Whidbey Island (LSD-41) Class	7
Harpers Ferry (LSD-49) Class	4
Strategic Submarines	**14**
Ohio (SSBN-726) Class	14
Other Submarines	**54**
Los Angeles (SSN-688) Class	26
Seawolf (SSN-21) Class	3
Virginia (SSN-774) Class	21
Ohio (SSGN-726) Class	4
Combat Logistics Ships	**29**
Lewis and Clark (T-AKE-1) Class	12[2]
Henry J. Kaiser (T-AOE-17) Class	15
Supply (T-AOE-6) Class	2
Fleet & Auxiliary Support	**33**
Total	**298**

Notes:
1. A second unit of the class has been commissioned but is not counted as a 'battle force' ship pending full completion of combat systems installation.
2. A further two members of the class are listed as Fleet & Auxiliary Support Vessels.

A summary of battle force units is provided in Table 2.1A.1.

The Pentagon is pursuing a modernisation programme which will require retirement of older, maintenance-intensive assets and those which provide only a marginal operational advantage. Simultaneously the USN is developing and/or procuring new systems with the goal of maintaining an operational advantage against peer and near-peer opponents. Parallel to this procurement program, some in-service ships, aircraft and weapon systems are being upgraded with new technology inserts.

An overview of some of the more important combat types follows.

AIRCRAFT CARRIERS

Despite ongoing debate about the optimal size and composition of the USN's aircraft carrier fleet – including studies to determine whether smaller carriers should be added to the fleet mix – the large, nuclear-powered fleet carrier (CVN) remains the centrepiece of USN power projection capabilities. In addition to fielding an extremely potent combat force – especially when its missile-armed escort vessels are considered – the deployment of a carrier task force to a crisis zone carries a strong symbolic message of resolve that can deter aggression. Since 2006, the US government is required by law to maintain an inventory of eleven operational aircraft carriers, including those undergoing refuelling and overhaul. The current inventory consists of ten *Nimitz* (CVN-68) class carriers and the first-of-class *Gerald R. Ford* (CVN-78).

***Nimitz* (CVN-68) Class:** *Nimitz* was commissioned in 1975, with an expected service life of 50 years. Like the other ships of her class, she routinely deploys with an airwing of more than 60 aircraft, although she can accommodate more than ninety fixed-wing units and helicopters. The final vessel, *George H.W. Bush* (CVN-77), was commissioned in 2009. The vessels of the *Nimitz* class will retire sequentially, beginning with CVN-68 in 2025. On the basis of expected service life, it will only be around 2060 that the last of the class is decommissioned.[5]

***Gerald R. Ford* (CVN-78) Class:** Roughly the same size as the *Nimitz* class, the *Ford* class promises to introduce revolutionary new technologies to enhance both efficiency and combat power. They eliminate steam service lines, relying instead on more efficient and maintenance-friendly electric utilities. Their twin A1B nuclear reactors are expected to produce 25 percent more power than the A4W reactors on the *Nimitz* class. Moreover, their electric plant has sufficient capacity to accommodate future insertion of new technologies, including directed energy weapons. Other new technologies include an Electromagnetic Aircraft Launch System (EMALS) and Advanced Arresting Gear (AAG), which are expected to enable a significantly higher aircraft sortie generation rate when compared with the legacy steam catapults and hydraulic arresting wires on the *Nimitz* class. EMALS and AAG also optimise the applied energy to suit specific aircraft mass and velocity, reducing stress on the airframe and enabling the launch and recovery of aircraft which are too light or too heavy for a steam catapult.

Ford also utilises a space-saving new radar system. CVN-78's Dual Band Radar combines the X-band

The lead *Ford* class aircraft carrier *Gerald R. Ford* (CVN-78) has now achieved initial operational capability and will undertake her maiden deployment before the end of 2022. Three other members of the class are under construction or on order. *(US Navy)*

(NATO I/J-band) SPY-3 multifunction radar and an S-band (NATO E/F-band) SPY-4 volume search radar with no moving parts and an improved cooling system. However, the follow-on vessels of this class will be equipped with the lower cost SPY-6(V3) variant of the Enterprise Air Surveillance Radar.

CVN-78 was commissioned in 2017 but propulsion system defects and delays in achieving operational status for several key technologies postponed operational availability. These issues have now been resolved to the navy's satisfaction and initial operational capability (IOC) was declared in December 2021. After completion of scheduled maintenance, the ship is expected to begin its maiden deployment in late summer or early autumn of 2022; four years later than originally planned.

Procurement of the next three vessels in the class was initiated in FY2013, FY2018 and FY2019, respectively. Construction of the first of these – *John F. Kennedy* (CVN-79) – is progressing largely to schedule, utilising lessons learned from the construction of CVN-78; the ship launched in 2019. Delivery of CVN-79, *Enterprise* (CVN-80) and *Doris Miller* (CVN-81) to the USN is scheduled in four-year intervals, in 2024, 2028 and 2032, respectively. At this point it is unsure whether the navy will procure more than four *Ford* class vessels, or make changes to the composition of the carrier force. Recent force structure studies have suggested inventories between eight and twelve CVNs, potentially augmented by up to six conventionally powered light aircraft carriers (CVLs). Advocates of adding CVLs stress that they would support the distributed operations concept, especially in a China-war scenario.

LARGE SURFACE COMBATANTS
Large surface combatants are highly-survivable multi-mission ships able to conduct the complete naval warfare spectrum including surface warfare, anti-submarine warfare, anti-air warfare, and naval surface fire support. As mentioned previously, many are Aegis BMD-capable. All are equipped with VLS cells and carry – depending on the mission spectrum – a mix of Standard Missiles (SM-2, SM-3 and/or SM-6), Evolved Sea Sparrow Missiles (ESSMs), Tomahawk Land Attack Cruise Missiles (TLAMs), and Vertical Launch Anti-Submarine Rocket ASROC (VLA) missiles.

Ticonderoga (CG-47) Class: The *Ticonderoga*

(CG-47) class guided-missile cruisers first entered the fleet in 1983. Of twenty-seven ships commissioned through to 1994, twenty-two remain in service. They are equipped with the Aegis Weapon System. One of their primary missions is to deploy in support of aircraft carrier groups, hosting the formation's air defence staff. In addition to their VLS-hosted missiles, they carry Harpoon anti-ship missiles (ASMs), two 127mm guns and torpedo launchers.

The FY2023 budget request calls for retirement of five of the class, citing increasingly arduous maintenance and the need to free up resources for procurement of new ship classes. Going forward, the USN wants to divest the entire cruiser fleet by FY2027. It remains uncertain whether the US Congress will approve the full retirement plan. Previous attempts to divest the cruisers have been blocked, citing capability gaps and slow procurement of a possible successor.

Arleigh Burke (DDG-51) Class: These guided-missile destroyers first entered service in 1991 and are still being built. With seventy vessels currently active, these multi-mission warships constitute the mainstay of the surface fleet. All are equipped with

the Aegis Weapon System. Non-VLS-based weapons include torpedoes, a 127mm gun, and close-range defensive armament. Another nineteen ships of the class are under construction or contract, with further procurement planned.

The class has been progressively upgraded with new weapons, sensors and ship systems. It is currently being produced in both its third and fourth major configurations, respectively designated as the Flight IIA and the Flight III variants. Each variant has become heavier due primarily to additional and heavier equipment, including the addition of an aircraft hangar and two MH-60R helicopters aboard Flight IIA and Flight III vessels. While *Arleigh Burke* originally displaced 8,300 tons, the Flight III variant will weigh in at 9,700 tons. Flights I, II and IIA are equipped with the SPY-1D multifunction radar, while the Flight III will introduce the SPY-6(V)1 Air and Missile Defense Radar (AMDR). The new radar permits the ship to perform anti-air warfare and BMD intercepts simultaneously.

Zumwalt (DDG-1000) Class: The USN describes *Zumwalt* as the most technologically advanced surface combatant in the world. The first USN surface combatant to be equipped with an integrated

There are now seventy *Arleigh Burke* class destroyers in service, with a further twenty-nine under construction, authorised or planned. However, a start will be made on retiring the earlier members of the class from FY2027 onwards. This photograph shows the Flight IIA variant *Gravely* (DDG-107) entering Portsmouth Harbour, United Kingdom on 11 June 2022. *(Derek Fox)*

power system, the class retains significant capacity for future upgrades, including deployment of energy weapons or very high-powered sensors. With procurement of the class truncated at three units – only one of which is in full commission – the USN is still developing a concept of operations for these vessels. Captain Matthew Schroeder, DDG-1000 programme manager, confirmed in March 2022 that the USN plans to equip the *Zumwalt* class with hypersonic Conventional Prompt Strike (CPS) missiles when these enter service in 2025. Reconfiguration of USS *Zumwalt* to receive the CPS is scheduled to begin in October 2023.

Next Generation Large Surface Combatant – DDG(X): Whilst construction of the *Burke* class destroyers continues for the time being, its hull is considered to have no more growth potential for future technologies, especially weapons and sensors with high energy requirements. The USN is therefore planning to acquire a so-called next-generation large surface combatant as a follow-on to both the *Ticonderoga* and *Burke* classes. The programme is currently designated as DDG(X). Research and development work currently underway is expected to allow procurement of the first vessel to be initiated in 2030. While DDG-51 Flight III combat systems are likely to form the baseline capability of the initial next-generation destroyers, top-level requirements for the new ship include an integrated power system and new armament options such as directed energy weapons and improved weapons. The overall intent seems to be to follow an evolutionary rather than revolutionary approach so as to avoid some of the developmental setbacks that occurred with the *Zumwalt* class design.[6]

SMALL SURFACE COMBATANTS

The USN's small surface combatant category covers a wide range of vessels including multi-mission and mission-dedicated classes of varying survivability.

Littoral Combat Ships (LCS-1 and LCS-2 Classes): Once lauded as a maritime 'Swiss army knife' capable of quick transition between anti-submarine, surface and mine warfare missions, the Littoral Combat Ship has become a symbol of mismatched aspirations and poor programme implementation. Structural failings and mechanical breakdowns, as well as delays developing the various mission-specific equipment sets that form an integral part of the

The Flight II *Arleigh Burke* class variant *Decatur* (DDG-73), pictured whilst operating in the US Third Fleet's AOR in June 2022. Although construction of the latest *Burke* class variants continues for the time being, work has started on a next-generation large surface combatant with more potential to adopt future technologies. *(US Navy)*.

The latest *Independence* variant Littoral Combat Ship *Augusta* (LCS-34) being floated out by builders Austal USA in May 2022. Although a number of ships of the type are still under construction, some existing Littoral Combat Ships are already being retired as the US Navy apparently loses faith with the type. *(Austal USA)*

concept, have delayed the Littoral Combat Ships' progression to normal operational deployment cycles.

Thirty-five Littoral Combat Ships – sixteen *Freedom* (LCS-1) class and nineteen *Independence* (LCS-2) class variants – have been ordered, of which two prototypes have already been decommissioned and twenty-four units are in service. The latest, FY2023 plans envisage six LCS-1 and fifteen LCS-2 class vessels remaining in the fleet in the longer term, with as many as nine of the *Freedom* class being retired in the course of the fiscal year. Again, USN leadership expects some pushback from Congress against decommissioning such new ships; one argument already being presented points to the need for more, not fewer battle force vessels. If nothing else, Littoral Combat Ships can assume lower-intensity missions, freeing up other combatants for more arduous duties.

Constellation **(FFG-62) Class:** These new guided-missile frigates will be multi-mission combatants capable of the full spectrum of naval warfare. The USN chose to eschew experimentation and selected the operationally proven Italian variant of the multi-

mission FREMM class as the basis of the FFG-62 design. The ships will be built in Wisconsin at Fincantieri's Marinette Marine shipyard, although the USN reserves the right to contract a second shipyard if it chooses to increase the construction rate. Procurement began in FY2020. Lead ship construction is expected to begin before the end of 2022, with commissioning and IOC likely in 2027 and 2030 respectively. The FY2023 budget request foresees a production rate of three vessels every two years, with a total procurement goal of twenty vessels.

FFG-62 will be the first USN class to utilise a combined diesel-electric and gas (CODLAG) propulsion system, which promises to reduce fuel consumption and maintenance demands. This, along with a requirement to replace major European components of the ship with US-sourced parts, has led Congress to require land-based testing of the FFG-62's entire engineering plant prior to sea-testing the first operational unit. Some additional risk is being incurred through design changes which are required to accommodate USN weapons and sensors and to increase the overall combat power of the base design. Primary combat power will reside in

thirty-two VLS cells plus sixteen anti-ship missiles in deck-mounted box launchers.

Avenger **(MCM-1) and *Cyclone* (PC-1) Classes:** Eight of an original fourteen *Avenger* class mine countermeasures vessels are still in service. Four each are stationed in Sasebo, Japan and Manama, Bahrain. Retirement of these units has been postponed due to delays in fielding the mine countermeasures mission module for the littoral combat ship, which is the *Avenger* class's designated successor.

Five out of what was once fourteen *Cyclone* class coastal patrol vessels are based in Bahrain to support US anti-terrorism operations in the region. A further five were transferred to the Royal Bahrain Naval Force following their decommissioning in February 2022.[7]

MAJOR AMPHIBIOUS UNITS
The USN currently has the world's largest amphibious fleet. It comprises two *Blue Ridge* (ACC-19) class command ships and thirty-two major amphibious warships. *Blue Ridge* is home-ported at Yokosuka and acts as the Seventh Fleet flagship, while *Mount Whitney* (ACC-20) performs the same role for the Sixth Fleet at Gaeta.

Amphibious Assault Ships (LHD-1 and LHA-6 Classes): The nine amphibious assault ships resemble small aircraft carriers. Indeed, they have been deployed with a complement of up to twenty STOVL jets rather than their standard mix of vertical lift transport aircraft and a smaller warplane contingent. Their primary mission is to execute contested amphibious landings by transporting and then quickly airlifting marines and their equipment to shore. The embarked STOVL aircraft provide air-to-air and air-to-ground support for their helicopters, MV-22 Osprey tiltrotor aircraft and infantry.

The *Wasp* (LHD-1) class started entering service in 1989. It now consists of seven units following the loss of *Bonhomme Richard* (LHD-6) to fire in 2020. Their airlift capability is augmented by a well-deck capable of deploying three LCAC air-cushion landing craft or two LCU-type conventional landing craft. The lead vessel of the follow-on *America* (LHA-6) class entered service in 2014 and she was joined by *Tripoli* (LHA-7) in 2020. They feature an aircraft-centric configuration with an enlarged hangar deck and aviation-specific storage capacity

The *Cyclone* class patrol ship *Tornado* (PC-14) pictured in September 2020, a few months before being decommissioned. Only five of the once fourteen-strong class now remain in US Navy service as the fleet transitions to a structure more suited to deal with great-power rivalry. *(US Navy)*

but no well-deck. The well-deck has been added back to the third vessel of the class, *Bougainville* (LHA-8), which is currently under construction.

Amphibious Transport Docks and Dock Landing Ships (LPD-17 and LSD-41 Classes): The *San Antonio* (LPD-17) class amphibious transport docks started entering service in 2006 as the replacement for five earlier amphibious ship classes. They have a well-deck for two LCACs or a range of other amphibious craft and can accommodate up to five rotorcraft. They incorporate enhanced survivability features and a reduced radar cross-section. Eleven of thirteen planned Flight I vessels are operational with the twelfth currently completing post-delivery trials. Acquisition of a revised Flight II design will be truncated at just three vessels under current plans.

The USN also operates eleven of the broadly similar *Whidbey Island* (LSD-41) class and *Harpers Ferry* (LSD-49) class dock landing ships following retirement of *Fort McHenry* (LSD-43) in 2021. Their large well-decks are considered less relevant for current amphibious doctrine and most of the remainder will be retired over the next five years.

Light Amphibious Warship: The USMC plans to acquire up to thirty-five light amphibious warships (LAWs). These smaller, c. 4,000-tonne shallow-draft vessels are needed to support the EABO concept, which calls for widely dispersed operations by platoon-to-company sized USMC units. Requirements include the ability to transport a minimum of 75 marines, 4,000–8,000ft² of cargo space, an unrefuelled range of 3,500 nautical miles, and survivability equivalent to that of a frigate. Five firms have received contracts to produce concept designs but initial procurement, once expected to begin in FY2023, has been deferred to FY2025, probably for budgetary reasons.

SUBMARINES

The USN currently operates five submarine classes of two types, continuing to modernise the force with new weapons and sensors to meet developing threats. All USN submarines utilise nuclear propulsion to maximise range and the duration of submerged missions.

The navy's attack submarines (SSNs) conduct independent offensive operations against enemy ships and submarines, including mine warfare, as well as land-attack and ISR missions. They provide

Fort Lauderdale (LPD-28) is the twelfth and latest *San Antonio* class amphibious transport dock to be delivered, being accepted by the US Navy on 11 March 2022. She incorporates a number of design enhancements that will be used in the Flight II *San Antonio* design. *(Huntington Ingalls Industries)*

covert transportation and support for Special Operations, including carriage of dorsal-mounted dry deck shelters containing appropriate equipment. They also escort carrier groups as force protection. Armament options include conventional torpedoes, TLAMs, and Harpoon anti-shipping missiles fired either through torpedo tubes or dorsal-mounted missile silos.

***Los Angeles* (SSN-668) Class:** The *Los Angeles* class were first deployed as long ago as 1976. Of sixty-two built, twenty-six remain in service. These boats belong to the Flight II – which added VLS silos for Tomahawk cruise missiles – and Flight III – which feature enhanced electronics suites and a reduced acoustic profile – construction runs. The remaining members of the class are steadily being withdrawn as they reach life expiry, putting pressure on overall USN submarine numbers.

***Seawolf* (SSN-21) Class:** Procurement of these boats ended after only three units were ordered. Originally planned for an extended production run, these vessels were designed to challenge high-performance Soviet attack and strategic submarines

in very deep waters. Today they are widely deployed in the ISR role due to their advanced sensors and extremely low acoustic signature. The third unit, *Jimmy Carter* (SSN-23), is equipped with a 30m-long extension designated as a Multi-Mission Platform. This accommodates additional payloads for classified missions and research projects, and permits launch and recovery of unmanned remotely operated vehicles.

***Virginia* (SSN-774) Class:** Entering service in 2004 as the successor to the *Los Angeles* class boats, the SSN-774 design remains under construction. Innovations introduced with this class included fly-by-wire ship control systems that optimise handling in littoral and shallow waters. Photonic masts housing visual and infrared light cameras replaced periscopes. The control room was enlarged and reconfigured to provide enhanced situational awareness. Pump-jet propulsors replaced propellers, reducing acoustic signature. Finally, a modular, open-architecture enables frequent upgrades of on-board systems to maintain state-of-the-art capabilities.

Twenty-one *Virginia*s have been delivered to date. A further seventeen are under construction or on order and future plans envisage ongoing procurement at a rate of two units per year. As with many other USN vessels, incremental improvements have been introduced in various Flights or Blocks, of which the most recent is the Block V variant. The primary innovation to most of this variant is the addition of the Virginia Payload Module (VPM); a new section inserted midships and containing four missile payload tubes. Each tube accommodates seven Tomahawk cruise missiles, adding a total of twenty-eight weapons to the boat's arsenal. Plans call for future construction of Block VI and Block VII variants incorporating additional, yet to be developed technologies.

The USN's ballistic missile-armed submarines (SSBNs) constitute part of the United States' strategic triad, augmenting strategic bombers and ground-based intercontinental ballistic missiles. SSBNs are considered the most survivable portion of the triad, as they conduct almost their entire patrol submerged with their precise location hidden from potential adversaries. They are currently armed with Trident II D-5 submarine-launched ballistic missiles (SLBMs), each of which can be equipped with a number of multiple independently targetable re-entry vehicles. A D-5 life extension programme has extended the lives of existing missiles to c. 2040.

Ohio (**SSBN-726**) **Class:** Entering service in 1981, fourteen of eighteen original class *Ohio* class submarines remain in service as strategic submarines, each carrying twenty Trident II SLBMs. Eight are stationed in the Pacific Northwest at Naval Base Kitsap in Washington state, reflecting the challenges posed by three nuclear-armed potential adversaries in the Pacific. The remaining six are stationed at Kings Bay, Georgia on the US east coast.

The remaining four *Ohio*s were converted to guided missile submarines between 2002 and 2008. Each of the four ships now patrols with up to 154 TLAMs carried in twenty-two Multiple All-Up-Round Canisters (MAC). In lieu of cruise missiles, some MACs can carry unmanned underwater or aerial vehicles, Special Forces equipment, or extra perishables to prolong underwater cruise duration. Extra berthing is present for up to sixty-six Special Forces personnel.

Columbia (**SSBN-826**) **Class:** Development of the *Columbia* class has been the USN's top priority since

US Navy attack submarine construction is currently focused on the *Virginia* (SSN-774) class, which are being built in progressively improved Blocks. The Block IV boat *New Jersey* (SSN-796) is seen here in the course of roll-out from her construction hall prior to launch in April 2022. *(Huntington Ingalls Industries)*

The *Ohio* class strategic submarine *Henry M. Jackson* (SSBN-730) begins to submerge after an underway change of command. The fourteen *Ohio* class submarines that remain allocated to the strategic role form the most survivable element of the United States' nuclear 'triad'. *(US Navy)*

2013. A turbo-electric-drive and pump-jet propulsion system is intended to make the new boats faster and quieter than the *Ohio* class. The propulsion reactor's nuclear fuel core will be good for the submarine's entire service life, obviating the need for a multi-year refuelling phase. While the planned displacement of 21,000 tonnes is greater than that of the *Ohio* class, overall dimensions will be similar to enable berthing and maintenance at the same facilities. Each ship will have sixteen missile tubes. The navy plans to acquire twelve units by 2042. Construction of the first of class – *District of Columbia* – officially began in June 2022. A target delivery date of 2027 should allow her first patrol mission to take place in 2031.

USN SPECIAL OPERATIONS AND RIVERINE FORCES

The USN maintains a large, c. 9,000-strong, special operations command. Active-duty operational units include two Naval Special Warfare Groups (NSWGs), one based in California and one in Virginia. Each group controls four SEAL (Sea-Air-Land) commando teams. Two additional NSWGs are responsible for SEAL delivery vehicle (mini-submarine) operations and for Special Boat Team operations. While NSWGs remain ready for a wide range of missions, they are adjusting to the Pentagon's renewed focus on great power conflict. This includes integration of SEAL teams and Special Boat Teams into aircraft carrier group and amphibious ready group training exercises to prepare to support fleet operations in a future war against China or Russia.

The USN also maintains two Coastal Riverine Groups which conduct intelligence, surveillance and reconnaissance (ISR), interdiction, infrastructure security, ship escort and special operations support missions. These 'brown water' units patrol inland waterways, as well as estuaries, bays and similar coastal waters.

US MARINE CORPS

The USMC currently has approximately 175,000 Marines on active duty. Operational forces are assigned to three Marine Expeditionary Forces (MEFs), which combine an infantry division, an air wing, and logistics/support units. II MEF and its subordinate units are based on the US Atlantic coast and are oriented toward operations in Europe, Africa, the Middle East and Latin America/the Caribbean. I and III MEFs are oriented toward the Pacific, with the bulk of III MEF permanently stationed in Japan. Each MEF also contains a medium-sized Marine Expeditionary Brigade and smaller Marine Expeditionary Units – all with their own air and logistical support – that facilitate a scalable crisis response.

The USMC is also re-orienting itself toward great-power conflict. Some units are honing Arctic warfare skills with an eye towards operations in Scandinavia or along the North American Arctic coast. The greater portion is looking toward China. To realise the high-tempo distributed operations and EABO concepts, the USMC is divesting some heavier formations in order to enhance mobility. High-tech communications networks, precision weapons with stand-off-range, and other technological innovations are intended to enhance the combat power of the lighter and more distributed force. A new operational formation, designated as the Marine Littoral Combat Regiment (MLR), is being developed and tested. The MLR will have three major components: a Littoral Combat Team organised around an infantry regiment augmented by an anti-surface missile battery; a Littoral Anti-Air Battalion to provide not only air defence but also air traffic control and forward rearming and refuelling of USMC aircraft; and a Combat Logistics Battalion. The MLR's forces will conduct distributed operations as reinforced platoons under the EABO concept. A minimum of three MLRs are planned, with the first to be established in FY2023 on Hawaii.[8]

NAVAL AVIATION

It is frequently said that US naval aviation, which encompasses both USN and USMC aircraft, 'constitutes the second most powerful air force in the world'; after the United States Air Force. Whilst this statement is debatable, the USN's naval airpower certainly represents a uniquely capable maritime force component.

A major element of naval aviation is the carrier air wing (CVW). The USN maintains nine such units – four orientated towards the Atlantic based at Naval Air Station (NAS) Oceana, Virginia and five towards the Pacific at NAS Lemoore California and Marine Corps Air Station Iwakuni, Japan – to serve on

A US Marine provides anti-air defence with a FIM-92E Stinger during Exercise Noble Jaguar 2021 at Combined Arms Training Center, Camp Fuji, Japan in September 2021. The exercise focused on coastal defence and counter-landing operations across a distributed maritime environment as part of the USMC's reorientation towards high-tempo distributed Expeditionary Advanced Base Operations (EABO) concepts. *(US Marine Corps)*

deployed aircraft carriers. Core elements of each air wing typically comprise:

- Four strike fighter (VFA) squadrons, each with twelve F/A-18E/F Super Hornets.
- One electronic attack (VQA) squadron with five E/A-18G Growlers.
- One airborne early warning (VAW) squadron with four E-2D Advanced Hawkeyes.
- One helicopter sea combat (HSC) squadron with eight MH-60S Seahawks.
- One helicopter maritime strike (HSM) squadron with eleven MH-60R Seahawks.
- One fleet logistic support (VRC) squadron detachment with two CA-2A Greyhounds.

Some of the helicopters are deployed on warships attached to the carrier strike group rather than the aircraft carrier itself.

With the introduction of new aircraft and changes in operating doctrine, the composition of the carrier air wing is changing. In August 2021 *Carl Vinson* (CVN-70) deployed with an upgraded wing to test future composition options. Changes included substituting a squadron of F-35C fighters for one F/A-18 unit; increasing the electronic attack capability to seven aircraft and the airborne early warning unit to five; and embarking three CMV-22B Ospreys to replace the C-2A logistics aircraft. Overall, the tested configuration enhanced the wing's strike range and capability while also enhancing survivability through better stealth and electronic warfare capabilities.

While the newer F/A-18E/F and E/A-18G airframes are expected to serve into the 2050s, and the F-35C is just entering front-line service, the USN is already planning its Next Generation Air Dominance (NGAD) system. NGAD is expected to be a family of airframes or 'capabilities', probably centred on a manned fighter/attack aircraft currently designated as the F/A-XX. It will be armed with long-range precision weapons, presumably including hypersonic missiles. It will be supported by several unmanned airframes configured for a variety of missions including ground attack, air-to-air combat, electronic warfare, and, potentially, airborne early warning. A greater number of airframes will support distributed operations, especially in the far-reaching Pacific AOR. The NGAD programme office officially opened in May 2020. The project is currently in the concept development phase, but the USN

A US Marine Corps F-35C Lightning II strike fighter prepares for launch from *Abraham Lincoln* (CVN-72) in February 2022. The composition of US Navy carrier air wings is changing as new equipment is introduced. *(US Navy)*

hopes to introduce the NGAD into the fleet in the 2030s.[9]

THE UNMANNED FUTURE

Unmanned air, ground, and sea systems are gaining importance as force multipliers. One senior US naval officer has postulated that 50–60 percent of future carrier air wing assets could be unmanned.[10] The USN is currently testing the MQ-25A Stingray, which will become the world's first operational, carrier-based large unmanned aircraft. It will provide aerial refuelling for manned aircraft and likely conduct ISR missions. Successful initial integration into the air wing of *George H.W. Bush* (CVN-77) was demonstrated in December 2021. The first operational deployment is scheduled for 2026 aboard *Theodore Roosevelt* (CVN-71).

The USN is also pursuing large unmanned underwater vehicle (UUV) and unmanned surface vessel (USV) projects. These vessels will act as force multipliers, significantly enhancing the capacity to conduct distributed operations and permitting units to move close to enemy forces or territory without endangering human crews. Corvette-sized large USVs could carry as many as thirty-two VLS cells and feature multiple payload options. Extra-large

UUVs (XLUUV) could be c. 25m long and carry torpedoes or mines. The USN's most recent long-range shipbuilding plan, released in April 2022, commits 'to actively testing concept of operations (CONOPS) and employment of these platforms to iteratively assess and fully develop their capabilities in a practical and realistic manner'.[11]

Experimentation and development programmes are intensifying in line with this objective. The USN formally established Unmanned Surface Vessel Division One in May 2022. The unit currently operates four prototype USVs, all of which are slated to participate in the RIMPAC 2022 exercise scheduled for August 2022. In July 2020 a US$35m contract was awarded for the design and construction of a MUSV prototype and detailed design and construction of the first operational large USV class has been scheduled for FY2025. The USN also ordered five, 'operationally-relevant' Orca XLUUVs in 2019, with deliveries slated to begin in 2023. An Orca XLUUV test vessel was launched in April 2022.

FUTURE FLEET STRUCTURE UNCERTAINTIES

Given the ever-changing geopolitical and techno-

The *Los Angeles* class submarine *Springfield* (SSN-761) loads a dummy Harpoon anti-surface missile at Perth, Western Australia during weapons handling training. The US Navy's future plans intend to grow the force of attack submarines but – like much of the projected fleet structure – precise numbers are uncertain. *(US Navy)*

logical backdrop, there remains much uncertainty concerning the future composition of the US fleet. Numerous internally prepared assessments regarding the optimal force needed to master future challenges have been overthrown by military or civilian leadership in recent years. Having learned from this experience – and, perhaps, demonstrating a certain exasperation – the USN's Warfighting and Requirement staff opted to present Congress with three alternative plans for the 2023–52 timeframe in the latest, FY2023 long-range shipbuilding plan.[12] The three options would result, respectively, in a fleet size of 316, 327, or 367 manned vessels by 2052. The first two options could be achieved without significant change to the expected defence budget trajectory, although the report warns that the currently planned procurement pace for certain ship classes cannot be maintained at the present level of funding. The third and largest fleet force option would require an additional annual growth of US$75bn (in 2022 constant US$ purchasing power) in capital procurement spending over the life of the plan. The report cautions that the ability of the defence industrial base to execute the third option remains uncertain.

All the options presented reflect the influence of the DMO concept. Numbers of large surface combatants and (implicitly) major amphibious units will fall, whilst there will be more small surface combatants, minor amphibious vessels, logistics assets and attack submarines. However, there are considerable variations in category numbers between the three proposals, particularly with respect to surface combatants and amphibious ships.

It must be stressed that the USN's long-range shipbuilding plan is updated yearly, with greater or lesser changes from one iteration to the next. Developing technology, revived assessments of the threat environment and – perhaps most importantly – budget uncertainty all but guarantee that the fleet numbers forecast will continue to evolve. However, it is hard to escape the conclusion that adapting to the return to great power competition is challenging the USN's efforts to devise an appropriate future fleet structure, which remains work in progress.

Notes

1. The USN strategic blueprint *A Blue Arctic* (Washington DC: US Department of the Navy, 2021) proposes a mix of permanent, rotational and temporary force stationing and materiel prepositioning in the region to counter ongoing Russian 'militarization of its northern flank' .

2. The US Navy Secretary's 2021 strategic guidance *One Navy-Marine Corps Team* (Washington DC: US Department of the Navy, 2021), p.2 states: 'As our central governing concept, the top priority for the Department of the Navy will be to develop concepts of operations and capabilities that bolster deterrence and expand our warfighting advantages vis-a-vis the People's Republic of China.'

3. Ronald O' Rourke's *Navy Aegis Ballistic Missile Defense: Background and Issues for Congress RL33745* (Washington DC: Congressional Research Service, 2022) provides a succinct overview of the Aegis BMD program including history, technical issues, and future planning.

4. This section inevitably provides only a sketch of a complex organisational structure.

5. The design and development of the *Nimitz* class is described in detail in Chapter 3.3.

6. For further detail see Ronald O'Rourke, *Navy DDG(X)*

Next-Generation Destroyer Program: Background and Issues for Congress IF11679 (Washington DC: Congressional Research Service, 2022).

7. Unlike the other small surface combatants mentioned, the *Cyclone* class boats are not included within the total battle force count.

8. Details of the USMC's reorganisation are being constantly refined and revised. The latest Force Design 2030 Annual Review was published in May 2022 and can be found at: www.marines.mil/Force-Design-2030/

9. For further information on the future of USN aviation, see *Navy Aviation Vision 2030-2035* (San Diego: Naval Aviation Enterprise, 2021).

10. Rear Admiral Gregory Harris, Director of Air Warfare 2019–21, speaking at the March 2021 Navy League symposium

11. See *Report to Congress on the Annual Long-Range Plan for Construction of Naval Vessels for Fiscal Year 2023* (Washington DC: Office of the Chief of Naval Operations, 2022).

12. Ibid.

Author:
Conrad Waters

2.2 REGIONAL REVIEW

ASIA AND THE PACIFIC

On 15 September 2021, in a surprise joint announcement, the then Australian Prime Minister Scott Morrison, British Prime Minister Boris Johnson and US President Joseph Biden revealed the creation of a trilateral security partnership to be called AUKUS (Australia, the United Kingdom and the United States). Aimed at strengthening the partner nations' ability to support mutual security interests and building on longstanding bilateral ties, the alliance is particularly focused on enhancing cooperation in defence technology. The first initiative to be taken under the AUKUS framework is realisation of a shared ambition to support Australia acquiring a nuclear-powered submarine capability for the Royal Australian Navy (RAN).

The announcement had several immediate and significant consequences. Despite subsequent claims by the British Prime Minister that the partnership 'is not intended to be adversarial towards any other power' the new security pact has been seen as an obvious attempt by the Anglo-Saxon triumvirate to counter growing Chinese influence in the Indo-Pacific region. As such, it drew a predictably negative response from the Chinese government, which stated that AUKUS 'has seriously undermined regional peace and stability'. Many of the leading Association of South East Asian Nations (ASEAN) members have also been ambivalent about the agreement. Whilst nervous of future Chinese hegemony, they are reluctant to see Sino-American tensions playing out in their own sphere of influence and see the partnership as exacerbating the two superpowers' rivalry. Of course, this is not a universal view. Many local nations

that are more closely aligned with the United States will doubtless see the partnership as a welcome step towards correcting a balance of power that has been steadily tilting in China's favour.[1]

One other country that was very unhappy about the new partnership was France. Australia's decision to acquire nuclear-powered attack submarines meant the termination of its programme to buy twelve 'Shortfin Barracuda' *Attack* class conventionally-powered variants of Naval Group's *Suffren* class design, detonating the French company's most lucrative export contract. As well as the financial consequences, AUKUS also represented a setback to France's efforts to expand its own influence in a region where it retains several overseas territories. France also appears to have had little idea that the announcement was coming. French Foreign Minister, Jean-Yves Le Drian's description of developments as a 'stab in the back' conveys something of the shock experienced by a jilted partner suddenly supplanted by a hitherto secret relationship.

From a practical perspective, there is much to be said in favour of Australia's submarine decision. The *Attack* class offered incremental improvements over the RAN's existing *Collins* class design but suffered in comparison with the endurance, speed and flexibility of a nuclear-powered solution. These factors became relevant as growing tensions with China increased the likelihood of Australia's new submarines having to operate at distance across South East Asia over a lifespan that could extend throughout much of the current century. It would, of course, have been possible for Australia to switch

its procurement efforts to France's nuclear-powered *Suffren* class. However, these boats use a technological solution that involves periodic refuelling of their reactors; a requirement that would involve significant investment in supporting infrastructure by a country that lacks its own civilian nuclear power industry. The 'whole life' reactor designs used in current American and British submarines therefore appear to be a more attractive option. It should also be noted that Australia's experience of its dealings with Naval Group was not an entirely happy one; there were many local press reports that the relationship had become strained. However, cancellation of the *Attack* programme does have downsides. A total of AS\$3.4bn (c. US\$2.4bn) invested in the project has now been lost. Moreover, the arrival of replacements for Australia's increasingly elderly submarine flotilla will be pushed further to the right.[2]

Meanwhile, geopolitical manoeuvring in the Asia-Pacific region is moving closer to Australian shores. On 19 April 2022, China announced that a security pact had been signed with the Solomon Islands, a south-west Pacific archipelago to the north-east of Australia of considerable strategic importance. Although ostensibly aimed at strengthening the internal security of a nation that has suffered major unrest under Prime Minister Manasseh Sogavare's polarising regime, there are fears that China will use the agreement to develop naval facilities in the islands. The development has certainly caused unease amongst US-allies in the region against a backdrop of Chinese efforts to expand its influence across numerous other Pacific island states.[3]

The US Navy nuclear-powered attack submarine *Santa Fe* (SSN-763) pictured exercising with four RAN *Collins* class patrol submarines off Western Australia in February 2019. In September 2021, Australia announced that it had decided to adopt nuclear propulsion for its next submarine design. *(Royal Australian Navy)*

Table 2.2.1: FLEET STRENGTHS IN ASIA AND THE PACIFIC – LARGER NAVIES (MID 2022)

COUNTRY	AUSTRALIA	CHINA[1]	INDONESIA	JAPAN	S KOREA	SINGAPORE	TAIWAN	THAILAND
Aircraft Carrier (CV)	–	2	–	–	–	–	–	–
Support/Helicopter Carrier (CVS/CVH)	–	–	–	4	–	–	–	1
Strategic Missile Submarine (SSBN)	–	7	–	–	–	–	–	–
Attack Submarine (SSN)	–	9	–	–	–	–	–	–
Patrol Submarine (SSK/SS)	6	50	4	22	19	4	4[4]	–
Fleet Escort (DDG/FFG)	11	90	7	38	24	6	26	8
Patrol Escort/Corvette (FFG/FSG/FS)	–	75	24	6	7	14	2	11
Missile Armed Attack Craft (PGG/PTG)	–	75	22[2]	6	18	–	c.30	–
Mine Countermeasures Vessel (MCMV)	4	25	9	20	10	4	c. 10	5
Major Amphibious Units (LHD/LPD/LSD)	3	10	7[3]	3	2	4	1	1

Notes:

1: Chinese numbers approximate. 2: Some additional Indonesian patrol gunboats are able to ship missiles. 3: Includes two vessels configured as hospital ships. 4: Taiwan's submarines are reported to have limited operational availability.

MAJOR REGIONAL POWERS – AUSTRALIA

Australia's decision to adopt nuclear propulsion for its next generation of submarines will have a considerable impact on both local shipbuilding and naval force structure. In the short term, the revised requirement makes it imperative that a life-extension programme is implemented for the existing *Collins* class, a project that was already being planned to accommodate the likely delivery schedule of the *Attack* class before the change of strategy was announced. All six of the boats will undergo a 'life of type' extension at ASC's facilities in Osborne, South Australia, commencing with *Farncomb* in 2026. The upgrades, which are to include new propulsion and electrical distribution systems as well as improvements to the sensor suite, should extend the life of each boat by approximately 10 years once the refit is complete. It has also been reported that the possibility of equipping the upgraded submarines with Tomahawk cruise missiles – already being acquired for the surface fleet – is under consideration.

In the longer term, the plan to build at least eight nuclear-powered boats instead of the twelve *Attack* class submarines previously envisaged will require substantial changes to industrial and supporting infrastructure that are still being worked out in detail. A Nuclear-Powered Submarine Task Force under the leadership of Vice Admiral Jonathan Mead RAN has been established to advise the Australian government on the optimal pathway to acquire the new capability with a brief to report back within 18 months of the AUKUS announcement. The task force will, inter alia, explore the design of the submarines to be acquired; how their crews and supporting workers will be trained; and what infrastructure will be required to sustain the boats in a safe and efficient way. There is no indication as of yet as to whether an American or British submarine design is preferred, with current work on the US Navy SSN(X) and Royal Navy SSNR programmes offering alternative routes to acquiring the new flotilla. It has already been established that an additional submarine base will be built on Australia's east coast – either at Brisbane, Newcastle or Port Kembla – to supplement the existing facility at Fleet Base West, near Perth. A major question that remains to be answered is whether the new submarines can be brought on line before the *Collins* class exceed the limits of their life extension.[4]

The revisions to the submarine programme mean that the *Hunter* class programme to acquire nine anti-submarine frigates evolved from the British Type 26 Global Combat Ship is currently the main naval procurement project underway. This is also proving to be not entirely plain sailing. Whilst BAE Systems Maritime Australia commenced prototype fabrication of five representative ship blocks to test production processes at its Osborne facility in December 2020, the start of actual production of the lead ship has been deferred from the end of 2022 to mid-2024 as the ship's design is matured. The Australian ships will incorporate significant country-specific revisions from their British 'cousins', including:

- Incorporation of the Aegis combat system combined with a Saab Australian tactical interface.
- Specification of the CEAFAR2 phased array as the main multi-function radar.
- Integration of Australian-specific weapons systems.
- Utilisation of Australian communications systems.
- Embarkation of the MH-60R SEAHAWK helicopter.

All these changes have pushed up full-load displacement to a reported 10,000 tonnes; close to the ship's design margins. Although a successful Systems Definition Review was concluded early in 2022 that established the Australian variant's design baseline, this has led to inevitable calls that the project be reconsidered in spite of few realistic alternative options.[5] The likely impact on any further major revision of shipbuilding plans to the local industrial base should also not be taken lightly.

Considerably closer to delivery is the RAN's Project SEA 1180 Phase 1 for twelve *Arafura* class offshore patrol vessels based on the NVL (formerly

The new RAN offshore patrol vessel *Arafura* – based on the NVL OPV-80 design – pictured being readied for launch at the Osborne Naval Shipyard in South Australia in December 2021. She is expected to enter service before the end of 2022. *(Royal Australian Navy)*

Table 2.2.2: ROYAL AUSTRALIAN NAVY: PRINCIPAL UNITS AS AT MID 2022

TYPE	CLASS	NUMBER	TONNAGE	DIMENSIONS	PROPULSION	CREW	DATE
Principal Surface Escorts							
Frigate – FFG	**HOBART** (F-100)	3	6,300 tonnes	147m x 19m x 5m	CODOG, 28 knots	200	2017
Frigate – FFG	**ANZAC**	8	3,600 tonnes	118m x 15m x 4m	CODOG, 28 knots	175	1996
Submarines							
Submarine – SSK	**COLLINS**	6	3,400 tonnes	78m x 8m x 7m	Diesel-electric, 20 knots	45	1996
Major Amphibious Units							
Amph Assault Ship – LHD	**CANBERRA** (JUAN CARLOS I)	2	27,100 tonnes	231m x 32m x 7m	IEP, 21 knots	290	2014
Landing Ship Dock – LSD	**CHOULES** (LARGS BAY)	1	16,200 tonnes	176m x 26m x 6m	Diesel-electric, 18 knots	160	2006

Lürssen) OPV-80 platform. The lead ship of the class was launched during an official ceremony held at the Osborne Naval Shipyard in South Australia on 16 December 2021 and will join the fleet before the end of 2022. The first pair of *Arafura* class vessels is being completed at Osborne to help maintain local shipbuilding skills in advance of assembly of the *Hunter* class. However, the remainder will be built in Henderson in Western Australia by a joint venture between the recently renamed German group and local Australian group company Cimvec. In addition to the ten vessels currently allocated to the partnership, a variant of the design is being considered for up to eight new mine countermeasures 'mother ships' and hydrographic survey vessels set to be acquired under Project SEA 1905 Phase 1. This holds out the prospect of an extended production run for the German design.

The *Arafura* class will be supplemented by smaller 'Evolved Cape' class patrol boats derived from eight ships delivered to the Australian Border Force from 2013 onwards. The RAN already operates two of these vessels acquired under an innovative lease arrangement involving National Australia Bank but is starting to receive eight units of its own under contracts announced in May 2020 and April 2022. The first of these, named *Cape Otway*, was accepted in March 2022. The next, *Cape Peron*, is expected in July. Although arguably better suited for coastal operations than the larger *Arafura* type, a cynic might argue that their acquisition is as much as maintaining employment at builder Austal's Henderson facility – that lost out to Cimvec with respect to offshore patrol vessel production – as meeting a long-term operational need. However, the new vessels' arrival is helping to compensate for the withdrawal of the life-expired *Armidale* class patrol boats, thereby preventing a capability gap. *Maitland* was the third of these to leave RAN service when she was decommissioned in a ceremony at Darwin on 28 April 2022.[6]

As illustrated by Table 2.2.2, there has been no significant change in the structure of the RAN's major units over the last year. However, renewal of the replenishment force has been completed with the commissioning of the second *Supply* class replenishment oiler, *Stalwart*, on 13 November 2021 after the installation of Australian-specific mission equipment. Her arrival allowed the retirement of the modified commercial tanker *Sirius*, which was decommissioned at Fleet Base West on 18 December 2021 after over 15 years of RAN service.

The new Australian 'Evolved Cape Class' patrol boat *Cape Otway* seen arriving at Darwin, her new home port, in June 2022. She is of similar design to the Trinidad and Tobago Coast Guard's *Scarborough* pictured in the North and South America chapter. *(Royal Australian Navy)*

MAJOR REGIONAL POWERS – CHINA

According to US Department of Defense assessments, the Chinese People's Liberation Army Navy (PLAN) is numerically the largest in the world with – as of 2020 – a front-line 'battle force' of c. 355

ships and submarines, including more than 145 major surface combatants.[7] Having spent the last decade first closing the gap between and then surpassing US Navy fleet numbers, the PLAN's rate of overall growth is now seemingly starting to slow as its focus increasingly turns to bridging the qualitative disparity with its strategic competitor. The United States acknowledges that considerable progress has been made in this respect, with the PLAN being regarded as 'being largely composed of modern, multi-role platforms'. This is reflected in Table 2.2.3 summarising current PLAN fleet strength, which illustrates the large number of major warships that have entered service in the last decade. The capabilities of China's other maritime forces – including its coast guard and maritime militia – in exerting pressure in the pursuit of the country's extensive maritime claims should not be overlooked.

As is the case for all navies, the PLAN has both strengths and weaknesses. Given its historical focus on near seas protection, it has developed strong anti-access/area denial (A2/AD) capabilities – particularly above the waves. The PLAN is also steadily improving its power projection capabilities, although it still has a long way to go in matching the power of the US Navy's carrier strike groups and is regarded as having significant logistical support deficiencies. Whilst it is enhancing its anti-submarine warfare (ASW) inventory, it is regarded as lacking a robust deep-water anti-submarine capability.[8] Another potential problem is inducting and training the large numbers of crew that need to become proficient in operating warships that are often two or more generations in advance of their predecessors. The strict limitations placed on Chinese society in order to manage the COVID-19 pandemic are reportedly exacerbating this problem in the short term.[9]

In spite of these limitations, the PLAN has continued to make significant headway in the last

Table 2.2.3: PEOPLE'S LIBERATION ARMY NAVY: PRINCIPAL UNITS AS AT MID 2022

TYPE	CLASS	NUMBER	TONNAGE	DIMENSIONS	PROPULSION	CREW	DATE
Aircraft Carriers							
Aircraft Carrier – CV	Type 001A (Modified Kuznetsov)	1	65,000 tonnes	315m x 35/75m x 10m	Steam, 32 knots	Unknown	2019
Aircraft Carrier – CV	Type 001 LIAONING (Kuznetsov)	1	60,000 tonnes	306m x 35/73m x 10m	Steam, 32 knots	Unknown	2012
Principal Surface Escorts							
Destroyer – DDG	Type 055 NANCHANG ('Renhai')	6	c. 12,000 tonnes	180m x 20m x 7m	COGAG, 30 knots	c.300	2019
Destroyer – DDG	Type 052D KUNMING ('Luyang III')	24	7,500 tonnes	156m x 17m x 6m	CODOG, 28 knots	280	2014
Destroyer – DDG	Type 051C SHENYANG ('Luzhou')	2	7,100 tonnes	155m x 17m x 6m	Steam, 29 knots	250	2006
Destroyer – DDG	Type 052C LANZHOU ('Luyang II')	6	7,000 tonnes	154m x 17m x 6m	CODOG, 28 knots	280	2005
Destroyer – DDG	Type 052B GUANGZHOU ('Luyang I')	2	6,500 tonnes	154m x 17m x 6m	CODOG, 29 knots	280	2004
Destroyer – DDG	Project 956E/EM HANGZHOU (Sovremenny)	4	8,000 tonnes	156m x 17m x 6m	Steam, 32 knots	300	1999
Destroyer – DDG	Type 051B SHENZHEN ('Luhai')	1	6,000 tonnes	154m x 16m x 6m	Steam, 31 knots	250	1998
Destroyer – DDG	Type 052 HARBIN ('Luhu')	2	4,800 tonnes	143m x 15m x 5m	CODOG, 31 knots	260	1994
Frigate – FFG	Type 054A XUZHOU ('Jiangkai II')	31	4,100 tonnes	132m x 15m x 5m	CODAD, 28 knots	190	2008
Frigate – FFG	Type 054 MA'ANSHAN ('Jiangkai I')	2	4,000 tonnes	132m x 15m x 5m	CODAD, 28 knots	190	2005
Frigate – FFG	Type 053 H3 LIANYUNGANG ('Jiangwei II')	8	2,500 tonnes	112m x 12m x 5m	CODAD, 27 knots	170	1992
Frigate – FSG	Type 056/056A BENGBU ('Jiangdao')	72[1]	1,500 tonnes	89m x 12m x 4m	CODAD, 28 knots	60	2013

Plus c. 5 remaining obsolescent frigates of the Type 053 H1/H1G TAIZHOU/BEIHAI ('Jianghu II & V') classes that remain active in second-line roles.

Submarines							
Submarine – SSBN	Type 094/094A ('Jin')	c. 6	9,000 tonnes	133m x 11m x 8m	Nuclear, 20+ knots	Unknown	2008
Submarine – SSBN	Type 092 ('Xia')	1	6,500 tonnes	120m x 10m x 8m	Nuclear, 22 knots	140	1987
Submarine – SSN	Type 093/093A ('Shang')	c. 6	6,000 tonnes	107m x 11m x 8m	Nuclear, 30 knots	100	2006
Submarine – SSN	Type 091 ('Han')	3	5,500 tonnes	106m x 10m x 7m	Nuclear, 25 knots	75	1974
Submarine – SSK	Type 039A/039B (Type 041 'Yuan')	c. 20	2,500 tonnes	75m x 8m x 5m	AIP, 20+ knots	Unknown	2006
Submarine – SSK	Type 039/039G ('Song')	13	2,300 tonnes	75m x 8m x 5m	Diesel-electric, 22 knots	60	1999
Submarine – SSK	Project 877 EKM/636 ('Kilo')	12[2]	3,000 tonnes	73m x 10m x 7m	Diesel-electric, 20 knots	55	1995

Plus c. 10 obsolescent patrol submarines of the Type 035 ('Ming' Class), some in reserve. A Type 032 'Qing' trials submarine has also been commissioned for strategic missile trials.

Major Amphibious Units							
Amph. Assault Ship – LHD	Type 075 HAINAN ('Yushen')	2	40,000 tonnes	237m x 36m x 8m	CODAD, 20+ knots	Unknown	2021
Landing Platform Dock – LPD	Type 071 KULUN SHAN ('Yuzhao')	8	18,000 tonnes	210m x 27m x 7m	CODAD, 20 knots	Unknown	2007

Notes:
1. Many of the 22-strong Type 056 variant are now being refitted for coast guard use.
2. It has reported that the two older Project 877 EKM 'Kilos' are being sold for scrap.

year, as the following summaries related to principal warship types makes clear.

Aircraft Carriers and Amphibious Vessels: 17 June 2022 saw the PLAN launch its third aircraft carrier, the Type 003 *Fujian*. She is noteworthy in being the first Chinese carrier of entirely indigenous design and – in contrast to her two predecessors – will be configured for catapult assisted take-off but arrested recovery (CATOBAR) operations. Her launch at the Jiangnang shipyard near Shanghai was reportedly delayed by strict pandemic containment measures undertaken by the Chinese authorities but it is possible that she will commence sea trials around the end of 2023. Conventionally powered but approaching the size of the US Navy's CVN-68 and CVN-78 classes, she will embark a new generation of aircraft that will likely include the carrier variant of its Shenyang FC-31 stealth fighter. Information circulating on the Internet in late 2021 suggests that a prototype of this aircraft is currently undertaking trials. Also slated for the new carrier is the Xian KJ-600 airborne early warning aircraft, the Chinese equivalent of the US Navy's E-2 Hawkeye.

The PLAN's inventory of amphibious shipping is also moving forward with deliveries of the new Type 075 LHD-type amphibious assault ships. An initial batch of three of these vessels has been completed by Shanghai's Hudong-Zhonghua Shipbuilding, of which two are already in commission. They are likely, in due course, to be followed by a second batch, which could be built in an improved Type 076 configuration. There have been rumours that – like the Type 003 – these will potentially be fitted with electromagnetic catapult technology, although possibly optimised for drone operation.

Major Surface Combatants: The PLAN continues to commission new surface combatants at a rapid pace, with construction increasingly focused on larger and more sophisticated vessels. The last year has seen the fleet of large, c. 12,000-tonne Type 055 'Renhai' class destroyers double to six units, with both Jiangnang and Dalian Shipbuilding delivering units to the fleet. Each shipyard has been allocated four units from an initial batch of eight ships, with deliveries expected to be concluded before the end of 2022.

Jiangnang and Dalian are also the assigned shipyards – on a roughly 3:1 ratio in favour of the Shanghai yard – for the smaller, c. 7,500-tonne Type 052D 'Luyang III' class destroyers. These remain in

The final Chinese Type 056A corvette *Aba* – delivered in January 2021 – pictured on a combat training exercise on 13 June 2022. Earlier Type 056 variants of this design – all less than a decade old – are already being converted for second line, coast guard service. *(Zhang Bin/China Military Online)*

production, with the further five delivered in the past year taking the total active fleet to twenty-four. One additional ship is believed to be ready for delivery from the Dalian shipyard but there might then be a pause in activity to examine the potential for further improvements to a series of ships that dates back to the initial pair of Type 052B 'Luyang' class vessels that were commissioned in 2004.

The last year has also seen delivery of the first of an additional batch of Type 054A 'Jiangkai II' series frigates after a near three-year pause since the delivery of the 30th ship in the class early in 2019. The new *Ziyang* was built by Huangpu Wenchong Shipbuilding, Guangzhou, which shared construction of the earlier vessels with Hudong-Zhonghua of Shanghai. She incorporates several incremental improvements over the previous ships, including a revised system of fire-control radars. At least six additional ships have been launched at Guangzhou and Shanghai, with some open-source information suggesting that the current batch may extend to twenty units. However, there has also been speculation that frigate production will soon transition to the long-awaited Type 054B/Type 055 design,

which will be reportedly larger, faster and incorporate a stealthier diesel-electric or integrated electrical propulsion power plant.[10]

Some of the new frigate construction may be directed towards replacing the initial, 22-strong batch of Type 056 corvettes, many of which are now being re-purposed for coast guard service. Although all have been delivered within the past decade, they lack the towed array sonar fitted to the later Type 056A variant, which itself encompassed a production run of as many as fifty vessels. The adaptation of these modern and well-equipped surface combatants for coast guard use indicates both the significance of China's maritime constabulary arm in its overall naval strategy and also the fact that the warship construction programme has now advanced to the stage that it is possible to release relatively modern ships for second-line duties.

Submarines: As always, developments with respect to the PLAN's underwater waters are difficult to assess with certainty. At present, the navy is believed to operate six Type 094/094A 'Jin' class nuclear-powered strategic submarines and a similar number

A view of two 'Yuan' series submarines belonging to the PLAN's Northern Fleet in the course of ammunition loading in March 2022. It is believed that around twenty of these boats are currently in service, with construction of the latest variants continuing. *(Wu Haodong/China Military Online)*

of Type 093/93A 'Shang' class attack submarines. These are supplemented by small numbers of 'legacy' nuclear-powered boats, probably now consigned to secondary roles. A new generation of both types of submarine is believed to be under development at the massive Bohai yard at Huludao in north-east China. In May 2022, satellite imagery revealed details of a new submarine – commonly regarded as being a further variant of the existing Type 093 series – that appears to incorporate vertical-launch cells for cruise missiles and a shrouded pump-jet propulsor. It is also possible that the new boat could be intended as a trials platform for the new series of Type 095 and Type 096 submarines that are reportedly under construction. The latter will be armed with the new JL-3 submarine-launched ballistic missile, which could potentially target US cities from within Chinese waters.

The conventionally-powered equivalents of the PLAN's nuclear submarines are the various iterations of the Type 039A 'Yuan' class series. Precise numbers are difficult to ascertain, although the US Department of Defense estimates that at least twenty-five will be in service by the middle of the current decade. This total, together with older Type 093 'Song' and Russian-built Project 636 'Kilo' class boats, would provide a total of around fifty submarines, sustaining the notional two, eight-strong patrol submarine flotillas sometimes attributed to each of China's three separate fleets. It is believed that a few old Type 039 'Ming' class submarines are also being retained in service to support training activities, although – interestingly – the two, more modern Project 877 'Kilo' class submarines may now have been withdrawn for scrap. Photographs have also emerged of a new, prototype small submarine that might be the basis of a different class of boat focused on littoral operations in the South China Sea.[11]

Mogami (FFM-1) is one of two 30-FFM class multi-mission frigates inducted into the JMSDF in early 2022. Another eight members of the class are either under construction or have been authorised as the JMSDF attempts to bolster fleet numbers. *(JMSDF)*

Table 2.2.4: JAPAN MARITIME SELF-DEFENCE FORCE: PRINCIPAL UNITS AS AT MID 2022

TYPE	CLASS	NUMBER[1]	TONNAGE	DIMENSIONS	PROPULSION	CREW	DATE
Support and Helicopter Carriers							
Support Carrier – CVL[2]	IZUMO (DDH-183)	2	27,000 tonnes	248m x 38m x 7m	COGAG, 30 knots	470	2015
Helicopter Carrier – CVH	HYUGA (DDH-181)	2	19,000 tonnes	197m x 33m x 7m	COGAG, 30 knots	340	2009
Principal Surface Escorts							
Destroyer – DDG	MAYA (DDG-179)	2	10,500 tonnes	170m x 21m x 6m	COGLAG, 30 knots	300	2020
Destroyer – DDG	ATAGO (DDG-177)	2	10,000 tonnes	165m x 21m x 6m	COGAG, 30 knots	300	2007
Destroyer – DDG	KONGOU (DDG-173)	4	9,500 tonnes	161m x 21m x 6m	COGAG, 30 knots	300	1993
Destroyer – DDG	HATAKAZE (DDG-171)	0 (2)	6,300 tonnes	150m x 16m x 5m	COGAG, 30 knots	260	1986
Destroyer – DDG	ASAHI (DD-119)	2	6,800 tonnes	151m x 18m x 5m	COGLAG, 30 knots	230	2017
Destroyer – DD	AKIZUKI (DD-115)	4	6,800 tonnes	151m x 18m x 5m	COGAG, 30 Knots	200	2012
Destroyer – DDG	TAKANAMI (DD-110)	5	6,300 tonnes	151m x 17m x 5m	COGAG, 30 knots	175	2003
Destroyer – DDG	MURASAME (DD-101)	9	6,200 tonnes	151m x 17m x 5m	COGAG, 30 knots	165	1996
Destroyer – DDG	ASAGIRI (DD-151)	8	4,900 tonnes	137m x 15m x 5m	COGAG, 30 knots	220	1988
Frigate – FFG	MOGAMI (FFM-1)	2	5,300 tonnes	133m x 16m x 5m	CODAG, 30+ knots	90	2022
Frigate – FFG	ABUKUMA (DE-229)	6	2,500 tonnes	109m x 13m x 4m	CODOG, 27 knots	120	1989
Submarines							
Submarine – SSK	TAGEI (SS-513)	1	4,300 tonnes	84m x 9m x 8m	Diesel-electric, 20+ knots	70	2022
Submarine – SSK	SORYU (SS-501)	12	4,200 tonnes	84m x 9m x 8m	AIP, 20+ knots[3]	65	2009
Submarine – SSK	OYASHIO (SS-590)	9 (2)	4,000 tonnes	82m x 9m x 8m	Diesel-electric, 20+ knots	70	1998
Major Amphibious Units							
Landing Platform Dock – LPD	OSUMI (LST-4001)	3	14,000 tonnes	178m x 26m x 6m	Diesel, 22 knots	135	1998

Notes:

1. Figures in brackets refer to trials or training ships.

2. In the course of conversion to operate F-35B STOVL strike fighters.

3. The last two units of the class have their AIP plant replaced by lithium-ion batteries; an arrangement also adopted in the follow-on *Tagaei* class

MAJOR REGIONAL POWERS – JAPAN

The deteriorating international environment has resulted in Japan deciding to review its existing National Security Strategy, with the replacement for the existing 2013 document due to be revealed before the end of 2022. Its publication will be accompanied by the early revision of the country's long-term National Defense Program Guidelines and five-year Medium Term Defense Program for FY2019–FY2023, thereby providing new clarity on the Japan Maritime Self Defense Force's (JMSDF's) likely trajectory in the years ahead. The Japanese Liberal Democratic Party headed by new Prime Minister Fumio Kishida supports doubling defence spending to two percent of GDP, a significant change from a policy that has capped military funding to around half this amount since the mid-1970s. Whilst it is unclear that an increase of this magnitude will be approved, it seems likely that the Japan Self Defense Force (JSDF) will be better funded in the years ahead.

The current fleet structure outlined in Table 2.2.4 reflects progress towards achieving the twenty-two submarine/fifty-four principal surface combatant structure contained in current defence policy. Importantly, the lead vessels of two significant new classes were inducted over the past year. The surface fleet was bolstered by the arrival of the first two members of the of '30-FFM' multi-purpose frigate design. *Mogami* (FFM-1), the nominal lead ship, was delivered at Mitsubishi Heavy Industries' Nagasaki shipyard on 28 April 2022; a month later than the commissioning ceremony for her sister *Kumano* (FFM-2) at Tamano after experiencing slight construction delays. Displacing around 5,500 tonnes in full load condition, the frigates are intended to perform surveillance and defensive duties in Japan's home waters. Their multi-role orientation, which includes an ability to deploy unmanned vehicles, will allow them to replace both the older surface escort vessels and the wooden-hulled minehunters that have traditionally under-

taken these roles. This is partly reflected by the assignment of the first two ships to the Mine Warfare Force based at Yokosuka. Three additional members of the class had been launched as of June 2022, whilst the ninth and tenth units were approved in the FY2022 defence budget.

Also joining the fleet – on 9 March 2022 – was the lead '29SS' submarine *Taigei* (SS-513). Representing an incremental improvement on the previous *Soryu* (SS-501) design, she follows the last two members of this earlier class in adopting lithium-ion batteries for extended underwater operation. A second boat, *Hakugei* (SS-514), was launched on 14 October 2021 and four additional class members are either under construction or have been authorised. All the boats of the class are being constructed at Kobe; either in the Mitsubishi Heavy Industries or Kawasaki Heavy Industries plants that are both located in that city. *Taigei's* acceptance takes the submarine flotilla to the long-planned target of twenty-two front-line boats.

The lead *Taigei* class patrol submarine pictured at the time of her induction into the JMSDF in March 2022. She represents an evolution of the final, lithium-ion battery equipped members of the previous *Soryu* class. *(JMSDF)*

Both *Izumo* class 'helicopter carrying destroyers' are being subject to incremental upgrades to allow them to deploy the Japan Air Self Defense Force's F-35B Lightning II strike fighters. This is *Izumo* (DDH-183) in late October 2021, shortly after she had participated in initial landing trials involving US Marine Corps F-35Bs. *(US Navy)*

Although the plans to induct the modular *Mogami* class allowed a reduction in the mine countermeasures force, the JMSDF has not completely abandoned traditional mine warfare concepts. Accordingly, the FY2022 budget has made provision for a fifth *Awaji* (MSO-304) class minesweeper as part of longer-term plans for up to nine of the type. The budget also reflected a desire to counterbalance expanding Chinese underwater activity with funding for a fourth *Hibiki* (AOS-5201) oceanic surveillance ship and a new oceanographic research vessel. In similar fashion, the need to sustain the JSDF's ability to operate across the increasingly exposed Ryukyu Islands is reflected in allocations for a logistics support vessel and a utility landing craft of new design. They will be operated by a tri-service JSDF unit that is expected to be stood up in 2024.

Operationally, the highlight of the year was the landing of two US Marine Corps F-35B strike fighters aboard *Izumo* (DDH-183) on 3 October 2021. Both *Izumo* class 'destroyers' are being refitted to operate Japan Air Self Defense Force F-35Bs but the modifications are being implemented incrementally. As a result it will not be until 2027 at the earliest before they are fully capable of operating the new aircraft. Meanwhile, the fleet has suffered a spate of collisions that included an incident between the training submarine *Oyashio* (TSS-3608) and a fishing boat on 10 March 2022; between the destroyer-escort *Jintsu* (DE-230) and the mine countermeasures control ship *Uraga* (MST-463) on 22 May 2022; and between *Uraga*'s sister *Bungo* (MST-464) and the minesweeper *Aishima* (MSC-688) on 23 June of the same year. Whilst the causes of the incidents are likely unrelated, they follow on from another, more serious incident involving the submarine *Soryu* and a commercial bulk carrier in February 2021. It has already become apparent that the higher operational tempo that now pertains in the Pacific has put US Navy operating procedures under stress and this may also be the case with the JMSDF as well.

MAJOR REGIONAL POWERS – SOUTH KOREA

Last year's *Seaforth World Naval Review* highlighted the Republic of Korea Navy's growing 'blue water' aspirations and, particularly, the progress that was being made towards developing the country's first aircraft carrier. Although parliamentary approval for initial development funding was achieved in 2021, the so-called CVX project has subsequently hit a significant speed bump with the advent of a new political administration in South Korea that is less favourably disposed towards the programme's implementation. The recent growth in South Korean defence spending has come to an at least temporary halt, with funding diverted to help deal with the aftermath of the pandemic. Amongst other projects, the navy is also pursuing an ambitious programme of submarine construction that could eventually extent to the acquisition of nuclear-powered submarines. These submarines – equipped with conventionally-armed ballistic missiles – form an important part of the strategic strike deterrent that the Republic is developing against North Korea's nuclear-armed programmes. Accordingly, they are likely to be given a higher priority in any ongoing budget squeeze.[12]

The capabilities of South Korea's current, third-generation KSS-III submarines have been highlighted by the commissioning of the lead boat of the type, *Dosan Ahn Chang-Ho*, on 13 August 2021. Displacing around 3,800 tonnes in submerged condition, the 84m-long boat is equipped with a diesel-electric propulsion plant supplemented by a PEM-type air-independent propulsion (AIP) system of indigenous manufacture. Unusually for a conventionally-powered submarine, she is equipped with six vertical launch tubes for the Hyunmoo 4-4 short-range ballistic missile in addition to the usual outfit

An impressive aerial view of the Republic of Korea Navy's new amphibious assault ship *Marado* in June 2022. The Korean Navy's plan to follow her delivery with a new CVX aircraft carrier is encountering significant political headwinds. *(US Navy)*

of torpedo tubes. The newly-delivered submarine carried out a successful full test firing of the missile on 15 September 2021. This was followed by a two-missile salvo in April 2022. The KSS-III series is being built in three batches of three boats, with all three of the initial batch now in the water following the launch of *Shin Chae-ho* by Hyundai Heavy Industries (HHI) on 28 September 2021. Construction of the second batch is also well underway, with Daewoo Shipbuilding & Marine

Table 2.2.5: REPUBLIC OF KOREA NAVY: PRINCIPAL UNITS AS AT MID 2022

TYPE	CLASS	NUMBER	TONNAGE	DIMENSIONS	PROPULSION	CREW	DATE
Principal Surface Escorts							
Destroyer – DDG	KDX-III SEJONGDAEWANG-HAM	3	10,000 tonnes	166m x 21m x 6m	COGAG, 30 knots	300	2008
Destroyer – DDG	KDX-II CHUNGMUGONG YI SUN-SHIN	6	5,500 tonnes	150m x 17m x 5m	CODOG, 30 knots	200	2003
Destroyer – DDG	KDX-I GWANGGAETO-DAEWANG	3	3,900 tonnes	135m x 14m x 4m	CODOG, 30 knots	170	1998
Frigate – FFG	FFX-2 DAEGU	2	3,600 tonnes	122m x 14m x 4m	CODLOG	140	2017
Frigate – FFG	FFX INCHEON	6	3,000 tonnes	114m x 14m x 4m	CODOG, 30 knots	140	2013
Frigate – FFG	ULSAN	4	2,300 tonnes	102m x 12m x 4m	CODOG, 35 knots	150	1981
Corvette – FSG	POHANG	7	1,200 tonnes	88m x 10m x 3m	CODOG, 32 knots	95	1984
Submarines							
Submarine – SSK	KSS-3 DOSAN AHN CHANG-HO	1	3,800 tonnes	84m x 8m x 8m	AIP, 20+ knots	50	2021
Submarine – SSK	KSS-2 SON WON-IL (Type 214)	9	1,800 tonnes	65m x 6m x 6m	AIP, 20+ knots	30	2007
Submarine – SSK	KSS-1 CHANG BOGO (Type 209)	9	1,300 tonnes	56m x 6m x 6m	Diesel-electric, 22 knots	35	1993
Major Amphibious Units							
Amph Assault Ship – LHD	LPX DOKDO	2[1]	18,900 tonnes	200m x 32m x 7m	Diesel, 22 knots	425	2007

Notes:
1. *Marado*, the second ship of the class, is built to a slightly different design.

Good progress is being made with South Korea's KSS-III submarine programme, with all three of the initial batch having been launched and the first in commission. This photograph shows the formal launching ceremony for the second boat, *Ahn Moo*, at DSME's Okpo yard in November 2020. *(Republic of Korea Navy)*

Engineering (DSME) currently working on two of this trio. This KSS-III Batch 2 variant will be longer (c. 89m) and heavier (4,000 tonnes) than the initial batch. They will be equipped with lithium-ion batteries for improved endurance and an increased number of ten vertical launch tubes.

Current fleet status is summarised in Table 2.2.5. The number of surface combatants has temporarily dipped with the withdrawal of elderly *Po Hang* class corvettes before arrival of their replacements; the much larger and more powerful FFX Batch II *Daegu* class frigates. All eight of these ships are now in the water following the launch of a new *Po Hang* by DSME in September 2021 and two HHI-built ships – *Cheonan* and *Chuncheon* – in November 2021 and March 2022 respectively. HHI also laid the keel of the prototype FFX Batch III type – to become the first of a new *Ulsan* class – on 25 April 2022. These ships will continue the process of incremental improvement seen across the various batches, including adoption of an integrated mast incorporating an active phased-array radar. HHI's warship production facilities are certainly busy at the moment, as they are also heavily committed to building the new KDX III Batch II Aegis-equipped destroyers. The keel of the first of these ships – to be

named *Jeongjo the Great* – was laid at Ulsan on 5 October 2021. In addition, the company was awarded the contract for the second of these three ships early in November. In contrast to the first batch, these latest destroyers will be equipped for ballistic missile defence and will also incorporate a new missile loadout that will include the latest indigenously-designed missiles.

OTHER REGIONAL FLEETS

Indonesia: The Indonesian Navy continues to pursue a modernisation strategy that encompasses maintaining a comparatively small but expanding force of front-line warships supplemented by a much larger flotilla of increasingly up-to-date patrol and logistic support assets. In broad terms, lack of resources has meant that the first leg of this strategy has been difficult to implement given the much greater amount of investment it requires. However, 2021–22 has seen the announcement of several important acquisition plans that – if realised in their entirety – would take the Indonesian Navy a long way towards its objectives. These encompass an agreement with Italy's Fincantieri to acquire six new-build FREMM and two second-hand *Maestrale* class frigates announced in June 2021; a contract for two

licence-built variants of British Babcock's 'Arrowhead 140' frigates agreed in September 2021; and signature of a memorandum of understanding between France's Naval Group and local shipbuilder PT PAL in February 2022 that envisages the local construction of two 'Scorpène' type submarines equipped with AIP. There have also been rumours that another deal to acquire Japanese *Mogami* class frigates is under consideration.

Whilst ostensibly promising, this naval investment spree gives rise to a number of questions. The most significant is whether Indonesia's comparatively modest defence budget can actually support the level of spending envisaged. The planned acquisitions take place at the same time as costly deals for Rafale and F-15 multi-role fighters have also been agreed. The resulting financial strain is reflected in the Indonesian Ministry of Defence requesting a defence budget of c. US$22bn for 2023, more than double the current total. Given that this request is unlikely to be achievable, it looks probable that recourse to external loans will be required to fund some of the new programmes; a device that can only be viewed as a temporary expedient. It is also noteworthy that the new naval acquisitions tear up previous long-term collaboration – with Dutch Damen in the field of surface combatants and South Korea's DSME with respect to submarines – in favour of a somewhat eclectic mix of new partners. It seems that the previous, April 2019 agreement with DSME to purchase a second batch of three Type 209 *Nagapasa* class has been one casualty of the revised approach. This will actually delay achieving the Indonesian Navy's target to expand its submarine flotilla from the existing four to between ten and twelve submarines by the end of the decade.

Conversely, the Indonesian Navy is achieving much greater success modernising its second-line strength through the construction of relatively basic but still effective warships by local industry. The range of ongoing programmes is extensive, including amphibious transport docks, tank landing ships, missile-armed fast attack craft and patrol boats. Developments over the past year include:

■ **Tank Landing Ships:** Further progress had been made with deliveries of *Teluk Bintuni* class tank landing ships; a c. 2,300-tonne, 117m design ordered from three local shipyards. Nine of these vessels have been authorised to date to replace 'legacy' shipping. Eight are now in service following the deliveries of *Teluk Weda* and *Teluk Wondama* by the PT Bandar Abadi Shipyard in Batam in October 2021 and of *Teluk Youtefa* and *Teluk Palu* by PT Daya Radar Utama of Lampung in July 2021 and May 2022. The ninth vessel, *Teluk Calang*, is in the final stages of outfitting at Lampung.

◼ **Hospital Ships:** The Indonesian navy operates a number of specialised hospital ships converted from the *Tanjung Dalpele/Makassar* series of amphibious transport docks. 2022 saw delivery of the first of the series built as a hospital ship from the keel up with the commissioning of *dr. Wahidin Sudirohusodo* on 14 January. Builders PT PAL of Surabaya – Indonesia's premier naval shipbuilding yard – are also close to completing a second member of the class.

◼ **Missile Armed Fast Attack Craft:** PT PAL are also working on latest iterations of the large, 60m KCR-60 *Sampari* class fast attack craft design, which are destined to be armed with Exocet surface-to-surface missiles. The fifth of the class, *Kapak,* was launched on 5 December 2021, being followed by her sister *Panah* on 20 April 2022. Work is also underway to upgrade at least some of the older vessels to the latest standard, commencing with the third vessel, *Halasan.* Improvements will include installation of a Danish Terma combat management system, specified for the latest vessels from build.

◼ **Patrol Vessels:** The various KCR missile-armed fast attack craft are supplemented by more numerous PC-designated patrol craft. The most recent type to enter construction is the PC-60 *Dorang* class, two of which were launched from the PT Caputra Mitra Sejati in Banten province in March 2022. Previously announced plans involved the procurement of up to forty-two PC-40 patrol vessel variants of the KCR-40 *Clurit* class fast attack craft design. However, just as the KCR-60 superseded KCR-40 production, it may well be that some of this patrol ship inventory will now be of the enlarged PC-60 type. Work is also underway on a larger, 90m offshore patrol vessel design, reportedly equipped with Turkish electronics.

2022 has also seen the reincarnation of the unusual *Klewang* class fast attack trimaran after the prototype was destroyed by fire shortly after launch in 2012. A replacement, named *Golok*, was delivered by builders PT Lundin in January 2022. It is likely that exten-

The Indonesian Navy's lead Sigma 9113 type corvette *Diponegoro* leads the larger Sigma 10514 frigate *Gusti Ngurah Rai* during exercises with the US Navy in October 2021. Despite the success of its Dutch-designed warships, Indonesia is now switching to a broad range of alternative suppliers for its next classes of major surface combatant. *(US Navy)*

sive trials of the innovativ carbon-fibre vessel will be required before a decision is taken on whether or not to proceed with series production. There are reports that acquisition of the Kongsberg strike missile is being considered for the currently lightly-armed vessel, thereby adding yet another weapons system into the Indonesian Navy's diverse mix.

Malaysia: Recent Royal Malaysian Navy procurement strategy has been based on a '15 to 5 Transformation Plan' aimed at reconfiguring the navy to comprise five major warship types. These would encompass (i) four submarines; (ii) twelve frigate-sized littoral combat ships; (iii) eighteen corvette-like new generation patrol vessels; (iv) eighteen littoral mission ships; and (v) three multi-role support ships for a total overall fleet of fifty-five combatants. Progress towards achieving this structure has been slight. With the exception of two submarines and six patrol vessels that were in service when the plan was adopted, only four Chinese-built *Keris* class littoral mission ships have been delivered to date. The order was completed in December 2021 with the delivery of *Rencong* by Wuchang

Shipbuilding, following on from the acceptance of *Badik* the previous October. Displacing around 700 tonnes, these 69m vessels are armed with a 30mm cannon and two 12.7mm machine guns. They can hardly be said to amount to a major addition to Malaysia's fleet strength.

Although limited defence budgets have been one factor in delaying the plan, the inability of local industry to support its implementation has been another major factor. The main problem has been the botched implementation of a contract to build a first batch of six littoral combat ships by Boustead Heavy Industries' shipyard at Lumut in Perak. The *Maharaja Lela* class frigates were first ordered in 2011 to Naval Group's 'Gowind' design and were due to be delivered from 2019 onwards. The lead ship was launched in 2017 but construction difficulties during her outfitting stage essentially brought the project to a halt. The Malaysian Government eventually decided to proceed with the ships' completion in 2021 and this was followed by agreement of a revised contract at the start of June 2022. By that stage, the overall programme was calculated as being delayed by around three and a half years, with delivery of the first ship not now expected until 2025.

With the way forward on the littoral combat ship programme now seemingly determined, the Royal Malaysian Navy's next priority is the order of a second batch of littoral mission ships. It seems that the navy is set on acquiring a much more potent capability than that provided by the *Keris* class, with light frigate designs from Damen, HHI and Turkey amongst those put forward for the design. This approach is seemingly at odds with that set out in the original Transformation Plan, which envisaged acquisition of a set of standardised modular designs to ease subsequent maintenance costs. As such, it is clear that the plan is unlikely to be realised in its original form.[13]

New Zealand: In December 2021, New Zealand published its new *Defence Assessment 2021*; a comprehensive review of the current challenges to New Zealand's defence interests, as well as defence officials' advice to Government on changing New Zealand's defence policy settings. Identifying strategic competition and the impacts of climate change as the two principal challenges to the country's security interests, it recommended a shift to a proactive, prioritised approach to defence strategy with a primary focus on the Pacific. Although actual implementation of these conclusions will be subject to further government work on defence policy, its conclusion that, 'Even ahead of this work, we judge that capabilities to deliver presence, awareness and response in and through the maritime domain will be critical …' suggests maintaining naval capabilities will remain central to New Zealand Defence Force (NZDF) objectives.[14]

In the short term, however, it has been a mixed year for the Royal New Zealand Navy. Positively, the frigate *Te Mana* departed Canada on her homeward voyage on 31 May 2022. This brought the protracted and costly midlife modernisation of the navy's two frigates to a satisfactory conclusion. The upgrades – including installation of the Lockheed Martin CMS 330 combat management system, new Thales SMART-S Mk 2 radar and CAMM surface-to-air missiles – are intended to extend the two ships' service lives through to 2030. However, replacement may take longer in practice. Meanwhile work has also commenced on the first of four Poseidon P-8A maritime patrol aircraft that will significantly expand the air force's surveillance capabilities when they are delivered from 2023 onwards.

A less favourable development has been suspension of the acquisition of an Antarctic and Southern Ocean patrol vessel, for which a request for information was floated in mid-2021. The main reason for the postponement appears to be financial, although pressures managing the other major projects the NZDF currently has underway have also seemingly played a part. The navy will also say a final farewell to the coastal patrol vessels *Rotoiti* and *Pukaki*, which were decommissioned in 2019 as a result of a previous defence review. In March 2022 it was announced the two vessels had been sold to the Irish Naval Service. They will make the long journey to the other side of the globe in 2023 after refit.

North Korea: The last year has seen North Korea step up its programme of ballistic missile launches. These included the first launch of an intermediate-range ballistic missile since 2017 on 30 January 2022, followed by the first launch of an intercontinental ballistic missile – claimed to be the new, larger Hwasong-17 – over the same timescale on 24 March.[15] There has also been speculation that the Democratic People's Republic of Korea is preparing to resume nuclear warhead testing amongst discussion over whether recent pronouncements from the country's leadership suggest a greater willingness to use tactical nuclear weapons than previously assumed. Neither of the missiles that undertook these new tests has yet been subject to underwater launch, although the development of such a capability cannot be ruled out in the future. In the meantime, the country's sole 'Sinpo/Gorae' type strategic submarine has also reportedly undertaken at least one test firing of a shorter range KN-23 ballistic missile over the past year.

The Philippines: The Philippine Navy has benefited from a raft of procurement announcements over the past few months as the departing Duterte administration attempted to conclude key elements of the 2018–2022 'Horizon 2' phase of the Revised Armed Forces of the Philippines Modernization Program (RAFPMP) before leaving office. The key beneficiary of the spending splurge appears to have been HHI. On 28 December 2021 it announced the signature of a c. US$550m contract to supply two new corvettes, which are reportedly based on its 3,100-tonne, 118m HDC-3100 design. If these reports are confirmed, the new ships would be larger than the existing pair of *Jose Rizal* class frigates deliv-

The mid-life upgrades of the Royal New Zealand Navy's *Anzac* class frigates have been completed with *Te Mana*'s return from Canada. This photograph shows her transiting the Pacific on her homeward voyage in June 2022. *(Royal New Zealand Navy)*

ered by the South Korean shipbuilder in 2020–1. Subsequently, on 27 June 2022, HHI announced details of another award, this time encompassing the supply of six 2,400-tonne offshore patrol vessels at a total cost of US$557m. The new patrol ships will be armed with a 76mm gun and will be able to operate a helicopter and/or unmanned aerial vehicles. The contract will be a disappointment to Australia's Austal, which previously had high hopes of building the required ships in its local facility in the Philippines.

Although HHI has gained the majority of new orders, there have been other beneficiaries. On 24 June, 2022 Indonesia's PT PAL was awarded a contract for a second pair of *Tarlac* class amphibious transport docks, which are derived from the Indonesian Navy's South Korean-designed *Makassar* class. The Philippine Navy will also gain from the donation of a second South Korean *Po Hang* class corvette as a further sweetener to the HHI deals. In another significant development, the Philippine Marine Corps will acquire three batteries of Indo-Russian BrahMos surface-to-surface missiles, each comprising three launch vehicles equipped with three missiles each. All-in-all, the series of orders marks a notable improvement in both surveillance and A2/AD capabilities across the contested South China Sea. A key question, however, will be whether the recent improvements in naval capability will be sustained in the 'Horizon 3' stage of the modernisation programme following assumption of political control by the new Marcos administration on 1 July 2022.

Singapore: The Republic of Singapore Navy has seen a number of existing and planned acquisition programmes delayed by the pandemic but is now starting to recover lost ground. The immediate priority is to progress deliveries of the four new Type 218SG submarines, which are being built by ThyssenKrupp Marine Services (tkMS) at Kiel. The lead boat, *Invincible*, was previously due to be delivered in 2021 but as of mid-2022, she was still undergoing final trials before rescheduled delivery to Singapore before the end of the year. Acceptance of the remaining boats was initially planned to be

Commissioned in March 2021, *Antonio Luna* is the second of the Philippine Navy's Hyundai Heavy Industries-built *Jose Rizal* class light frigates. She is seen here approaching Pearl Harbor in June 2022 to participate in the RIMPAC exercises. The Philippine Navy has subsequently turned to HII to build new two frigate-sized 'corvettes' and a new class of patrol vessel. *(US Navy)*

The Republic of Singapore's lead Type 218SG submarine *Invincible* pictured at the time of her naming ceremony in February 2019. The subsequent COVID-19 pandemic had delayed her delivery and she was still completing trials as of mid-2022. *(tkMS)*

complete before 2024 but it is uncertain whether the ground lost by the pandemic can be made up in time.

The next major acquisition programme is likely to be that for the long-planned Multi-Role Combat Vessel, which will replace the six existing *Victory* class corvettes. As the new ships are all planned to be in service by the end of 2030, there is a degree of urgency to launching the project. They are likely to be a modular design utilising Singapore's expertise in unmanned and autonomous vehicles to deploy a range of robotic systems. Singapore also envisages replacing its current flotilla of manned mine countermeasures vessels with unmanned technology from 2027 onwards. Another major programme – announced in March 2022 – will be a midlife upgrade for the existing *Formidable* class frigates. This will encompass the upgrade of command and control, combat and logistical support technology with the involvement of Singapore's Defence Science and Technology Agency, as well as its DSO National Laboratories.

Taiwan: Taiwan's Republic of China Navy continues to make incremental progress that – whilst paling into insignificance compared with the development of the neighbouring PLAN – is resulting in material improvements to its overall capabilities. The most significant development over the past year has been the keel-laying of the country's first Indigenous

Defense Submarine (IDS) at the China Shipbuilding Corporation's Kaohsiung yard on 16 November 2021. The lead vessel of a planned class of eight boats, she is reportedly scheduled for delivery in 2025. Whilst this schedule seems aggressive given Taiwan's lack of previous experience of submarine construction, advancement of the programme is both a major achievement and a serious complication to any future PLAN operation to invade the island.[16]

Taiwan's surface fleet has also been making headway with the delivery of *Ta Chiang*, the first series-built unit of the *Tuo Chiang* class catamaran-hulled missile corvette design. She was commissioned at a ceremony held in the presence of Taiwan's president, Tsai Ing-wen, on 9 September 2021. *Ta Chiang* incorporates a number of changes over the prototype vessel, including the ability to embark surface-to-air missiles in lieu of some of her surface-to-surface missile capability. She forms one of a batch of three ships, the second of which commenced construction in October 2021. Eventually, a total fleet of twelve is planned. The basic design has also been used as the basis for a series of *Angping* class offshore patrol vessels for the Coast Guard Administration of Taiwan. Three of these vessels have been delivered to date and – dependent on source – up to fifteen may eventually be procured. Although normally lightly-armed, they

are designed to be fitted with anti-ship missiles in case of emergency. This capability was demonstrated in May 2022 when the lead ship, *Angping*, fired a HF-2 surface-to-surface missile during an exercise with her naval counterparts.

Also adding to Taiwan's A2/AD capabilities are the new quartet of FMLB fast minelaying boats. All four of these diminutive 375-tonne vessels have now been delivered following acceptance of the final pair in December 2021. The 'fast' in their designation apparently refers not to their speed – they are reportedly capable of only 14 knots – but the rapidity with which their precision minelaying system can sow a minefield. Each vessel is equipped with four independent sets of minelaying rails that can be deployed by means of an automated console located on the bridge. The system is designed to automatically record the position of each mine as it is laid.

Thailand: The Royal Thai Navy's most important programme is the establishment of a three-strong submarine flotilla comprised of Chinese manufactured S26T submarines, a derivative of the PLAN's 'Yuan' series. The first of these boats was contracted in 2017 for delivery in 2023 but the project is now facing significant headwinds. The new submarine is supposed to be powered by German-made MTU396 diesel engines. However, China has failed to obtain the necessary export licences and Taiwan

Two views of the first series-built *Tuo Chiang* class catamaran-hulled corvette *Ta Chiang* at the time of her delivery in September 2021. Another member of the class is currently under construction and a total of twelve vessels is planned. Along with new submarines and fast minelaying vessels, these missile-armed catamarans form an important part of Taiwan's A2/AD strategy to prevent any invasion from the Chinese mainland. *(Office of the President of the Republic of China)*

has rejected proposals to use an alternative propulsion system. It had not proved possible to find a way out of this impasse as of mid-2026 and the entire programme now appears to be under threat. The navy has already agreed to the further postponement of orders for the other two units due to budgetary pressures arising from the pandemic.

Prospects for development of the surface fleet look somewhat brighter. Delivery of *Chang* – a Chinese-built Type 071E variant of the PLAN's 'Yuzhao' class – is on schedule for the end of 2022 following launch by Shanghai's Hudong-Zhonghua Shipbuilding on 23 December 2021. The navy is also looking to resurrect longstanding plans to acquire a second *Bhumibol Adulyadej* class frigate, a project that might involve at least partial local construction of the South Korean DSME design. Acquisition of a further offshore patrol vessel is also envisaged. This will likely involve procurement of an additional, locally-built *Krabi* class variant of the British Batch 2 'River' class to add to the pair that are already in service.

The navy retired the last of its missile-armed fast attack craft on 30 September 2021 when *Ratcharit*, the final member of the three Italian-built *Ratcharit* class vessels to remain in service, was paid off for the final time. Three Singapore-built *Prabparapak* class fast attack craft have also been retired in recent years, leaving none of the type in the active fleet.

Vietnam: A full status report on the Vietnam People's Navy is provided in Chapter 2.2A.

Notes

1. A good review of the AUKUS pact is provided by a House of Commons Library research briefing by Louisa Brooke-Holland, John Curtis & Claire Mills entitled *The AUKUS Agreement* (London: House of Commons Library, 2021). Many of the quotations used in this introduction are taken from the briefing.

2. For an analysis of the technological aspects of Australia's decision to acquire nuclear-powered submarines, see Peter Layton's 'Australia's Nuclear Submarine Surprise', *Maritime Security & Defence* – December 5/2021 (Bonn: Mittler Report, 2021), pp.7–12. The edition is available for download at: msd-mag.com/profile/print-issues

3. A comprehensive analysis of the implications of the security pact is undertaken by Euan Graham in 'Assessing the Solomon Islands' new security agreement with China' posted to the Institute of Strategic Studies blog site – iiss.org/blogs – on 5 May 2022.

4. Vice Admiral Mead was interviewed by Brendan Nicholson of the Australian Strategic Policy Institute's *The Strategist* – aspistrategist.org.au – in an article entitled 'Australia considering next-generation US and UK designs for nuclear submarines' posted to the site on 10 May 2022.

5. One of the major critics of the *Hunter* class programme has been the Australian Strategic Policy Institute. Amongst advocates of the class's cancellation on its website is Vice Admiral David Shackleton, RAN (retd), a former Chief of Navy. He argues in favour of the USN's Flight III *Arleigh Burke* design – largely on the basis of its greater number of missile cells – with further *Hobart* construction viewed as a temporary fall-back position. See *The Hunter Frigate: An Assessment* posted to the ASPI website on 28 April 2022 and available at: aspi.org.au/report/hunter-frigate-assessment. In the editor's view, the merits of going back to the drawing board to adopt a design that originates from the 1980s and is widely seen as having reached its capacity for further evolution seem questionable.

6. Official announcements leave some doubt as to whether the RAN's 'Evolved Capes' are seen as a temporary expedient pending full commissioning of the *Arafura* class or a longer-term part of the force structure. Interestingly, they are not commissioned RAN ships, taking the prefix ADV (Australian Defence Vessel). *Maitland*'s decommissioning is reportedly not the end of her career, as Austal will reportedly convert her into an autonomous trials vessel in conjunction with L3Harris.

7. See *Military And Security Developments Involving The People's Republic Of China 2021: Annual Report To Congress* (Washington DC: US department of Defense, 2021).

8. The PLAN is, however, undertaking steps to bolster its capabilities in this area. This includes the commissioning of surface combatants equipped with full ASW suites that include variable-depth sonar and the induction of other modern ASW equipment. In the air, the large Z-18F and medium Z-20F helicopters are being supplemented by the new Shaanxi Y-8Q maritime patrol aircraft. A detailed overview of PLAN efforts in this area was provided by Anika Torruella, Alessandra Giovanzanti, Georgios Papangelopoulos and Matteo Scarano in 'Blue-water build up', *Jane's Defence Weekly* – 18 May 2022 (Coulsdon: Jane's, 2022), pp.22–9.

9. Some of these problems are described by Minnie Chan in 'China's navy goes back to work on big ambitions but long-term gaps remain' posted to the *South China Morning Post* site – scmp.com – on 20 August 2020.

10. See, for example, another Minnie Chan article, 'China naval steel order sparks speculation over bigger, faster frigate' posted to the *South China Morning Post* site on 7 May 2022.

11. An excellent source of information on PLAN – and wider – submarine developments is defence analyst's H I Sutton's *Covert Shores* website; available at hisutton.com.

12. A comprehensive review of the likely fortunes of the navy's aircraft carrier and nuclear-powered submarine aspirations was provided by Daehan Lee in an article entitled 'Prospect: CVX And K-SSN In South Korea's New Administration' posted to the *Naval News* website – navalnews.com – on 17 May 2022.

13. A more detailed update on Royal Malaysian Navy modernisation is provided by Gabriel Dominguez in 'Slow progress; The Royal Malaysian Navy's modernisation challenges', *Jane's Defence Weekly* – 9 February 2022 (Coulsdon: Jane's, 2022), pp.24–9.

14. See *Defence Assessment 2021: A Rough Sea Can Still Be Navigated* (Wellington: New Zealand Ministry of Defence, 2021). A copy can be downloaded at: defence.govt.nz/assets/publication/file/Defence-Assessment-2021.pdf

15. Some reports suggest that there were previous, non-publicised tests of the Hwasong-17 before the first, publicly-confirmed launch. Other sources doubt whether it was the new missile that was involved in the test firing. The Henry L. Stimson Center think tank's *38 North* project at 38north.org and H I Sutton's *Covert Shores* site remain good sources of information on North Korean weapon development.

16. The *Reuters* website posted an interesting review of Taiwan's submarine programme entitled 'Silent Partners – T-Day: The Battle for Taiwan' on 29 November 2021. It is currently available at: reuters.com/investigates/special-report/taiwan-china-submarines. The report describes Taiwan's efforts to circumvent Chinese efforts to prevent the programme accessing crucial submarine technologies, highlighting the role of the United States and United Kingdom in supporting the programme. The article notes that British licences for the export of submarine-related equipment to Taiwan amounted to at least £158m (c. US$190m) in the period between 2018 and 2021.

Author:
Mrityunjoy Mazumdar

2.2A FLEET REVIEW

THE VIETNAM PEOPLE'S NAVY

Marching to Modernity?

Vietnam, like other coastal states in the highly contested South China Sea (the East Sea in Vietnamese), is dependent upon the sea and on resources contained within its exclusive economic zone (EEZ) for its economic well-being. As such, the Vietnam People's Navy – and other sea services such as the Vietnam Coast Guard, Fisheries Control Service, Maritime Militia and Maritime Border Guard – are crucial to national prosperity. This chapter examines how the Vietnam People's Navy (VPN) is rapidly modernising to meet the needs of a complex and challenging maritime security environment.

THE STRATEGIC BACKGROUND

Vietnam has extensive maritime interests. In addition to its c. 3,250km coastline, Vietnam is a major claimant to rights in the South China Sea, including the Paracel (Hoang Sa in Vietnamese) and Spratly (Trường Sa) Islands, as well as extensive EEZ interests. In reality, Vietnam's claims over the Paracel Islands are symbolic given that China seized them by force from the then South Vietnam in 1974. The situation with respect to the Spratlys is more complex, with Vietnam maintaining a significant presence despite the loss of Johnson South Reef (Gac Ma) to another Chinese incursion in March 1988. More broadly, its economic claims overlap those of other nations; not only of China through its infamous nine-dash line but also of Brunei, Malaysia, the Philippines and Taiwan. It has been estimated that – out of total EEZ claims of c. 1.4m km² – only a little over 400,000km² are undisputed.[1]

Irrespective of the many competing claims to the South China Sea's economic resources, it is the territorial dispute with China that poses the greatest threat to Vietnam's maritime interests. Often on the receiving end of Chinese provoca-

The Vietnam People's Navy has undergone a major transformation over the past decade, inducting new surface combatants and submarines as part of an anti-access/area-denial strategy aimed at countering China's expansion in the South China Sea. This is the Project 11661E 'Gepard 3.9' light frigate *Đình Tiên Hoàng* (HQ-011) in March 2017. Inducted in March 2011, she is one of a quartet of frigates of the type that form the core of the surface fleet. *(Chris Sattler)*

tions, Vietnam has been almost alone amongst the sea's contiguous states in taking an assertive stance against China's sweeping claims, a source of tension that has been exacerbated by various elements of the Belt and Road initiative. The most tangible of these has been Chinese funding for modernisation of the Cambodian naval base at Ream, a development exacerbating concerns in Hanoi that its western neighbour could essentially become a Chinese client state.[2]

However, Vietnam has to manage relations with China delicately given the imbalance of power, as well as the longstanding political and economic ties between the one-party, Communist nations. This has resulted in an approach that has been described as 'balanced hedging'. On the one hand, Hanoi maintains strong relations, particularly in the economic sphere, with Beijing. On the other, it is modernising its armed forces and maritime law enforcement capabilities to counter Chinese expansionism. An anti-access/area-denial (A2/AD) approach encompassing naval platforms, land-based missiles and aircraft has also been bolstered by efforts in the diplomatic field. These have included leveraging its membership of the Association of Southeast Asian Nations (ASEAN) to seek to curb Chinese ambitions, whilst building ties with the United States and its allies, who have similar aims.[3]

There is a general agreement among observers that – as tensions in the South China Sea intensify – the challenge in preventing disputes and standoffs from escalating into an armed conflict is increasing. Moreover, there is always a danger that China's powerful military might decide to initiate a limited conflict that it believes it can win so as to prove its prowess to conduct sustained at-sea joint operations in support of its expansionist vision. The fact that Vietnam is, despite strengthening ties, less likely to achieve US support than America's established regional allies in any such conflict might also be an important consideration.[4]

China aside, current conventional military threats to Vietnam can be considered limited given that past tensions with its other immediate neighbours – Cambodia and Laos – have largely abated. However, Vietnam faces the usual range of maritime security problems afflicting all regional states. Of these, piracy, illegal unregulated and unreported fishing, smuggling, drug trafficking and the impacts of climate change are probably the most significant.

In short, the VPN must focus on protecting its territorial and economic interests in the South China Sea from potential Chinese aggression whilst maintaining good order at sea for the benefit of its 'blue economy'.

HISTORY OF THE VIETNAM PEOPLE'S NAVY

The Vietnam People's Navy (*Hải quân nhân dân Việt Nam*) considers 7 May 1955 as its founding date.[5] It was then that the so-called Coastal Defence Department was established under the auspices of the Ministry of National Defence. However, its origins date back to the dying days of the Second World War and efforts by the armed wing of the Viet Minh nationalist movement to prevent a return of a French-controlled Indochina. Formal steps were taken by the Viet Minh-led government to establish a naval force as early as 1946 but it would take nearly a decade of fighting with France before the signing of the Geneva Accords in July 1954 paved the way for the end of colonial rule and the establishment of a permanent naval structure.

Amongst other consequences, the Geneva Accords resulted in the division of Vietnam between the communist-led Democratic Republic of Vietnam (DRV) in the north and the Western-supported Republic of Vietnam (RVN) in the south. Although the accords envisaged nationwide elections to select a unified government, the southern regime – buoyed by the United States' support – refused to accept the arrangement, triggering a further 20 years of conflict. This ultimately ended in the defeat of South Vietnam – and its American allies – in 1975 and the formal reunification of Vietnam the following year.

The VPN was to play a steadily growing role in this conflict. The formal establishment of the DRV's Coastal Defence Department was preceded by the creation of a coastal training school (code named C45) and a ship repair workshop (C46) in April 1955. The first naval units were limited in scope, comprising around twenty small wooden hulled patrol boats organised into the *Song Lo* and *Bach Dang* flotillas. However, this initial force

The VPN expanded rapidly during the course of the Vietnam War through the delivery of equipment from the Soviet Union and China. Amongst these ships, coastal torpedo and, later, missile boats formed its most powerful 'punch'. The four surviving Project 206T 'Shershen' class fast attack craft, delivered in the 1980s, are the spiritual successors to these early warships. Here, a torpedo is seen being loaded on *Ship 306* of the class. (*Vietnam People's Navy*)

The period that followed the end of the Vietnam War and the county's unification saw a break in relations with China, pushing Vietnam into a close strategic alliance with the Soviet Union. Five Project 159 'Petya' series anti-submarine frigates were delivered during this period; they remain in front-line service to this day. *(Vietnam People's Navy)*

The Vietnamese-built TT400TP-class patrol boat *HQ-274* stands watch as the Japanese amphibious transport dock *Kunisaki* (LST-4003) docks at Da Nang in June 2014. The Vietnam People's Navy is increasingly involved in defence diplomacy – including receiving visits from foreign warships to its own ports – as it seeks to build regional friendships. *(US Navy)*

expanded rapidly, being renamed the Navy Department in 1959 and the Navy Command in 1964. By that time it numbered around 100 vessels, ranging from coastal torpedo and patrol boats through landing craft to logistic support vessels. Many smaller units were constructed locally, although the Soviet Union and China became the major sources of supply for more complex types. According to research produced by Vietnam's Institute of Military History in 2008, the Soviet Union delivered 52 combat and 21 support vessels during the course of the conflict, with China adding a further 30 and 127 respectively.[6]

Besides largely defensive combat operations against South Vietnamese and US naval forces – possibly most famously in the initial 1964 Gulf of Tonkin incident – the VPN was increasingly involved in providing logistics support for DRV forces operating in the south. A seaborne version of the famous Ho Chi Minh trail – using small craft and fishing trawlers – was developed to infiltrate personnel and materiel. Over the course of the war, it is claimed that over 25,000 troops and more than 100,000 tonnes of supplies – including at least 40 tanks – were transported by specialist VPN detachments.

After the fall of the RVN in 1975, the VPN subsumed large numbers of former South Vietnamese naval platforms – as well as 're-educated' personnel – into its ranks. Estimates of precise numbers of captured ships vary; from US estimates of around 300 vessels to nearly 1,000 ships and craft in Vietnamese sources. Despite the inevitable logistical support and maintenance issues, the impact on VPN combat capabilities was significant, bringing ships as large as corvettes and tank landing ships into its order of battle. Some of the newly acquired ships subsequently received Soviet weaponry. The Soviet Union also continued to be a major source of new warships. Most notably five Project 159 series (NATO: 'Petya II/III') light frigates were transferred between 1978 and 1984.

The period following the end of the Vietnam War remained busy for the VPN. The deployment of an organised garrison for the Vietnamese-occupied areas of the Spratly Islands – seized from South Vietnam in the war's final days – was followed by the re-unified Vietnam's overthrow of the Khmer Rouge regime in Cambodia through a lightning offensive at the start of 1979 in which the navy played an important supporting role. The resulting breakdown in relations with China – a major supporter of the Khmer Rouge – saw Vietnam fall more closely under the Soviet Union's influence, a fact reflected in the increasing reliance on Soviet sources of naval equipment, as already noted above.[7] The Soviet Union also acquired basing rights to the huge US-built port and airfield facilities at Cam Ranh Bay, arrangements which persisted until Russia's final withdrawal in 2002.

Although Sino-Vietnamese relations were later to thaw, links with Russia remained generally close in the post-Cold War era. It was therefore to Russia that Vietnam turned when a strengthening economy – and increasing South China Seas-related concerns – saw it embark on a major programme of naval modernisation from the early years of the current millennium onwards. A key element of this programme has been the establishment of Vietnam's own submarine flotilla. Modernisation has been accompanied by a process of organisational change, including the creation of an independent Coast Guard in November 2008 to bring new focus to constabulary operations.[8] The Coast Guard, particularly, has seen the development of new sources of equipment supply, including Japanese, US and indigenously-built vessels.

The VPN has also become increasingly involved in defence diplomacy as part of efforts to counter Chinese influence and build regional friendships. It has been involved in undertaking several joint patrols with neighbouring countries such as Cambodia and Thailand, and is increasingly venturing into more distant seas. This has seen it undertake port visits as far afield as India and Russia's Far East.

NAVAL ROLE AND ORGANISATION

The Vietnam People's Navy is a separate 'service' or branch of the Vietnam People's Army. According to Vietnam's National Ministry of Defence, the VPN is the 'core service for protecting the sovereignty, sovereign rights, territorial unity and integrity of Vietnam's seas and islands and for building the country's national defence posture at sea'. Along with the country's other sea services, the VPN also participates in disaster prevention and relief, search and rescue, and various constabulary roles as part of a broader brief of protecting and managing Vietnam's maritime interests.

Being a Communist state, the Vietnam People's Army's organisational structure and military doctrine is closely modelled upon the Soviet-era military. As such, the naval headquarters is organised along former Soviet Navy lines, with a 'watchdog' political branch responsible for indoctrination of personnel into Communist Party of Vietnam ideology playing a very important role at all levels. The main elements of the command structure are as follows:

- **Naval Headquarters:** This is headed by the Navy Commander, who is assisted by a Deputy Navy Commander and Chief of Staff. It is organised into a General Staff Branch (*Bộ Tham mưu*) for military affairs, a Political Branch (*Cục Chính trị*) for party and political work and other branches or departments for technical matters.
- **The General Staff Branch:** This is headed by the Deputy Navy Commander and Chief of Staff, who is assisted by a Deputy Chief of Staff and a number of Vice-Commanders. It advises the Navy Commander and exercises operational and administrative command and control over all aspects of the navy.
- **The Political Branch:** This is headed by the Political Commissar, who is supported by a Deputy Political Commissar. It operates at all levels of the VPN from headquarters down.

Operationally, the VPN is organised into five Naval Regional Commands numbered from one to five, as well as a number of separate units such as the Naval Academy at Nha Trang, the various elements of the naval infantry, and logistical and research formations. The numbering system of naval regions can be regarded as reflecting the political importance of each naval region.

- **Region One:** Headquartered in Hai Phong near the Vietnamese capital city of Hanoi. It is responsible for the north-east and part of the north-central coast.
- **Region Two:** Headquartered in Nhơn Trạch near Ho Chi Minh City (the former Saigon) and responsible for the south-east coast.
- **Region Three:** Headquartered in Da Nang. Its area of operations includes parts of the north-central and south-central coasts, including the disputed Paracel Islands.
- **Region Four:** Headquartered in Cam Ranh and responsible for parts of the south central coast, including the Spratly Islands. Despite its relatively lowly numerical status, Region Four has responsibility for some of the VPN's most modern warships, whilst the base at Cam Ranh incorporates some of the navy's most important infrastructure.
- **Region 5:** Headquartered in Phú Quốc Island. Its area of operations includes the maritime borders with Cambodia, Thailand, and Malaysia, as well as the Mekong Delta.

Broadly speaking, each naval region has a similar organisational structure. This includes the headquarters and affiliated units encompassing combat and

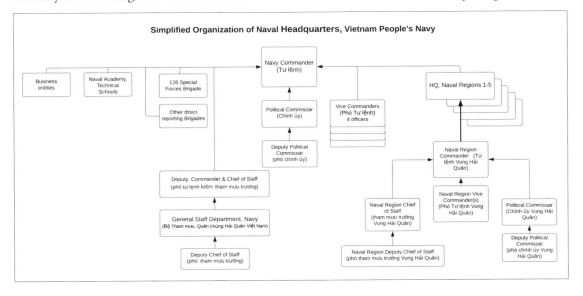

VIETNAM'S OTHER NAVIES

Vietnam's other military and paramilitary sea services all operate significant fleets of patrol vessels and auxiliaries that, in many instances, work in close coordination with the VPN. These include:

- **The Army:** A number of non-VPN regular army formations operate small combat and amphibious craft for riverine and coastal missions. Other entities – such as the General Logistics Department – also own maritime assets, such as transports, logistic ships and tugs.

- **The Maritime Militia:** Reporting to the General Staff of the Vietnam People's Army through the Department of Militia and Self-Defence, the maritime militia is being strengthened by standing (permanent) militia units that will eventually be rolled out across fourteen provinces. Ships of the first six standing maritime militia flotillas are currently in the course of delivery. The vessels – essentially fishing boats painted

in blue with dark grey upperworks – are steel hulled with strengthened bows, with most being based on the 42m TK-1482 type used by the Fisheries Surveillance Service. A total force of 126 vessels is eventually planned. It is expected that the permanent maritime militia will replicate so-called 'grey-zone' activities of similar Chinese units, including surveillance and sovereignty-enforcement.

- **The Border Guard:** A sister branch of the Vietnam People's Army, the Border Guard is responsible for the management and protection of the country's land and sea borders. It operates numerous small and medium-sized patrol vessels, as well as landing ships and various similar craft.

- **The Coast Guard:** Also part of the Vietnam People's Army but reporting directly to the Ministry of Defence, the Coast Guard is responsible for constabulary and humanitarian missions in Vietnamese waters. It operates

seven large offshore patrol vessels – including two former US Coast Guard *Hamilton* class (WHEC-715) class cutters – as well as more than forty seagoing patrol ships and various high speed and support craft. An increasing number of vessels are of modern, local construction. There is also a small maritime aviation element utilising CASA C-212 aircraft.

- **The Vietnam Fisheries Resource Surveillance Service:** Controlled by the Ministry of Agriculture and Rural Development, the civilian Fisheries Service operates a large force of armed patrol and fishing vessels, largely of the 700-tonne KN-750 and 400-tonne TK-1482 types.

All these assets add up to a fairly significant array of patrol and auxiliary ships to complement the VPN's assets in times of conflict. However, their numbers are overshadowed by the growing Coast Guard and militia fleets that form an integral part of Chinese efforts to asset dominance over the South China Sea.

support shipping brigades, coastal and naval infantry units, and support formations. The main bases tend to be clustered around the regional command headquarters. For example Region One has several bases

in the Hai Phong region including one for combat ships at Hạ Long. There are also smaller bases within each region housing independent units, including island bases in the Spratlys.

In addition to those formations under regional command, it appears that some units come under the direct responsibility of VPN Headquarters. These include the 189th Submarine Brigade, the 954th Naval Aviation Brigade, Special Forces and a number of training, engineering and logistical support activities.

Vietnamese sources indicate that overall VPNs personnel strength is around 45,000–50,000, although the actual figure could be higher given its extensive involvement in commercial activities.[9]

NAVAL VESSELS

A summary of current VPN major units is provided in Table 2.2A.1, with comments on individual warship categories following.

Submarines: Vietnam has been a submarine operator since 1997 when it received two 'Yugo' type midget submarines – designated *HQ-41* and *HQ-42* – from

The Project 636.1 'Kilo' class submarine *Đà Nẵng* (HQ-186) is one of six of the class that forms the VPN's new submarine flotilla. She was commissioned in February 2017. (*Vietnam People's Navy*)

North Korea. Along with a number of North Korean semi-submersible infiltration craft, these were primarily intended for Special Forces operations by what is now the 196th Submarine Commando Regiment. The current operational status of these submarines is unclear. There have been reports that Vietnam is building its own indigenous midget-submarine class, which may well be intended as replacement for the North Korean vessels.

The current core of Vietnam's submarine capability comprises six Project 636.1 'Kilo' class submarines ordered in December 2009 under a contract reportedly valued at US$2bn. They were commissioned between 2014 and 2017, constituting the 189th Submarine Brigade at Cam Ranh Bay. They are equipped with torpedoes and the SM-54E 'Club-S' export variant of the 'Kalibr' series of cruise missiles. On 2 June 2017, HQ-182 *Hà Nội* successfully carried out the first submarine missile firing by the VPN.

Sensibly, Vietnam has invested heavily in support infrastructure and training facilities for its new submarines. This has included upgraded infrastructure and facilities to repair submarines at the X52 Shipyard adjacent to the Cam Ranh Bay submarine base and acquisition of a multifunctional simulator for the brigade's training centre developed by Russia's Rubin. Initial training for 'Kilo' class crews

took place in Russia and – as for all those serving on Russian-sourced platforms – crew members need to be reasonably proficient in Russian given equipment markings are in this language. More recently, the VPN has also sent personnel to the Indian Navy's submarine training centre, INS *Satavahana.* Here they train in undersea warfare doctrine and tactics, as well as the English language.

In July 2021, the VPN also commissioned HQ-927 *Yết Kiêu*, a locally-built submarine search and rescue ship based on a Damen Multipurpose Submarine Search-And-Rescue Ship (MSSARS) 9316 design. This ship is equipped with, inter alia, a LR11 submarine rescue vessel supplied by the British-arm of Forum Energy Technologies that is capable of rescuing up to seventeen people at a time and operate at depths of up to 600m.

Major Surface Combatants: The VPN operates eleven large surface combatants, four of which are missile armed. This quartet of vessels are the most capable surface warships in the navy's inventory, comprising modern Russian-built Project 11661E 'Gepard 3.9' light frigates commissioned in pairs in 2011 and 2018. The first two are focused on anti-surface warfare whilst the latter pair are reportedly equipped with additional anti-submarine warfare equipment. All are armed with eight Kh-35 'Uran'

(SS-N-25 'Switchblade') surface-to-surface missiles and can operate a Kamov Ka-28 helicopter. This used to be housed in an unusual half-hangar arrangement that left part of the rotorcraft exposed to the elements. Since 2019, the design has been modified to incorporate an extended, probably telescoping arrangement. The frigates have been extensively deployed for military diplomacy, undertaking foreign flag-waving visits as far as China, India and Russia. They are currently allocated to the 162nd Brigade of Naval Regional Command Four, based at Cam Ranh.

Plans dating back to around 2015 for two more 'Gepards' have yet to materialise, although some reports suggest that this pair are to be assembled locally might explain the delay. Another explanation put forth is that complications in acquiring Ukrainian Zorya gas turbines following Russia's 2014 Crimea invasion put an end to this plan.

Two former Republic of Korea Navy *Po Hang* class corvettes were donated by South Korea in 2015 and 2017. Despite their age – they were initially commissioned in 1986 – these ships remain effective platforms and there have been various unconfirmed reports of modernisation work. Whilst the initial ship – *HQ-18* (ex-*Gimcheon*) – appears to have been transferred with some equipment removed – the following *HQ-20* (the former *Yeosu*) has retained much

The VPN's four Project 11611E type frigates – *Trần Hưng Đạo* (HQ-015) is seen left – are typical of the modern Russian-sourced vessels that form the core of its combat capabilities. However, some 'Western' equipment, such as the South Korean *Po Hang* class corvette *HQ-20* pictured right, is being acquired. Both these photographs were taken in October 2018. *(Tetsuya Katikani/Arjun Sarup)*

Table 2.2A.1 VIETNAM PEOPLE'S NAVY FLEET COMPOSITION – MID 2022

PRINCIPAL UNITS

TYPE	CLASS	NUMBER	TONNAGE	DIMENSIONS	DATES[1]	CLASS[2]
Submarines (6)						
Submarine – SSK	Project 636.1' Kilo'	6	3,200 tonnes	73m x 10m x 7m	2014–17	*HQ-182, HQ-183, HQ-184, HQ-185, HQ-186, HQ-187*
Major Surface Combatants (11)						
Frigate – FFG	Project 11661E 'Gepard 3.9'	4	2,200 tonnes	102m x 13m x 5m	2011–17	*HQ-011, HQ-012, HQ-015, HQ-016*
Frigate – FF	PO HANG	2	1,200 tonnes	88m x 10m x 3m	2017–18	*HQ-18, HQ-20*
Frigate – FF	Project 159A/AE 'Petya'	5	1,200 tonnes	82m x 9m x 3m	1978–84	*HQ-09, HQ-11, HQ-13, HQ-15, HQ-17*
Missile Boats (21)						
Fast Attack Craft – FAC	Project 1241.8 'Molniya'	8	550 tonnes	60m x 12m x 2m	2007–17	*HQ-375, HQ-376, HQ-377, HQ-378, HQ-379, HQ-380, HQ-382, HQ-383*
Fast Attack Craft – FAC	Project 12418 BPS 500	1	525 tonnes	62m x 12m x 2m	2001	*HQ-381*
Fast Attack Craft – FAC	Project 1241RE 'Tarantul'	4	500 tonnes	56m x 12m x 2m	1996–2000	*HQ-371, HQ-372, HQ-373, HQ-374*
Fast Attack Craft – FAC	Project 205U 'Osa II'	8	250 tonnes	39m x 8m x 2m	1979–81	*HQ-354, HQ-355, HQ-356, HQ-357, HQ-358, HQ-359, HQ-360, HQ-361*
Patrol Ships (c. 30)						
Fast Attack Craft – MTB	Project 206M 'Turya'	5	250 tonnes	40m x 8m x 2m	1984–6	*HQ-331, HQ-332, HQ-333, HQ-334, HQ-335*
Fast Attack Craft – MTB	Project 206T 'Shershen'	4	170 tonnes	35m x 7m x 2m	1973–80	*HQ-306, HQ-307, HQ-311, HQ-312*
Patrol Ship – PV	TT-400TP	6	450 tonnes	54m x 9m x 2m	2012–15	*HQ-272, HQ-273, HQ-274, HQ-275, HQ-276, HQ-277*
Patrol Ship – PV	Project 1041.2 'Svetlyak'	6	400 tonnes	50m x 9m x 2m	2002–12	*HQ-261, HQ-263, HQ-264, HQ-265, HQ-266, HQ-267*

Two elderly c. 50m TP-01/TP-01M patrol vessels – *HQ-251* and *HQ-253* – as well as six to eight older c. 38m 'Shanghai' series patrol craft – *HQ-201–203, HQ-205–206* and *HQ-209–211* – are also probably still in service. There are also numbers of smaller patrol craft, many operated by Vietnam's other maritime services.

TYPE	CLASS	NUMBER	TONNAGE	DIMENSIONS	DATES	CLASS
Mine Countermeasures Vessels (8)						
Oceanic Minesweeper – MCMV	Project 266 'Yurka'	2	550 tonnes	52m x 9m x 3m	1979	*HQ-851, HQ-852*
Coastal Minehunter – MCMV	Project 1265E 'Sonya'	4	450 tonnes	48m x 9m x 2m	1987–90	*HQ-861, HQ-862, HQ-863, HQ-864*
Inshore Minehunter – MCMV	Project 1258 'Yevgenya'	2	100 tonnes	25m x 6m x 1m	1986	*HQ-871, HQ-872*
Major Amphibious Ships (9)						
Tank landing Ship – LST	LST-542	2	4,200 tonnes	100m x 15m x 4m	1975	*HQ-501, HQ-502*
Tank Landing Ship – LST	Project 771 'Polnochny'	3	850 tonnes	75m x 10m x 2m	1979–80	*HQ-511, HQ-512, HQ-513*
Logistic Support Ship – LSV	Damen 5612	4	650 tonnes	57m x 12m x 1m	2021	*HQ-526, HQ-529, HQ-528, HQ-529*

There are significant numbers of additional landing craft and other amphibious vessels, ranging from two, medium-sized c. 68m indigenously-designed logistic landing ships (*HQ-521* and *HQ-522*) through to former Soviet and US Navy mechanised landing craft.

Notes:

1. Dates refer to induction of serving ships into the VPN.

2. The 'HQ' prefix is no longer displayed on ship hulls but it is uncertain whether or not it continues to be used in any official documentation. Only a few ships are named. These includes the six submarines – *Hà Nội* (HQ-182); *Thành phố Hồ Chí Minh* (HQ-183); *Hải Phòng* (HQ-184); *Khánh Hoà* (HQ-185); *Đà Nẵng* (HQ-186); and *Bà Rịa-Vũng Tàu* (HQ-187) – and four new frigates – *Đinh Tiên Hoàng* (HQ-011), *Lý Thái Tổ* (HQ-012), *Trần Hưng Đạo* (HQ-015) and *Quang Trung* (HQ-016). Five auxiliaries are also named: the sail training ship *Lê Quý Đôn* (HQ-286), the survey vessel *Trần Đại Nghĩa* (HQ-888), the K122 class troop transport *Trường Sa* (HQ-571), the similar K123 class hospital ship *Khánh Hòa-01* (HQ-561) and the submarine rescue ship *Yết Kiêu* (HQ-927).

3. Please refer to the text for an overview of the many support and ancillary vessels in service with the VPN.

of the Republic of Korean Navy weapons outfit.

The five ageing 'Petya' class light frigates transferred in the decade after independence complete the major combatant force. At least some have reportedly been upgraded with Indian-supplied anti-submarine equipment. Imagery that emerged in 2021 showed one hull undergoing extensive modernisation, including a new superstructure arrangement.

Missile-Armed Fast Attack Craft: The VPN has a total inventory of twenty-one missile-armed corvettes and fast attack craft. The oldest are eight Project 205U 'Osa II' class missile boats acquired from the Soviet Union between 1979 and 1981. They are equipped with four cylindrical KT67ER launchers for P15U 'Termit' (SS-N-2B 'Styx') surface-to-surface missiles. The Indian Navy has supplied spares to keep these boats operational.

Four Russian built 1241RE 'Molniya' ('Tarantul') were ordered in the 1990s. These 56m vessels have twice the endurance and range of the 39m 'Osa' class and are much better adapted for

open seas. They are equipped with four P-20 series (SS-N-2D 'Styx') missiles that – although obsolescent – have a large warhead and long range.

In 1996, two waterjet-powered BPS 500 missile boats designed by Russia's Severnoye Design Bureau were ordered for assembly at the Ba Son Shipyard in Ho Chi Minh City. The first ship – *HQ-381* – was launched in 1998 but did not enter service until late 2021. Vietnamese reports suggest problems with vibration and an inability to fire missiles whilst moving at high speeds caused the cancellation of the second hull.

These problems apparently prompted a move to return to a proven platform in the form of the Project 1241.8 variant of the 'Molniya'. Two were built at the Vympel Shipbuilding Plant in Russia for delivery in 2007, with six more subsequently being assembled locally at Ba Song. These were delivered in pairs between 2014 and 2017. Main armament comprises sixteen Kh-35 surface-to-surface missiles, which reportedly have a range of over 120km.

Other Fast Attack and Patrol Vessels: The VPN is

believed to operate five Project 206M ('Turya') class high-speed torpedo boats delivered by the Soviet Union in the 1980s. Although equipped with hydrofoils, imagery suggests that this equipment is no longer used in Vietnamese service. Four surviving Project 206T ('Shershen') class high-speed torpedo boats – out of sixteen or so transferred between 1973 and 1983 – also remain in the inventory.

There are also twelve relatively modern patrol ships. Six are Project 10412 'Svetlyak' class craft that were delivered between 2002 and 2012. They were followed into service by six locally-constructed TT-400TP gunboats that were accepted from 2012 onwards. Reportedly of Ukrainian design, these were built by the Hong Ha shipyard in Hai Phong. Both types have a main armament of a single 76mm gun.

From available imagery, it is likely that around six to eight older patrol vessels of the 'Shanghai', TP-01 and derivative types remain operational to bolster the more modern craft. Significant numbers of coastal and riverine patrol craft are also in existence, although many are operated by the Coast Guard and Vietnam's other maritime services.

At the tactical level, the missile, gun and torpedo ships of combat flotillas are structured to work cooperatively in attacking targets. In an article published in the VPN's official newspaper, an officer of the 170th Brigade explained that during an exercise, 'Our ships cooperated with the other warships of the brigade. According to the plan, with one target, the rocket ship attacked first, the artillery ship attacked later, and then the torpedo boat attacked in the rear.'

Mine Countermeasures Vessels: The VPN operates eight mine countermeasures vessels, all of Soviet/Russian origin. These comprise two Project 266 'Rubin' ('Yurka') class oceanic vessels, four Project 1265E 'Yakhont' ('Sonya') class coastal vessels and two Project 1258 'Korund' ('Yevgenya') inshore types. The two larger classes are known to have been upgraded with new equipment but the status of the inshore minehunters is uncertain.

Historically, the VPN used improvised smaller craft for mine clearance operations in heavily mined areas such as Hai Phong harbour, so it is reasonable to assume that such craft also exist for this purpose today.

Amphibious Ships: The VPN maintains a relatively large force of amphibious shipping, much comprising former US equipment seized at the end

The Project 10412 'Svetlyak' class ship *HQ-264* seen on patrol in Vietnamese waters. The VPN operates a relatively modern flotilla of large patrol craft. *(Vietnam People's Navy)*

The Project 1265E 'Sonya' class mine countermeasures vessel *HQ-862* photographed from a visiting US Navy warship in 2014. Whilst the Vietnam People's Navy's mine countermeasures force is relatively elderly, some units are starting to receive modern minehunting equipment. *(US Navy)*

of the Vietnam War. These include two 100m former 'County' class tank landing ships and small numbers of mainly LCM and LCU types. Although some have received upgrades such as new engines, they are steadily being replaced by locally-built construction.

Other significant amphibious units include three c. 850-tonne Polish-built Project 771 'Polnochny' series vessels delivered shortly after reunification and two slightly smaller ships of indigenous origin. These were joined in 2021 by four locally-built Damen Stan Lander 5612 landing ships; three from a cancelled Venezuelan order. Ten T4 utility landing craft obtained from the Soviet Union at the end of the 1970s may also still be in service.

Separately from the VPN, the sea transport arm of the General Department of Logistics also operates a large assortment of landing craft, freighters, tugs and other small ships. These include a new c. 300-tonne VDN-150 type that might form the basis of a replacement for many of the VPN's 'legacy' assets.

Auxiliary and Support Shipping: The VPN is supported by a considerable force of auxiliary shipping, often under-reported. Some of these vessels are assigned to the maritime militias and other Vietnamese sea services (see text box), although numbers of offshore supply vessels, other transport and logistic shipping, tugs and yard craft are under direct VPN control. Amongst more noteworthy vessels are:

- **The survey vessel** *Trần Đại Nghĩa* **(HQ-888):** Built to Damen's HSV-6613 design by the Song Thu Corporation at Da Nang and delivered in 2011, HQ-888 was possibly acquired to support charting of the new submarine flotilla's likely operational areas. She is supplemented by a number of auxiliary survey vessels.
- **The hospital ship** *Khánh Hòa* **(HQ-561):** The VPN's first hospital ship, the 2,000-tonne HQ-561 was commissioned early in 2015. Facilities include a treatment room, operating theatre, dental surgery and a fifteen-bed hospital ward. A sister vessel – *Trường Sa* (HQ-571) – serves in the transportation and logistic support roles.

The VPN's auxiliary force is being modernised with the acquisition of new vessels. This is the hospital ship *Khánh Hòa* (HQ-561), commissioned early in 2015. *(Vietnam People's Navy)*

- **The replenishment ship HQ-905:** A sister to the similar CSB-7011 ordered for the Vietnam Coast Guard, HQ-905 was built by the Hong Ha shipyard. Completed in 2019, she is capable of long-term operation at sea, transporting nearly 900 tons of fuel, more than 400 tons of fresh water and 850 tons of cargo. It is not known whether or not she is replenishment at sea-capable.

- **The sail training ship *Lê Quý Đôn* (HQ-286):** Ordered from Poland in 2013 and delivered in 2015, HQ-286 is a 1,000-tonne, three-masted barque attached to the VPN's naval academy. The academy is located at the site of the former RVN Naval academy at Nha Trang and is the primary training centre for officers of the VPN and para-military sea services such as the Coast Guard and Border Guard.

LAND-BASED FORMATIONS

The VPN's sea-going assets are supplemented by a large number of land-based formations, including naval infantry, anti-shipping missile and coastal radar units. These play an important role not only in the defence of the coastal mainland but also with respect to Vietnam's network of outposts in the South China Sea.

Naval Infantry: The VPN maintains a large force of naval infantry (marines), with units of varying strengths attached to all five Naval Regional Commands. Detailed open-source information on these formations is scarce, although the 101st Marine Brigade in Naval Region Four and 147th Marine Brigade in Naval Region One appear to be the largest and likely have all-arms capabilities. Smaller marine detachments serve on the outlying islets and man-made DK-1 rigs that have been constructed to reinforce Vietnam's presence across the SCS. Equipment has traditionally been of Russian origin but there has been an influx of Israeli weaponry in recent years.

A separate commando unit – the 126th Brigade – provides the VPN's Special Forces.

Mobile Coastal Missile Units: The VPN currently operates five mobile coastal missile brigades, comprising a key element of its overall A2/AD architecture. These are:

- **The 679th Coastal Missile Brigade:** Based at Hai

VIETNAM'S OUTPOSTS IN THE SOUTH CHINA SEA

Vietnam occupies large numbers of islands, reefs and other garrison points across the South China Sea. The Asia Maritime Transparency Initiative (AMTI) suggesting there are around fifty outposts spread across twenty-seven features. According to AMTI's analysis, Vietnam's outposts in the South China Sea fall into three categories: occupied islets, concrete buildings atop reefs (sometimes compared to pillboxes) and isolated rig-like structures known as *Dịch vụ-Khoa* (DK1).

Roughly translating as 'economic, scientific and technological service stations', the DK-1 rigs were built from 1989 onwards as a response to Chinese expansion into the Spratly Islands. Around twenty were built in seven clusters, six in the Spratly Island archipelago. Prefabricated in Vietnam with Russian technical assistance, around fourteen remain in use following losses to inclement weather. Most of these remaining rigs are of an improved type and have better storm resistance.

Maintenance of these isolated garrisons presents a major logistical challenge, with resupply and relief carried out by VPN vessels of the Tru'ò'ng Sa fleet. Whilst providing a valuable physical presence – and assisting with situational awareness – they are vulnerable to blockade, raid and invasion owing to their isolation and limited firepower. The majority are too small to contain sophisticated weapons and surveillance equipment, with their naval infantry likely armed with light weapons in most cases.*

Note
* An interesting – and pessimistic – analysis of Vietnam's strategic situation in the South China Sea is provided by Shang-su Wu in an article 'The Development of Vietnam's Sea-Denial Strategy' contained in the *Naval War College Review* Vol 70, No.1 (Newport RI: US Naval War College, 2017), pp.143–61 and available at: digital-commons.usnwc.edu/nwc-review/vol70/iss1/11

Phong and assigned to Naval Region One, this is equipped with the Cold War-era Soviet 4K-44 'Redut-M' (SSC-1) system armed with P-35 (SS-N-3B 'Shaddock') series surface-to-surface missiles. The VPN reportedly uses Ka-28 helicopters to provide targeting data for these elderly but

PT-76 amphibious light tanks pictured operating with the Project 771 'Polnochny' series tank landing ship *HQ-511* during a training exercise. Vietnam maintains a large force of naval infantry, including at least two all-arms brigades. *(Vietnam People's Navy)*

long-range (c. 500km) and supersonic missiles.

■ **The 680th Coastal Missile Brigade:** Based at Da Nang and assigned to Naval Region Three, this is believed to use the 4K51 'Rubezh' (SSC-3) system armed with P-20 'Styx' series surface-to-surface missiles. Although dated, these c. 80km range missiles still pack a powerful punch.

■ **The 681st Coastal Missile Brigade:** Based at Phan Thiết, west of Ho Chi Minh City, in Naval Region Two, this unit is equipped with the modern K-300P 'Bastion P' (SSC-5 'Stooge') complex that uses the P-800 'Oniks'/'Yakhont' (SS-N-26 'Strobile') supersonic surface-to-surface missile. Range is reportedly 350km. Two 'Bastion P' batteries were delivered to Vietnam in 2010 and comprise the most modern weapons in its coastal artillery.

■ **The 682nd Coastal Missile Brigade:** Based at Tuy Hòa, north of Cam Ranh, in Naval Region Four, this brigade is equipped with the VPN's other 'Bastion P' battery.

■ **The 685th Coastal Missile Battery:** This is also located in Naval Region Four to protect the VPN's most important naval base at Cam Ranh. Local reports suggest that it uses Israeli Elbit-produced ACCULAR and EXTRA medium and long-range rockets. There are reports that some of these systems have been deployed to Vietnamese-occupied islets in the Spratly

Islands as a defence against potential amphibious landings.

Given the gap in the brigade numbering system, some Vietnamese sources suggest additional coastal missile units will be established. It has been speculated that these could be equipped with a locally-made variant of the Russian 3M24 'Uran' anti-ship missile known as VCM-01

Coastal Radar Units: Situational awareness is maintained by a fairly extensive network of naval coastal radar sites organised under the Naval Regional Commands. Soviet-origin surveillance radars have been largely replaced by commercial 'Western' types, particularly after Thales became involved in modernising the coastal radar network in the early part of the last decade.

NAVAL AVIATION

The VPN gained its own naval air arm in July 2013 when the former 954th Air Regiment – a maritime-orientated air force unit – was transferred to navy control as the 954th Naval Air Brigade. Based at Cam Ranh, it operates six Viking Air DHC-6 Twin Otter turboprops in the maritime surveillance and transportation roles, as well as around eight Ka-28 'Helix' anti-submarine, two Eurocopter EC-225 utility and a single Ka-32T search and rescue rotor-

craft. The Ka-28s' principal function is to deploy aboard the 'Gepard' class frigates in the anti-submarine and utility roles. The unit also operates a number of UAVs of various types.

FUTURE CHALLENGES TO MODERNISATION

The latest Vietnamese Defence White Paper – *2019 Viet Nam National Defence* – states that, by 2030, the Vietnam People's Army is to be '… built to become a revolutionary, regular, highly-skilled, and gradually modernised force with some services and arms advancing straight to modernity'.[10] Without being explicitly stated, it is clear that VPN is one of the services for which this accelerated march to modernity is intended. The question is to what extent this ambition is achievable.

After good progress in the last decade, the VPN's progress appears to have slowed significantly. The reasons for this are multi-faceted. They include changed political priorities following the fall from grace of Prime Minister Nguyễn Tấn Dũng in 2016, associated constraints on funding and a deep-rooted Vietnam People's Army mind-set that has prioritised political action and internal regime preservation over progress towards a professional military. Concerns over potential corruption associated with the 'big ticket' acquisitions of the past may be another problem, particularly given the

The VPN maintains five mobile coastal missile brigades as part of its anti-access/area denial strategy. The oldest system still in use is the 4K51 'Rubezh' (SSC-3) system armed with P-20 'Styx' series surface-to-surface missiles, which is deployed by the 680th Coastal Missile Brigade. *(Vietnam People's Navy)*

The Russian Ka-28 'Helix' anti-submarine helicopter – pictured here aboard *Đinh Tiên Hoàng* (HQ-011) – forms the mainstay of the VPN's aviation capabilities. *(Chris Sattler)*

emphasis on financial probity being driven by Vietnam's current political leadership. Certainly, dealing with corruption is a significant challenge for the Vietnamese military given the extent to which its activities are intertwined with commercial enterprises.[11]

Another potential problem is the country's heavy reliance on Russian military technology; a reliance which dates back to the break in relations with China after reunification, if not before. Growing Sino-Russian ties and the enhanced difficulties with Russian trade following the Ukraine War make this a questionable policy and there is greater use of 'Western' – including Israeli, Japanese and South Korean – equipment across the maritime services than before. However, changing the military's Soviet-orientated mind-set – and its associated desire for equipment produced by the Union's successor states – will not be an easy task.[12]

CONCLUSION

The VPN has certainly undergone a major modernisation in recent years, with its induction of a powerful submarine flotilla a point of particular note. However, more needs to be done. Anti-air, anti-submarine and intelligence, surveillance and reconnaissance capabilities are all not yet quite state-of-the art. Whilst unmanned assets are increasing, low numbers of maritime surveillance aircraft seem a particular problem.

Moreover, since 2016, the VPN's modernisation drive has seemingly slowed. Whilst there is evident political interest in continuing this process, a conservative mind-set that places a heavy emphasis on internal security is likely a hurdle to necessary change. What is clear is that the VPN – and its sister services – face difficult external challenges in the face of China's continuing rise. The question remains whether or not the VPN will be provided with the right equipment – and develop an appropriate mind-set – to counter an evolving security environment.

Notes

1. The nine-dash line refers to line segments on various maps that delineate China's extensive claims over the waters of the South China Sea.

2. The Belt and Road initiative is a global infrastructure development strategy adopted by the Chinese government principally aimed at improving connectivity – and thus trade – with Europe, the Middle East and Africa. Dependent on perspective, it has been viewed either as a welcome boost to international prosperity or an example of Chinese neo-colonialism. The initiative is being accompanied by an increasing Chinese maritime presence in the seas encompassed by the strategy, including a first overseas base at Djibouti. The expansion of Ream, in the Gulf of Thailand, is seen as a further element of this maritime expansion, in spite of Chinese denials. See, for example, 'Cambodia and China deny naval base scheme as Australian PM voices concern' posted to *The Guardian* website on 8 June 2022.

3. A good overview of Vietnam's political approach to managing South China Sea tensions is contained in the International Crisis Group's *Report No. 318: Vietnam Tacks Between Cooperation and Struggle in the South China Sea* posted to crisisgroup.org on 7 December 2021. It asserts that 'No single option can help Vietnam deal with China effectively, and only combined can these tactics offer some strategic leverage'.

4. This argument was expounded by Rand Corporation analyst Derek Grossman in 'Vietnam Is the Chinese Military's Preferred Warm-Up Fight' first posted to *The Diplomat* news site on 14 May 2019. He states, 'At some point the military will need to test its new capabilities and the training it has honed over time. If the People's Liberation Army has any say in the matter, which it might, then it would very likely prefer to fight Vietnam ... as a warm-up to larger battles'.

5. Readers seeking a linguistic challenge can access the official history of the VPN in the Vietnamese language at the navy's internet site; baohaiquanvietnam.vn. A direct link to the document is currently: baohaiquanvietnam.vn/ storage/posts/L%E1%BB%8CH%20S%E1%BB%AC%20H QNDVN.pdf

6. These numbers are difficult to verify and it is possible ships attributed to the Soviet Union include some Soviet designs built in China. Soviet-sourced warships transferred during the war are believed to have included four 200-tonne Project 201M (NATO 'SO-1') submarine chasers delivered in the early 1960s; twelve Project 123K (P-4) torpedo boats transferred at around the same time; and a number of the larger P-6 type, at least some built in China. These were followed by two Project 386 ('Poluchat 1') patrol boats and, significantly, four Project 183R ('Komar') class missile boats, the latter armed with two P-15 'Termit' (SS-N-2 'Styx') series surface to surface missiles. Warships supplied by China are understood to have included a small number of 50-tonne patrol craft in the mid-1950s; large numbers of 80-tonne Type 055A ('Swatow') patrol boats between 1958 and 1964; and a handful of larger Type 062 ('Shanghai') series vessels in the mid-1960s.

7. There was a short but bloody border war between China and Vietnam in February-March 1979, a clash in which the two countries' navies played little part.

8. First formed in 1998, the Coast Guard was previously a subordinate command of the VPN.

9. In addition to its core defence role, the VPN runs several commercial 'economic-defence' entities involved in shipping, logistics and port operations, shipbuilding, oil and gas, fisheries and the cultivation of marine aquaculture. Ships from these units are deployed on both military and commercial tasks, as well as in support of government-related activities such as (currently) COVID-19 prevention and control.

10. *2019 Viet Nam National Defence* (Hanoi: Socialist Republic of Viet Nam – Ministry of National Defence, 2019), which is available by searching the web. The phrases 'modern' and 'modernity; are used no fewer than forty-three times in the document.

11. These explanations are expanded upon by Nguyen The Phuong, 'Why is Vietnam's Military Modernisation Slowing?' first posted to the Singapore-based *ISEAS Yusof Ishak* institute's website as Article 2021/96 and now available on their *Fulcrum* website at: fulcrum.sg/why-is-vietnams-military-modernisation-slowing/

12. See further Le Hong Hiep's 'Will Vietnam Be Able to Wean Itself Off Russian Arms?' published on the *Fulcrum* website on 4 April 2022. Commenting to *World Naval Review*, Collin Koh of Singapore's Institute of Defence and Strategic Studies at the Rajaratnam School of International Studies (RSIS) explained, 'Putting together Nguyen's and Le's arguments, one gets a more holistic picture of the structural impediments that hold back the VPN from pushing its modernisation further than just hardware and software upgrades. As it stands, the Russia-Ukraine conflict is likely to put into question the VPN's long-term procurement strategy given how heavily it relies on Soviet/Russian equipment. Vietnam can be expected to feel this impact in similar fashion to India. This carries further ramifications: Western equipment is more expensive than Russian kit, whilst to supplant Soviet/Russian kit the VPN will also have to drastically overhaul its entire infrastructure of training, logistics and support – all of which costs more money.'

REGIONAL REVIEW

Author:
Conrad Waters

THE INDIAN OCEAN AND AFRICA

On Wednesday 4 August 2021, the Indian Navy's first indigenous aircraft carrier (IAC) – *Vikrant* – departed Cochin Shipyard (CSL) to undertake an initial series of sea trials. By June 2022, this first, five-day series of tests had been followed by two further periods at sea as the new ship progressed towards delivery and ultimate commissioning. The latter ceremony is widely reported as being planned for Monday 15 August 2022; the 75th anniversary of Indian independence from the British Empire. *Vikrant*'s imminent arrival reflects both the technological progress the Indian Navy has made over recent years but also some of the challenges it faces as it attempts to counter the rise of China's People's Liberation Army Navy (PLAN).

Looking at the positives first, *Vikrant* undoubtedly represents an important technical achievement for the Indian shipbuilding sector. Only a handful of nations currently possess the industrial prowess to build an aircraft carrier and even fewer one of largely national design. India claims that *Vikrant*'s level of indigenous content exceeds 75 percent, an important step along the road to *Atmanirbhar Bharat* or a self-reliant India.[1] Moreover, the carrier's completion comes at a time when Indian shipyards are also delivering an increasing flow of equally sophisticated warships. Notably 21 November 2021 saw the commissioning of the lead Project 15B destroyer, *Visakhapatnam*, an event followed four days later by a similar ceremony for the fourth *Kalvari* ('Scorpène') class submarine, *Vela*. On 17 May 2022, builders Mazagon Dock Shipbuilders Ltd

(MDSL) of Mumbai hosted an unusual joint launch of the final member of the Project 15B class, *Surat*, and their second Project 17A class frigate, *Udaygiri*. It is hoped that shipyard improvements will allow these vessels to be delivered more quickly and efficiently than previous ships.

This hope reflects, in essence, the problem that continues to afflict the Indian Navy's plans for fleet recapitalisation and, ultimately, expansion: the fact that the country's largely state-owned naval shipbuilding sector has consistently struggled to produce ships on time and to budget. *Vikrant* herself has been long in the making; design work on the IAC commenced late in the last Millennium and her keel was laid in February 2009. Over this period, China has commissioned two aircraft carriers of her own and has gone a long way in constructing a third. *Vikrant* has also proved to be an expensive investment; total cost has been reported as amounting to INR230bn (c. US$3bn). This is not much less than the unit cost of the larger British *Queen Elizabeth* class carriers in spite of India's much lower-cost economy.

Some improvements are being achieved. For example, *Visakhapatnam* was completed in a period of around eight years from keel-laying to delivery; a material improvement over the 11 years required to build the first of the preceding Project 15A *Kolkata* design. However, more needs to be done. Aided by new block assembly techniques, the lead Project 17A frigate *Nilgiri* – laid down in December 2017 – was reportedly due for delivery by August 2022, a date

that will be considerably exceeded. All-in-all, construction schedules remain considerably longer than for comparable Chinese warships. There are also other problems to be overcome. These include the overly bureaucratic and time-consuming nature of Indian procurement approvals and an arguable over-reliance on Russia as a source of supply of critical components. The latter is becoming an increasingly critical issue given potential disruption to supplies arising from the Russo-Ukraine war.

A demonstration of the importance of overcoming these challenges was provided on 24 December 2021 when the Myanmar Navy inducted its second submarine – named *Minye Kyaw Htin* – at a ceremony marking the fleet's 74th anniversary. Unlike the service's first submarine, a former Indian Navy 'Kilo' class boat commissioned the previous year, the 'new' submarine is a Type 035 'Ming' class unit of PLAN origin. Although unlikely to alter the local balance of power, the unexpected transfer of the elderly submarine was clearly driven by China's desire to reinforce its ties with Myanmar's ruling military junta against a backdrop of India's efforts to expand its own links with the country. Her arrival was therefore yet another manifestation of the ongoing struggle for influence that continues to be fought out across the Indian Ocean region by the two nations. With China supplying more sophisticated ships to other regional allies, notably Pakistan, it seems increasingly imperative for India to accelerate its own process of fleet renewal if its relatively strong maritime position is to be assured.

A computer-enhanced image released to celebrate the commencement of sea trials by *Vikrant*, India's first indigenous aircraft carrier, on 4 August 2021. The image makes an interesting comparison with the unadjusted image that appears in the World Naval Aviation chapter, on which it was based. *(Indian Navy)*

Table 2.3.1: FLEET STRENGTHS IN THE INDIAN OCEAN, AFRICA AND THE MIDDLE EAST – LARGER NAVIES (MID 2022)

COUNTRY	ALGERIA	EGYPT	INDIA	IRAN	ISRAEL	PAKISTAN	SAUDI ARABIA	SOUTH AFRICA
Aircraft Carrier (CV)	–	–	1	–	–	–	–	–
Strategic Missile Submarine (SSBN)	-	-	1	–	–	–	–	–
Attack Submarine (SSN/SSGN)	–	–	–	–	–	–	–	–
Patrol Submarine (SSK/SS)	6	8	16	4	5	5	–	3
Fleet Escort (DDG/FFG)	2	11	22	–	–	8	7	4
Patrol Escort/Corvette (FFG/FSG/FS)	10	5	11	8	3	2	5	–
Missile Armed Attack Craft (PGG/PTG)	c. 12	c. 30	7	c. 25	8	10	9	1
Mine Countermeasures Vessel (MCMV)	2	c. 14	–	1	–	3	3	4
Major Amphibious (LPD)	1	2	1	–	–	–	–	–

Notes:

1 Algerian fast attack craft and Egyptian fast attack craft and mine-countermeasures numbers approximate.

2 Iranian fleet numbers exclude large numbers of indigenously-built midget and coastal submarines, as well as numerous additional missile-armed patrol boats operated both by the Iranian Navy and Revolutionary Guard .

3 The South African attack craft and mine countermeasures vessels serve in patrol vessel roles. Not all the latter are operational.

INDIA

In February 2022, India announced an INR5.25 trillion (c. US$70bn) defence budget for 2022–3, a nominal year-on-year increase of almost 10 percent.[2] As noted in previous editions of *World Naval Review*, defence spending continues to be seriously impacted by heavy personnel and pensions costs relating to India's large standing army, leaving the more capital-intensive air force and navy starved of resources. This is increasingly recognised as a major concern and a new, short-term service concept – known as Agnipath – has been proposed to help address the problem in the longer term.[3] In the interim, Indian Navy procurement spending has benefitted from delayed implementation of some army capital programmes, being expected to increase to as much as INR465Bn (c. US$6bn) in the coming year. However, this still remains inadequate to cover all projected acquisition costs, inevitably slowing the launch of new projects. Much may depend on the appointment of a new Indian Chief of Defence Staff following the death of the first-ever appointee to the role, Indian Army General Bipin Rawat, in a helicopter crash on 8 December 2021. Rawat had promoted the supremacy of the army over the 'supporting arms' of the navy and air force, opposing programmes such as the Indian Navy's proposed second indigenous aircraft carrier. A more balanced approach might result in an improved outlook for this and other naval schemes.

Current Indian Navy strength is summarised in Table 2.3.2. In overall terms, the picture is one of a navy holding its own in terms of fleet size, with newly completed warships being largely sufficient to sustain – but not grow – overall fleet strength. As such, longstanding plans to expand the fleet to c. 200 ships of all types seem little closer to fruition. A summary with respect to major warship categories follows.

Aircraft Carriers and Major Amphibious Ships: The imminent arrival of India's new indigenous aircraft carrier is giving increased priority to the acquisition of new fighter jets to operate from the ship. These will supplement and, perhaps, ultimately replace the navy's existing MiG-25K series aircraft, which have proved to be less than satisfactory in service. The naval variant of France's Rafael and the US F/A-18E/F Super Hornet are in the running for a government-to-government contract for the supply of twenty-six aircraft; down from an initial requirement for fifty-seven.[4] Both types are opti-mised for conventional catapult assisted take-off but arrested recovery (CATOBAR) operation but have demonstrated an ability to use the ski-jump config-uration fitted to Indian carriers.

Meanwhile, a new request for information was circulated in August 2021 for the supply of four amphibious assault ship-like LPDs. This follows on from the collapse of a previous bidding process after two of the three contenders experienced financial difficulties. The tender documents set out ambitious requirements for a 'through deck' design capable of accommodating at least sixteen helicopters and drones (of which four should be capable of simulta-neous operations), as well as four mechanised and four personnel landing craft. Armament is to include a 32-cell short range surface-to-air missile system, four AK-630 close-in weapons systems and, interest-ingly, sixteen surface-to-surface missiles. Delivery of the first ship is anticipated no later than five years after contract award. The other ships are to follow at annual intervals.

Major Surface Combatants: The Indian Navy's procurement of major surface combatants continues to follow a three-strand approach encompassing indigenous Project 15B *Visakhapatnam* class

Table 2.3.2: INDIAN NAVY: PRINCIPAL UNITS AS AT MID 2022

TYPE	CLASS	NUMBER	TONNAGE	DIMENSIONS	PROPULSION	CREW	DATE
Aircraft Carriers							
Aircraft Carrier (CV)	Project 1143.4 **VIKRAMADITYA** (KIEV)	1	45,000 tonnes	283m x 31/60m x 10m	Steam, 30 knots	1,600	1987
Principal Surface Escorts							
Destroyer – DDG	Project 15B **VISAKHAPATNAM**	1	7,400 tonnes	163m x 17m x 7m	COGAG, 30+ knots	300	2021
Destroyer – DDG	Project 15A **KOLKATA**	3	7,400 tonnes	163m x 17m x 7m	COGAG, 30+knots	330	2014
Destroyer – DDG	Project 15 **DELHI**	3	6,700 tonnes	163m x 17m x 7m	COGAG, 32 knots	350	1997
Destroyer – DDG	Project 61 ME **RAJPUT** ('Kashin')	3	5,000 tonnes	147m x 16m x 5m	COGAG, 35 knots	320	1980
Frigate – FFG	Project 17 **SHIVALIK**	3	6,200 tonnes	143m x 17m x 5m	CODOG, 30 knots	265	2010
Frigate – FFG	Project 11356 **TALWAR**	6	4,000 tonnes	125m x 15m x 5m	COGAG, 30 knots	180	2003
Frigate – FFG	Project 16A **BRAHMAPUTRA**	3	4,000 tonnes	127m x 15m x 5m	Steam, 30 knots	350	2000
Corvette – FSG	Project 28 **KAMORTA**	4	3,400 tonnes	109m x 13m x 4m	Diesel, 25 knots	195	2014
Corvette – FSG	Project 25A **KORA**	4	1,400 tonnes	91m x 11m x 5m	Diesel, 25 knots	125	1998
Corvette – FSG	Project 25 **KHUKRI**	3	1,400 tonnes	91m x 11m x 5m	Diesel, 25 knots	110	1989
Submarines							
Submarine – SSBN	**ARIHANT**	1	7,500+ tonnes	112m x 11m x 10m	Nuclear, 25+ knots	100	2016
Submarine – SSK	Project 75 **KALVARI** ('Scorpène)	4	1,800 tonnes	68m x 6m x 6m	Diesel-electric, 20 knots	45	2017
Submarine – SSK	Project 877 EKM **SINDHUGHOSH** ('Kilo')	8	3,000 tonnes	73m x 10m x 7m	Diesel-electric, 17 knots	55	1986
Submarine – SSK	**SHISHUMAR** (Type 209)	4	1,900 tonnes	64m x 7m x 6m	Diesel-electric, 22 knots	40	1986
Major Amphibious Units							
Landing Platform Dock – LPD	**JALASHWA** (AUSTIN)	1	17,000 tonnes	173m x 26/30m x 7m	Steam, 21 knots	405	1971

destroyers and Project 17A *Nilgiri* class frigates, supplemented by Russian-designed frigates of the Project 11356 *Talwar* class. As referenced in the introduction, the Project 15B programme is starting to produce results. *Visakhapatnam* is now in commission whilst second of class *Mormugao* is close to delivery after commencing sea trials from MDSL on 19 December 2021. However, completion of the two other ships of the class by MSDL is far less advanced. Given the likely imminent retirement of the three remaining elderly members of the *Rajput* class, it therefore seems that destroyer numbers will fall in the short term before stabilising at an eventual total of ten.

The medium-term prospects for frigate numbers are also somewhat mixed. Following retirement of *Gomati*, the final serving member of the Project 16 *Godavari* class, on 28 May 2022, all the remaining twelve-strong force comprises ships delivered during the current Millennium. They should therefore be good for a few years yet. Moreover, there are a further seven Project 17A and four Project 11356 vessels under construction or on order. Less positively, both programmes are encountering problems and are likely to be delayed in their completion.

Construction of the Project 17As – shared between MDSL (four units) and Kolkata's Garden Reach Shipbuilders & Engineers or GRSE (three units) – is running significantly behind schedule. Whilst all seven are now in the course of assembly following a keel laying for the last of MDSL's quartet on 28 June 2022, only three have been launched to date. Accordingly, the class's planned completion by the end of 2025 looks increasingly unrealistic. Meanwhile, the Project 11356 programme – encompassing completion of two further members of the *Talwar* class at Russia's Yantar shipyard in Kaliningrad followed by the local assembly of a further pair at Goa – saw the launch of the first of the new batch, *Tushil*, on 28 October 2021. Unfortunately, further progress looks particularly vulnerable to the outbreak of the Ukrainian conflict. Importantly, the class's main gas turbines are supplied by Mykolaiv-based Zorya-Mashproekt, whose production has been badly disrupted by the onset of the war. Whilst engines for the Russian-built ships are believed to have been delivered before the start of hostilities, those for the Goa-built ships were seemingly only contracted towards the end of 2021. If this is correct, their delivery will inevitably be delayed, if it ever happens at all. More broadly,

A photograph of the lead Project 15B destroyer *Visakhapatnam* taken at India's President's Fleet Review in February 2022. The destroyer is the major addition to the Indian Navy's surface fleet over the past year, commissioning on 21 November 2021. *(Arjun Sarup)*

the Indian Navy must be increasingly concerned about future deliveries of spare parts for engines that power the bulk of its major combatants.

Further into the future is a programme for a flotilla of next-generation corvettes, which are likely to be frigate-sized in their dimensions and capabilities. Initiation of the procurement of a reported eight-strong class was given through an 'acceptance of necessity' in June 2022 at an estimated cost of INR360bn (c. US$4.7bn) but – on the basis of past experience – it is likely to be many years before the new ships are delivered. In the meantime, the number of existing corvettes is already beginning to shrink with the retirement of the 32-year-old *Khukri* – the lead Project 25 vessel – on 23 December 2021.

Submarines: The last year has seen good progress with implementation of the final stages of the *Kalvari* class submarine programme, another MDSL project which has previously suffered from delays. As already referenced, the fourth boat – *Vela* – was commissioned on 25 November 2021. The fifth

member of the class – *Vagir* – subsequently commenced trials in February 2022, whilst the sixth and final unit – *Vagsheer* – was launched on 20 April 2022. This brings the project close to a satisfactory conclusion.

Developments with the follow-on Project 75I for a further six submarines have been less satisfactory. The acquisition is designed to operate under a 'strategic partnership' model under which two Indian companies – MDSL and the privately-owned Larsen & Toubro – will link with one of a list of shortlisted foreign shipbuilders to compete for the final contract award. A request of proposal for the contract was issued in July 2021. However, the process is now close to foundering because the majority of the shortlisted overseas companies – France's Naval Group, Germany's tkMS, Russia's Rosoboronexport, South Korea's DSME and Spain's Navantia – have been unwilling or unable to comply with the technical and commercial terms of the bid. Even if a way forward is found, it seems unlikely that a contract will be awarded before 2024, likely pushing back deliveries of the new boats into the

2030s. Given the age of much of India's existing submarine fleet, this will put numbers under pressure at a time when rival Pakistan is taking delivery of new Chinese-built boats.

The little open-source news available on the secretive strategic submarine programme suggests that the second *Arihant* class submarine – *Arighat* – was still in the final stages of pre-delivery trials in early 2022 despite previous reports of likely earlier delivery. It appears that a half-sister known only by the code name S4 was launched from the Shipbuilding Centre at Visakhapatnam on 23 November 2021, although this has not been publicly confirmed.[5] This latest submarine is believed to be a stretched variant of the previous boats that will carry eight – rather than four – ballistic missile launch tubes.

Other Ships: In addition to its projects relating to surface warship and submarine construction, the Indian Navy maintains a myriad of ongoing programmes for smaller combatants and support vessels that are at different stages in the procurement process. Amongst the largest and most advanced is that for sixteen Anti-Submarine Warfare Shallow Water Craft (ASW-SWC); small, c. 750-tonne vessels armed with anti-submarine rocket launchers and torpedoes. Under contracts awarded in April 2019, these have been allocated equally to GRSE and CSL, who are each building their part of the order to their own, bespoke design. GRSE has subcontracted construction work on at least five of its allocation to Larsen & Toubro's shipyard at Kattupalli, which had laid the keels of the first three vessels as of June 2022. By this time work was also underway on two of the GRSE vessels, as well as at least five of the batch allocated to CSL. The contracts envisaged first deliveries taking place in October 2022 but this seems unlikely at the current rate of construction. The new ships will, inter alia, replace the existing *Abhay* class corvettes, which have now been reduced to just two vessels

following the retirement of *Akshay* on 3 June 2022.

Also leaving service on the same day as *Akshay* was the *Veer* class fast attack craft *Nishank*. This leaves seven of an original thirteen-strong class – a derivative of the Russian 'Tarantul' type – in service. In 2021 it was announced that CSL was the lowest bidder for six replacement next-generation missile vessels. However, there had been no notification of a contract award by mid-2022.

Another project that is struggling to reach the contract stage is the construction of five new fleet replenishment tankers that are to be built by Hindustan Shipyard with the assistance of the Turkish TAIS consortium. The parameters of the programme have been in place for a number of years but conclusion of an agreement has been continuously postponed, possibly because of disquiet over Turkish industry's support for the rival Pakistan Navy.

There is better news with respect to a flotilla of four new survey ships. In similar fashion to some of the ASW-SWC units, these have been ordered from GRSE but are being built in conjunction with to Larsen & Toubro. *Sandhayak*, the lead, GRSE-built unit, was launched on 5 December 2021 and was followed down the slipway by the Larsen & Toubro-built *Nirdeshak* on 26 May 2022. The remaining pair have also started assembly at Larsen & Toubro's Kattupalli facility.

OTHER INDIAN OCEAN NAVIES

Bangladesh: The Bangladesh Navy has benefitted from significant quantitative and qualitative upgrades over the last decade, largely through the arrival of new and second-hand vessels of Chinese origin. Most of these – including the two 'Ming' class submarines that were commissioned in March 2017 to form an embryonic underwater flotilla and the four 'Jiangwei II' and 'Jianghu III' frigates that form the core of the surface fleet – are still relatively elderly, obsolescent vessels. Others, particularly the quartet of C13B (Type 026) *Shadhinota* class corvettes delivered in two batches between 2015 and 2019, provide a more modern but limited capability.

Having undertaken this initial phase of fleet renewal, naval procurement has seemingly taken a pause as plans are developed for further acquisitions. These will be more focused on developing indigenous construction capabilities. The major ongoing project is for a second batch of five c. 350-tonne *Padma* class patrol vessels, which are being assem-

Construction of the Indian Navy's *Kalvari* class 'Scorpène' type submarines is now drawing to a satisfactory conclusion. This photograph shows the sixth and final boat, *Vagsheer*, being floated out by MDSL on 20 April 2022. *(Indian Navy)*

bled at the local Khulna Shipyard with Chinese help.[6] The first of these, named *Shaheed Daulat*, was launched on 14 February 2022. A more ambitious plan relates to the acquisition of up to six new indigenous guided-missile frigates, which are to be built at Chittagong Dry Dock in conjunction with a foreign partner. A number of overseas designs – including the British Arrowhead 140 and Turkish 'Milgem' – have been proposed for the new project.

Myanmar: Whilst the arrival of Myanmar's new Chinese-built submarine undoubtedly drew most headlines over the past year, it is possibly the navy's ongoing progress with local construction that has most significance in the medium term. The submarine's December 2021 commissioning coincided with that of *Inma*, the second member of the indigenous, c. 1,500-tonne *Inlay* offshore patrol vessel class. Less far advanced is the new 135m frigate referenced in last year's *World Naval Review*, which is likely to be the navy's first warship equipped with a vertical launch system. It has been speculated that she will be launched within the next 12 months.[7] When completed, she will join a surface flotilla that comprises three smaller indigenous frigates of the *Kyan Sittha* and *Aung Zeya* classes and three locally-built *Anawrahta* class corvettes, all supplemented by two former Chinese 'Jianghu II' frigates transferred in 2012.

Pakistan: The Pakistan Navy's modernisation programme has picked up pace over the last year, with a start being made on the delivery of new surface combatants. As is the case for an increasing number of Asian fleets, heavy reliance is being placed on Chinese shipyards to deliver the required capability enhancements. The country's Hudong–Zhonghua shipyard has now completed an initial pair of Type 054A-P *Tughril* class frigates, with the lead ship being accepted in November 2021 prior to a formal commissioning ceremony at Karachi on 24 January 2022. Her sister, *Taimur*, followed her into service on 23 June 2022. Hudong–Zhonghua is now focused on completing a second pair of ships – *Tipu Sultan* and *Shah Jahan* – which were launched on 3 August 2021 and 23 December 2021 respectively. The new frigates are broadly similar to their Chinese Type 054A equivalents but have a different radar outfit focused on SR2410C multi-function and SUR17B surveillance arrays. When combined with the Pakistan Navy's existing quartet of F-22P

Tabuk – pictured here during exercises with the US Navy in November 2021 – is the second of two Damen OPV1900 *Yarmook* class corvettes delivered to the Pakistan Navy in 2020. It appears that she has yet to be fully armed. Pakistan's fleet is – after considerable delays – benefitting from a significant flow of new warships. *(US Navy)*

Zulfiqar class frigates, they will give it a relatively homogenous front-line force of eight major surface combatants.[8]

The Chinese-built frigates will be supplemented in service by four *Babur* class variants of the Turkish 'Milgem' light frigate design. Two pairs of these c. 3,000-tonne ships are being built by Istanbul Naval Shipyard (INS) and Pakistan's Karachi Shipyard & Engineering Works (KSEW) under a contract signed in 2018. Each yard has launched one ship to date, with INS launching *Babur* on 15 August 2021 and KSEW following with *Badr* on 20 May 2022. Unlike their Turkish counterparts, the Pakistan Navy ships will be equipped with a vertical launch system for the Albatros-NG extended range variant of the CAMM surface-to-air missile. The quartet are then likely to be followed by an indigenous 'Jinnah' class frigate programme, which will be built by KSEW on the basis of a transfer of technology agreement with Turkish industry. It is thought that a class of six of these ships is eventually envisaged. When combined with the two Damen

OPV1900 *Yarmook* class corvettes delivered in 2020, this would allow the surface fleet to achieve a medium-term target of twenty frigates and corvettes.

Renewal of the surface fleet is being mirrored in a parallel upgrade of underwater forces. This is focused on a programme for eight *Hangor* class submarines, an export variant of the Chinese Type 039B 'Yuan' series. Assembly is being equally shared between China's Wuchang Shipbuilding and KSEW. The latter held a first steel-cutting ceremony for *Tasnim* – its initial unit and the fifth boat of the overall class – in December 2021. Deliveries of the Chinese-built vessels are expected to commence over the course of the coming year. Their arrival is likely to allow withdrawal of the two elderly French-built *Agosta* class boats but the navy's more recent modernised 'Agosta-90B' variants will stay in service for the foreseeable future. This will give a total patrol submarine flotilla of eleven boats, not far short of India's fifteen-strong force of patrol submarines.

Amongst other recent developments has been delivery of the c. 650-tonne *Haibat*, the fourth and final member of the *Azmat* class of fast attack craft. Her commissioning in late March 2022 followed a considerable gap from the three earlier ships in the class, which are derived from China's Type 037 series of missile boats. This is possibly due to the incorporation of a greater level of indigenous design input from Pakistan's Maritime Technologies Complex. Her arrival might allow a start to be made on retiring some of Pakistan's older missile boats, which are now reaching the end of their operational lives.

Sri Lanka: The Sri Lanka Navy's plans for further reorientation towards blue water constabulary operations will undoubtedly be impacted by the country's economic crisis, with the exhaustion of foreign currency reserves even seeing the private sale of fuel suspended in mid-2022. A second former US Coast Guard national security cutter – the former *Douglas Munro* (WHEC-724) – was transferred to Sri Lanka in October 2021 but required refit before delivery to her new home. It is now not clear whether this voyage will go ahead given the current economic backdrop.

AFRICAN NAVIES

South Africa saw the first addition to its naval strength in recent memory with the delivery of *King Sekhukhune I*, the first of the three c. 700-tonne multi-mission inshore patrol vessels ordered under Project Biro. Handed over in May 2022, she was formally commissioned on 15 June. Her two sistership ships will follow at approximately annual intervals. Built by Damen Shipyards Capetown, the new ships are based on Damen's Stan Patrol 6211 design and incorporate a Sea Axe bow. Constructed with a steel hull and aluminium superstructure, they have a maximum speed of around 26 knots and an endurance of 4,000 nautical miles. Main armament comprises a Super Sea Rogue remotely-controlled weapons station fitted with a 20mm cannon. The principal sensor is an RTS 3200 Frequency Modulated Continuous Wave Optronics Radar Tracker (FORT). The MMIPVs will replace the South African Navy's remaining 'Warrior' class fast attack craft, which have been operating as interim patrol vessels following conversion between 2012 and 2014. Only one of these vessels – *Makhanda* – remains active, with *Isaac Dyobha* – the only other survivor of a once ten-strong class – now preparing to reduce to reserve. More broadly, ongoing constraints on South Africa's defence budget continue to have a negative impact on fleet readiness. For example, previous plans to upgrade the naval station at Durban to a fully operational base have now shelved because of financial constraints. However, funding has been made available for the navy's other major procurement programme; a new hydrographic survey vessel being acquired under Project Hotel. The ship is being built by Sandock Austral Shipyards of Durban and remains

The multi-purpose inshore patrol vessel *King Sekhukhune I* is the first of three units based on the Damen Stan Patrol 6211 design being delivered to the South African Navy. *(Damen)*

on schedule to be delivered in the first half of 2023.[9]

The procurement of constabulary and logistic support assets remains a priority for other Sub-Saharan African navies against a continued backdrop of the need to secure the maritime economy from piracy and other criminal activity. Although the Gulf of Guinea remained a focal point of maritime lawlessness, a combination of local and international action saw a sharp decline in reported incidents from eighty-one in 2020 to thirty-four in 2021, contributing to the lowest recorded level of international piracy since 1994.[10] Considerable efforts are underway to bolster maritime patrol forces, a process typified by **Cote d'Ivoire**'s recent announcement that it is soon to take delivery of a former French P400 type patrol vessel and two new OPV-45 patrol vessels from Israel Shipyards. France and Israel remain amongst the leading suppliers of choice to the region. The vessels being procured range from simple coastal patrol craft to relatively sophisticated offshore combatants, the latter perhaps best typified by **Senegal's** order for three OPV 58S patrol ships from France's Piriou. The second of these vessels was launched at Concarneau on 2 February 2022, whilst the first is already outfitting and should be ready for delivery in 2023.

Nigeria's navy has been notable in undertaking a programme of renewal in recent years, with acquisitions ranging from Chinese Type 056 corvette-derived P18N offshore patrol vessels through to an extended series of coastal fast patrol boats delivered by France's OCEA. The start of April 2022 saw a further expansion of this process with the delivery of a new 100m tank landing ship – named *Kada* – from Damen Shipyards, Sharjah, in the United Arab Emirates. A second member of the class is planned. Amongst other major developments has been an order for two OPV-76 offshore patrol vessels from Turkey's Dearsan, an acquisition that should considerably enhance the navy's long-range patrol capabilities. Nigeria is also continuing to develop indigenous shipbuilding through local construction of more basic assets. *Oji*, a third c. 50m coastal 'seaward defence vessel' of improved design was commissioned in December 2021 and two further vessels of the type are currently being built by the Nigerian Naval Dockyard in Lagos.

Turning to North Africa, **Egypt's** recent Saudi

Seen here being fitted out at the Piriou yard in Concarneau is *Walo*, the first of three 'high end' OPV 58S patrol vessels being built for Senegal. *(Bruno Huriet)*

The Nigerian Navy's new tank landing ship *Kada* has been built at Damen Shipyards, Sharjah, in the United Arab Emirates. An order for a second member of the class is planned. *(Damen)*

The British Royal Fleet Auxiliary's solid stores support ship *Fort Rosalie* (left) pictured in company with the German Navy's Type 702 combat support ship *Berlin* on the River Clyde. In a surprise move, the Egyptian Navy has acquired *Fort Rosalie* and her sister *Fort Austin* for further service, saving them from the scrapyard. *(Michael Leake)*

El Kasseh 3 is the third of a series of mine countermeasures vessels ordered from Italy's Intermarine for the Algerian Navy. This photograph shows her at La Spezia in the course of completing sea trials in April 2022. *(Lorenz Amiet)*

Arabian-backed programme of naval modernisation and expansion continues to bear fruit. Recapitalisation of the submarine fleet with a quartet of new-build Type 209/1400(mod) submarines has been completed with the delivery of *S44* at tkMS Kiel on 7 July 2021. The German company also continues to make progress on four MEKO 200-EN frigates ordered in preference to further Naval Group 'Gowind' corvettes in 2018. Fabrication of three of these has been sub-contracted to the Rönner Group, with final integration taking place at Kiel. The first of the trio – named *Al Aziz* – commenced trials in April 2022 and should be delivered before the end of the year. The fourth vessel is to be built in Egypt at Alexandria Shipyard in Alexandria, where construction reportedly commenced in December 2021. The facility continues to complete the last pair of the three 'Gowind' corvettes allocated to it, with the third ship – *El Moez* – commencing sea trials in mid-2021. In another development that provides an interesting insight into the extent of the Egyptian Navy's ambitions, Egypt has acquired the veteran British solid stores replenishment vessels *Fort Rosalie* and *Fort Austin*. The two ships – to be renamed *Abu Simbel* and *Luxor* – had been put up for sale for scrap following the 2021 Integrated Review but will now be refurbished by Merseyside's Cammell Laird before transfer to their new owner.

Elsewhere in North Africa, **Algeria's** naval procurement continues to experience something of a pause after the frenetic activity of the last decade that saw, inter alia, the arrival of four Project 636 'Kilo' class submarine variants, five major surface combatants and the amphibious transport dock *Kalaat Béni Abbès*. The third *El Kasseh* (improved *Lerici*) class minehunter being built by Italy's Intermarine commenced sea trials in the second half of 2021 but it is not apparent that she has yet been delivered. An undefined number of offshore patrol variants of China's popular Type 056 corvette are also reportedly under construction, continuing the navy's past policy of sourcing equipment from a wide range of suppliers.

MIDDLE EASTERN NAVIES

Israel is another regional country that has embarked on a significant programme of naval modernisation. This saw progress on several fronts over the past year. Most significantly, January 2022 saw Germany's tkMS conclude a framework agreement

for the supply of three new *Dakar* class submarines, which will replace the existing trio of Batch I *Dolphin* class boats from the early years of the next decade. The new submarines are to be of a completely new design that will be specifically engineered to fulfil the operational requirements of the Israeli Navy. However, precise details are scant. Speculative reports suggest that they will be considerably larger than the existing submarines and be fitted with vertical launch cells for cruise or even ballistic missiles. Meanwhile, it appears that *Drakon*, the last of the three Batch II *Dolphin* class boats being completed by tkMS under a previous contract, is now close to acceptance after the COVID-19 pandemic impacted pre-delivery trials.

In the meantime, tkMS has completed its part in another Israeli Navy project with the delivery of the SA'AR 6-class corvettes *Atzmaut* and *Nitzachon* on 27 July 2021. They are, respectively, the third and fourth units of a four-ship order placed in 2015. The new warships subsequently departed Germany for final outfitting of weapons and sensors by Israel Shipyards in Haifa, where the lead member of the class, *Magen*, has already completed this process. In February 2022, Rafael Advanced Defense Systems confirmed that a programme of live fire tests of C-Dome – the naval configuration of the well-known Iron Dome air-defence system – had been performed aboard the new corvette. Israel Shipyards is also working on finalising the details of its new 'Reshef' design; a variant of its SA'AR 72 concept that is intended to replace the Israeli Navy's existing eight SA'AR 4.5 type fast attack craft. Key features of the new ship include a high payload to displacement ratio and a hybrid diesel-electric/diesel propulsion system. The latter combines efficient low speed operation on electrical motors with an ability to achieve speeds of up to 30 knots from the vessel's main diesels. A contract for the new class is expected before the end of 2022.[11]

Elsewhere in the Middle East, **Saudi Arabia**

Saudi Arabia's new 'Avante 2200' corvette *Al-Jubail* is the first of a class of five ships that are scheduled to be handed over by 2023. She was delivered on 31 March 2022. *(Navantia)*

continues to move forward with the Saudi Naval Expansion Programme II (SNEP II), which is largely focused on renewal of its Persian Gulf-based Eastern Fleet.[12] On 31 March 2022, Navantia delivered *Al-Jubail*, the first of five 'Avante 2200' corvettes ordered from Spanish shipbuilder Navantia under a €1.8bn (c. US$2.1bn) contract announced in July 2018. Enlarged variants of the four *Guaiquerí* class offshore patrol vessels previously sold to Venezuela, they are equipped to a more capable 'combatant' standard that includes a Mk 41 vertical launch system and an Hazem combat management system (CMS). The latter is believed to be a Saudi Arabian modification of the Catiz CMS developed by Navantia. All five of the class are now in the water following launches of *Jazan* on 24 July 2021 and *Unayzah* on 4 December 2021. Final deliveries are expected to take place in 2023. Work also continues at Fincantieri's Marinette Marine on four, larger

The 'offshore patrol vessel' *Musherib* – in reality a heavily-armed fast attack craft – is one of a number of vessels that Fincantieri had delivered to the Qatar Emiri Navy over the last year. *(Fincantieri)*

multi-mission surface combatants; upgraded variants of the US Navy's *Freedom* (LCS-1) class Littoral Combat Ship. It is interesting to speculate whether the Royal Saudi Navy's confidence in the programme will have been impacted by the American decision to retire most of their own examples of the design before the Saudi vessels have even entered service.

The **United Arab Emirates**, perhaps the other most significant Middle Eastern maritime power, also has significant naval acquisitions underway. The most advanced of these is that for 'Gowind' type corvettes ordered from France's Naval Group in 2019. Two of these are being built at the Lorient yard, which launched the lead vessel, *Bani Yas*, in December 2021. The other, *Al Emarat*, followed in May 2022. Displacing around 2,800 tonnes, these 102m vessels will be the largest in the Emirati navy. Construction is supposedly taking place in partnership with local Abu Dhabi Ship Building, which previously played a leading role in the *Baynunah* class corvette project. However, the company's precise role in the project is unclear. In the meantime, the yard is focused on the new 'Falaj 3' programme for four, heavily-armed offshore patrol vessels. These are to be based on the Republic of Singapore Navy's *Fearless* class.

Qatar's rapid naval expansion – undertaken largely in association with Fincantieri – has been one of the most notable regional maritime developments of recent years. A seven-ship naval expansion programme initially agreed in June 2016 encompasses an amphibious transport dock, four *Al Zubarah* class air-defence 'corvettes' and two smaller but heavily armed *Musherib* class 'offshore patrol vessels'. The project is now starting to come to fruition starting with the delivery of *Al Zubarah* on 28 October 2021. This has been followed by the acceptance of *Musherib* on 29 January 2022 and the second corvette, *Damsah*, on 28 April. In May 2022, Fincantieri announced the start of the final element of the programme with a formal keel laying ceremony for the as yet-unnamed LPD-type amphibious transport dock at its yard in Palermo, Sicily. The selection of the facility – more usually associated with the construction of commercial vessels – for the ship's construction is interesting and possibly reflects the heavy workload faced by the group's usual naval yards arising from national and export orders.

It has been a mixed year for **Iran's** naval forces. The most newsworthy event was the four-month Atlantic deployment of the multi-role support vessel *Makran* and supporting 'Mowj' class frigate *Sahand*. Initially expected to be focused on the Caribbean and particularly Venezuela, the voyage took the Iranian ships to the Baltic. Once there, they participated in Russia's Navy Day celebrations in late July 2021. The deployment proved the Iranian Navy's ability to operate at distance from its own bases and provides an additional – if relatively modest – increase in the range of asymmetric threats the US Navy and its allies need to worry about. The Iranian Navy – and separate Iranian Revolutionary Guard Corps (IRGC) Naval Forces – continue to rely on a mix of largely indigenously manufactured anti-access/area denial capabilities to deter the perceived threat from the United States and its allies. However, there are indications that their development and deployment are stretching the limits of its capacity. In December 2021, *Talayieh*, the most recent of the 'Mowj' series, fell of its blocks whilst the dry dock being used for its construction was being flooded-up in the latest of a number of setbacks to impact Iranian naval vessels.[13] Whilst the damage is likely repairable, the accident will inevitably create another delay to a programme that has struggled to deliver a meaningful number of operational ships.

Notes

1. Interestingly, a report optimistically titled 'India's first indigenous aircraft carrier INS Vikrant to be handed over to Navy in May' posted to *The New Indian Express*'s website – newindianexpress.com – on 28 April 2022 quoted Cochin Shipyard Limited officials as stating the new carrier's indigenous content was 60 percent. This suggests, perhaps, that official claims of a higher Indian content have been overstated.

2. The Indian defence budget is a complex topic and this paragraph gives the briefest of overviews. Indian academic Laxman K Behera provides a much more detailed explanation on an annual basis, this year posted to the *Observer Research Foundation*'s orfonline.org website on 23 February 2022 under the title, 'Bigger, Not Necessarily Better: India's Defence Budget 2022-23'.

3. The Agnipath reforms envisage new armed service personnel being enlisted on initial four-year contracts that do not carry pension rights, with only a quarter subsequently being offered more lucrative, long-term service. Claimed to be aimed at creating 'a much more youthful and technically adept war fighting force by ensuring a fine balance between youthful and experienced personnel', the scheme has been widely seen as a means of reducing personnel costs to allow more money to be spent on equipment. It has been badly received by potential recruits, leading to widespread civil disturbance.

4. It appears that the planned order has been reduced in the hope that future contracts can be directed towards an indigenous Twin Engine Deck Based Fighter (TEDBF) that is currently under development by HAL.

5. This development was reported by Christopher Biggers in 'India quietly launches third Arihant-class SSBN', *Jane's Defence Weekly* – 12 January 2022 (Coulsdon: Janes, 2022), p.16.

6. An additional seven variants of the design have been constructed by Dockyard & Engineering Works and Khulna Shipyard for the Bangladesh Coast Guard. The last of these, *Joy Bangla*, was delivered on 10 January 2022.

7. See Ridzwan Rahmat, 'Myanmar completes hull section of new frigate at Thanlyin', *Jane's Defence Weekly* – 13 April 2022 (Coulsdon: Jane's, 2022), p.16.

8. The Pakistan Navy's former six-strong flotilla of ex-British Type 21 frigates has now been reduced to just one ship, *Tariq* (previously HMS *Ambuscade*). It is also difficult to see the sole FFG-7 frigate *Almagir* – formerly *McInerney* (FFG-8) – being retained in service once the new frigates arrive.

9. The *defenceWeb* news portal – www.defenceweb.co.za – contains considerable additional information related to African navies over this chapter's inevitably brief summary.

10. Full details of global piracy are provided in the news section of the ICC's Commercial Crime Services website, accessible at: icc-ccs.org

11. For further details on current Israeli Navy programmes see the editor's interview with 'Israel Shipyards Ltd', *Maritime Defence Monitor* – April 1–2/2022 (Bonn: Mittler Report, 2022), pp.47–9 and available for download at: msd-mag.com/profile/print-issues

12. Another of the editor's articles in the April 2022 edition of *Maritime Defence Monitor*, 'Status report: Naval Programmes in the Persian Gulf' provides more information on current regional procurement.

13. See H I Sutton, 'Iran's Drive to Modernize Navy Faces Latest in String of Setbacks' posted to the *USNI News* site – news.usni.org – on 16 December 2021.

Author:
Conrad Waters

2.4 REGIONAL REVIEW

EUROPE AND RUSSIA

On Sunday 27 February 2022, Chancellor Olaf Scholz addressed a special session of Germany's Bundestag to set out his government's response to Russia's invasion of Ukraine three days before. In a major change to previous German policy, he pledged that his country would achieve NATO's longstanding target of spending two percent of national economic output – GDP – on defence by 2024. This objective will be assisted by a special €100bn (US$100bn) fund to make good well-publicised deficiencies in Germany's armed forces.[1] This announcement – subsequently followed by similar commitments to increased military budgets in a number of other European capitals – has been seen as a major watershed. It essentially marks the end of the three-decade long 'peace dividend' declared at the end of the Cold War, the culmination of a steady policy shift that can be seen as tracing its origins to Russia's annexation of Crimea in March 2014.

Although this funding boost will likely result in an eventual uplift to the fortunes of many European fleets, these improvements will be years in the making. Moreover, they may well initially be reflected more in enhanced readiness and operational sustainability than any significant increase in naval orders of battle. Much will need to be done to make good deficiencies in areas such as availability of ammunition and spare parts, as well as to bring existing formations up to full strength after the reversal of previous discredited concepts such as the *Bundeswehr*'s 'dynamic availability management'.[2] Additional funding will also be subject to competi-

tion as all branches of the armed forces seek to repair previous deficiencies. A boost to naval budgets might not necessarily be seen as the highest priority response to the outbreak of a new European land-based conflict.

Nevertheless, the German example suggests spending on naval equipment procurement will increase. Although aviation programmes are likely to the main beneficiaries of the €100bn special fund, it is expected that there will be an uplift in German purchases of the new Type 212CD submarines from the currently contracted two to, perhaps, as many as six. The surface fleet will also likely benefit from the eventual exercise of the options for two additional F126 frigates contained in the existing deal. There are also reports of a third batch of K130 type corvettes to standardise the class on the latest, batch two, configuration and allow the sale of older vessels to friendly nations. Similarly, it is expected that France's next Military Planning Law will place a strong emphasis on naval forces, including the possible procurement of a second nuclear-powered aircraft carrier. Implementation of such a significant acquisition would be a notable development that would inevitably require substantial resourcing given the budgetary squeeze already likely to result from France's need to recapitalise its strategic nuclear force over roughly the same timescale.

The other major question is whether Europe's depleted naval shipbuilding infrastructure will be able to support the increased requirement for new vessels. As noted in the Introduction, Germany's

ThyssenKrupp Marine Systems (tkMS) is already attempting to position itself to meet the uplift in demand by acquiring the MV Werften shipyard in Wismar, one of a number of facilities that had fortuitously been put up for sale following the pandemic-related collapse in orders for cruise liners that had previously sustained them. The purchase marks a major change in strategy by the German company, which had divested a number of shipyards a few years previously. However, it is not only additional infrastructure that will be required. For example, it appears that the Wismar yard is to be earmarked to support expanded submarine construction. This will, presumably, require a significant effort retraining the existing workforce in the skills required for this particular specialisation.

Another aspect of the change in the European security environment is the expansion of the NATO alliance as a result of the decision by Finland and Sweden to request membership of the security pact. It is expected that the necessary accession protocols will be completed early in July 2022. Expansion will then be subject to ratification by each of the alliance's existing members. Once the process is completed, NATO will have a total of thirty-two member states. Although both countries have long enjoyed close relations with their NATO partners, their formal participation in the alliance is a welcome development. Notably it does much to turn the Baltic Sea into a 'NATO lake', reducing something of the previously perceived vulnerability of the alliance's northern flank.

The German Navy's K130 corvette *Oldenburg* pictured on exercise in May 2022. The significant hike in German defence spending that is planned as a response to the Russo-Ukrainian war could see the vessels of this type that are already in service replaced by a new batch of upgraded variants.

TABLE 2.4.1: FLEET STRENGTHS IN WESTERN EUROPE – LARGER NAVIES (MID 2022)

COUNTRY	FRANCE	GERMANY	GREECE	ITALY	NETHERLANDS	SPAIN	TURKEY	UK
Aircraft Carrier (CVN/CV)	1	–	–	1	–	–	–	2
Support/Helicopter Carrier (CVS/CVH)	–	–	–	1	–	–	–	–
Strategic Missile Submarine (SSBN)	4	–	–	–	–	–	–	4
Attack Submarine (SSN)	6	–	–	–	–	–	–	5
Patrol Submarine (SSK)	–	6	11[2]	8	4	2	12	–
Fleet Escort (DDG/FFG)	14	12	13[2]	16	6	11	16	18
Patrol Escort/Corvette (FFG/FSG/FS)	12	5	–	–	–	–	10	–
Missile Armed Attack Craft (PGG/PTG)	–	–	18	–	–	–	19	–
Mine Countermeasures Vessel (MCMV)	13	10[1]	3	10	5	6	11	11
Major Amphibious (LHD/LPD/LPH/LSD)	3	–	–	3	2[3]	3	–	5

Notes:

1 Two further units used as support vessels.

2 Headline figures overstate the actual position, as some old units are of doubtful operational status.

3 Also one joint support ship with amphibious capabilities.

Suffren, the first of the French Navy's new 'Barracuda' type nuclear-powered attack submarines, was declared ready for operational service on 3 June 2022. This picture shows her in July 2020 during the course of her pre-delivery trials. *(Bernard Prézelin)*

MAJOR REGIONAL POWERS – FRANCE

Pending any major changes in defence priorities arising from the Russo-Ukrainian war, the French Navy is making good progress with the programmes being implemented under the current 2019–2025 Military Planning Law. Whilst there has been little year-on-year change to the fleet structure outlined in Table 2.4.2, the pace of change is likely to accelerate over the next few years as important capabilities are delivered.

Submarines: A major step in the recapitalisation of France's underwater flotilla took place on 3 June 2022 with a ceremony to mark the *admission au service actif* of the first of France's six new 'Barracuda' type nuclear-powered attack submarines, *Suffren*. The event follows an extensive series of trials and training that followed the boat's delivery in November 2020 and was reportedly delayed by the need to rectify a minor problem with one of the submarine's turbo-generators. With *Suffren* now fully operational, attention will turn to delivery of *Duguay-Trouin*, the second member of the six-strong class. She was rolled out of the assembly hall at Cherbourg in November 2021 but is not expected to be floated out until the late summer of 2022. This is somewhat later than previously envisaged, in turn pushing her delivery back to 2023.

The delay to *Duguay-Trouin* will add to the pres-

TABLE 2.4.2: FRENCH NAVY: PRINCIPAL UNITS AS AT MID 2022

TYPE	CLASS	NUMBER	TONNAGE	DIMENSIONS	PROPULSION	CREW	DATE
Aircraft Carriers							
Aircraft Carrier – CVN	CHARLES DE GAULLE	1	42,000 tonnes	262m x 33/64m x 9m	Nuclear, 27 knots	1,950	2001
Principal Surface Escorts							
Frigate – FFG	AQUITAINE (FREMM)	7[1]	6,000 tonnes	142m x 20m x 5m	CODLOG, 27 knots	110	2012
Frigate – FFG	FORBIN ('Horizon')	2	7,100 tonnes	153m x 20m x 5m	CODOG, 29+ knots	195	2008
Frigate – FFG	LA FAYETTE	5	3,600 tonnes	125m x 15m x 5m	CODAD, 25 knots	150	1996
Frigate – FSG	FLORÉAL	6	3,000 tonnes	94m x 14m x 4m	CODAD, 20 knots	90	1992
Frigate – FS[2]	D'ESTIENNE D'ORVES (A-69)	6	1,300 tonnes	80m x 10m x 3m	Diesel, 24 knots	90	1976
Submarines							
Submarine – SSBN	LE TRIOMPHANT	4	14,400 tonnes	138m x 13m x 11m	Nuclear, 25 knots	110	1997
Submarine – SSN	SUFFREN	1	5,300 tonnes	100m x 9m x 7m	Nuclear, 25+knots	65	2020
Submarine – SSN	RUBIS	5	2,700 tonnes	74m x 8m x 6m	Nuclear, 25+ knots	70	1983
Major Amphibious Units							
Amph Assault Ship – LHD	MISTRAL	3	21,500 tonnes	199m x 32m x 6m	Diesel-electric, 19 knots	160	2006

Note:

1 Includes one slightly modified *Alsace* variant.

2 Now officially reclassified as offshore patrol vessels.

sure on the submarine force resulting from the severe fire aboard the previous generation *Rubis* class boat *Perle*. She has now returned to Toulon to complete her final refit and refuelling following the complex operation carried out at Cherbourg to replace her damaged sections with those from her previously-decommissioned sister *Saphir*. It is expected that sea trials will commence before the end of 2022, allowing her to return to operational service the following year. Meanwhile, *Rubis* herself is scheduled to be decommissioned within the next few months after already receiving a five-year long life extension due to delays with the 'Barracuda' programme. This will leave four of the class in the fleet.

Surface Combatants: The transition of the French Navy's surface fleet from legacy ships to the new FREMM multi-role frigates is now almost complete. June 2022 saw *Latouche-Tréville*, the final member of the 'FASM 70' *Georges Leygues* class anti-submarine frigates, return to Brest for the final time ahead of a decommissioning ceremony scheduled for 1 July. Meanwhile, *Lorraine* – the eighth and final French FREMM – commenced running sea trials from Lorient early in 2022 prior to her scheduled delivery in November. Like her sister *Alsace*, she has been completed in FREMM-DA (*frégate européenne multimissions de défense aérienne*) configuration. This includes four octuple Sylver A50 vertical launch system (VLS) modules capable of firing the long-range Aster 30 surface-to-air missile and upgrades to the 'Herakles' multifunction radar and SETIS combat system.

Work is already well underway on France's next generation surface combatant, the FDI *frégate de défense et d'intervention*. On 16 December 2021, Naval Group held a formal keel-laying ceremony at Lorient for *Amiral Ronarc'h*, the first of five French members of the class. The c. 4,500-tonne ship had already been under fabrication for over two years and is expected to be delivered during 2024. Intended to be a smaller and more cost-effective successor to the FREMM, the new design has already gained success in the export markets with the selection of its 'Belh@rra' export variant to meet the Hellenic Navy's requirement for new warships. Three of the five existing *La Fayette* class stealth frigates – *Courbet*, *La Fayette* and *Aconit* – have been subject to limited upgrades to extend their service lives until the new class is completed. *Courbet* was

Jacques Chevallier, the first of four new replenishment oilers – force replenishment vessels in French Navy parlance – was floated out from the Chantiers de l'Atlantique shipyard at Saint Nazaire on 29 April 2022. (Bruno Huriet)

the first to complete the nine-month process and is now back in the operational fleet. The enhancements include replacement of the obsolescent 'Crotale' surface-to-air missile launcher with the MBDA 'Sadral' system and a limited anti-submarine capability based on Thales' 'KingKlip' Mk 2 hull-mounted sonar.[3]

Design work continues on the *porte-avions de nouvelle génération* (PANG) next-generation aircraft carrier programme prior to the expected commencement of physical construction at Chantiers de l'Atlantique in Saint Nazaire in 2025. In December 2021, the US State Department approved the potential sale of electromagnetic EMALS catapults and AAG advanced arresting gear for the new ship at an estimated cost of US$1.3bn.

Minor Warships and Auxiliaries: 29 April 2022 saw launch of *Jacques Chevallier*, the first of four force replenishment vessels –*bâtiments ravitailleurs de force* or BRF – at Chantiers de l'Atlantique. She is expected to commence sea trials before the end of

2022 and be delivered in the first half of 2023. Acquired to meet the French Navy's FLOTLOG requirement to replace the elderly *Durance* class replenishment oilers, the new design is based on the Italian Navy's logistic support ship, *Vulcano*. The quartet were ordered from a consortium that also includes France's Naval Group at a reported cost of €1.9bn (US$1.9bn) early in 2019. Displacing some 31,000 tonnes at full load, the new ships will be the largest French naval vessels by tonnage after the aircraft carrier *Charles de Gaulle*. They will have a capacity for 13,000m³ of liquid cargo and will also be able to carry fuel, ammunition, spare parts and other solid stores.

Another lead ship launched for the French Navy during the last year is the new *Auguste Bénébig,* the first of six new *patrouilleurs outre-mer* (POM) destined for overseas service in French Polynesia, La Réunion and New Caledonia. The ship was launched from Socarenam's Saint-Malo yard on 15 October 2021. She is expected to complete sea trials in the course of 2022 before departing for Nouméa,

New Caledonia in 2023. Construction of a further three vessels is also currently underway in anticipation of completing the whole programme by 2025. Socarenam are also working on a subcontract from CNIM to build a total of fourteen *engins de débarquement amphibie standard* (EDA-S) tank landing craft for use with the navy's Toulon-based amphibious flotilla and in the overseas territories. An initial pair of these 29m, roll-on, roll-off vessels – named *Arbalette* and *Arquebuse* – were delivered in November 2021.

In October 2021, Naval Group signed a contract with the French DGA defence procurement agency for the detailed design of the new *patrouilleurs océaniques* (PO). Larger than but broadly similar to the smaller POM type, these are intended to serve in mainland France, replacing the remaining re-rolled *avisos* of the A-69 type. An innovative construction scheme envisages Naval Group coordinating the overall design process but actual construction being subcontracted to a number of smaller yards, such as Piriou and Socarenam. There is a degree of urgency in beginning construction given the age of the existing ships and it is hoped that the first will be completed by 2025.

MAJOR REGIONAL POWERS – ITALY

Table 2.4.3 outlines the Italian Navy's composition as at mid-2022. In spite of Italy's relatively limited defence budget, which is not expected to meet NATO's two percent of GDP target until 2028, the Italian Navy continues to benefit from a range of procurement programmes that are the envy of many of its European peers. The last 12 months have seen both further progress with existing construction and the award of new contracts.

One of the more significant developments in the last year was the commencement of initial trials by the new amphibious assault ship *Trieste* from Fincantieri's Muggiano shipyard near La Spezia on 12 August 2021. The largest ship to be built under the 'Naval Law' of 2014/15, she will undertake a secondary role as a substitute aircraft carrier for *Cavour* when *Giuseppe Garibaldi* retires from this mission. The new ship is expected to be delivered before the end of 2022 once an intensive programme of testing and post-trial rectification has been completed.

Just as is the case for France, construction of FREMM multi-mission frigates is now starting to wind down. Fabrication of replacements for the two ships sold to Egypt in 2020 commenced on 25 February and 12 October 2021, with both expected in Italian service before the end of 2025. Their arrival will complete the original ten-ship programme. Construction of surface combatants is otherwise focused on the *Paolo Thaon di Revel* class multi-purpose offshore 'patrol ships', which are effectively frigates in all but name. The lead ship was commissioned on 18 March 2022 and will be followed into service by a further six units by 2026. All of these vessels have now been laid down. The modular nature of the class means that units can be built in 'light', 'light plus' and 'full' configurations, each incorporating progressively greater load-outs of weaponry. The first four vessels will all be completed in light or light plus configurations but *Giovanni delle Bande Nere* – the fifth ship, launched from Fincantieri's Riva Trigoso yard on 12 February 2022 – will receive the enhanced 'full' outfit.

The 2021–2023 *Multiannual Programming Document* published in August 2021 provides greater clarity on what will follow.[4] A key priority is the construction of two new large destroyers to replace the pair of obsolescent *Luigi Durand de la Penne* class vessel, a programme that is expected to transition into the construction phase within the next two to three years. The estimated total programme cost of €2.7bn gives some idea of the new ships' likely level of sophistication. A project to modernise the existing *Andrea Doria* class air-defence destroyers will also be implemented around the middle of the decade. Another important programme that will keep Fincantieri's yards busy is the planned construction of a series of eight additional patrol ships that will be built as part of the European Union's European Patrol Corvette (EPC)

Table 2.4.3: ITALIAN NAVY: PRINCIPAL UNITS AS AT MID 2022

TYPE	CLASS	NUMBER	TONNAGE	DIMENSIONS	PROPULSION	CREW	DATE
Aircraft Carriers							
Aircraft Carrier – CV	CAVOUR	1	28,100 tonnes	244m x 30/39m x 9m	COGAG, 29 knots	800	2008
Aircraft Carrier – CVS	GIUSEPPE GARIBALDI[1]	1	13,900 tonnes	180m x 23/31m x 7m	COGAG, 30 knots	825	1985
Principal Surface Escorts							
Frigate – FFG	CARLO BERGAMINI (FREMM)[2]	8	6,700 tonnes	144m x 20m x 5m	CODLOG, 27 knots	145	2013
Frigate – FFG	ANDREA DORIA ('Horizon')	2	7,100 tonnes	153m x 20m x 5m	CODOG, 29+ knots	190	2007
Destroyer – DDG	DE LA PENNE	2	5,400 tonnes	148m x 16m x 5m	CODOG, 31 knots	375	1993
Frigate – FFG	MAESTRALE	3	3,100 tonnes	123m x 13m x 4m	CODOG, 30+ knots	225	1982
Frigate – FF	PAOLO THAON DI REVEL	1	5,800 tonnes	143m x 17m x 5m	CODAG, 32+ knots	90	2022
Submarines							
Submarine – SSK	TODARO (Type 212A)	4	1,800 tonnes	56m x 7m x 6m	AIP, 20+ knots	30	2006
Submarine – SSK	PELOSI (Improved SAURO)	4	1,700 tonnes	64m x 7m x 6m	Diesel-electric, 20 knots	50	1988
Major Amphibious Units							
Landing Platform Dock – LPD	SAN GIORGIO	3	8,000 tonnes	133m x 21m x 5m	Diesel, 20 knots	165	1987

Note:

1 Now operates largely as a LPH.

2 Class includes *Bergamini* (GP) and *Fasan* (ASW) variants.

Seen here at Fincantieri's Muggiano yard in April 2022, Italy's new amphibious assault ship *Trieste* is in the course of final trials before delivery. With her twin island structure and ski-jump giving her more than a passing resemblance to the British *Queen Elizabeth* class aircraft carriers, she will undertake a secondary role as a substitute carrier for Italy's *Cavour*. *(Lorenz Amiet)*

project. Italy has been assigned the coordination role for this programme, which is being taken forward under the European Union's Permanent Structured Cooperation (PESCO) framework.

The renewal of the fleet's auxiliary shipping has received a further boost with the order for a second logistic support ship, a sister ship for the existing *Vulcano*. The c. €410m contract will be completed at Fincantieri's Castellammare di Stabia shipyard near Naples, which has previously constructed sections for both Italian and French vessels of the type. Delivery is expected to take place by 2025 and an order for a third vessel is envisaged. Also ordered during the last year was a new submarine rescue ship to replace the life-expired *Anteo*. Contracted to the T Mariotti shipyard in Genoa, the as-yet unnamed vessel is also expected to be operational by 2025.

The new rescue ship will operate with Italy's growing flotilla of Type 212 series submarines. On 11 January 2022, Fincantieri announced that production activities had commenced at Muggiano on the first of two U212NFS (Near Future Submarines). These are an evolution of the navy's earlier quartet of Type 212A *Todaro* class boats, which were built in conjunction with Germany's tkMS. Like the *Todaro* class, the new units will be equipped with air-independent propulsion but they will also incorporate significant technological enhancements contributed by the Italian defence sector. It is envisaged that the two new boats will be delivered in 2027 and 2029, replacing the third batch of *Sauro* class submarines. The programme also includes options for an additional pair of U212NFS submarines that, if exercised, would allow replacement of the *Sauro* class to be completed on a like-for-like basis.

The Italian Navy's PPA oceanic patrol vessels are essentially frigates in all but name. They are being delivered in a number of different configurations, each outfitted to a different level of warfighting potential. *Giovanni delle Bande Nere*, pictured here at Muggiano in April 2022, will be delivered in the most potent 'full' configuration. *(Lorenz Amiet)*

MAJOR REGIONAL POWERS – RUSSIA

It is difficult to undertake any assessment of recent Russian naval developments without viewing events through the prism of the Russo-Ukrainian war. The more detailed but preliminary analysis of the naval aspects of the 'special military operation' contained in Chapter 1.2 suggests that the navy has experienced a decidedly mixed conflict. On the one hand, the war has demonstrated the Russian Navy's ability to deploy large numbers of warships in a complex military operation – an achievement that would have been improbable only a decade ago – and the potency of its large and growing arsenal of precision land-attack cruise missiles. On the other hand, it has revealed the vulnerabilities arising from its still-significant reliance on obsolescent, Soviet-era ships, associated weaknesses in anti-air and anti-missile defences, and likely deficiencies in training and operational procedures.

At this stage, it is unlikely that even the Russian military themselves have yet to determine how the fleet will need to change to address the war's lessons. The fact that these changes will need to be imple-

mented against the backdrop of a weakened economy and the need to rebuild conflict-depleted land forces will be an additional complication. It seems unlikely that the high current priority given to the strategic and wider submarine fleets will be diminished given the more acute East-West rivalry. However, the future trajectory of the surface navy must be open to considerable uncertainty.

For the time being, the composition of the Russian Navy is summarised in Table 2.4.4, with overviews of principal warship types following.

Submarines: The Russian Navy's ongoing focus on its underwater assets continues to pay dividends, with the last year seeing a number of new submarines enter its ranks. Prominent amongst these boats was *Knyaz Oleg*, the fifth member of the 'Borey' class of strategic submarines and the second Project 995A variant. She was commissioned at a ceremony in Severodvinsk on 21 December 2021 after a series of trials that included the successful test-firing of a RSM-56 'Bulava' (SS-N-32) intercontinental ballistic missile from the White Sea into

the Kura proving ground on the Kamchatka Peninsula on 21 October of that year. Her sister boat and sixth member of the class, *Generalissimus Suvorov*, was launched by the Sevmash plant at Severodvinsk on Christmas Day 2021. Four additional members of the class – all Project 995A boats – are under construction at Sevmash following a joint keel-laying ceremony for *Knyaz Potemkin* and *Dmitry Donskoy* on 23 August 2021. In addition, it has been reported that orders for the eleventh and twelfth boats will be placed in 2023. They would, in effect, complete replacement of the Soviet-era Project 677BDR and Project 677BDRM 'Delta III' and 'Delta IV' strategic submarines that maintained the underwater element of Russia's nuclear deterrent in the post-Cold War era. The numbers of these 'legacy' boats in service is steadily shrinking, with the 'Delta IV' *Ekaterinburg* the latest to be approved for disposal.

The nuclear-powered Project 855M 'Yasen-M' attack submarine *Novosibirsk* was commissioned alongside *Knyaz Oleg* on 21 December 2021. She is the second modified variant and third member of the overall class. Another six of the type are under construction, with the third 885M – *Krasnoyarsk* – launched on 30 July 2021 prior to commencing sea trials in June 2022. After a long initial gestation period – the prototype boat, *Severodvinsk*, took 20 years to build – these submarines are now being delivered at regular intervals, materially strengthening Russia's underwater arm. In October 2021, *Severodvinsk* undertook an initial test firing of the 3M22 Tsirkon (SS-N-33) hypersonic missile, further adding to the class's potential.

Progress also continues with renewing the navy's force of conventional diesel-electric submarines. The major effort is re-equipping the Pacific Fleet with a second batch of six Project 636.3 'Improved Kilo' class boats following the previous completion of deliveries of a first batch destined for the Black Sea Fleet. The third of this new batch, *Magadan*, was commissioned on 12 October 2021 whilst the fourth, *Ufa*, was launched on 31 March 2022. Two more boats laid down at the Admiralty Shipyard in Saint Petersburg in August 2021 will complete this series. Whilst there have previously been reports that a third batch will be constructed for service in the Baltic, this plan may have been overtaken by renewed construction of the Project 677 'Lada' class design. *Sankt Peterburg* – the lead member of this troubled class – was commissioned as long ago as

The vulnerabilities arising from Russia's continued use of obsolescent Soviet-era warships to make up the bulk of its blue water naval forces have been revealed by the Russo-Ukrainian war. This is the *Slava* class cruiser *Marshal Ustinov*, a sister to the ill-fated *Moskva*, pictured from a Norwegian reconnaissance aircraft in January 2022. *(Norwegian Armed Forces)*

2010 whilst the second, redesigned boat, *Kronshtadt*, is still completing an extended series of trials. However, in June 2022, the Admiralty Shipyard made a start on the fourth and fifth members of the class that were ordered back in 2019. This might suggest confidence that the previous problems experienced by the design are now close to resolution.

Work also continues on a number of experimental submarines. Perhaps the most notorious of these is the Project 09852 submarine *Belgorod*. Reconstructed from an incomplete Project 949A 'Antey' ('Oscar II') class attack submarine, the new boat is designed, inter alia, to deploy the 2M39 'Poseidon' nuclear-armed underwater drone. She reportedly commenced sea trials in late June 2021 and is now believed to be close to acceptance.

Aircraft Carriers and Amphibious Warships: Modernisation of the sole Russian Project 1143.5 aircraft carrier, *Admiral Kuznetsov*, continues to suffer from delays. The refit commenced in 2017 but is not now expected to be completed before 2024 after previous setbacks that have included a floating dock collapse and a shipboard fire. The problems in retraining and qualifying naval aircrew after such a long gap will inevitably be considerable.

There has been little news on progress with the two project 23900 *Ivan Rogov* class amphibious assault ships laid down at the Zaliv shipyard in the Crimea in mid-2020 but it seems unlikely they will be delivered before the end of the decade. The second batch of two, enlarged Project 11711 *Ivan Gren* class large landing ships is more advanced. The hull of the first of this pair – *Vasily Trushin* – was

rolled out of its assembly shed at Kaliningrad's Yantar yard in June 2022 to allow installation of the superstructure to commence.[5]

Surface Combatants: The Russian Navy's three-tier construction programme for revitalising the surface fleet has made only modest progress over the last year due both to industrial challenges and production mishaps.

It is envisaged that the top tier of the new surface fleet will be the c. 5,500-tonne Project 22350 *Admiral Gorshkov* class frigates being built by Saint Petersburg's Severnaya Verf. Two of these ships have been completed, six are under construction and two are on order. The third member of the class, *Admiral Golovko*, was launched in May 2020 but had yet to commence sea trials as of mid-2022. She

TABLE 2.4.4: RUSSIAN NAVY: SELECTED PRINCIPAL UNITS AS AT MID 2022

TYPE	CLASS	NUMBER[1]	TONNAGE	DIMENSIONS	PROPULSION	CREW	DATE
Aircraft carriers							
Aircraft Carrier – CV	Project 1143.5 KUZNETSOV	1	60,000 tonnes	306m x 35/73m x 10m	Steam, 32 knots	2,600	1991
Principal Surface Escorts							
Battlecruiser – BCGN	Project 1144.2 KIROV	2	25,000 tonnes	252m x 29m x 9m	CONAS, 32 knots	740	1980
Cruiser – CG	Project 1164 MOSKVA ('Slava')	2	12,500 tonnes	186m x 21m x 8m	COGAG, 32 knots	530	1982
Destroyer – DDG	Project 956/956A SOVREMENNY	c. 3	8,000 tonnes	156m x 17m x 6m	Steam, 32 knots	300	1980
Destroyer – DDG	Project 1155.1 CHABANENKO ('Udaloy II')	1	9,000 tonnes	163m x 19m x 6m	COGAG, 29 knots	250	1999
Destroyer – DDG	Project 1155 UDALOY	c. 7	8.500 tonnes	163m x 19m x 6m	COGAG, 30 knots	300	1980
Frigate – FFG	Project 22350 GORSHKOV	2	5,500 tonnes	135m x 16m x 5m	CODAG, 30 knots	210	2018
Frigate – FFG	Project 11366M GRIGOROVICH	3	4,000 tonnes	125m x 15m x 4m	COGAG, 30 knots	200	2016
Frigate – FFG	Project 1154 NEUSTRASHIMY	2	4,400 tonnes	139m x 16m x 6m	COGAG, 30 knots	210	1993
Frigate – FFG	Project 1135 BDITELNNY ('Krivak I/II')	c. 2	3,700 tonnes	123m x 14m x 5m	COGAG, 32 knots	180	1970
Frigate – FFG	Project 20385 GREMYASHCHIY	1	2,500 tonnes	106m x 11m x 5m	CODAD, 27 knots	100	2020
Frigate – FFG	Project 20380 STERGUSHCHIY	7	2,200 tonnes	105m x 11m x 4m	CODAD, 27 knots	100	2008
Frigate – FFG	Project 11611 TATARSTAN ('Gepard')	2	2,000 tonnes	102m x 13m x 4m	CODOG, 27 knots	100	2002
Submarines							
Submarine – SSBN	Project 95/955A YURY DOLGORUKY ('Borey')	5	20,000+ tonnes	170m x 13m x 10m	Nuclear, 25+ knots	110	2010
Submarine – SSBN	Project 941 DONSKOY ('Typhoon')	1[2]	33,000 tonnes	173m x 23m x 12m	Nuclear, 26 knots	150	1981
Submarine – SSBN	Project 677BDRM VERKHOTURYE ('Delta IV')	5[3]	18,000 tonnes	167m x 12m x 9m	Nuclear, 24 knots	130	1985
Submarine – SSBN	Project 677BDR ZVEZDA ('Delta III')	1[3]	12,000 tonnes	160m x 12m x 9m	Nuclear, 24 knots	130	1976
Submarine – SSGN	Project 855 SEVERODVINSK ('Yasen')	3	13,500+ tonnes	120m x 14m x 9m	Nuclear, 30+ knots	90	2013
Submarine – SSGN	Project 949A ('Oscar II')	c. 7	17,500 tonnes	154m x 8m x 9m	Nuclear, 30+ knots	100	1986
Submarine – SSN	Project 971 ('Akula I/II')	c. 10	9,500 tonnes	110m x 14m x 10m	Nuclear, 30+ knots	60	1986
Submarine – SSK	Project 677 ST PETERSBURG ('Lada')	1	2,700 tonnes	72m x 7m x 7m	Diesel-electric, 21 knots	40	2010
Submarine – SSK	Project 877/636 ('Kilo')	c. 20	3,000 tonnes	73m x 10m x 7m	Diesel-electric, 20 knots	55	1981

Notes:
1 Table only includes main types and focuses on operational units and/or ships under active modernisation or refit.
2. Now used as a trials platform.
3. One additional unit of each type is being used in experimental roles.

will be the first of the class to go to sea with new Russian-built gas turbines manufactured by UEC Saturn, which were substituted for the Ukrainian units used in the earlier pair after their supply was terminated after the 2014 Crimean invasion. Russian news reports suggest that the ship will be delivered before the end of 2022 but the complexities of integrating the revised power plant should not be underestimated.

The second tier of surface combatant construction encompasses the extended range of Project 20380/20385/20386 corvettes.[6] Six Project 20380 *Steregushchiy* and a sole Project 20385 *Gremyashchiy* class variant have been delivered to date out of the twelve Project 20380, six Project 20385 and single Project 20386 vessels firmly contracted. A second Project 20385 class vessel, *Provornyy*, was reportedly close to completion when badly damaged by fire at Severnaya Verf on 17 December 2021. The fire, which is believed to have extended across the full length of the composite superstructure, was finally extinguished by the efforts of around 170 firefighters

with – it is claimed – no damage to the ship's hull. Nevertheless, the superstructure will need to be completely replaced, pushing back scheduled delivery to the middle of the decade.

With construction of the twelve-strong class of Project 21631 'Buyan M' small missile ships at the inland Zelenodolsk yard now close to completion, construction of third-tier combatants is largely concentrated on the follow-on Project 22800 'Karakurt' type. Three of a planned sixteen-strong fleet were rapidly commissioned from the Pella yard between 2018 and 2020 but there have been no further deliveries. This may be a consequence of the decision to split construction of the class across at least five shipyards, with the need for each to develop the skills required to build the new design potentially stretching out construction.

Minor Warships and Auxiliaries: Russian Navy procurement continues to support construction of a wide-range of minor warfighting and auxiliary vessels, ranging from multi-role icebreakers to small

patrol boats. A snapshot of the more prominent programmes includes:

■ **Project 22160 Offshore Patrol Ships:** Six of these ships have been ordered from the Zelenodolsk and Zaliv yards for service with the Black Sea Fleet. Four have been delivered to date, with *Sergey Kotov* the latest to join the fleet in mid-2022. A multi-role modular design, the class has been prominent in the Russo-Ukrainian war where their potential vulnerability in a combat environment has led to some dissatisfaction. According to unofficial statements reported by the TASS news agency, this has led to plans for a second batch to be abandoned.[7]

■ **Project 21890 'Grachonok' Class Guard Boats:** Built by three separate shipyards, some twenty-six of these 31m patrol craft have been delivered to the navy and border guard since late 2009. The most recent deliveries were a pair accepted from Zelenodolsk in June 2022. Additional units of the type are under construction.

■ **Project 03160 'Raptor' Class Patrol Boats:** Around seventeen of these 17m high-speed patrol boats – similar in appearance to the Swedish CB-90 type – have been delivered by the Pella shipyard to date. The class has proved vulnerable to aerial drones in the Russo-Ukrainian conflict, with at least four reportedly destroyed.

■ **Project 12700 'Alexandrite' Mine Countermeasures Vessels:** Five of these vessels have been delivered by Saint Petersburg Sredne-Nevsky Shipyard to date following the acceptance of *Georgy Kurbatov* in August 2021. Originally scheduled to be the second member of the class, her completion was badly delayed by a fire in June 2016. A further five members of the class are either undergoing trials or in the course of construction after the laying down of *Polyarny* on 12 June 2022.

■ **Project 23550 Multi-Role Icebreakers:** Two of these large, 8,500-tonne ships are under construction at the Admiralty Shipyard for naval service, with a further two allocated to the Vyborg Shipyard for the border guard. Like the Project 22160 class, they are based on a modular design concept that allows them to be equipped with surface-to-surface and land attack cruise missiles.

The Project 22350 *Admiral Gorshkov* class frigate *Admiral Kasatonov* is the second member of her class and one of the few modern Russian major surface combatants in service. A number of sister-ships are currently under construction but their delivery has been delayed due to the need to replace their Ukrainian-sourced gas turbines with ones of Russian origin. *(Norwegian Armed Forces)*

The construction of the Project 23550 class reflects a broader push to renew Russia's icebreaking capabilities as global warming increases strategic interest in the Arctic. December 2021 saw the commissioning of *Sibir*, the second of a class of at least five 33,000-tonne Project 22220 nuclear-powered icebreakers operated by the civilian but state-owned FSUE Atomflot enterprise. Already the largest and most powerful vessels of their type ever constructed, they will be followed by three, even larger Project 10510 'Leader' icebreakers that will reportedly displace over 70,000 tonnes at full load. The keel of the first of these behemoths, to be named *Rossiya*, was laid at the Zveda shipyard in Russia's Far East on 5 July 2021. Delivery is expected in 2027. The Arctic certainly appears to becoming the focal point of its very own Cold War as global tensions increase.

MAJOR REGIONAL POWERS – SPAIN

The summary of the Spanish fleet's current major warships provided by Table 2.4.5 shows no change year-on-year. The only major new procurement was signature of the formal contract for the long-awaited BAM-IS submarine rescue ship on 5 November 2021. The new vessel will be built at Navantia's Puerto Real shipyard in the Bay of Cadiz, with delivery scheduled for mid-2025.

Although news with respect to new procurements was sparse, two significant existing contracts made progress. May 2022 saw commencement of sea trials in the Bay of Cartagena of the lead S-80 Plus class submarine, *Isaac Peral*, thereby taking the boat's planned 2023 delivery a step closer. Fabrication of the second boat, *Narciso Monturiol*, is also moving closer to completion with the integration of the vessel's fin (sail) to the rest of her hull prior to a planned 2023 launch. Significant efforts are also being made at the Cartagena Arsenal to support the new submarines, which are larger and longer than the S-70 *Galerna* class boats that they will replace.

Physical construction has also started on the new F-110 class frigates. The event was marked by a formal steel-cutting ceremony for the first ship, *Bonifaz*, presided over by Spanish Prime Minister Pedro Sánchez at Navantia's Ferrol shipyard on 6 April 2022. The lead ship is expected to be delivered in 2027, somewhat later than originally planned, and will be followed by her four sisters at roughly annual intervals. They will replace the six obsolescent F-80 (FFG-7) *Santa María* class frigates, the oldest of which is now over 35 years old.

The lead Spanish S-80 Plus submarine, *Isaac Peral*, pictured in the course of preliminary sea trials from Cartagena in May 2022. She is expected to enter service in the course of 2023. *(Navantia)*

Physical construction work on Spain's new F110 class frigates has started at Ferrol. The event was marked by a formal steel-cutting ceremony presided over by Spanish Prime Minister Pedro Sánchez for the first ship, *Bonifaz*, on 6 April 2022. *(Navantia)*

Table 2.4.5: SPANISH NAVY: PRINCIPAL UNITS AS AT MID 2022

TYPE	CLASS	NUMBER	TONNAGE	DIMENSIONS	PROPULSION	CREW	DATE
Principal Surface Escorts							
Frigate – FFG	ÁLVARO DE BAZÁN (F-100)	5	6,300 tonnes	147m x 19m x 5m	CODOG, 28 knots	200	2002
Frigate – FFG	SANTA MARÍA (FFG-7)	6	4,100 tonnes	138m x 14m x 5m	COGAG, 30 knots	225	1986
Submarines							
Submarine – SSK	GALERNA (S-70/AGOSTA)	2	1,800 tonnes	68m x 7m x 6m	Diesel-electric, 21 knots	60	1983
Major Amphibious Units							
Amph Assault Ship – LHD	JUAN CARLOS I	1	27,100 tonnes	231m x 32m x 7m	IEP, 21 knots	245	2010
Landing Platform Dock – LPD	GALICIA	2	13,000 tonnes	160m x 25m x 6m	Diesel, 20 knots	185	1998

A notable event took place at the end of June 2022 with the final retirement of the navy's last two SH-3D 'Sea King' helicopters. The rotorcraft first entered service with the Spanish Navy in the anti-submarine role in 1966 but have more recently been employed as transport helicopters.

MAJOR REGIONAL POWERS – UNITED KINGDOM

The British Royal Navy has spent the last year starting to implement the main tenets of the integrated security review published in March 2021.[8] At an operational level, the success of the Carrier Strike Group 2021 (CSG 21) at raising the Royal Navy's international profile has been replicated on a smaller scale by the forward deployment of modest naval forces across the globe. This task has fallen largely to the Batch 2 'River' class offshore patrol vessels. The work of *Spey* and *Tamar* – which departed their Portsmouth home base in September 2021 on a five-year mission to the Indo-Pacific region – has gained a particularly high profile. Their activities have ranged from *Tamar*'s surveillance of North Korean shipping in the East China Sea to *Spey*'s participation in disaster recovery operations following the Hunga-Tonga volcanic eruption. Elsewhere, Gibraltar-based *Trent* deployed with a contingent of Royal Marines from 42 Commando to perform security and capacity-building activities in the Gulf of Guinea. The Bahrain-based Type 23 frigate *Montrose* has also hit the headlines by intercepting missiles and other weaponry being smuggled out of Iran.

Fleet composition is summarised in Table 2.4.6. As is often the case, there is something of a 'jam tomorrow … but never jam today' flavour with respect to force structure, with overall fleet numbers declining due to retirement of obsolescent equip-ment before the arrival of replacements. This is detailed further below.

Submarines: The Royal Navy's force of nuclear-powered attack submarines has temporarily fallen to just five following the decommissioning of the *Trafalgar* class boats *Trenchant* and *Talent* at a joint ceremony at Devonport on 20 May 2022. *Trenchant* had actually finished her final mission over a year previously in March 2021 whilst *Talent* had reportedly completed her final patrol earlier in 2022. Their retirement leaves only *Triumph* from the class in the fleet. The main reason for the depletion in submarine numbers is the protracted delivery of the replacement *Astute*s, which continues to run behind schedule. *Audacious*, the fourth member of the class, completed her maiden operational deployment to the Mediterranean in the first half of 2022 whilst *Anson*, the fifth boat, was in the final stages of harbour acceptance trials at BAE Systems' Barrow-in-Furness shipyard as of mid-2022. Significant efforts are being made to accelerate deliveries of the remaining two members of the class, as well as to improve the availability of existing boats.[9] As such, it is hoped that the planned force level of seven submarines will be achieved by 2026. In September 2021, contracts worth a total of £170m (US$200m) were awarded to BAE Systems and Rolls-Royce to undertake design and concept work on the next generation of attack submarine; the Submersible Ship Nuclear Replacement (SSNR).

BAE Systems and Rolls-Royce subsequently gained much larger contracts totalling over £2bn (US$2.4bn) in May 2022 to deliver the third phase of the *Dreadnought* class strategic submarine programme. This phase will take the project through to the commencement of sea trials for the lead boat of the four-vessel class. In the meantime, the protracted overhaul and refuelling of the current generation *Vanguard* is expected to be completed before the end of 2022. The refit, which commenced as long ago as December 2015, has taken twice as long as expected due to a combination of technical problems and working restrictions imposed during the COVID-19 pandemic.

Surface Combatants: Physical construction work on *Venturer*, the first of the Royal Navy's five new Type 31 'Inspiration' class frigates, commenced with a first steel-cutting ceremony in Babcock's new ship hall at Rosyth on 23 September 2021. The ship's keel was subsequently laid on 26 April 2022. It is envisaged that she will be launched in 2023 and delivered in 2025 prior to entering operational service in 2027. The new, £60m (US$70m) facility is intended to support the simultaneous construction of two frigate-sized vessels and should assist with achieving the challenging target of completing the entire programme by 2030.

Progress with the Type 26 'City' class frigates on the Clyde has been less satisfactory. A number of problems relating to design maturity, equipment supply delays and the impact of the pandemic have slowed production of the lead ship, *Glasgow*. As a result, her in-service date is likely to be pushed back to 2028, over a year later than initially planned. This will be around 11 years from the start of production, a performance bettered by the oft-criticised Indian warship shipyards in building comparable ships.[10] It appears that BAE Systems are finally planning material investment – including a new covered ship hall – at their somewhat antiquated Govan yard. It is to be hoped that this will facilitate a better performance building the planned second batch of five Type 26 frigates, the order for which has yet to be placed.

Table 2.4.5: BRITISH ROYAL NAVY: PRINCIPAL UNITS AS AT MID 2022

TYPE	CLASS	NUMBER	TONNAGE	DIMENSIONS	PROPULSION	CREW	DATE
Aircraft Carriers							
Aircraft Carrier – CV	**QUEEN ELIZABETH**	2	65,000 tonnes	284m x 73m x 11m	IEP, 26 knots+	1,600	2017
Principal Surface Escorts							
Destroyer – DDG	**DARING** (Type 45)	6	7,500 tonnes	152m x 21m x 5m	IEP, 30 knots	190	2008
Frigate – FFG	**NORFOLK** (Type 23)	12	4,900 tonnes	133m x 16m x 5m	CODLAG, 30 knots	185	1990
Submarines							
Submarine – SSBN	**VANGUARD**	4	16,000 tonnes	150m x 13m x 12m	Nuclear, 25+ knots	135	1993
Submarine – SSN	**ASTUTE**	4	7,800 tonnes	93m x 11m x 10m	Nuclear, 30+ knots	100	2010
Submarine – SSN	**TRAFALGAR**	1	5,200 tonnes	85m x 10m x 10m	Nuclear, 30+ knots	130	1983
Major Amphibious Units							
Landing Platform Dock – LPD	**ALBION**	2[1]	18,500 tonnes	176m x 29m x 7m	IEP, 18 knots	325	2003
Landing Ship Dock – LSD (A)	**LARGS BAY**	3	16,200 tonnes	176m x 26m x 6m	Diesel-electric, 18 knots	60	2006

Notes:
1. One at extended readiness.

There have been a number of positive developments with respect to the existing Type 45 destroyers over the past year. The long-delayed power improvement programme intended to resolve the class's propulsion issues took a major step forward in June 2022 when *Dauntless*, the first ship to complete the programme, returned to sea from Cammell Laird's Merseyside yard. Work is also underway on *Daring* and *Dragon*, the latter at a second production line for the improvements at Portsmouth. However, it will not be until 2028 until the improvement, which involves the upgrading of diesel-generation capa-

The Royal Navy is experiencing something of a 'jam tomorrow … but never jam today' moment as existing assets are withdrawn before replacement, often with new technology. The hydrographic survey ship *Echo* became the latest in a number of second-line warships to be prematurely decommissioned when she paid off at Portsmouth on 30 June 2022. *(Crown Copyright 2022)*

A picture of the Royal Navy *Astute* class submarine *Anson* undertaking its first trim dive at BAE Systems' Barrow-in-Furness facility in February 2022. The Royal Navy's force of nuclear-powered attack submarines has temporarily fallen to just five boats pending *Anson*'s delivery. *(BAE Systems)*

bility, will be completed on all six ships. By then, the class should also be benefitting from a series of improvements to their air-defence systems as part of the Sea Viper evolution programme. These include an increase in missile loadout from forty-eight to seventy-two by incorporation of an additional twenty-four cells for the short-range Common Anti Air Modular Missile (CAMM) rounds currently associated with the Sea Ceptor system. Additionally, in a first for a European fleet, modifications to their longer-range Aster 30 missiles and associated radar and command system upgrades will give the class an anti-ballistic missile capability.

Minor Warships and Auxiliaries: The number of minor warships in service continues to decline as a result of technological change and funding constraints. Notably, the introduction of autonomous minehunting capabilities is seeing an ongoing rundown in manned mine countermeasures vessels, with the *Sandown* class *Ramsey* and *Blyth* being decommissioned in August 2021 prior to planned transfer to Ukraine's navy. An additional

vessel, *Shoreham*, commenced a short farewell tour of Britain's south coast in May 2022 before her own scheduled withdrawal. Also departing the fleet was the survey vessel *Echo*, which was decommissioned at Portsmouth on 30 June 2022. Like the mine-hunters, autonomous systems will form part of her replacement. Portsmouth previously hosted the decommissioning of the former Gibraltar-based patrol boats *Scimitar* and *Sabre* on 30 March 2022; their replacements *Cutlass* and *Dagger* are described in Chapter 3.2.

The Royal Fleet Auxiliary has also been impacted by the need for savings, placing both 'Wave' class fleet tankers in extended reserve to save £79m by the end of the decade. However, the fleet solid support ship programme for three new replenishment ships is moving ahead at a reported cost of c. £1.7bn. Four consortia are bidding for the contract, which will see the vessels delivered between 2028 and 2032. The decision on a preferred bidder, expected early in 2023, is seen by many as a litmus test of the extent to which a refreshed National Shipbuilding Strategy, published on 10 March 2022, will result in addi-

tional shipbuilding work flowing to British yards. The strategy provides a list of government ship-building 'opportunities' available to British industry over the next 30 years. However, it stops short of mandating that work is placed in the United Kingdom.[11]

MID-SIZED REGIONAL FLEETS

Germany: Germany's naval renewal was already making significant headway prior to the announce-ment of Chancellor Scholz's budget boost. On 7 July 2021, tkMS announced what was claimed to be the largest contact in the company's history after the conclusion of negotiations to supply Type 212CD submarines to Germany and Norway. The €5.5bn contract covers the construction of four boats for Norway and two for Germany. The Norwegian submarines will be delivered from 2029 onwards, with the German units being completed in 2032 and 2034. Norway's Kongsberg will be an important collaborator in the project. With an overall length of 73m and a surface displacement of c. 2,500 tonnes, the new boats are significantly larger than pervious iterations of the Type 212 series. They will also benefit from significant technical enhancements. As mentioned in the introduction, it appears that the German component of the contract will be expanded as part of the budget settlement.

The last year has seen a series of announcements relating to equipment selections for the four new F126 class frigates. First steel cutting for the lead ship is expected in 2023 to meet a planned 2028 delivery date. The ships will be built in Germany at the yards of NVL – the new name for Lürssen's stand-alone warship business – and German Naval Yards Kiel. However, the lead contractor is the Netherlands' Damen. The participation of Dutch industry in the programme is a legacy of the trou-bled construction of the previous F125 *Baden-Württemberg* class. This project was brought to a close in January 2022 with the delivery of *Rheinland Pfalz*, the fourth and final member of the class. She is to be commissioned in July. Her arrival will allow the retirement of the last F122 *Bremen* class frigate *Lübeck*. She completed her final mission in June 2022 prior to her planned decommissioning. Meanwhile construction continues on the second batch of K130 *Braunschweig* class corvettes, which are spanning the production gap between the F125 and F126 series frigates. The first of the batch, *Köln*, was christened at a ceremony at NVL's Blohm &

Germany's previously problematic construction of F125 stabilisation frigates has been brought to a satisfactory conclusion by the delivery of the final member of the class, *Rheinland-Pfalz*, early in 2022. *(tkMS)*

Voss shipyard in Hamburg on 21 April 2022. She subsequently commenced sea trials at the end of June.

Although the Royal Navy's CSG 21 deployment garnered most headlines, the German Navy undertook its own Far Eastern voyage in 2021–2, reportedly the first for almost two decades. The six-month mission was carried out by the F123 *Brandenburg* class frigate *Bayern* between 2 August 2021 and 18 February 2022. Involving a series of port calls and training activities, the deployment was seen as a sign of Germany's political willingness to become more actively involved in ensuring the region's stability. The Chinese government's decision to deny the warship a Shanghai stopover suggests this more active policy is not entirely popular with Germany's largest trading partner.

The Netherlands and Belgium: If the expression 'jam tomorrow ... but never jam today' reflects the current state of play impacting Britain's Royal Navy, its relevance to the Royal Netherlands Navy is even greater. The new Dutch White Paper, *A Stronger Netherlands, A Safer Europe,* published on 1 June 2022 commits to bolstering defence spending to meet the NATO target of two percent of GDP in 2024 and 2025, increasing funding by an additional €5bn on a structural basis. Whilst little of the additional money is actually allocated to naval programmes, the acquisition of naval cruise missiles and a ballistic missile defence capability is back on the agenda. The problem, however, is that many years will likely elapse before the new capabilities enter operational service. In the interim, a legacy of inadequate funding and poor decision making will see the fleet shrink in the short term.[12]

It is the Dutch submarine flotilla that is set to be hit the hardest. Delays in selecting a new submarine mean that it will no longer be possible to maintain all the existing *Walrus* class boats in service until their replacements arrive. As a result, two of the current quartet will be decommissioned to provide spare parts to keep the remaining pair operational. The procurement process for the new class is also being restructured in the hope that a winning bid from proposals due to be provided from Naval Group, Saab and tkMS can be determined before the end of 2023.

The recapitalisation of the surface fleet – being carried out in conjunction with the Belgian Naval Component – is achieving mixed results.

The German F123 *Brandenburg* class frigate *Bayern* has completed the navy's first deployment to the Far East for almost two decades in yet another sign of increased European interest in forging security ties to the region. This picture shows her exercising with the Royal Australian Navy in November 2021. *(Royal Australian Navy)*

An unidentified Royal Netherlands Navy *Walrus* class submarine pictured on the Clyde in March 2019. Delays in acquiring replacement submarines mean that two of the existing class of four boats will need to be retired to provide spare parts for the other pair until new vessels eventually arise. *(Michael Leake)*

Importantly, physical construction of the mine countermeasures 'motherships' being acquired by the two navies is now underway. A keel-laying ceremony for *Oostende*, first of the six planned Belgium vessels took place at Piriou's Concarneau yard on 30 November 2021. It was followed by a similar event at Kership's Lanester facility for *Vlissingen* – the lead ship of the six Dutch members of the class – on 14 June 2022. Deliveries are expected to commence around the end of 2024, when the first 'toolbox' of autonomous mine clearance systems from a new factory being built by ECA in Belgium is also due to be ready. In the meantime, the Netherlands' inventory of 'legacy' *Alkmaar* ('Tripartite') class mine warfare vessels has been reduced to just five ships with the formal decommissioning of *Urk* on 22 June 2022.

Progress with the joint project for two pairs of 'ASWF' anti-submarine warfare-optimised frigates is less advanced, with construction contracts yet to be placed. It seems that previous efforts to reduce the cost of the programme were taken too far and the current design is now too small to meet the requirements demanded of it. As a result, a further enlarged

iteration is being planned to address the problem. It is hoped that this process will be completed by early 2023. Another programme impacted by previous delays is the modernisation of the quartet of *De Zeven Provinciën* LCF frigates. Previous funding restrictions mean that a new APAR Block 2 radar that forms part of the scheme has been delayed. As a result, it is not now worth upgrading all of the class given their short remaining expected service lives. As a result, only two will now be modified.

Greece: The long overdue recapitalisation of the Hellenic Navy's surface fleet has taken a major step forward with the September 2021 decision to acquire three French FDI-HN frigates. The decision was subsequently ratified by contract signature on 24 March 2022. The agreement includes an option for a fourth vessel. Its reported value is c. €3bn. Two of the frigates will be delivered in 2025 and the third in 2026; a production schedule that only looks possible if construction of some of the ships destined for the French Navy are delayed. The Hellenic Navy's ships will reportedly be more heavily-armed than their French equivalents and incorporate a

number of specific systems needed to meet Greek requirements.

Although Greek industry will be involved as subcontractors to the programme, the decision to build the entire class overseas is surprising given that it was previously assumed the need to revitalise Greek yards would be given a high priority. This could well reflect a political angle to the deal; more specifically French support for the Greek position in tensions with Turkey. However, it also appears that initial plans to upgrade the country's MEKO-200HN *Hydra* class corvettes may, at least in part, be replaced with local construction of additional surface combatants, thereby dealing with the industrial requirement. If this path is followed, it would appear that Naval Group's 'Gowind' series would be strong contenders for the additional contract, although other bidders are reportedly still in the running. The Hellenic Navy has also been in discussions to acquire second-hand Dutch frigates and mine countermeasures vessels as they are replaced with new warships, although this may be contingent on Damen's involvement in the follow-on contract.

Turkey: The progress made by Turkey towards achieving the status of a major regional power is reflected in the new amphibious assault ship *Anadolu*'s start of a series of pre-delivery sea trials

The Turkish Navy's new amphibious assault ship *Anadolu* commenced sea trials in February 2022. Plans have been drawn up that will see the ship's air group include navalised Baykar TB3 drones in another indication of the increased influence of unmanned technologies on naval operations. *(Devrim Yaylali)*

Turkey's 'Milgem' national ship programme is spawning both export contracts and a number of national variants. This is the recently commissioned intelligence-gathering ship *Ufuk* in June 2022. *(Devrim Yaylali)*

commencing on 27 February 2022. Although the navy's previous hopes of operating the ship – a derivative of Spain's *Juan Carlos I* – as a light aircraft carrier have been thwarted, plans have been drawn up that will see the ship's air group include AH-1W Super Cobra attack helicopters transferred from the army and, importantly, the Baykar 'Bayraktar' TB3 drone. The new unmanned aerial vehicle (UAV), reportedly a navalised version of the existing TB2, is anticipated to undertake its first flight before the end of 2022. The Turkish Navy is already a significant user of land-based unmanned aircraft, with TB2, TAI 'Anka' and TAI 'Aksungur' drones already included in its inventory. Recent trials using an indigenously-manufactured synthetic aperture radar have demonstrated the potential for UAVs to be used in the mine-detection role. The possibility of deploying the larger 'Aksungur' as an anti-submarine warfare asset is also being explored.

Turkey's submarine programme has taken another step forward with the rolling-out of *Hizir Reis* – second of the six AIP-equipped Type 214TN boats – from the Gölcük Naval Shipyard on 23 May 2022. All six of the class are now in production following

the start of work on the final boat, *Selman Reis*, on the same day. It is anticipated that the first unit, *Piri Reis*, will be delivered before the end of 2022. She will be followed by her sisters at annual intervals. Construction will then transition to a new national 'MILDEN' submarine, on which work will commence around the middle of the decade. In the meantime, local defence and security group STM have announced the start of construction of a test pressure hull for a 500-tonne STM500 mini-submarine, which is designed principally for shallow-water use. It is uncertain whether it is intended for the domestic or export market.

Surface warship construction continues to be dominated by derivatives of the 'MILGEM' national surface ship programme. As well as the four original 'Ada' corvette variants of the design, the intelligence-gathering ship *Ufuk* – which utilises the same hull form and superstructure as the corvettes – is also now in operational service. In addition, work continues on *Istanbul*, the first of the stretched 'Istif' class ships. Three follow-on members of the class are planned. Unlike the previous Istanbul Naval Shipyard-built ships, it is envisaged that they will be

built by private sector yards under requests for proposals issued at the end of 2021. However, no firm contracts have yet been placed. The naval shipyard is being kept occupied building *Akhisar*, the first of up to ten 'Hisar' class offshore patrol vessels. Laid down in August 2021, she is essentially a cut-down variant of the 'Ada' class with a simplified propulsion system and a 'fitted for but not with' weapons configuration. Another programme that should shortly enter into construction is that for the FAC55 fast attack craft currently being designed by STM under a contract placed in August 2020.

Turkey's focus on enhancing its local defence industry is also evident in its efforts in combat management and weapons system development. This has included the evolution of the original national GENESIS combat management system (CMS) into the current ADVENT CMS; the introduction of the 'Atmaca' surface-to-surface missile into operational service; and ongoing testing of the AKYA heavyweight torpedo. The latter was subject to a test firing utilising the indigenous MUREN sub-surface CMS in March 2022 utilising the upgraded Type 209/1400 submarine *Preveze*. Turkey is therefore developing not only the capability to design and build its own warships but also the capacity to equip them with its own weapons and sensors.[13]

OTHER REGIONAL FLEETS

Black Sea and Mediterranean: The Russo-Ukrainian War is having an inevitable impact on naval procurement plans of the countries that border the Black Sea. The status of **Ukraine's** ambitious naval modernisation programme is particularly uncertain. Various elements of this scheme – including joint production of 'Ada' type corvettes with Turkey and fast attack craft with Britain's Babcock – were at relatively early stages of implementation when hostilities commenced. Others, notably French OCEA's construction of FCB 98 Mk 1 patrol boats for the country's border guard, were somewhat more advanced. Given the war's uncertain trajectory – as well as the closure of the Dardanelles and Bosphorus to naval traffic – the fate of these programmes will remain uncertain for some time to come.

Elsewhere in the region, the war is likely to give additional impetus to current and planned construction that has previously been impeded by funding constraints. The highest priority is the induction of modern surface combatants. In November 2020,

Bulgaria's MTG Dolphin has commenced construction of the first of two multipurpose modular patrol vessels that are being constructed to NVL's OPV 90 design. These are enlarged and more heavily-armed variants of the 80m offshore patrol vessels sold to Australia and Brunei. *(NVL)*

Delays in the procurement of modern warships mean that the Romanian Navy still relies on legacy Cold War-era assets such as the frigate *Mărăşeşti* for a significant part of its fighting strength. *(US Navy)*

Bulgaria signed a contract with Germany's Lürssen (now NVL) for two 'Multipurpose Modular Patrol Vessels' (MMPVs) based on the group's OPV-90 design. Despite the name, the new vessels are essentially large corvettes armed with surface-to-air and surface-to-surface missiles and equipped with a Saab combat management system. MTG Dolphin of Varna, which has been allocated actual construction, held a first steel-cutting ceremony for the first unit – named *Hrabri* – on 3 December 2021. This was followed by formal keel-laying on 17 June 2022. She is scheduled for delivery before the end of 2025, with her sister following a year later.

Fleet renewal in neighbouring **Romania** is further behind. In July 2019, the country announced that Naval Group, acting in partnership with local company Santierul Naval Constanta (SNC), would undertake a major programme of fleet renewal. This encompassed the modernisation of the existing Type 22 frigates and the construction of four new 'Gowind' corvettes. Contemporary reports suggested that the first of the newly-built vessels could be delivered during 2022. However, as of June 2022, a contract had yet to be finalised against a backdrop of legal challenges and speculation in the local press about tensions within the Naval Group/SNC alliance. However, the June 2022 announcement of the signature of a letter of intent between France and Romania to enhance naval collaboration suggests that a breakthrough might be imminent.

There have been fewer developments of note with respect to the smaller European Mediterranean countries. **Croatia** continues to work on its four follow-on 200-ton *Omiš* class patrol boats, with delivery of the first of this serial production batch expected within the year. **Malta's** flagship 1,800-tonne patrol vessel is also making good progress, having now reached the final outfitting stage.

Northern Europe and the Atlantic: Turning first to the Baltic and Scandinavia, the last year has seen a number of important developments. On 4 May 2022, **Denmark** carried out its first test firing of a Standard Missile-2 (SM-2) from the *Iver Huitfeldt* class frigate *Niels Juel* as part of a programme intended to integrate the area defence missile with the three-strong frigate class. Although the frigates were equipped from build with Thales APAR and SMART-L radar systems and Mk 41 vertical launch cells to undertake this role, there was insufficient money available to purchase the SM-2 when the ships

Two photographs of the Royal Danish Navy's first test firing of a Standard Missile-2 (SM-2), which was carried out from the frigate *Niels Juel* on 4 May 2022. Funding restrictions have meant that more than a decade has elapsed between the class's initial entry into service and the acquisition of the weapons needed for them to fulfil their primary area air defence mission. *(Royal Danish Navy)*

first commissioned. Funding for the new missiles was finally made available during the period of the current Danish Defence Agreement. It is believed fifty SM-2s have been acquired under the Foreign Military Sales regime. The delay in procuring SM-2 is indicative of the hard choices forced on many European navies during the post-Cold War era that now look short-sighted in the light of recent events.

Meanwhile, **Sweden** – celebrating the navy's 500th anniversary in 2022 – has been making further progress with its ambitious programme of underwater modernisation. In March 2022, a contract was signed with Saab for the mid-life upgrade of the third and final *Gotland* class submarine, *Halland,* as part of steps to achieve the five-submarine force structure outlined in the 'Total Defence' 2021–2025 programme. Subsequently, on 30 June 2022, Saab laid the keel for the first of the new A26 *Blekinge* class submarines at Karlskrona; five years after the initial order was placed. The two boats are due to be delivered in 2027 and 2028. The navy hope to persuade the government to expand submarine numbers in due course given the ongoing deterioration in East/West relations. Preliminary work on a new, larger UB30 design is already underway. Project definition efforts also continue on the new 'Visby Generation 2' combatant. This will replace the quartet of *Gävle* class corvettes and *Stockholm* class patrol vessels on a one-for-one basis over the next decade.

Construction of **Finland's** new *Pohjanmaa* class corvettes being acquired under the Squadron 2020 programme has yet to commence as a result of delays caused by maturing their detailed design. It appears that the project has been pushed to the right by between six to twelve months. This makes achieving the previous target of bringing the entire quartet into operational service by the end of 2028 increasingly unlikely. A tender has also been launched to acquire replacements for the remaining 'Kuha' and 'Kiiski' class inshore minesweepers, all of which date from the mid-1970s.

On 4 March 2022, **Poland** announced that Babcock International's 'Arrowhead 140' frigate

design – the export variant of the British Royal Navy's Type 31 – had been selected as the platform design provider and technology partner for Poland's 'Miecznik' (Swordfish) frigate programme. Its proposal won out over a MEKO-A300PL concept offered by tkMS, after a previously shortlisted Navantia design based on the F-100 frigate failed to make the final cut. The programme will eventually encompass the local assembly of three vessels by the PGZ Miecznik consortium, with the lead ship expected to begin construction in 2023 to meet a planned 2027 delivery date. In a further announcement made in June 2022, the acquisition of a second batch of three 'Kormoran II' mine countermeasures vessels was also announced. The final two members of the original batch are now close to entering service. *Albatros* – the second ship – commenced sea trials in June 2021, with *Mewa*, the first and final member of the batch, following her at the end of the year. There is, however, no further news on the 'Orka' submarine programme against a backdrop of delays that has seen the underwater flotilla shrink to the single Project 877E 'Kilo' class submarine *Orzeł*.

Conversely, the outlook for **Norway's** underwater arm is now far more positive. Here, the signature of the Type 212CD submarine contract in July 2021 secures the longer-term future of the submarine flotilla as the existing Type 210 *Ula* class boats – now all into their fourth decade of service – start to approach life-expiry. Whilst the programme will inevitably be a significant draw on naval funding, midlife upgrades of the *Nansen* class frigates and *Skjold* class fast attack craft are also being pursued.

The modernisation of **Portugal's** small flotilla of major surface combatants took a major step forward in October 2021 with the return of the 'M' class frigate *Bartolomeu Dias* from mid-life upgrade at Den Helder. The programme was originally supposed to be completed in 2020 but had been delayed, inter alia, by the impact of the pandemic. Her sister-ship, *Dom Francisco de Almeida*, remains in the Netherlands as part of the same programme, which should be brought to a conclusion within the next 12 months. Meanwhile, in June 2022, the navy launched a limited tender process for a new multi-purpose platform capable of performing roles ranging from oceanic surveillance through to humanitarian relief and climate research. Provisional images of the new vessel suggest an innovative design optimised for unmanned vehicles, including a through length, ski-jump

The success of the Polish Navy's 'Kormoran II' class mine countermeasures vessel design has resulted in a second batch of three ships being ordered in June 2022. This picture shows *Mewa*, the third and final member of the first batch, at the time of the announcement. *(Maciej Nędzyński/Polish Armed Forces)*

A tkMS graphic of the Type 212CD (common design) variant of the Type 212 series of submarines, which is being acquired by Germany and Norway in a joint programme. The new submarine is significantly larger than the Type 212A variants that are currently in service. *(tkMS)*

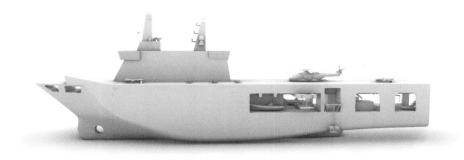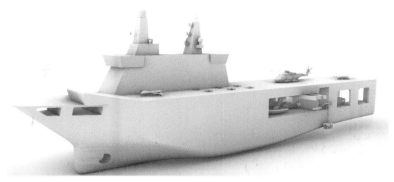

Two graphics of the Portuguese Navy's new multipurpose platform design, for which tenders are now being sought. An innovative, low-cost ship, she is optimised for the deployment of aerial, surface and underwater drones to carry out a range of tasks ranging from oceanic surveillance and pollution control through to humanitarian missions. The inclusion of a ski-jump to facilitate unmanned aerial vehicle operation is a notable feature. *(Portuguese Navy)*

equipped flight deck for helicopters and aerial drones.

Ireland's naval service is expected to experience a temporary dip to just six operational vessels in the second half of 2022 with the pending retirement of its flagship offshore patrol vessel *Eithne* and the former British Royal Navy *Peacock* class patrol ships *Ciara* (ex-*Swallow*) and *Orla* (formerly *Swift*). The departure of the patrol ships will soon be made good by the planned 2023 arrival of the former Royal New Zealand Navy 'Lake' class inshore patrol vessels *Rotoiti* and *Pukaki* under a €23m deal announced in March 2022. The former New Zealand ships are smaller and require fewer sailors to operate than the vessels they will replace; an important consideration given the Irish Naval Service's ongoing crewing problems. *Eithne* will ultimately be replaced by a long-planned multi-role vessel. However, this procurement has yet to reach the tender stage.

Notes

1. It was not immediately entirely clear whether the special fund – to be made available over a five-year period – was to be in addition to or in support of the pledge to meet the two percent commitment. It seems from subsequent developments that the latter is more likely to be the case.

2. Dynamic availability management essentially institutionalised equipment shortages in the German military by accepting that formations would only normally be equipped with around 70 percent of the heavy weaponry required to be fully operational. The idea was that units on deployment would be temporarily bolstered with additional systems to become fully effective. The concept – which did much to hollow out German military capabilities – was already being reversed before Chancellor Scholz's announcement.

3. For further information on the *La Fayette* class modernisation programme, see Martin Manaranche, 'French Navy's La Fayette-Class Frigate Mid-Life Update' posted to the *Naval News* website on 31 July 2021.

4. *Documento Programmatico Pluriennale Della Difesa per il Triennio* 2021-2023 (Rome: Italian Ministry of Defence, 2021), available at: difesa.it/Content/Documents/2021 0804%20DPP%202021-2023%20-ult.pdf

5. This information was revealed in a press release issued by the Yantar shipyard on 30 June 2022.

6. A detailed review of the Project 20380 series was provided by Nikolai Novichkov in 'Steregushchiy Class Corvettes: Russia's Green Water Combatants for the 21st Century', *Seaforth World Naval Review 2022* (Barnsley: Seaforth Publishing, 2021), pp.120–35.

7. The editor views this criticism as unfair. The class's modular configuration was supposed to allow the upgrading of a basic constabulary design for higher-intensity combat operations by the installation of containerised weaponry. It appears that it has been a lack of this containerised equipment – as well as the limited local availability of ships with 'high end' anti-air capabilities following *Moskva*'s loss – that have hindered the class's use in operations against Ukraine in the Black Sea. This has resulted in the temporary expedient of fitting land-based 9K330 Tor (S-A-15 'Gauntlet') surface-to-air missile launchers to their flight decks to beef-up their air defences.

8. *Global Britain in a competitive age: The Integrated Review of Security, Defence, Development and Foreign Policy, Cm. 403* (London: HMSO, 2021). This is readily accessible by searching the Internet.

9. A good review of the Royal Navy's efforts to improve submarine availability was provided in the article 'Getting boats to sea – efforts to improve Royal Navy submarine availability' posted to the *Navy Lookout* site – navylookout.com – on 6 June 2022.

10. The comparison is a little unfair. The construction of India's current lead Project 15B destroyer *Visakhapatnam* – a ship of comparable size and sophistication to the Type 26 – took just over eight years (from 12 October 2013 to 28 October 2021) but this does not make any allowance for working up to full operational status. In addition, the design of the Project 15B series is closely correlated to the previous Project 15A whilst the Type 26 is entirely new.

11. See *CP5605 National Shipbuilding Strategy* (London: National Shipbuilding Office, 2022), available at: gov.uk/government/publications/refresh-to-the-national-shipbuilding-strategy

12. An English-language summary of *the Defence White Paper 2022: A Stronger Netherlands, A Safer Europe* (The Hague: Netherlands Ministry of Defence, 2022) is available at: english.defensie.nl/downloads/publications/2022/06/01/summary-defence-white-paper-2022. Jaime Karremann's marineschepen.nl website remains the 'go to' source of additional information and analysis on Dutch and Belgian naval programmes.

13. Devrim Yaylali's *Bosphorus Naval News* blog at: turkishnavy.net remains the premier English language source for Turkish Navy developments. The author thanks Mr Yaylali for his assistance in commenting on this section.

3.1 SIGNIFICANT SHIPS

HMNZS AOTEAROA

Providing New Zealand's Maritime Sustainment Capability

Author: Guy Toremans

On 29 July 2020, the Royal New Zealand Navy's (RNZN's) new Polar sustainment vessel, *Aotearoa*, was commissioned into the fleet. First approved some six years earlier, the Maritime Sustainment Capability project has produced New Zealand's largest ever warship and one that provides some notable additional capabilities over and above those often found in a typical auxiliary replenishment oiler (AOR). This chapter looks at the process that led to the construction of this innovative design and describes the main characteristics of the resulting ship.

INITIAL PROJECT DEVELOPMENT

The RNZN's aspiration to replace its previous fleet oiler *Endeavour* dated to the first decade of the current millennium.[1] Early thinking in the New Zealand Defence Force (NZDF) favoured acquisition of a broad Maritime Projection and Sustainment Capability (MPSC). This would have led to the procurement of a multi-purpose platform that could provide more than a standard afloat replenishment capability. In particular, incorporation of aviation and amphibious facilities in the new vessel would support a supplementary military sealift capability and enable the conduct of humanitarian aid and disaster relief (HA/DR) missions,

thereby supplementing the facilities already afforded by the multirole vessel *Canterbury*.

Following confirmation of the requirement for a new vessel in New Zealand's *Defence White Paper 2010*, the NZDF formally established the MPSC project through approval of a project charter in

2011.[2] A concept study was completed early in 2012, being quickly accepted as the basis for developing a new projection and sustainment platform of a size and displacement eclipsing anything previously seen in the RNZN. This was one of two broad options in an Indicative Business Case approved by

It was initially hoped to incorporate some of the amphibious capabilities found in New Zealand's existing multi-role support ship *Canterbury* in the replacement for *Endeavour*. Ultimately, however, the initial project development process saw these ambitions scaled back in favour of more modest – but still significant – enhancements. *(Australian Department of Defence)*

New Zealand's new *Aotearoa* class Polar sustainment vessel is the largest vessel ever delivered to the Royal New Zealand Navy. Although falling short of the navy's original aspirations for a maritime projection and sustainment capability, she still provides additional capabilities over and above those found in a typical replenishment oiler. *(RNZN)*

the New Zealand Cabinet the same year. The other was a like-for-like *Endeavour* replacement. When a detailed business case for the project was subsequently considered by the Cabinet in June 2014, a better understanding of cost/capability drivers and trade-offs saw the sealift capacity being dropped to free up resources for other capital acquisitions. Instead, a 'medium-level capability' offering some improvements over *Endeavour* would be taken forward, as highlighted in the text box above. The more limited requirement was reflected in a change of nomenclature from the Maritime Projection and Sustainment Capability (MPSC) to the Maritime Sustainment Capability (MSC) project. It was also determined that the possibility of 'winterising' the design should be considered to provide an ability to support operations in Antarctic waters.[3]

PROJECT APPROVAL

With the project implementation business case approved, the way was cleared for a request for tenders, which were issued in March 2015. Five companies provided tender responses, from which a shortlist of two was selected for further evaluation in the second half of the year. These two companies – South Korea's Daewoo Shipbuilding & Marine Engineering (DSME), teamed with BMT Defence Services, and Hyundai Heavy Industries (HHI), partnered with Rolls-Royce – were asked to provide best and final offers. The offers were to include an Antarctic support option with an amended technical specification and cost structure. In December 2015, following an extensive technical evaluation, HHI – then the world's largest shipbuilder – was selected as the preferred bidder.[4]

New Zealand's Maritime Sustainment Capability (MSC) project – as ultimately delivered in the form of *Aotearoa* (bottom) – provides a number of specific capability improvements over her predecessor, *Endeavour* (top). These include increased and more diverse fuel stowage, the ability to transport ammunition and improved helicopter facilities. Importantly, an option to support operations in the Arctic was also taken up. *(Australian Department of Defence/US Navy)*

New Zealand's *Defence White Paper 2016* – published in June of that year – confirmed that the new MSC vessel would be ice-strengthened and winterised to facilitate support to New Zealand's Antarctic programme. Subsequently, on 18 July 2016, New Zealand Defence Minister Gerry Brownlee announced that the government had approved the purchase of the new naval tanker from HHI. The relevant contract was signed the following week on 25 July. The project's total value was reported at NZ\$493m (c. US\$320m), of which NZ\$64m (c. US\$40m) related to the vessel's 'winterisation'.

Although destined to be built in South Korea, the design used was based on Roll-Royce's 'Environship' Leadge Bow concept; the first time that the group's wave-piercing bow had been used in the naval sector.[5] Rolls-Royce was also contracted to supply and integrate a flexible hybrid-electric propulsion and power system optimised to perform efficiently at a range of operating speeds. Other equipment supplied by Rolls-Royce included the all-electric replenishment-at-sea (RAS) system, the steering gear, the high lift rudders, the controllable-pitch propellers and a bow thruster.

CONSTRUCTION AND DELIVERY

The first steel for the new ship was cut in January 2018 at the SinHwa Technology Company in Pohang, South Korea. The steel was fabricated into assembly blocks and the first of these was laid in the dry dock at HHI's Ulsan shipyard during a formal keel laying ceremony on 13 August 2018. Just eight months later, in April 2019, the ship was floated out of the building dry dock for final outfitting. A formal naming ceremony took place on 25 October 2019. The ship was christened *Aotearoa* – the Maori name for New Zealand – meaning 'land of the long white cloud'.

Throughout the build programme, personnel from the Ministry of Defence and NZDF worked in Ulsan as part of an Integrated Project Team (IPT) overseeing construction; several of the latter were subsequently to become part of *Aotearoa*'s commissioning crew (or 'plank owners'). From mid-2019, the RNZN also commenced a structured training programme for prospective members of the crew that included courses both in New Zealand and overseas. Some underwent RAS training at the British Royal Navy's School of Seamanship at HMS *Raleigh*, Cornwall, whilst others were sent to

A graphic of the Hyundai Heavy Industries proposal – based on the then Rolls-Royce 'Environship' Leadge Bow concept – selected for the MSC project at the end of 2015. *(RNZN)*

An image of *Aotearoa* taken in October 2018 whilst the vessel was in the course of construction at Hyundai Heavy Industries' Ulsan shipyard, South Korea. In an indication of the rapid pace of her construction, it is notable that her keel had been laid two months previously. *(RNZN)*

Aotearoa pictured in her building dock at Ulsan immediately before being floated out in April 2019. Following final outfitting, she commenced builder's sea trials at the end of the year. *(RNZN)*

Aotearoa pictured at sea during the course of acceptance trials in March 2020. Although the COVID-19 pandemic had some impact on the later stages of the project, delivery was only one month later than initially envisaged. *(RNZN)*

Australia and Norway. Inevitably, the rapid escalation of the COVID-19 pandemic posed unforeseen challenges to the final phases of sea trials and equipment configuration. HHI's supply chain was affected, with several overseas suppliers being unable or unwilling to send technicians to Ulsan. The pandemic also had an impact on a number of the training courses scheduled for the RNZN crew.

Prior to her delivery, *Aotearoa* underwent a full range of builder's and acceptance trials to ensure that the ship and her onboard systems complied with the contractual criteria. Builder's sea trials took place in December 2019 and were followed by the start of the acceptance trials programme early in 2020. Following completion of these trials and some minor rectification work, *Aotearoa* returned to sea for another round of tests relating to her refuelling and station-keeping capabilities. These tests included the simulation of a fully-loaded condition to check the ship's handling and manoeuvring characteristics, as well as dummy RAS evolutions with the Philippine Navy's HHI-built frigate *Jose Rizal*. The latter validated *Aotearoa*'s hydrodynamic interaction, providing additional information about how she handled alongside another vessel.

After final quality assurance work – and a paint touch-up – *Aotearoa* received her certification from Lloyd's Register and was provisionally accepted for delivery to New Zealand on 8 June 2020. Despite the pandemic's impact on the later stages of the project, this was only one month later than initially envisaged. With strict COVID-19 rules in place, South Korean health authorities tested the 49-strong delivery crew (comprising thirty-eight HHI technicians and eleven New Zealand 'observers') before the ship's departure from Ulsan two days later. Briefly accompanied by the Republic of Korea Navy's *Cheonji* class combat support ship *Daecheong*, *Aotearoa* undertook a flawless 15-day delivery voyage without port visits, finally anchoring in the Hauraki Gulf, off Rangitoto Island. Here a medical team went onboard to conduct further COVID tests, all coming back negative. The following day, 26 June 2020, she sailed into Waitematā Harbour to be welcomed by the hydrographic and diving support vessel *Manawanui* (with VIPs and media embarked), an aerial fly-past and many small vessels. Officially transferred into RNZN control on 8 July 2020, *Aotearoa* was commissioned at a ceremony at Devonport Naval Base, Auckland on the 29th of that month. Following commissioning, the vessel

Aotearoa arrives at Devonport Naval Base on 26 June 2020 after her delivery voyage from South Korea in the midst of the early stages of the COVID-19 pandemic. *(RNZN)*

commenced customisation with her military communications suite, whilst outstanding work within HHI's remit was also completed. This essentially prepared the new ship for the complex period of work-up towards operational readiness that lay ahead.

Aotearoa's construction was accompanied by significant investment in Devonport Naval Base, the ship's homeport. It was evident that facilities required expansion to accommodate the 173m ship. Accordingly, the existing Calliope South Wharf was extended from 270m to 320m by new western and eastern ends; the latter incorporating a 'Dolphin' bollard structure. New pneumatic fenders were also fitted to cope with the new vessel's mass and the original deck was replaced by a composite deck with precast planks and a concrete topping slab.

DESIGN DESCRIPTION

Requirements Overview: The MSC project, as ultimately fulfilled by the *Aotearoa* design, was intended to fulfil four main operational needs.[6] These were:

- **Operational Need 1:** To conduct maritime force logistic support.
- **Operational Need 2:** To maintain deployable bulk fuel reserves.
- **Operational Need 3:** To provide an effective and appropriate maritime platform.
- **Operational Need 4:** To support other government agencies with specific fitted capabilities.

These operational requirements resulted in a design equipped to perform both RAS and vertical replenishment (VERTREP) functions, the latter requiring maintenance and refuelling systems for an embarked helicopter. Stowage for a wide range of fuel and stores was also provided, including Class 1 (food and water); Class 2 (general stores); Class 3 (petroleum and other liquids); Class 5 (ammunition); and Class 9 (spare parts). The requirement for an 'effective and appropriate maritime platform' encompasses parameters such as endurance; speed; communications and weapons systems; damage control; and accommodation. The need to support other government agencies is essentially reflected in *Aotearoa*'s winterisation.

Key resultant design characteristics are set out in Table 3.1.1.

Platform: An auxiliary oiler replenishment-helicopter (AOR-H) type vessel, *Aotearoa* has an overall length of 173.2m, a beam of 24.5m, a loaded draught of 8.4m and a full load displacement of c. 26,500 tonnes. This makes her the largest ship ever built for the RNZN.

The ship's innovative 'Environship' hull design,

Displacing some 26,500 tonnes, *Aotearoa* is the largest ship ever to have served with the Royal New Zealand Navy. Primarily intended to provide logistic support for the RNZN and other allied forces, her 'winterisation' means that she can also assist other New Zealand government agencies in Antarctic waters. *(US Navy)*

with its wave-piercing axe bow hull, is intended to optimise *Aotearoa*'s hydrodynamic characteristics, seaworthiness and crew comfort. This bow shape, featuring a vertical stem above a bulbous bow and a relatively long and narrow forward hull, allows the ship to cut through waves rather than riding over their tops, thus reducing pitch motions and resistance in some sea conditions.

Intended to deploy regularly to the Southern Ocean and Antarctica – missions that can take her as far south as the Ross Ice Shelf and the Scott Base – *Aotearoa* is designed to perform in a harsh maritime environment. She can operate in conditions up to Sea State 9 and is able to perform RAS and helicopter evolutions as far as Sea State 5. Her winterisation package is intended to allow her to withstand the adverse conditions of Antarctic waters and is in accordance with the Polar Class 6 notation.[7] This package includes a reinforced hull with an increased number of hull scantlings (hull ribs) and the use of a higher grade of steel plating of additional thickness to counter hull fatigue in cold temperatures. Other elements encompass steam heating of the side ballast tanks and flight deck, as well as electrical trace heating of the weather decks and pathways. Equipment – such as the propellers and rudders – that could be subject to ice impact loads has been strengthened. *Aotearoa* is also fitted with twin anti-roll stabilisation and bilge keels constructed with a segmented design to minimise the risk of ice damage.

Particular attention has been given to ship safety. The hull design is based on a structure that allows the ship to remain afloat with three adjacent compartments flooded, and to maintain propulsion and power generation with two adjacent compartments flooded. Longitudinally the double-hull is divided into eleven sections by ten watertight and gastight bulkheads. The ship is also split into five fire and two separate damage control zones, each of the

Table 3.1.1.

AOTEAROA (A11) PRINCIPAL PARTICULARS

Building Information:

Laid Down:	13 August 2018[1]	Launched:	24 April 2019	Delivered: 8 June 2020[2]
Builders:	Hyundai Heavy Industries, Ulsan, South Korea.			

Dimensions:

Displacement:	26,500 tonnes full load displacement
Overall Hull Dimensions:	173.2m x 24.5m x 8.4m.

Equipment:

Armament:	2 x 12.7mm Rafael Mini-Typhoon RCWS. Heavy machine guns.
	Fitted for but not with 1 x CIWS.
Aircraft:	Flight deck and hangar. Can sustain one medium helicopter.
Sensors:	3 x SharpEye Mk 11 navigation/helicopter control radars.
Communications:	Saab TactiCall integrated communications system, including MF, HF, VHF and UHF and satellite links.
Cargo Capacity:	9,500 tonnes of total liquid cargo capacity. 22 x TEU containers.
RAS & Handling Equipment:	2 x RAS rigs (1 x starboard; 1 x port).
	1 x 25-tonne Palfinger Marine DKF800 deck crane. 2 x 1.8-tonne MEP Pellegrini Marine Equipment cargo-handling cranes.

Propulsion Systems:

Machinery:	CODLAD Hybrid Propulsion. 2 x 5.4MW Bergen B33:45L9P main diesels and 2 x 1.2MW Kongsberg electric motors powered by 4 x 2.6MW MTU 20V4000M53B diesel generators. 1 x 2.5MW Kongsberg TT3000 tunnel bow thruster.
Speed:	Sustained speed of c. 16 knots (20 knots max). Endurance is c. 6,750 nautical miles.

Other Details:

Complement:	64 core crew, including 10 officers. Accommodation for a total of 100 personnel.

Notes:
1. First steel was cut in January 2018.
2. Date of provisional acceptance. The ship was commissioned into the RNZN on 29 July 2020.

latter being equipped with its own damage control station, independent air-conditioning modules, electrical power, fire-fighting pumps and power-distribution panels. Fire-retardant materials and equipment are used throughout the ship's compartments, while ammunition and pyrotechnics magazines are surrounded by buffer zones. The control of flooding, fires and fumes is based on their rapid detection through automated sensors linked to the integrated platform management system (see further below) and the subsequent isolation of these compartments to prevent the relevant hazard spreading. This is assisted by the degree of duplication of key systems.

Both the main and auxiliary engine rooms are fitted with their own independent Inergen fire-fighting system; supported by water-mist systems, a Survitec fixed foam system and water sprinklers. The galley is also fitted with water-mist systems as well as a CO_2 drenching capability within the exhaust ducting. There are gastight doors installed around the cargo deck for protection against the possibility of cargo fuel vapours igniting a fire. Her flight deck and the cargo deck are fitted with SKUM aqueous film-forming foam (AFFF) remotely-controlled cannons, while the hangar is equipped with foam drenching technology.

The ship's boats are housed in twin recesses to either side of the main superstructure. There are two Zodiac J3 rigid hulled inflatable boats (RHIBs) for rescue and utility purposes and two specially-designed, fully-enclosed Palfinger LBT1090T Polar Code-compliant lifeboats. The latter's orange-painted hulls make a distinct impression. Supplementary lifesaving equipment includes Viking 25DK and Viking 35DK life rafts.

Propulsion: *Aotearoa* utilises a combined diesel-electric and diesel (CODLAD) propulsion train. This comprises two 5.4MW Bergen Engines B33:45L9P

Aotearoa (2020)

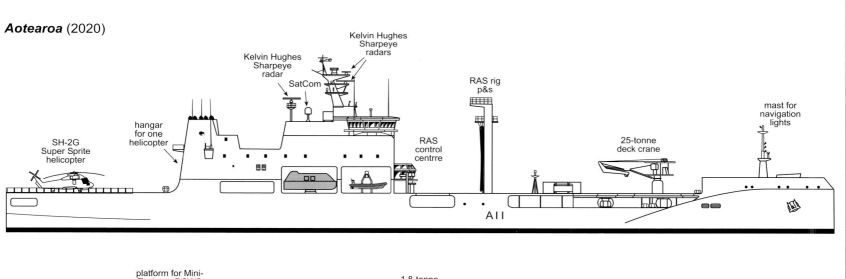

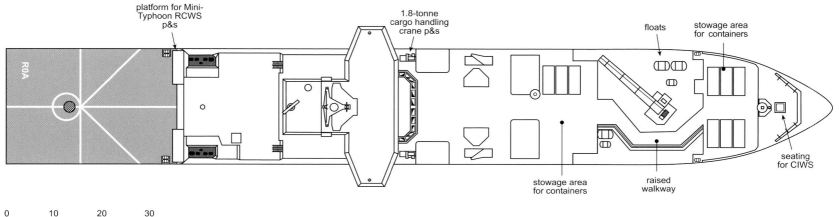

0   10   20   30

METRES

© John Jordan 2022

A graphic showing the general layout of *Aotearoa*'s hybrid CODLAD propulsion plant. *(Rolls-Royce)*

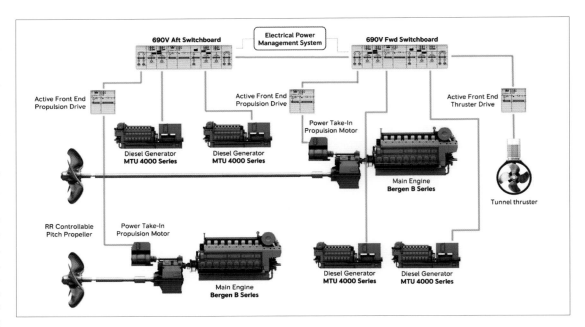

main diesels and four 2.6MW MTU 20V4000M53B diesel generators, the latter supplying two 1.2MW Kongsberg electrical propulsion motors and a 2.5MW Kongsberg TT3000 tunnel bow thruster by means of the ship's electrical distribution system. This flexible propulsion arrangement allows the ship to loiter in a hybrid-mode at speeds of up to 8 knots by using only her electrical motors. Higher speeds of up to 20 knots (16 knots sustained) can be achieved through utilisation of the main diesels in combination with the electric motors. Maximum endurance is in the region of 6,750 nautical miles. The propulsion train is linked to twin shafts fitted with five-bladed controllable pitch propellers via two reduction gearboxes. *Aotearoa* is also fitted with twin flap rudders and a 410KW emergency diesel generator. Another notable design feature is the ship's Selective Catalytic Reduction system, which is intended to ensure the ship meets International Maritime Organization (IMO) III emission guidelines.

Platform Management: *Aotearoa* is equipped with a range of state-of-the-art platform management technology focused on a Servowatch integrated platform management system (IPMS). This connects principal systems and sub-systems via a dual redundant data network to a comprehensive range of crew interfaces, thereby ensuring ongoing monitoring and control of the propulsion system, electrical distribution network and auxiliary systems. These control and monitoring functions are typically performed remotely through dedicated workstations equipped with high-resolution colour monitors. They are located in the machinery control room (MCR), on the bridge, and in other locations around the ship. A closed-circuit television (CCTV) system permits comprehensive monitoring of all key equipment from the bridge, thus negating the need to crew the MCR in normal circumstances.

The IPMS incorporates an integrated battle damage control system (IBDCS) that supports a fully automated damage analysis approach. The IBDCS records, processes and reports relevant information to the damage control teams via the workstations located in each of the two damage control headquarters. The vessel's stability in a damaged condition can be assessed with the aid of continuously updated tank level measurements, adjusted – as necessary – for any damaged compartments. The IPMS can also support onboard training functions.

Another important piece of technology is Hensoldt UK's integrated naval bridge system (INBS). Incorporating the usual multi-function displays and dual redundant data network, it consol-

An interior view of *Aotearoa*'s spacious bridge. State-of-the-art platform and bridge management technology means that most ship control functions can be performed from the bridge with a relatively lean crew. *(RNZN)*

An external view towards *Aotearoa*'s superstructure showing the replenishment control room (RASCO) at lower level and the bridge above. Atop the mast are two of the three SharpEye Mk 11 radar arrays that provide the ship's primary sensors. *(RNZN)*

idates information provided by the ship's Kelvin Hughes radars, a geographic electronic chart display and information system (GECDIS), a bridge alert management system and other key navigation aids such as the autopilot, compasses and AIS.

Sensors and Communications: The ship's most important sensors are three solid state Kelvin Hughes SharpEye radars. These encompass one SharpEye Mk 11 X band (NATO I/J bands) and two SharpEye Mk 11 S band (E/F band) arrays.[8] Self-contained systems benefitting from use of an innovative, lightweight carbon fibre housing, they are claimed to offer enhanced detection of small targets in clutter and at greater ranges than legacy radars.

Aotearoa is also fitted with a Farsounder Argos 1000 forward-looking obstacle avoidance sonar (OAS). This can detect objects in three dimensions up to 1km ahead. It is particularly useful for the vessel's Antarctic missions, assisting safe navigation through shallow seas and areas that might be strewn with ice and other obstacles.

The ship's communications are handled by a Saab TactiCall integrated communications system (ICS). This manages all internal and external communications, including sensitive encrypted data. This interfaces, inter alia, with the normal range of satellite and other radio communications links.

Cargo and Replenishment Capacity: *Aotearoa*'s total official liquid cargo capacity amounts to some 9,500 tonnes. The majority of this normally comprises marine diesel fuel but aviation fuel and water are also stowed. The ship is able to accommodate around 300 tonnes of dry cargo and has positions for up to twenty-two 20ft equivalent unit (TEU) containers on her deck. These can house bulk goods, refrigerated stores and ammunition. Four of these container positions are specifically dedicated to store dangerous goods, being monitored by the IPMS and linked to appropriate fire-fighting systems. The ship is also fitted with two reverse osmosis plants capable of producing up to 100 tonnes of fresh water a day.

Aotearoa is fitted with two reverse osmosis plants capable of producing up to 100 tonnes of fresh water a day. *(RNZN)*

The vessel is fitted with two identical NATO-compliant electric RAS stations, one to port and one to starboard, to allow two vessels to be replenished simultaneously. These abeam rigs allow the transfer of diesel and aviation fuel, as well as potable water and solid cargo. The fuel is pumped to the RAS stations by a network of pipes, with nitrogen used to fill the tanks as fuel is issued. RAS operations are managed from a replenishment control room (RASCO) located forward of the bridge. The ship can also provide fuel to helicopters, either on deck or by use of a helicopter inflight-refuelling system.

The ship's main equipment for solid cargo handling comprises a Palfinger Marine DKF800 deck crane mounted on the centreline. Of compact, knuckle boom design, this has a safe working limit of 25 tonnes. Its impressive operating reach of 23m facilitates the efficient loading and offloading of bulk goods and containers from the ship's side. There are also two smaller, MEP-Pellegrini Marine Equipment GNK 1.8-10EH stores cranes located to port and starboard just forward of the superstructure. Cargo routes are designed for easy movement of cargo to the RAS positions and cranes, with extra width and flat surfaces provided between the cargo deck forward of the superstructure and the aft flight deck and hangar. *Aotearoa* also incorporates a palletised cargo-handling system to facilitate the transfer of heavy loads. Other deck equipment includes five Arim Machinery and Engineering

One of the twin RAS towers that provide *Aotearoa* with the ability to replenish two vessels simultaneously. *(RNZN)*

Aotearoa's ability to embark and sustain a variety of helicopters – this is a SH-2G Super Seasprite sea control helicopter seen operating from the ship in 2021 – provides an important vertical replenishment capability whilst adding to the ship's warfighting potential. *(RNZN)*

A centreline Palfinger Marine DKF800 deck crane provides *Aotearoa*'s main capacity for handling solid cargo. This is seen being put to good effect as containers are unloaded at New Zealand's Scott Base in McMurdo Sound, Antarctica in February 2022. *(RNZN)*

AHM-KC-18 mooring winches and two Arim Machinery and Engineering AHL-KCM-B68 anchor windlasses.

The replenishment-at-sea teams have a RAS Ready Room to prepare for underway refuelling operations to store the crew's weather and protective clothing.

Self-Defence: *Aotearoa*'s ability to operate helicopters supports VERTREP replenishment whilst providing an important element of the ship's organic warfighting capabilities. The large 35m x 24.5m flight deck and associated 16m x 8.5m hangar allow the operation of one helicopter from New Zealand's inventory of NH90 transport, SH-2G Super Seasprite sea control and AW109 utility types. The flight deck is fitted with a night landing capability, a traversing system and helicopter refuelling equipment whilst the hangar is provided with an overhead gantry crane and workshops that allow for the maintenance and repair of embarked aircraft.

The main component of *Aotearoa*'s self-defence capability comprises two 12.7mm Rafael Mini-Typhoon remotely-controlled weapon stations (RCWS). Remotely operated and fully stabilised, they incorporate an integrated electro-optical tracking system with forward looking infra-red (FLIR) and day cameras. Maximum range is around 1,800m. The forward part of the bow deck also has also been fitted with infrastructure and services to retrofit a close-in weapons system (CIWS). The ship's defensive capabilities against asymmetric threats can also be supplemented by four manually operated heavy – 0.5in (12.7mm) – calibre machine guns.

Accommodation: *Aotearoa* has a core crew of sixty-four, with additional accommodation being provided for an additional thirty-six personnel, such as helicopter support teams (pilots and technicians), trainees and mission-specific teams. The core crew comprises ten officers, fourteen petty officers and

Standards of accommodation in *Aotearoa* are high. Junior ratings share four-berth cabins with ensuite bathroom facilities. *(RNZN)*

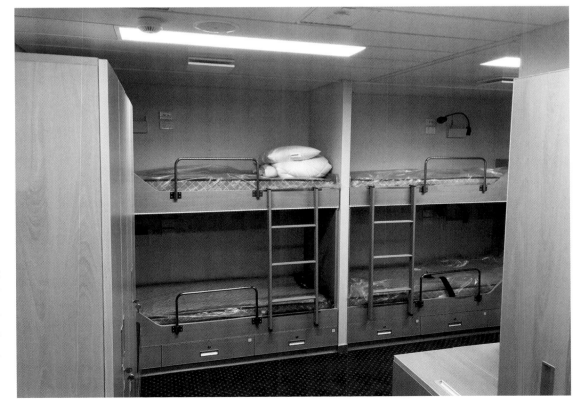

Aotearoa refuels the lead Australian *Anzac* class frigate (right) and her New Zealand counterpart *Te Kaha* during the Bersama Gold 21 exercise in the course of her maiden deployment. In addition to demonstrating *Aotearoa*'s replenishment capabilities, the photo is interesting in showing how the two sister frigates have evolved from their once identical design. *(Australian Department of Defence)*

forty ratings. Of these, twenty-six crew members work in the Operations Department, fourteen in the Supply/Support/Medical Department and twenty-four in the Engineering Department.

Given that the vessel is expected to deploy for extended periods, considerable attention has been paid to providing a high-quality lifestyle by incorporating the latest accommodation standards for all personnel, with a broadly egalitarian approach being adopted for officers, petty officers and junior ratings alike. The accommodation arrangement includes a mix of single, double and four-berth cabins, all equipped with ensuite bathroom and toilet facilities to facilitate the requirements of a mixed-gender crew. Cognisant of ship's diplomatic role and the need provide for formal or official entertainment, the commanding officer's accommodation comprises a living/office space; a bedroom; a private bathroom and a pantry. The latter allows meals to be

Aotearoa refuels the US destroyer *Howard* (DDG-93) in November 2021 during the final stages of her inaugural operational deployment. *Howard* was about to conduct the US Navy's first visit to New Zealand for six years at the time. *(US Navy)*

received from the galley and wardroom pantry via a 'dumb waiter' system and then passed through a serving hatch directly into the commanding officer's dining area. The ship's executive officer and chief engineer also have their own living/office space, bedroom and private bathroom, whilst the other officers, the chief bosun's mate and the vessel's warrant officer marine technician all have single cabins. Other petty officers, senior ratings and junior officers under training occupy two-berth cabins, with the junior ratings living in four-berth accommodation. Furniture, bulkhead and ceiling fittings are designed for easy removal and good noise insulation.

The galley, petty officers' and ratings' messes are located on the same deck. The officers' wardroom is located two decks above. Officers, petty officers and ratings each have their own dedicated lounges incorporating a recreational space to relax and watch television and movies. Wi-Fi is available throughout all recreation spaces. The ship also incorporates a library and training centre housing eight workstations for the crew's use, as well as a well-equipped gymnasium. The ship's cargo routes allow for a running track of about 400m in length to be laid out along the weather deck.

Onboard medical facilities include a surgery and treatment room, as well as a two-bed hospital. The latter is sufficiently well equipped to provide 'Role 1' medical care.[9]

Although not specifically designed to act as a command platform, the ship can embark a small staff, thus allowing the ship to operate as the focal point of a naval task group. Provision of a separate planning and conference room with secure video conferencing facilities and multi-function consoles provides the necessary connectivity to establish an effective, dedicated operational space without interfering with the ship's own activities.

OPERATIONAL EXPERIENCE

Despite the fact that she was only delivered some two years ago, *Aotearoa* has already handled quite a busy programme.

The first months of 2021 saw the ship going through an extensive set of sea acceptance readiness checks (SARCs) and practising RAS evolutions with the frigate *Te Kaha* and assets from the Royal Australian Navy's sea training group. The ship's first 'live' RAS was performed with the frigate *Stuart* off Australia's east coast in March 2021.[10] Subsequently,

Following a short-notice emergency deployment to Tonga to deal with the aftermath of the Hunga Tonga-Hunga Ha'apai eruption, *Aotearoa* departed for Antarctica in early February 2022 to perform the navy's first resupply of the country's Scott Base. These photographs show the ship navigating through the ice flows of the Ross Sea. *(RNZN)*

in September 2021, *Aotearoa* sailed to South East Asia for her maiden operational deployment, where she participated in the Five Power Defence Arrangements' Exercise Bersama Gold.[11] This was followed by interaction with the British Royal Navy's Carrier Strike Group 21 (CSG21) task force and a passex with units from the Indonesian Navy.

Following her return home in November 2021, *Aotearoa* commenced preparations for her most challenging mission to date, her first Antarctic resupply operation. However, events conspired to produce a change in plan. Instead of sailing directly to the Southern Ocean and Ross Sea, the replenishment vessel was tasked with providing HA/DR support to the Kingdom of Tonga after the archipelago was hit by a tsunami and extensive ash fall after the climax of an eruption on the submarine Hunga Tonga-Hunga Ha'apai volcano on 15 January 2022. The ship rapidly embarked five containers of relief supplies and filled her water tanks to maximum capacity, leaving Devonport Naval Base on 18 January for the 1,100 nautical mile voyage to Tonga's capital, Nuku'alofa. Berthing three days later on 21 January, she immediately commenced disembarking her humanitarian aid cargo. Over the following week, her desalination plants produced a

total of 520,000 litres of fresh water for distribution throughout the island. Her replenishment capabilities were also put to good use through the delivery of fuel to other ships involved in the humanitarian response, including the RNZN patrol vessel *Wellington* that had spearheaded the naval response. A particular complication of the mission was the need to maintain Tonga's COVID-free status, meaning that all activities had to be carried out according to strict COVID-19 prevention protocols and in a contactless way.

Following departure from Tongan waters on 28 January, *Aotearoa* immediately returned to New Zealand to make contactless port stops at Devonport and Lyttleton to embark supplies for her resupply mission in the Antarctic. She sailed from New Zealand on 3 February for the long crossing of the Southern Ocean, encountering her first icebergs the day after she reached 60° south on 6 February. After five days of weaving round the ice flows on the Ross Sea, she arrived at New Zealand's Antarctic Scott Base in McMurdo Sound on 11 February. This marked the first time in more than 50 years that a RNZN had conducted a resupply of the Antarctic base. Here, *Aotearoa* offloaded ten containers of materials for refurbishment of the research station

and other supplies. The crew then loaded several containers of equipment, waste and other rubbish no longer required at the Scott Base facility for return to New Zealand. The ship also transferred over a million litres of aviation fuel to the neighbouring American McMurdo Station. Again, all these activities were carried out with all possible precautions to avoid the transmission of COVID-19 and other illnesses.

Departing McMurdo Sound on 14 February, *Aotearoa* sailed for home via Ross Island. On the way back, her crew conducted a series of maritime safety trials and experiments for the Defence Technology Agency, also assisting the Meteorological Service with sea ice and wave forecasting in the Southern Ocean and Ross Sea by deploying thirty wave buoys. In addition, work was carried out with Maritime New Zealand on the application of emergency beacons. The 2,830 nautical mile voyage proved the vessel's capacity to handle the extreme and unique conditions found in the region, proving the design's capabilities in adverse conditions.

Following completion of a period of maintenance, *Aotearoa* is scheduled to remain active throughout the remainder of 2022. She has recently deployed to Hawaii in the Western Pacific to take part in the US-led RIMPAC 2022 exercise scheduled for July/August, with defence diplomacy visits to Singapore and other East Asian countries subse-

Aotearoa pictured operating with the US Navy Littoral Combat Ship *Charleston* (LSC-18) in September 2021. She provides a potent means for the navy to support the NZDF and its allies both in home and overseas waters.

quently planned. These will include participation in the Japanese Maritime Self-Defence Force's International Fleet Review that will take place in November.

CONCLUSION

It is clear that *Aotearoa* has already shown that she is a very useful vessel for the RNZN, quickly demonstrating her capability to operate effectively in conditions ranging from the tropical environment of South East Asia to the freezing weather of Antarctica. She furnishes the navy with the ability to support the NZDF and its allies both in home and overseas waters, providing a replenishment and sustainment capacity that is in relatively short supply in her key areas of operation. The project has also been a financial success, with total estimated project costs of c. NZ$495m as of June 2020 being almost exactly in line with the original approved budget.[12]

In summary, *Aotearoa* is a very capable ship that is going to serve New Zealand – and the Royal New Zealand Navy in particular – very well for many years to come.

Aotearoa approaches Auckland on 26 June 2020 at the end of her delivery voyage. She will serve New Zealand – and the Royal New Zealand Navy in particular – very well for many years to come. *(RNZN)*

Notes

1. *Endeavour* was inducted into the RNZN in April 1988 and decommissioned in December 2017. Built by HHI, *Endeavour* had a length of 138.1m, a width of 18.4m, a draft of 7.6m and a full load displacement of 12,390 tonnes. Capacity was initially around 7,500 tonnes of diesel fuel but this was reduced when her outer tanks were sealed off to meet double-hulled tanker standards.

2. See *Defence White Paper 2010* (Auckland: New Zealand Ministry of Defence, 2010). This and other New Zealand Ministry of Defence publications can be found at: www.defence.govt.nz/publications/

3. A more detailed description of the history of the MPSC and MSS projects is found in the New Zealand Ministry of Defence's *Major Projects Reports*. The most recent one to be published at the time this article was produced is that for 2020. The reports provide further granularity on the various design options that were considered during the capability definition phase of the projects, as well as on capability and operational requirements.

4. It is believed that the competing DSME proposal was based on Royal Norwegian Navy's logistic support vessel *Maud,* itself an evolution of BMT's Aegir 18/18R concept. This ship – and the Aegir family's larger 'Tide' class design – is described in the editor's '"Tide" Class Fleet Tankers & HMNoS *Maud*', *Seaforth World Naval Review 2020*

(Barnsley: Seaforth Publishing, 2019), pp.121–39.

5. The Environship Leadge Bow concept was produced by Rolls-Royce's commercial marine business, which was subsequently sold to Norway's Kongsberg with effect from April 2019.

6. These needs are set out in the *Major Projects Report 2020* (Auckland: New Zealand Ministry of Defence, 2021).

7. According to International Meteorological Organization (IMO) nomenclature, the Polar Class 6 (PC-6) notation allows summer and autumn operation in medium first-year ice, which may include older ice inclusions.

8. One of the S band radars is optimised for helicopter approach and control.

9. According to the NATO Handbook, Role/Echelon 1 medical support is that which is integral or allocated to a small unit, and which will include the capabilities for providing first aid, immediate lifesaving measures, and triage. Additionally, it will contribute to the health and well-being of the unit through provision of guidance in the prevention of disease, non-battle injuries and operational stress. Normally, routine sick call and the management of minor sick and injured personnel for immediate return to duty are a function of this level of care.

10. *Aotearoa* also undertook 'dry' hook ups with the Australian ships *Hobart* and *Parramatta* during this period of work up.

11. Usually known as Exercise Bersama Shield, 2021's edition was renamed Bersama Gold to celebrate the 50th Anniversary of the Five Power Defence Arrangements (FPDA) that encompass Australia, Malaysia, New Zealand, Singapore and the United Kingdom.

12. *Major Projects Report 2020* (Auckland: New Zealand Ministry of Defence, 2021), p.68. The forecast cost of NZ$495.4m was adjusted for the effect of foreign exchange movements.

13. The author acknowledges the assistance of the following RNZN and New Zealand Ministry of Defence personnel with gratitude.

– **Captain Simon Rooke:** *Aotearoa*'s first commanding officer.
– **Captain Simon Griffiths:** *Aotearoa*'s commanding officer since November 2021.
– **Ms Jennifer Wilson:** MSC Project Manager, NZ Ministry of Defence.
– **Mr Scott Sargentina:** Public Affairs Manager, Royal New Zealand Navy.

CUTLASS CLASS PATROL BOATS

Gibraltar's New Guardians

Author: **Conrad Waters**

First established in 1985, the British Royal Navy's Gibraltar Squadron is tasked with ensuring the security of the peninsula's territorial waters and the safety of visiting warships. Although its mandated area of operations is small, the squadron performs a demanding role in often challenging sea conditions. Spain's ongoing claims to the British Overseas Territory – ceded to Britain as a result of the Treaty of Utrecht in 1713 – have given rise to frequent naval incursions that require a rapid response. Moreover, the Naval Dockyard Port of Gibraltar remains an important naval logistics hub, with its two 'Z' berths on the South Mole routinely supporting visits by US and Royal Navy submarines.[1] The Gibraltar Squadron provides a vital force protection role escorting shipping to and from these base facilities.

From 2003 onwards, the Gibraltar Squadron's most important assets comprised a pair of *Scimitar* class fast patrol boats. Completed in 1993 as MV *Grey Fox* and MV *Grey Wolf*, the two vessels were initially operated by the Royal Marines on Loch Neagh in Northern Ireland during the Troubles. Following a review of security arrangements in the Mediterranean after the 9/11 terrorist attacks, they

Guardian of the Rock: *Cutlass* is one of two new fast patrol boats specifically ordered for the British Royal Navy's Gibraltar Squadron from Mersey-based MST Group. These photographs show her (left) patrolling Gibraltar's waters in May 2022 and (above) at high speed on the River Mersey in the course of trials in September 2021.

were subsequently commissioned into Royal Navy service as *Scimitar* and *Sabre* for service at Gibraltar. Their top speed of over 30 knots gave them a useful advantage compared with the c. 25-knot *Archer* (P2000) class vessels that had previously served with the squadron. However, with the pair becoming increasingly long in the tooth, the British Ministry of Defence's Defence Equipment & Support (DE&S) agency issued a request for expressions of interest in providing replacement vessels in June 2018.[2] The new patrol boats were required to achieve speeds in excess of 35 knots, be able to deploy in conditions up to Sea State 6–7 and be capable of both day and night time operation.

Following an exhaustive competitive tender process that concluded with a best and final offer stage, DE&S announced on 24 July 2020 that a £9.9m (c. US$12.5m) contract had been signed with Merseyside-based Marine Specialised Technology (MST) to build two new fast patrol boats. The contract notification stated that the construction of the new craft would take approximately 18 months, with one being delivered during the last three months of 2021 and the other following in the second three months of 2022. Later, in April 2021, it was revealed that the names *Cutlass* and *Dagger* had been assigned to the new vessels. The lead ship completed initial sea trials from

Liverpool in the autumn of 2021, subsequently being delivered to Gibraltar to undertake a further round of tests in local waters under the Blue Ensign. Following successful completion of the full trials programme, *Cutlass* was formally commissioned into the Royal Navy on 4 May 2022. Meanwhile *Dagger* arrived in Gibraltar in March 2022 and is due to be commissioned during the second half of the year.

THE DESIGN PARTNERSHIP

The *Cutlass* class has been delivered by MST Group working in partnership with the Specialised Ship Design business of the well-known BMT naval and

Table 3.2.1.

CUTLASS (HPB-1900 FAST PATROL BOAT) PRINCIPAL PARTICULARS

Building Information:

Ordered:	24 July 2020 **Commissioned:** 4 May 2022
Builders:	Marine Specialised Technology (MST Group) at their facility in Liverpool, United Kingdom

Dimensions:[1]

Displacement:	c. 35 tonnes full load displacement.
Overall Dimensions:	19.0m x 5.3m x 1.0m. Hull dimensions are 17.5m (15.5m waterline) x 4.8m.

Equipment:

Armament:	3 x 7.62mm GPMGs.
	Alternative armament of 3 x 12.7mm Browning machine guns.
Principal Sensors:	Furuno DRS-NXT series navigation/surface search radar. iSea-25HD electro-optical/infrared surveillance system.
Other Systems:	OpenSea360 mission system for bridge and platform management. Integrated communications.

Propulsion Systems:

Machinery:	3 x Volvo Penta D13-1000 diesels each rated at 735kW. 3 x Marine Jet Power MJP 350X water jets.
Speed:	Maximum speed is in excess of 40 knots in Sea State 2. Range is c. 400 nautical miles in Sea State 2.

Other Details:

Complement:	6 crew plus seating for 6 passengers. Bunk accommodation for crew.
Class:	Two ships: *Cutlass* (P295) & *Dagger* (P296).

Notes:

1. Dimension and range are based on data for the generic HPB-1900 design. Details for the Royal Navy vessels might vary slightly.

engineering consultancy. Established in 2002, the privately-owned MST was initially focused on the production of inflatables, rigid-hulled inflatables (RHIBs) and small high-speed workboats for the defence and security markets. Having developed an extensive client base in the military, paramilitary and 'blue light' sectors, the company has recently been expanding its product base to include larger patrol boats in line with its understanding of market requirements.

The *Cutlass* design forms part of a wider portfolio of MST 'HPB' high-speed patrol boats that encompasses vessels up to 28m in length. More specifically, *Cutlass* and *Dagger* are HPB-1900 –

19m – variants of this series. BMT are essentially MST Group's design partners for these vessels, which are exclusive to the Merseyside-based company. BMT therefore assisted MST with the design of the two boats' hull form and overall structure, with MST concentrating on internal fit-out, systems selection and systems integration. A number of other sub-contractors have also played an important role in the project. Notably, Dorset-based NORCO manufactured the main composite hull, deck and wheelhouse structures for the two craft at its Poole factory. Assembly, outfitting and final systems integration took place at MST's Liverpool facility.

DESIGN DESCRIPTION

Overview: Principal statistics for *Cutlass* and *Dagger* are set out in Table 3.2.1. Displacing around 35 tonnes in full load condition, the HPB-1900 design utilises a planing 'V'-shaped mono-hull of composite GRP construction. The hull was specifically designed with Royal Navy operations in mind, including the need to meet challenging seakeeping performance parameters set out in the original requirements. This approach also extended to design details; for example, strength in the boats' shoulders and quarters support passenger transfer and boarding operations. The lower (accommodation) deck houses crew sleeping, galley, messing and wash-

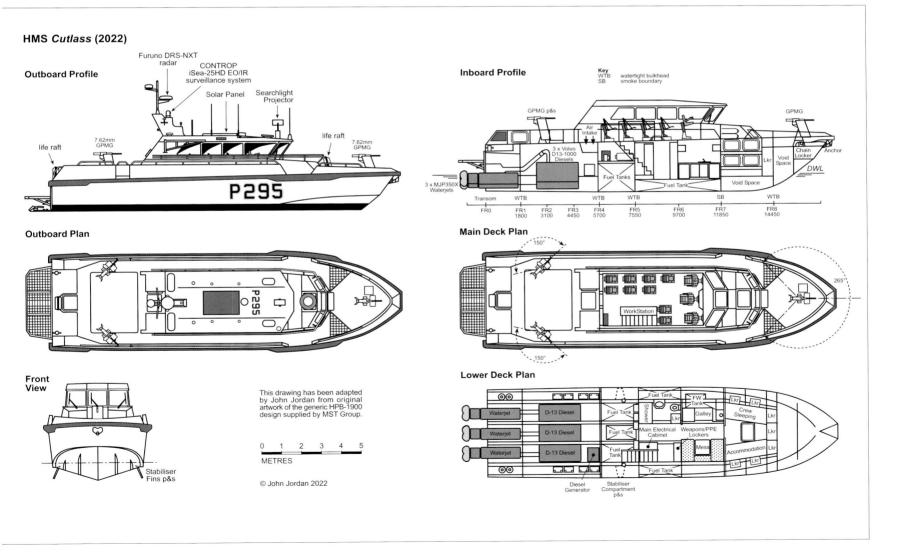

HMS *Cutlass* (2022)

room facilities forward, with the boat's propulsion train being located aft. It is subdivided by five main bulkheads into six principal compartments.

Moving upwards, the main deck is dominated by the centrally-located wheelhouse, which provides whole body anti-vibration seating for a core crew of six and up to six additional passengers. The incorporation of ballistic protection is stated as being an optional feature of the HPB-1900 design and photographs of *Cutlass* and *Dagger* indicate that this has been fitted, inter alia, to the wheelhouse and propulsion train, as well as to the three weapon stations. One of these is located forward of the wheelhouse, where it enjoys a broad, 265° firing arc. The other two weapon stations – each able to cover 150° – are located to port and starboard of the large aft working deck, which incorporates a transfer platform at its

stern. The wheelhouse roof provides a platform for the boat's short mast. This houses the boats' principal sensors and communications systems.

Propulsion and Platform Management: *Cutlass* and *Dagger* are powered by three six-cylinder 735kW (1,000hp) Volvo Penta D13-1000 diesels, each of which is linked to a Marine Jet Power MJP 350X water jet.[3] Optimised for high-speed performance, the MJP X series utilises an aluminium body and intake combined with a stainless steel duplex pump unit. The combination is capable of powering the craft to speeds in excess of 40 knots in Sea State 3, a performance that was confirmed during *Cutlass*' sea trials. This gives the class a significant margin of speed over most other vessels likely to be encountered in Gibraltar's waters, thereby providing an

important advantage with respect to their presence and interception roles. The two craft are equally capable of rapid acceleration and deceleration – for example, they are able to stop from maximum speed in just two boat's lengths – and have excellent manoeuvrability at both high and low speeds. Stability is aided by a fully integrated Humphree fin stabiliser and interceptor system that operates throughout the class's speed range and is reportedly effective even in severe conditions.[4]

Generic data on the HPB-1900 design suggests that fuel capacity is some 5,000 litres of diesel, which is sufficient to provide a range of up to 400 nautical miles in calm seas. A fresh water tank holding 350 litres of potable water is located adjacent to the compact galley on the lower deck. Electricity for the boats' systems and general hotel services is supplied by a separate diesel generator located in the main engine compartment. A reverse osmosis plant is fitted for potable water generation.

The class's bridge and platform management functions are provided by an OpenSea360 mission system supplied by Canadian information technology group CGI. A maritime mission system designed for smaller (sub-24m) high-speed craft, it is described by the company as offering a scalable, open-architecture solution that integrates platform systems, sensors, navigation and communications. Primarily selected to provide a paperless navigation system, OpenSea360 displays radar and other navigation information, as well as propulsion data. It also facilitates the management of many other systems, such as the control of lights, internal video cameras and ventilation. Using multi-function displays, it has a user interface that has been proven to enable full use of the system at speed in significant sea states. Notably, OpenSea360 controllers mounted in the armrests of the three forward crew positions means the system can be managed by the crew from the comfort and safety of their own seats. All in all, the system provides a level of automation that is a generation or more in advance of equipment found in previous Gibraltar-based patrol craft.

A view of *Cutlass*' bridge, showing the three whole body anti-vibration seating provided for the bridge team and the multi-function screens used by the OpenSea360 mission system. The level of equipment integration and automation provided by the mission system lowers the workload on the crew, giving them more ability to focus on the operation in hand. *(MST Group)*

Sensors and Armament: The essential patrol and presence focused mission set allocated to *Cutlass* and *Dagger* mean that the ship's suite of sensors is arguably of far greater importance than their weapons fit. The primary radar system is a Furuno DRS-NXT series solid-state Doppler radar; a system

Dagger seen leaving Gibraltar's dockyard port in May 2022, with the offshore patrol vessel *Trent* in the background. The image provides a good view of the iSea electro-optical surveillance system towards the foot of the mast, with a Furuno DRS-NXT series navigation radar above. A powerful searchlight is mounted atop the forward end of the wheelhouse roof. *(Crown Copyright 2022)*

that is often found as a navigation aid aboard pleasure craft, fishing vessels and other commercial shipping. It is located on the forward face of the mast that is attached to the aft end of the wheelhouse roof. Capable of performing surface surveillance out to ranges of up to 48 nautical miles, it has an alternate dual display mode to present both short and long-range radar images out to 12 nautical miles. In addition to acting as a navigation aid, the system also assists general situational awareness. An auto target acquire function can spot potentially hazardous objects out to 3 nautical miles and trigger an alarm, whilst up to 100 'targets' can be monitored at any one time.

A supplementary iSea-25HD electro-optical/infrared (EO/IR) surveillance system can also be found on the mast, just below the radar. Manufactured by Israeli firm CONTROP, this light-weight, 13kg optronic turret is part of a wider family

of iSea observation systems that the company states are especially designed for the maritime environment. Able to detect small boat-sized objects out to a range of around 8 nautical miles, it incorporates gyro-stabilisation and advanced image processing. In similar fashion to the Furuno radar, it interfaces with the OpenSea360 mission system.

The boats are also fitted with a powerful search-light, which is mounted on the centreline on the forward roof of the mainmast. Other equipment includes acoustic hailing devices and the normal suite of communications systems found in a vessel of this size. These include a full Global Maritime Distress and Safety System (GMDSS). It would also

be reasonable to assume that the boats are fitted with additional, Gibraltar-specific communications equipment to facilitate inter-agency operations with the appropriate local authorities.

The three weapon stations are located to provide 360° coverage. The normal weapons outfit comprises 7.62mm general purpose machine guns (GPMGs) that are fitted in shielded mountings.[5] A licensed variant of the widely-used Belgian FN MAM design, it has a maximum firing rate of 1,000 rounds per minute and an effective range in the region of 1,800 metres (or one nautical mile). The shielded weapons stations are also capable of being fitted with the heavier calibre 0.5in (12.7mm)

Although broadly similar in size and sophistication to high speed assault craft such as Sweden's CB-90, MST Group's HPB-1900 design is more properly regarded as a 'high end' inshore patrol boat. These images show *Dagger* off Gibraltar in 2022. *(Crown Copyright 2022)*

Browning machine guns in case of need. All of the weapon stations are manually operated. All-in-all, these weapons provide a proportionate response to the range of largely asymmetric threats that *Cutlass* and *Dagger* are likely to encounter.

ASSESSMENT

The *Cutlass* class is an innovative and technologically advanced design that will undoubtedly merit serious consideration by the many potential customers seeking to acquire this type of vessel. The two boats make an interesting comparison with sophisticated assault craft such as the internationally acclaimed Swedish CB-90 and the Finnish U-700 types, both of which could be considered as potential competitors. Certainly these vessels exhibit broad similarities in terms of overall size, speed and technology. However, the Scandinavian craft's primary amphibious assault and troop transportation roles are fundamentally different from those assigned to *Cutlass* and her sister, which are largely focused on patrol, enforcement and force protection missions. As such, the *Cutlass* class can be more properly regarded as forming the top end of a large number of inshore patrol craft designs focused on constabulary taskings, only a few of which achieve their level of systems automation.

The favourable reports received on *Cutlass'* initial sea trials – when it was stated that she had exceeded design expectations – have been followed by the swift entry of the lead ship into operational service. This progress speaks well of the achievements of the BMT/MST design and build partnership, particularly considering the headwinds created by the pandemic. Certainly, MST is optimistic that the HPB design portfolio will replicate the export sales achieved by many of their smaller craft. Tangible evidence of this optimism has been provided by the recent acquisition of the former McTay Marine shipyard in Bromborough, on the opposite bank of the River Mersey to the company's existing facility. This more extensive yard, which brings greater capacity and will facilitate the construction of larger vessels, is currently in the course of completing a £1m (c. US$1.25m) refurbishment.

MST has already gained one early additional success with its HPB series. In June 2021, the company announced that it won a further, £36m (c. US$45m) contract from the British Ministry of Defence, this time to supply eighteen high-speed patrol craft to support police activities. The programme is expected to extend for five years, with deliveries scheduled to commence in the second half of 2022. The new 15m HPB-1500 design is similar in overall concept to the *Cutlass* class but will be both smaller and slower. Equipped with two Marine Jet Power waterjets, the craft will be capable of achieving speeds of up to 30 knots and are to be operated by a three-strong crew (with the ability to accommodate four additional passengers). Although unarmed, they will also receive ballistic protection against light-calibre weapons. Interestingly, two of the class are destined for delivery to the Gibraltar Defence Police, where they will serve alongside their larger cousins.

Dagger seen passing Gibraltar's Europa Point. The successful delivery of the *Cutlass* class patrol boats could well spur additional sales of MST Group's HPB series. The Ministry of Defence has already ordered eighteen of the smaller HPB-1500 design for the maritime police. Two of these will join *Cutlass* and *Dagger* in patrolling Gibraltar's waters. *(Crown Copyright 2022)*

Notes

1. A 'Z' berth is a berth designated for occasional operational or recreational visits by nuclear-powered warships. It can be contrasted with an 'X' berth, which is a berth designated for frequent and regular use by nuclear-powered warships, or a berth in a dockyard or naval base which is suitable for the building, refit, repair or maintenance of nuclear-powered warships.

2. *Scimitar* and *Sabre* returned to the United Kingdom towards the end of 2020, being temporarily replaced by the *Archer* class patrol boats *Dasher* and *Pursuer* until the new *Cutlass* class arrived in Gibraltar as their permanent replacements. After further service in British waters, *Scimitar* and *Sabre* were decommissioned at a joint ceremony at Portsmouth Naval Base on 30 March 2022.

3. MST states that various alternative engine and propulsion options, including twin-engine propulsion trains, are available for the HPB-1900 hull.

4. An interceptor is a plate that is attached to the lower edge of a vessel's stern that creates additional lifting pressure beneath the boat, helping it to plane and ride more comfortably.

5. Some photographs of *Cutlass* at Gibraltar show her without her forward weapon station. The reason for this omission – and whether or not this is a temporary measure – is not known to the author.

6. The author acknowledges with gratitude the assistance of Ellie Taylor, Sales & Marketing Coordinator at MST Group, with respect to the production of this chapter.

3.3 SIGNIFICANT SHIPS

NIMITZ (CVN-68) CLASS AIRCRAFT CARRIERS

Fifty Years of Evolution

Author:
Norman Friedman

It is now 50 years since the aircraft carrier *Nimitz* (CVN-68) was launched on 13 May 1972. Since that time nine more nuclear carriers, all nominally her sisters, have been built; it is only now that the US Navy has switched to an entirely new design, the *Gerald R. Ford* (CVN-78) class. The remarkable longevity of the *Nimitz* design can be traced to its flexibility, which is partly due to its sheer size and to the absence of revolutionary alternatives. Perhaps at least as importantly, carriers are inherently modular, in the sense that their air wings can be replaced without demanding entirely new hulls or major new sub-systems. A lot has happened to naval aviation over the past five decades, but a big carrier has proven fully adaptable. Only recently has it been contended that something different is needed, and even now it can be argued that the new features of

the *Ford* have not been driven by the requirements of the evolving air wing.

DESIGN ORIGINS

The most critical driving force behind the *Nimitz* class design, as for all navies, has been economics. Navies are expensive. Unlike armies, their role is not immediately obvious to governments. They often operate around an enemy's periphery. As the Cold War began, it seemed that the main role of Western military forces was to defeat or, better, to deter a Soviet land attack in Europe. The implication was that Western navies should be shaped mainly to keep a NATO army alive and fighting, by ensuring the security of its supply line across the North Atlantic. That was much the naval role in the European theatre during the Second World War. The US Navy initially justified carrier striking forces by pointing to their ability to destroy Soviet submarines 'at source', meaning before they could leave their bases. The carriers' nuclear strike role engendered fierce inter-service rivalry, as the US

Air Force badly wanted a nuclear strike monopoly.

As the first post-war US carrier was completed, understanding of the naval role changed. From the mid-1950s on, both the US Navy and the British Royal Navy argued successfully that the Cold War was unlikely to turn hot in Europe, because war there might easily escalate into a nuclear holocaust. That was not to say that the Cold War itself would dissipate. Instead, its tensions would likely lead to wars on the Eurasian periphery, in places like Malaysia and Vietnam. In such places mobile sea-based airpower would be vital. That justified new US Navy carriers, the main question being their cost. In both cases, the need for new carriers collided with the need to keep the Cold War cold by deterrence, which from the 1960s on was enforced by very expensive strategic submarine forces. This was the context for the design of the *Nimitz* class. It had to be able to deliver conventional firepower in a war like the one being fought at the time it was being designed, in Vietnam. It also had to be able to deliver nuclear weapons in the

Left: *Nimitz* (CVN-68) pictured operating in the South China Sea in July 2020. Launched half a century ago on 13 May 1972, the longevity of the ten-strong *Nimitz* class is a tribute to the flexibility of the original design. *(US Navy)*

The US Navy's first nuclear aircraft carrier – *Enterprise* (CVAN-65) – pictured in the course of sea trials in October 1961. Her eight-reactor power plant was expensive to run and difficult to refuel. This drove efforts to produce ships with fewer, higher-powered reactors; a direction of travel reflected in the *Nimitz* class's two-reactor plant. *(HII Newport News Shipbuilding)*

event the Soviets confounded expectations and fought a European war.[1]

All warships incur two kinds of cost; the cost of construction and their lifetime cost. The latter includes increasingly expensive personnel, particularly highly-trained ones. For nuclear carriers, lifetime cost includes both the operating personnel and the cost of refuelling. When the ship is cut open for several years to get at her reactor for midlife refuelling, typically she receives all sorts of other upgrades. The opportunity to install them may encourage installations which otherwise might have been considered too expensive.

When the first US Navy nuclear carrier, *Enterprise* (CVAN-65), was authorised, US naval policy was to build a large carrier every year. That policy collided with the Polaris programme, but – even with construction plans scaled back – there was also intense pressure to limit the costs of the ships. To the extent that the complex eight-reactor power plant of the *Enterprise* was expensive (in manpower) to operate and difficult to refuel, this effort was reflected in designs for ships with fewer reactors, hence reduced performance. Meanwhile the reactor developers sought increased power per reactor, the advantage being that manning each reactor was apparently more or less fixed. By 1964 they could envisage a reactor about four times as powerful as each *Enterprise* reactor. In 1964 the estimated capital cost of a two-reactor ship was U$422m, compared with U$425m for four reactors. However, the lifetime cost of the two designs would have been

Table 3.3.1: *NIMITZ* (CVN-68) CLASS LIST

HULL[1]	NAME	APPROVED	ORDERED	LAID DOWN	LAUNCHED	DELIVERED	COMMISSIONED	RCOH
CVAN-68	Nimitz	FY 1967	31 March 1967	22 June 1968	13 May 1972	11 April 1975	3 May 1975	1998–2001
CVAN-69	Dwight D. Eisenhower[2]	FY 1970	30 June 1970	15 August 1970	11 October 1975	12 September 1977	18 October 1977	2001–05
CVN-70	Carl Vinson	FY 1974	5 April 1974	11 October 1975	15 March 1980	26 February 1982	13 March 1982	2005–09
CVN-71	Theodore Roosevelt	FY 1980	30 September 1980	31 October 1981	27 October 1984	17 October 1986	25 October 1986	2009–13
CVN-72	Abraham Lincoln	FY1983	27 December 1982	3 November 1984	13 February 1988	30 October 1989	11 November 1989	2013–17
CVN-73	George Washington	FY1983	27 December 1982	25 August 1986	21 July 1990	8 June 1992	4 July 1992	2017–
CVN-74	John C. Stennis	FY1988	30 June 1988	13 March 1991	13 November 1993	9 November 1995	9 December 1995	2021–
CVN-75	Harry S. Truman	FY1988	30 June 1988	29 November 1993	7 September 1996	30 June 1998	25 July 1998	
CVN-76	Ronald Reagan	FY1995	8 December 1994	12 February 1998	10 March 2001	20 June 2003	12 July 2003	
CVN-77	George H. W. Bush	FY2001	26 January 2001	19 May 2003	9 October 2006	11 May 2009[3]	10 January 2009[3]	

Notes:

1. The hull classifications of *Nimitz* and *Dwight D. Eisenhower* were changed from CVAN to CVN in June 1975.

2. The ship's name was changed from the originally approved *Eisenhower* shortly before the order was placed.

3. Unusually, *George H. W. Bush* was commissioned before she was completed so that President George W. Bush could host his father, the ship's namesake, at the ceremony whilst he was still in presidential office.

significantly different due to the heavy expense of nuclear-qualified personnel.[2]

THE *NIMITZ* CLASS PROGRAMME

A list of the *Nimitz* class aircraft carriers is provided in Table 3.3.1. The keel of the lead vessel was laid down on 22 June 1968, with the tenth and final ship being accepted on 11 May 2009. All members of the class were built to essentially the same base configuration.

The relative stability of the *Nimitz* class design owes a great deal to political factors. *Nimitz* (originally CVAN-68) was conceived in the era of Secretary of Defense Robert S. McNamara, who espoused economy by buying multiple units as a single package. Carriers were no exception. He wanted to buy three nuclear carriers (CVAN 68–70; later to be re-designated CVN 68–70) as one series of identical ships. These were to be authorised every two years, in FY1967, FY1969 and FY1971. However, money was tight, presumably due to the Vietnam War. As a result, the second ship – *Dwight D. Eisenhower* (CVAN-69) – was funded only in FY1970, followed by the third – *Carl Vinson* (CVN-70) – in FY1974. By that time defence money was even tighter, so the Ford Administration (1974–6) sought something much less expensive rather than a fourth *Nimitz*.[3]

As has been explained, these carriers were justified mainly on the grounds that the offensive strength of the US Navy was badly needed for peripheral wars like Vietnam. In the wake of Vietnam, Jimmy Carter became President, promising that the United States would fight no more such wars; what he called the 'North-South' problem would be solved by soft power. The only war in sight would be the East-West war in Europe. To balance his budget – and, he hoped, defeat inflation – President Carter would cut naval spending to what was needed to protect supplies flowing across the North Atlantic, meaning that investment should focus on anti-submarine warfare (ASW). The US Navy had to scramble to define its role in a war it had considered grossly unlikely for two decades. It began to lay out the case that threats to the flanks of a Soviet advance into Western Europe could drastically slow it. This explicit Maritime Strategy justified construction of the fourth nuclear carrier, which was ultimately included in the FY1980 programme. In theory, a fresh carrier design might have been attractive, but there was no time to complete one. The

The first units of the *Nimitz* class were envisaged as a three-ship programme, with one vessel to be acquired every two years. Financial constraints meant that orders were spread out over a longer period. This is the second *Nimitz* class carrier, *Dwight D. Eisenhower* (CVN-69), pictured early in her career whilst operating in the Mediterranean in 1980. Ordered under the FY1970 construction programme, she was commissioned in October 1977. *(US National Archives 6419997)*

FY1980 ship – *Theodore Roosevelt* (CVN-71) – therefore, was a lightly-modified *Nimitz*.

The next, Reagan, Administration understood the navy's case, and saw large-deck carriers as key to its national strategy. It was able to authorise new nuclear carriers. Moreover, the sole carrier builder, Newport News, was willing to invest heavily in its own infrastructure to reduce the ships' unit cost. Two ships were included in each of the FY1983 and FY1988 programmes. These were *Abraham Lincoln*

(CVN-72) and *George Washington* (CVN-73), followed by *John C. Stennis* (CVN-74) and *Harry S. Truman* (CVN-75). This pace again explains retention of the *Nimitz* design. There was certainly no opportunity for a fresh design when ships were being ordered in 1982 (FY1983), and not much time if Newport News was offering a good price for repeat ships in 1988.

Two more ships were authorised after the end of the Cold War so as to maintain a planned eleven-

Abraham Lincoln (CVN-72) was one of a pair of *Nimitz* class carriers authorised under the FY 1983 budget. The rapid build-up of the US Navy during the Reagan years meant that there was insufficient time available to produce an entirely new aircraft carrier design. *(US Navy)*

George H. W. Bush (CVN-77) pictured in the course of post-delivery trials in February 2010. Along with *Ronald Reagan* (CVN-76), she exhibited a number of visible differences from earlier members of the *Nimitz* class. *(US Navy)*

carrier fleet: these were *Ronald Reagan* (CVN-76) in FY1995 and *George H.W. Bush* (CVN-77) in FY2001. The only ship for which there was a real possibility of a new design was the last, CVN-77. New sketch designs were offered, but they were not considered worthwhile. These last two ships were the only units of the class, as built, showing very visible differences from the first eight.

The loss of internal US Navy design capability may also have been significant in the programme's later stages. When *Nimitz* was being built, US Navy designs typically went through three stages. They began as Preliminary Designs, sketches which embodied most or all of the characteristics of the ship as she would be built. The Bureau of Ships and its 1966 successor the Naval Ship Systems Command (NAVSHIPS) – and then the Naval Sea Systems Command (NAVSEA) – had a Preliminary Design section which created these designs. They were, among other things, a way to evaluate alternative proposals from the naval staff.[4] Once a preliminary design had been approved, a separate organisation created a Contract Design as a basis on which companies could bid. In the case of carriers, by 1968 only Newport News had the capacity to build a nuclear carrier, but it still began with a Contract Design. Once the shipyard received the building contract, it developed detailed working drawings; a considerable task.

This arrangement was upset in the 1990s. The Office of the Secretary of Defense (OSD) decided that the Navy should shift NAVSHIPS/NAVSEA from being engineering-oriented to being managerial in nature. This was what the other services already did. It seems that the US Navy did not realise how particularly effective its unique organisation was.[5] The consequence of reorganisation was the loss of the considerable experience which the naval preliminary designers had accumulated. Shipyards such as Newport News now needed much more capable design organisations, involving considerable investment. It helped that yards hired former NAVSEA design engineers, but they would not last. Their successors were unlikely to understand unique naval conditions and requirements, which too often were unexpressed when design contracts were let. *Ronald Reagan* was designed as design policy was about to change. With the next ship, *George H.W. Bush*, Newport News proposed real alternatives, but they were not attractive enough. *Gerald R. Ford* is a fresh design, although she is constrained by an OSD decision that she fit within the envelope defined by the *Nimitz*. The need for a fresh design can be seen as a reaction to the accumulation of viable alternatives to major ship systems. A shift to electric power has been a major contributing factor. Sceptics have argued that this has been less than successful in terms of reliability. Problems with the new ships are likely to prolong the lives of the *Nimitz* class.

THE *NIMITZ* CLASS DESIGN

Principal particulars of the *Nimitz* class design as first built are set out in Table 3.3.2. The design – Ship Characteristic Board No. 102 (SCB-102) – exhibits broad similarities to the run of post-war US Navy carriers that began with *Forrestal* (CVA-59), herself influenced by the abortive *United States* (CVA-58). The general arrangement of the flight deck, elevators and island structure is similar to that adopted with effect from *Kitty Hawk* (CVA-63).

General Design: Given that the Newport News Shipbuilding and Dry Dock Company was the only American shipyard capable of building a large nuclear-powered vessel by the time the *Nimitz* class was designed, the company's large graving dock essentially set the limit on what could be built. Taking account of that limit – and what had to be squeezed into her – *Nimitz* was given a somewhat fuller hull than would have been optimal for speed. She was equipped with four long C13-1 steam catapults for maximum aviation capability. The ships were intended to operate heavy bombers – the A3 Skywarrior and, later, the A-6 Intruder – so they needed the most powerful possible catapults and arresting gear.[6] The first three ships were later credited with a capacity of 2,570 tons of aviation ordnance and 2.8 million gallons of aviation fuel, in each case greater than the capacity of the earlier nuclear carrier, *Enterprise*. Total aviation payload is reported to be approximately 15,000 tons, presumably including aircraft, spares, fuel, and ordnance. Compared to the earlier, non-nuclear *Forrestal* class, *Nimitz* class carriers were said to carry 90 percent more aviation fuel and 50 percent more aviation ordnance.

Flight Deck Arrangements: The main changes compared to previous carriers were in the flight deck and in magazine arrangement. The object of flight deck redesign was to improve air flow abaft the new carriers. It turned out that the only way to do so was to reduce the angle of the angled deck. That in turn was determined by the requirement that the after

Two undated photos of *Nimitz* – then designated CVAN-68 – under construction at the Newport News Shipbuilding & Dry Dock Company. The dimensions of the company's graving dock provided some limitation on the size of ship that could be built. Note the angled runs of the two forward C-13-1 steam catapults. These long catapults were driven by the requirements of the heavy bombers that then formed part of the ship's air group. (*US National Archives 24740977/24741067*)

end of the landing runway pass between Nos. 3 and 4 elevators, and that its forward end should clear an aircraft on No. 2 (portside) catapult. Relocating No. 4 elevator to a centreline position (between the forward catapults) would have solved the problem, but that was rejected by the aviation community. Instead, the after ends of the two forward catapults were angled to starboard. That made it possible to make the forward end of the flight deck parallel to the centreline. Later ships of the class featured further modified flight decks.

The most obvious difference between the flight decks of the first three ships related to their bridle-catchers; the booms intended to catch catapult bridles discarded as aircraft left the deck. *Nimitz*, like earlier large carriers, had two of them in her bow. Her two sisters had only one. Later ships had none because newer aircraft had permanent catapult attachments.

Magazines: The key fact of internal arrangement, which could not be changed in any of the ships of the class, was the number and placement (and type) of the reactors. The two reactors were widely separated, for survivability. In a conventional arrangement, such a ship would have three magazines; one between the reactors and one at each end. That would have made for a longer magazine length than preceding carriers – which had a magazine at either end of the vessel – with a better chance that an enemy projectile would hit one of these vulnerable spaces. The design therefore merged what would have been the after magazine with the midships

Table 3.3.2.

NIMITZ (CVAN-68) PRINCIPAL PARTICULARS AS BUILT

Building Information:

Keel Laid:	22 June 1968 **Launched:** 13 May 1972 **Commissioned:** 3 May 1975
Builders:	Newport News Shipbuilding & Dry Dock Company, Newport News, VA (now a division of Huntington Ingalls Industries)

Dimensions:

Displacement:	c. 88,900 long tons (90,300 tonnes) designed, c. 91,400 long tons (92,900 tonnes) actual full load displacement.
Overall Dimensions:	331.6m x 78.5m x 11.2m. Waterline dimensions are 317.0m x 40.8m.

Equipment:

Aircraft:	Typical air group of up to 90 fast jets and helicopters. 4 x C13-1 catapults. 4 x deck-edge aircraft elevators.
Weapons:	Basic Point Defence Missile System. 3 x octuple Mk 25 launchers for Sea Sparrow SAMs controlled by Mk 115 manual illuminators.
Countermeasures:	ULQ-6 electronic warfare system. T Mk 6 Fanfare torpedo decoy system.
Principal Sensors:	SPS-43A 2D long-range air surveillance; SPS-48 3D air surveillance; SPS-10 surface search; various aircraft control radars.
Combat System:	Naval Tactical Data System (NTDS)

Propulsion System:

Machinery:	Nuclear. 2 x A4W pressurised water reactors and 4 x GE steam turbines generate a total of c. 260,000SHP through four shafts.
Speed:	Designed maximum speed is over 30 knots. Endurance is limited only by a nuclear core life of c. 25 years.

Other Details:

Complement:	A typical crew on completion comprised c. 3,100 personnel plus c. 2,600 additional personnel in the embarked air wing.[1]
Class:	See Table 3.2.1

Notes:

1. Reported personnel numbers vary, even in official sources.

magazine. Unlike the flight deck, this internal arrangement could not be changed within the class, although details of the magazines could be revised.

When *Nimitz* was completed, the US Navy claimed she could absorb three times as much damage as the *Essex* (CV-9) class carriers had survived in 1944–5. This point was often made when critics argued that the big carriers were vulnerable to Soviet anti-ship missiles; the US Navy likened these to Kamikazes.

It seems fair to argue that the *Nimitz* design was shaped by the permissive environment of the Vietnam War, in which the key capability was delivery of as much ordnance as possible. Maximum aviation ordnance capacity limited the amount of time spent replenishing. The benign environment seemed to justify economies. For example, a proposal to install a phased-array radar system was dropped.

Electronics: *Nimitz* was completed with a computerised combat system; the Naval Tactical Data System (NTDS). At the time, this was an exotic and expensive addition. In a carrier, NTDS was intended mainly to control fighters against enemy bombers. However, its role extended to landing control as well.

All three ships in the first batch had the same principal radars; a three-dimensional planar array (SPS-48) atop the bridge and the antenna of a long-range two-dimensional radar (SPS-43A) atop a mast abaft the island. SPS-48 was the first US Navy digital radar. There were also the usual air traffic

USS *Nimitz* (1980)

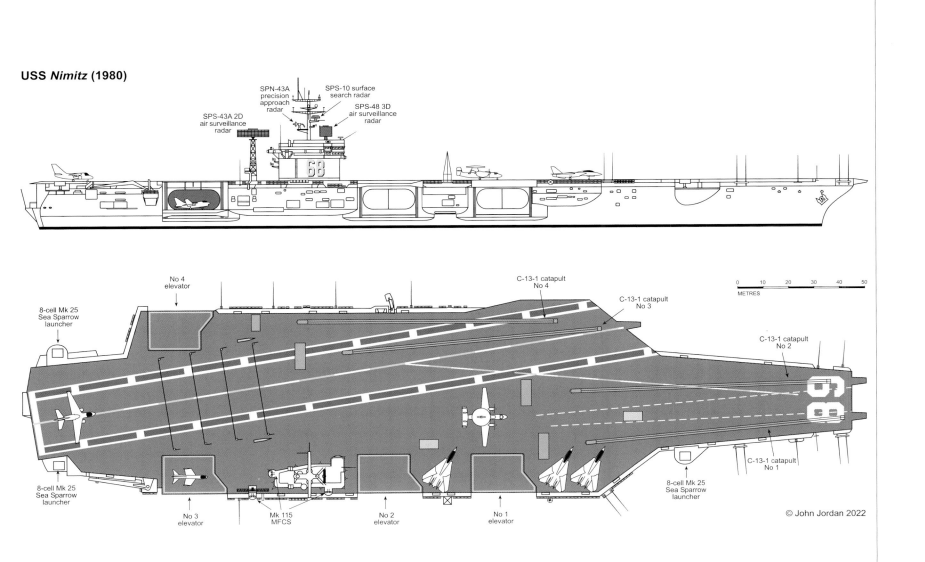

© John Jordan 2022

A close-up view of the island structure on *Dwight D. Eisenhower* (CVN-68) in 1984; still essentially unchanged from the arrangement fitted to the first two of the *Nimitz* class on build. A SPS-48 three-dimensional planar array is located forward of the island's mast. This has a SPS-10 surface-search set on a platform attached to its forward face and a SPN-43 air traffic control radar facing aft. The lattice mast aft of the island provides a platform for the long-range, two-dimensional SPS-43A surveillance antenna. *(US National Archives 6417337)*

control radars. Aircraft were shepherded into a landing pattern using the SPN-43, located on the mast above the island. It was a medium-range air-search radar which could back up SPS-43A. As an aircraft got closer, it was picked up by a precision-control radar (SPN-42). There were two such radars, to control two aircraft at a time. SPN-44 employed a dish antenna atop the island to measure the speed of an approaching aircraft. All of these specialised radars helped create a distinctive radar signature, a matter of increasing concern as it became easier to collect radar information, particularly from space. The carriers also had an inertial navigation system, which could initialise the navigational systems of A-6 bombers they carried.

Weaponry: Although previous carriers had Terrier and Tartar systems, to hold down cost *Nimitz* was at first to be limited to twin 3in/50 guns. However, she was completed instead with three box launchers for Sea Sparrow missiles, the first US Navy point defence system. One box launcher was sponsored out on her starboard side forward, and two others were on either side aft. Although the system changed in later ships, the positions were the only ones available.

The first Sea Sparrow system was extremely simple. It was controlled by a crewman who manually pointed his Mk 115 director at the incoming target, based on designation he received via his headphones. The missile launcher similarly was slewed in the desired direction. It was a modified ASROC launcher, the missiles being unmodified Sparrow air-to-air weapons.[7]

An aerial view of *Nimitz* (CVN-68) pictured at sea in May 1981. Two of her three box-like Mk25 Sea Sparrow missile launchers can be seen on platforms to port and starboard at her stern; these comprised her sole defensive armament when first completed. Note also that the angle of her landing deck was reduced compared with previous carriers to improve air flow, with a knock-on effect on catapult arrangements. *(US Navy)*

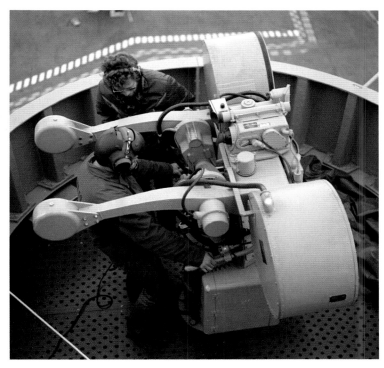

The first two *Nimitz* class carriers were fitted with the first iteration of the Sea Sparrow point defence missile system, seen here being tested on *Dwight D. Eisenhower* (CVN-68) in November 1981. The system was controlled by a crewman who manually pointed his Mk 115 director at the incoming target, based on designation he received via his headphones. (*US National Archives 6417798/9*)

It was obvious that more was needed: an air-search radar to detect incoming air targets, which it would automatically designate to the missile system. The launcher would slew automatically onto the bearing of the incoming target. Ideally, operation would be entirely automatic. In theory, however, the simple system was good enough, since the only targets the system would be engaging would be headed straight for the ship. The desired automated version of Sea Sparrow was developed under a NATO project, begun as a test case for NATO Armaments Group research and development procedures. At American suggestion, but employing NATO companies, the group developed NATO Sea Sparrow, which the US Navy saw as a second-generation system. Targets were designated by a ship's air-search radar. Launchers and fire-control radars slewed automatically onto the designated bearing. The new NATO system was expected to acquire a target about twice as far from the ship (about 24 nautical miles in the absence of jamming) and to deal with targets approaching at 1,500ft/sec, i.e., at about 800 knots. As *Nimitz* was being built, this automated system was coming together. It was ready for *Carl Vinson*, the third ship of the class.[8]

MODIFICATIONS: *CARL VINSON* (CVN-70)

In addition to NATO Sea Sparrow, *Carl Vinson* was the first of the class to be fitted with another new anti-missile system, the Phalanx close-in weapon system (CIWS). Comprising a 20mm Vulcan cannon with an elaborate fire-control system capable of detecting an incoming threat and triggering itself, Phalanx essentially combined with NATO Sea Sparrow to constitute a layered anti-missile defence.

Carl Vinson also had the automated SLQ-17 electronic warfare system, the replacement for the manual ULQ-6 on board the two earlier ships. In 1974, it was planned for all twelve operational carriers. In addition, *Vinson* introduced the commercial LN-66 navigational (i.e., surface-search) radar, which might be seen as a self-defence measure. Since it could be turned on instead of the US Navy-standard SPS-10, LN-66 made it more difficult for an enemy force to use radar intercepts to identify the ship as a carrier.

By the time *Vinson* was authorised, the then Chief of Naval Operations – Admiral Elmo Zumwalt Jr. – was in the course of reorganising the carrier force. The specialised anti-submarine carriers, converted Second World War *Essex* class vessels, were being retired without direct replacement. Zumwalt decided that all remaining carriers, which had been classified as attack carriers (CVAs), would be re-categorised as dual-purpose and capable of operating ASW aircraft. The carrier would function as their command centre, utilising an onboard Tactical Support Center (TSC) which could correlate what the aircraft and fleet ASW ships found. A shipboard TSC could also communicate with land TSCs to, for example, use what maritime patrol aircraft and seafloor acoustic arrays found. Initially the TSC was not integrated with the ship's anti-air warfare-oriented combat direction system, whose computers were already heavily loaded. *Vinson* was the first *Nimitz* to be fitted with a TSC during construction. She heralded the re-designation of nuclear carriers to CVN from CVAN.

A series of views of *Carl Vinson* (CVN-70) taken in January 1982, shortly before her delivery to the US Navy. She is fitted with the second-generation NATO Sea Sparrow point defence missile system and Phalanx CIWS, the first of the *Nimitz* class to be so equipped. Below decks, she was equipped with a Tactical Support Center (TSC) to facilitate anti-submarine warfare operations. *(US National Archives 6350940/42/44)*

Vinson also had the new SLQ-25 Nixie towed torpedo decoy, presumably replacing the earlier T Mk 6 Fanfare. It had been under development for some time, and was standard in major US Navy warships.

The modifications incorporated in *Vinson* were later extended to her two sister-ships. In the course of the 1980s, all three of this first batch of the *Nimitz* class carriers were updated with Kevlar splinter protection and new long-range radars.[9]

EVOLUTION: *THEODORE ROOSEVELT* (CVN-71) TO *HARRY S. TRUMAN* (CVN-75)

The carrier authorised in FY1980, *Theodore Roosevelt*, was further modified. While she was being built, the war in the Falklands was fought; the US Navy digested its implications. The most obvious were the need for better splinter protection and for better fire-fighting. Consequently, *Roosevelt* had improved armour – including the introduction of Kevlar and more robust magazine protection – and a Halon fire-fighting system.[10] Instead of a free-standing TSC, she had an Anti-Submarine Module (ASWM) integrated into her combat control system. Her upgraded NATO Sea Sparrow system was supported by a better radar intercept receiver (WLR-1H). She was also equipped with a new commercial-type navigational radar (SPS-64) and a new surface-search radar (SPS-67).

Lessons from the Falklands certainly included the need for better air defence. A third-generation Sea Sparrow system incorporated a dedicated target-acquisition radar, embedded in the Target Acquisition System (TAS) Mk 23. The US Navy already had a pulse-Doppler version of its standard surface-search radar (SPS-10), but in TAS Mk 23 a new dedicated radar fed a separate memory (for up to fifty-four targets) with logic to decide which was most urgent. It was introduced in the first of the Reagan-era *Nimitz* class vessels, *Abraham Lincoln*. She also had upgraded (Block I) Phalanx CIWS.

In *Abraham Lincoln* the SPS-43 long-range air-search radar was replaced by SPS-49(V)5, a higher-frequency, hence higher-precision, digital system. It became standard in all the large-deck carriers. She also introduced the stealthy SPN-46 landing control system. The SPN-43A marshalling radar remained but the smaller antennae visible in previous carriers were no longer needed. Low-pressure catapults replaced the earlier type; these carry the Mk C-13-2

designation. *Lincoln* also had a rearranged communications centre.

The other ship of this batch, *George Washington*, was completed with additional Kevlar fragment protection to safeguard topside areas and low-smoke cable, presumably further responses to Falklands War lessons. By the time she was being built, there was pressure to replace military-specification systems with less expensive commercial ones where this was possible; the ship's internal telephone system therefore used a commercial switchboard system employing fibre optics.

By this time the Navy was standardising on the SLQ-32 'design to price' electronic warfare system, so a version of it replaced the SLQ-17. Aircraft carriers initially were fitted with SLQ-32(V)3, but *Roosevelt* was fitted with SLQ-32(V)4 in 1997–8, and the others were similarly updated. The new very-short-range defensive missile envisaged as a result of the 1972 panic was now emerging as the Rolling Airframe Missile (RAM); it first flew in 1978. It was triggered by the electronic radiation of an incoming attacker, so SLQ-32 became its key sensor. Unlike a radar, this wide-open system would instantaneously detect threats, although it would not be able to find their range or their velocity. It could also detect high-divers more readily than radars concentrating on sea-skimmers as they popped over the horizon. In the *Nimitz* class, two RAM launchers replaced one Phalanx and one NATO Sea Sparrow launcher from around 1990 onwards.

The first of the next pair, *John C. Stennis*, was built of HSLA 100 steel, for better damage resistance. She had a new 3-D radar (SPS-48E) and a new air traffic control radar (SPN-43C). Other changes included a revised air-conditioning plant and the use of fibre optics for internal communications. Her counterpart in this batch, *Harry S. Truman*, had a modified bridge and a new IT-21 internal communications network.

Stennis and her sister were completed after the Gulf War demonstrated that US Navy carriers had insufficient connectivity. Their UHF satellite communication system, which used a pair of 'wash basin' antennas on the foremast, was not good enough. The US Air Force had controlled nearly all Allied air operations over Iraq via a centralised Air Tasking Order. Without sufficient satellite connectivity, US Navy carriers received their copies of the order as hard copies delivered by aircraft. To preclude such problems in the future, carriers needed as much satellite communication capacity as possible. Typically that meant extremely high frequency (EHF) and super high frequency (SHF) dishes in large spherical radomes (the higher the frequency, the greater the transmission rate). Examples included the EHF USC-38 and the SHF Challenge Athena (WSC-6 system). Smaller thimble-shaped antennas were added for the Global Broadcast satellite system. These systems were installed on board all existing US Navy large-deck carriers. Locations varied.

Among other things, the satellite data systems supported an evolving network which provided a wider picture of the situation, beyond that in a ship's combat data system. This wider picture is not quite compatible with the near-real-time one in the combat system, but it is increasingly important as the carrier is the flagship of a battle group which can wield long-range cruise missiles. Ideally the short-range and long-range data had to be integrated in the ship's combat system, but that proved very difficult. As long-range data systems matured in the 1980s, overloading of the existing NTDS combat system became more and more evident. A new Advanced Combat Direction System (ACDS), in effect a modernised NTDS, was developed. By 1998 a Block 0 version had been installed on board twelve carriers as well as other ships. In effect it was NTDS running on much more powerful computers. The successor Block 1 was supposed to integrate it with the increasingly important wide-area picture, which previously had been handled separately. Replacement of Block 0 by Block 1 began with the carrier *Eisenhower* in FY1996. Unfortunately the system failed its operational evaluation. For

Ordered in FY 1988, *John C. Stennis* (CVN-74) and her sister *Harry S. Truman* (CVN-75) – pictured here transiting the Straits of Gibraltar in 2004 – introduced HSLA 100 steel into *the Nimitz* class design. Other enhancements included a new SPS-48E variant of the 3D radar and an upgraded SPN-43C air traffic control radar. *(US Navy)*

Ronald Reagan (CVN-76) pictured in the course of 2016. Compared with previous ships she had her flight deck extended, the angled portion angled slightly further – by 0.3° – to port, and the arresting gear modified with three rather than four wires. She also has a revised island structure that incorporates the mast for her long-range surveillance radar. *(US Navy)*

example, it did not work effectively with the new Cooperative Engagement Capability (CEC). Of the nuclear carriers, only *Nimitz* and *Eisenhower* ever had the new system. Instead, work began on a version of the Surface Ship Self-Defense System (SSDS). Despite its name, it was a scalable ship combat data system adaptable to the largest ships. SSDS Mk 2 Mod 0 was installed on board *Nimitz* in 2001; the first Mod 1 version, tested in 2002, went aboard the carrier *Ronald Reagan*, and is now standard across the class.[11]

THE FINAL *NIMITZS* – *RONALD REAGAN* (CVN-76) AND *GEORGE H. W. BUSH* (CVN-77)

The last two ships were redesigned using a 'design budget' technique, an important object being to reduce life-cycle cost by about a fifth. The first ship of this pair, *Ronald Reagan*, had her flight deck extended, the angled portion angled slightly further – by 0.3° to port – and the arresting gear modified with three rather than four wires. The modifications made it possible to use both the port bow catapult and one of the waist catapults simultaneously. Flight deck operations are reoriented to the port side of the ship, making possible simultaneous landings and take-offs.

The starboard weapons elevator was moved into the island so that it interfered less with flight operations, essentially with how quickly aircraft could be turned around. It was accommodated in an island lengthened by about 20ft and which is one level lower than in previous ships. There is also an outboard weapons elevator. The island contains a two-level flight deck control position with a 270° view. The long-range SPS-49 radar, which was located on a separate mast on earlier ships of the class, was relocated onto the island structure. This frees flight deck parking space. *Ronald Reagan* may also have been the first ship with the new SPQ-9B target-acquisition radar, which replaces the earlier TAS Mk 23. She carries it atop her foremast, the satellite radome which occupies that place in earlier ships having been relocated.

Ronald Reagan had much more extensive fibre-optic cabling than in the past as part of the integrated communication and advanced networks (ICAN) project. She also introduced an integrated digital navigation system (NAVSSI), incorporating a ring-laser digital gyro. She had much more powerful air-conditioning plant than earlier ships. Her near-

George H. W. Bush (CVN-77) being prepared for float-out at Newport News Shipbuilding in September 2006. The bulbous bow – intended to improve hull efficiency and, presumably speed, by reducing drag – was another design change introduced with effect from *Ronald Reagan* (CVN-76). *(Newport News Shipbuilding)*

sister, *George H.W. Bush*, saw further enhancements. She completed with a composite mast and a revised propeller design. Reportedly she also has higher-capacity elevators, which can handle 100 tons compared with the previous 70 tons. Both ships have a large new bulbous bow. Reported aviation fuel capacity is 3.4 million gallons; over 20 percent more than that carried by the first batch when completed.

Initially there was considerable interest in building CVN-77 to a new design. In the mid-1990s there was intense interest in stealth, as most clearly reflected in the *Zumwalt* (DDG-1000) class design. The carrier programme office asked whether even a ship the size of a carrier could have her radar cross-section drastically reduced. The sides of the fore end of the flight deck could be angled to reflect signals away from a radar. The gap in front of the angled deck could be filled in. The island could be dramatically reduced, and the ship's radars replaced by active arrays, which would not reflect nearly as much as conventional radars. In one version of the

design, nearly all deck-edge elevators were eliminated in favour of a flight deck elevator forward and a second elevator dead aft. Newport News – now central to the design process – proposed the new 'pit stop' aircraft servicing concept that survives in the *Ford* class.[12] In the case of stealth, the carrier programme office decided that the operational sacrifices involved in achieving the goal were not worthwhile. Whatever was done, a viable carrier is a very large ship which is difficult to hide.

THE FUTURE

Each *Nimitz* class carrier is expected to have a service life of 50 years; a phenomenal lifespan for any modern warship. A key element in achieving this goal is the midlife refuelling and complex overhaul (RCOH) of each ship, a process described more fully in the accompanying Text Box (overleaf). RCOHs are also supplemented by more normal refit and maintenance availability periods that take place through a carrier's scheduled life.

All *Nimitz* class aircraft carriers are intended to undergo a midlife refuelling and complex overhaul (RCOH) around 25 years after first delivery. The process only occurs once in each carrier's life and includes refuelling the ship's two nuclear reactors, as well as significant repair and modernisation work. It is claimed that the RCOH represents 35 percent of all the maintenance and modernisation work planned during an aircraft carrier's operational service. The necessary work can only be carried out by Huntington Ingalls Industries' Newport News Shipbuilding. It should take between three and four years to complete, although it requires several additional years' planning. The current cost of a RCOH is c. US$3bn. At various times, proposals have been seriously considered to retire *Nimitz* class vessels at the half-life stage because of the cost involved in this endeavour.

Nimitz commenced the class's first RCOH in May 1998. This was the fourth RCOH to be performed on a US Navy carrier, *Enterprise* have being subject to three separate refuelling periods previously. A further four members of the class have completed the process and work on two additional carriers is underway.

The latest *Nimitz* class carrier to leave RCOH was *Abraham Lincoln*. The project commenced on 28 March 2013 following a slight delay due to budget uncertainties, with the ship being redelivered on 12 May 2017 following the successful completion of post-overhaul sea trials. In addition to the refuelling, the RCOH incorporated major upgrades to the carrier's flight deck, catapults and combat systems, as well as the reconstruction of her island. The last-mentioned included installation of a new 70-ton upper level structure to contain the ship's primary flight control systems. In addition, the ship's hull, shafting, propellers, rudders, piping, ventilation and electrical systems were all repaired and upgraded. With the exception of the new *Ford*, the RCOH currently makes her the most up-to-date carrier in the US Navy.

A potential problem with the successful completion of a RCOH is the emergence of unplanned work during the course of the project. This, along with the impact of the pandemic, is believed to account for delays to the current overhaul of *George Washington*, which commenced in August 2017. Latest estimates suggest she will return to the fleet at the end of 2022.

A new 70-ton upper level structure is craned aboard *Abraham Lincoln* (CVN-72) in April 2014 as part of the carrier's refuelling and complex overhaul (RCOH). RCOH represents 35 percent of all the maintenance and modernisation work planned during an aircraft carrier's service life. *(Huntington Ingalls Industries)*

George Washington (CVN-73) is pictured being manoeuvred out of dry dock at Newport News in September 2021. The impact of emerging work requirements and the COVID-19 pandemic has delayed completion of her RCOH, which is currently estimated to be finished at the end of 2022. *(Huntington Ingalls Industries)*

Table 3.3.3.

ABRAHAM LINCOLN (CVN-72) PRINCIPAL PARTICULARS POST RCOH

Equipment:

Aircraft:	Typical air group of up to 70 fixed wing aircraft and helicopters. 4 x C13-2 catapults. 4 x deck-edge aircraft elevators.
Weapons:	2 x octuple Mk 29 ESSM launchers with Mk 95 fire control. 2 x 21-cell Mk 49 RAM launchers. 2 x 20mm Phalanx CIWS. 3 x Mk 38 Mod 2 25mm RCWS.
Countermeasures:	Include SLQ-32A(V)4 ECM. Mk 137 Nulka decoy launchers. SLQ-25A Nixie torpedo countermeasures.
Principal Sensors:	SPS-49A 2D long-range air surveillance; SPS-48E 3D air surveillance; SPQ-9B surveillance and tracking. SPS-67 surface search. Various air control and navigation radars.
Combat System:	Surface Ship Self-Defense System Mk 2 Mod 1.

Notes:

1. Information is based on public sources, some of which are inconsistent.

USS *Abraham Lincoln* (2022)

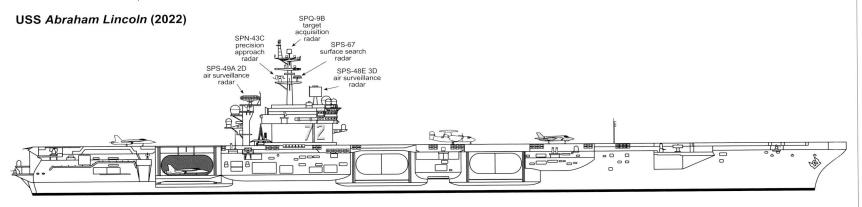

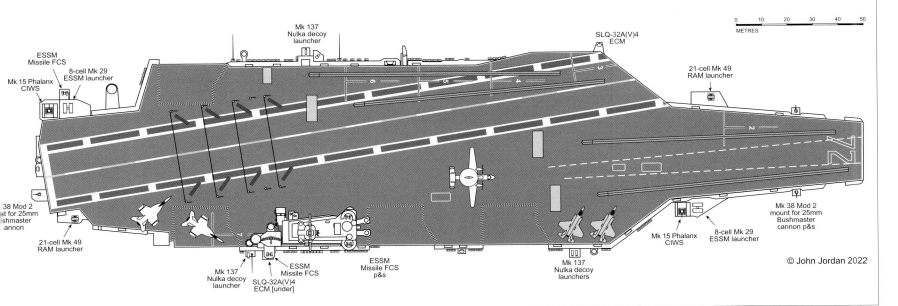

© John Jordan 2022

Carl Vinson (CVN-70) pictured transiting the Pacific Ocean in October 2018. She completed her RCOH back in 2009. Now entering her fifth decade of service, she shares the phenomenal lifespan achieved by the other early members of the *Nimitz* class. *(US Navy)*

With *Nimitz* having completed her RCOH between 1998 and 2001, the second half of her life is now drawing to a close. On current plans she will be retired from service in the course of FY2025; an event to be followed by disposal through recycling.

She is to be followed shortly thereafter by *Eisenhower*, with her final decommissioning being scheduled for FY2027 on the basis of current plans. The US Navy has been thinking about deferring one or both of these withdrawals in the light of delays in

bringing the following *Ford* class into operational service. It has previously been reported that *Nimitz* has the potential to last in service from 52 to as much as 55 years; an extension that would maintain her in the fleet until the end of the decade.

Whatever the outcome of these deliberations, it seems clear that the later members of the *Nimitz* class will be in service for a good number of years yet. At the present moment, *Stennis* is in the early phases of her midlife RCOH, with the remaining three carriers to follow thereafter. *Stennis* looks set to be the first ship of the class to be fitted with the single-faced AN/SPY-6(V)2 Enterprise Air Surveillance Radar (EASR) variant of the new SPY-6, continuing the process of evolution that has typified the class's history to date. Amongst numerous other changes, the class are also steadily being modified to sustain the F-35C Lightning II strike fighter during scheduled refits. *Carl Vinson* made the first operational deployment with the type in 2021, also embarking the new CMV-22B Osprey carrier on-board delivery variant at the same time.

On current plans, the two final members of the class will not be retired until the second half of the current century; nearly a hundred years after the design was first conceived. It is a notable achievement of the *Nimitz* design team, standing in marked contrast to the short shelf life of some of the S Navy's more recent ships.

These photographs show *Abraham Lincoln* (CVN-72) transiting the Philippine Sea in the course of training exercises with her sister-ship *Carl Vinson* (CVN-70) in January 2022. Having completed her RCOH in May 2017, *Lincoln* is arguably the most up-to-date *Nimitz* class carrier currently in service. However, with two other members of the class currently in overhaul and the final three ships yet to complete the process, the design's half-century of evolution is set to continue. On present plans, it will be well into the 2050s that the last *Nimitz* class carrier is finally retired. *(US Navy)*

Notes

1. Conversely, the coincidence of the British Polaris strategic deterrent programme with the need for new fleet carriers proved to be more than the defence budget could accommodate, resulting in the demise of the Royal Navy's CVA-01 project.

2. *Enterprise* was fitted with eight A2W reactors, the 'A' relating to the type of ship (aircraft carrier); the '2' to the generation of the plant (second) and the 'W' to the manufacturer (Westinghouse). *Nimitz* and her sisters are equipped with two A4W reactors. The intermediate A3W design was proposed for installation in *John F. Kennedy* (CVA-67) – using a configuration which would have had four nuclear reactors – but it was ultimately determined to complete her as a conventionally-powered ship.

3. The change in designation from attack to general-purpose aircraft carriers took place after CVN-68 and CVAN-69 had commenced construction, with *Nimitz* actually being delivered as CVAN-68. The third member of the class was laid down as CVN-70.

4. Preliminary Design was later called Feasibility Design. For nearly all US Navy warships, the end product closely resembled what emerged from Preliminary Design. The *Spruance* (DD-963) class was an important exception. The Preliminary Design looked much like other US Navy surface combatants of the time, with 'macks'. Once the feasibility of a gas-turbine destroyer had been demonstrated, Litton won a competition with the very different *Spruance* designed by Dr. Reuven Leopold (who was later the senior civilian in the US Navy ship design organisation). After that the *Perry* (FFG-7) and *Arleigh Burke* (DDG-51) classes were in-house designs, in the latter case a design by Litton being rejected.

5. The first ships associated with the new design organisation were the *Zumwalt* (DDG-1000) class and the Littoral Combat Ships of the *Freedom* (LCS-1) and *Independence* (LCS-2) classes. In neither case was there anyone in the naval organisation to show those who wanted the ship the consequences of desired characteristics, such as a degree of stealth and very high speed.

6. The 325ft (overall length) C-13-1 steam catapult had previously been used in *America* (CVA-66) and *John F. Kennedy* (CVA-67) but only one of their four catapults were of this longer design.

7. Despite its crudity, in 1966 this Basic Point Defense Missile System was credited with three to five times the effectiveness of the even less expensive guns. Initially

OSD opposed installing even this very limited defence on board carriers on the grounds that they already operated within a layered task force defence. It was desperate to limit spending as the cost of the Vietnam War escalated. The US Navy argued that carriers were the principal targets within every task force. Carriers already had air-to-air Sparrows on board, hence could readily maintain these missiles. Production deliveries began in October 1967, in time for *Nimitz*. By that time it was obvious that sometimes the fleet's layered air defence might not be effective. From the 1967 Middle East War onwards, the Soviets had deployed a substantial missile-armed fleet to the Mediterranean, and some of their ships might well be inside any fleet air defence envelope when they began to shoot.

8. The need for something like NATO Sea Sparrow, with a pulse-Doppler radar to spot low-flying attackers, was emphasised by a summer 1972 panic in the Pacific Fleet. Through the Vietnam War there had been periodic claims that the North Vietnamese were being given Styx missiles. It was also believed that they had coast defence missiles. Both justified considerable investment in countermeasures, but they were unlikely to affect carriers well offshore. About June 1972 there was a sudden scare that the North Vietnamese might soon receive means of deploying anti-ship missiles at greater ranges from the coast. The crisis may have been triggered when the cruiser *Sterrett* (DLG-31) reported, in April 1972, that she had shot down a Styx. At the time, US Naval Intelligence was able to assert confidently that no such missile had been involved, but surviving papers show that there was scepticism that the Office of Naval Intelligence could always be so sure. The depth of the panic is evident in reports that US Marines with Redeye anti-aircraft missiles were being stationed on the catwalks of carriers. It must have been obvious that the marines would endanger aircraft taking off. In addition to the decision to field a US version of NATO Sea Sparrow, the panic caused development of RAM, the fire-and-forget anti-missile weapon.

9. Kevlar was installed on board the ships between June 1983–September 1984 (CVN-68), October 1985–April 1987 (CVN-69), and in 1989 (CVN-70) during refit. SPS-49 replaced SPS-43A in CVN-68 and in CVN-70 in 1983, and in CVN-69 in 1986.

10. It has been reported that these arrangements reduced magazine capacity from 2,570 tons to c. 1,950 tons.

11. Another command system development deserves mention here: CEC. The CEC network distributes data of fire-control quality around the fleet. At least potentially it

enormously enhances the value of the semi-active Sea Sparrow missiles which defend carriers. Without CEC, the carrier cannot launch Sea Sparrows until its own radars detect an attacking enemy missile. At that point it can turn on a fire-control radar which illuminates the incoming attacker; the Sea Sparrow homes on reflected radiation. The ship's radar horizon is about 10 or 12 miles out. If the Sea Sparrow is fired as soon as an attacking missile pops over the horizon, it cannot hit until the attacker has come a lot closer. If it fails to destroy the attacker, little time is left for more shots. With CEC, the carrier will be able to fire as soon as some ship in the net detects the attacker. Current Sea Sparrows have autopilots which enable the carrier to fire them towards a threat without needing something on which to home at the outset. The system makes it possible to fire so that the Sea Sparrow is within interception distance as soon as the threat pops over the horizon (some Sea Sparrows now have active radars of their own). The first ship of the class to be fitted with CEC was *Eisenhower* (CVN-69), during 2000–02.

12. By the time the last two ships were being built, the advent of GPS-guided weapons had changed the logic of carrier operations. In the past, aircraft attacking a chosen target generally did so en masse, the idea being to saturate enemy defences. Carriers launched one or possibly two deck-load (Alfa) strikes each day, the aircraft carrying as much ordnance as possible. Tactics began to change late in the Vietnam War with the introduction of 'smart' guided weapons such as laser-guided bombs, but the real revolution came in the 1990s with the appearance of GPS-guided weapons. An aircraft could drop GPS bombs from well outside target defences, the range increasing if it flew higher. Laser guidance still required that several aircraft attack in sequence, because each could only drop a single bomb; debris thrown up from that bomb's explosion would disrupt the laser reflection further bombs would seek. With GPS, that was no longer true; one aircraft could make multiple hits. Alternatively, it could attack multiple targets in sequence. The criterion for effectiveness changed from the number of aircraft the ship could launch at one target to the number of separate sorties – separate targets – she could handle. That in turn made it important to be able to turn around aircraft as quickly as possible after they landed. The flight deck had to change. To see what was possible, late in 1997 *Nimitz* was tested to increase daily F/A-18 sorties from the usual 125-140 to more than 200. To do that, she embarked 20 more pilots and 100 additional maintenance personnel. This experiment was part of the run-up to the current *Ford,* one of whose key performance parameters was the number of strikes she could launch daily.

Author:
David Hobbs

4.1 TECHNOLOGICAL REVIEW

WORLD NAVAL AVIATION

A Review of Recent Developments

This year's review follows the format first adopted last year, focusing on national developments whilst noting the degree to which international co-operation has become a factor. The first carrier strike group deployment by the British Royal Navy's (RN's) *Queen Elizabeth* – which ended in December 2021 – is described in detail. Another area of focus relates to the US Navy and RN ambitions to introduce unmanned aircraft into carrier air wings by the 2030s, the objective being to increase mass and capability while decreasing operating costs.

UNITED KINGDOM – THE ROYAL NAVY

In November 2021 Admiral Sir Tony Radakin relinquished his appointment as First Sea Lord (1SL) to become Chief of the UK Defence Staff. He told an audience at the Royal United Services Institute (RUSI) that he requires the British armed forces to be more innovative and efficient in the immediate future. His successor as 1SL, Admiral Sir Ben Key, conferred with Admiral Mike Gilday,

US Chief of Naval Operations, on his first day in office to re-affirm the special relationship between the two navies and discuss areas for continued collaboration and co-operation. Key, a Fleet Air Arm observer, was formerly Chief of UK Joint Operations and commanded the aircraft carrier *Illustrious* in 2009. During their conversation he stressed the importance he places on the ability of *Queen Elizabeth* to operate both British and American F-35B jets, a capability he described as magnifying the importance of the two nations' trust in each other.

Admiral Key has spoken at length since becoming 1SL about the UK's return to a position based on global maritime interests with government recognition that navies are not just there to fight when necessary but are also primary instruments of national influence and reach, with aircraft carriers at their heart. He affirmed that *Queen Elizabeth*'s Carrier Strike Group 21 (CSG 21) deployment had shown 'levels of interoperability

and interchangeability that make us far greater than the sum of our parts'. Talking of the immediate future he said that the RN is developing plans to 'blend crewed and un-crewed systems, operating both F-35Bs and drones from the same flight deck … a future where the Royal Marines' Commandos will operate from multi-role support ships'. During a visit to the construction hall at Rosyth where the first Type 31 frigate is being built, Key spoke about how he wants to move from traditional means to untraditional, new and innovative methods of achieving the effects the RN wants. He expressed his belief that this is a once-in-a-generation moment in which a bolder transition to new and more lethal systems is the answer, 'not more people or more cash', and called on industry to play its part. Recognition of the Navy's importance was also given by the British House of Commons Defence Select Committee which stated in its Third Report of the 2021/2022 Session that the United Kingdom urgently needs a larger navy, identifying Russia and China as the main potential adversaries in the maritime domain.[1]

Ben Wallace, the British Secretary of State for Defence, has spoken of the importance that the United Kingdom places on a web of alliances that bring like-minded allies together at the time and place of their choosing, sharing data and flying from each other's ships. In the Atlantic and Mediterranean theatres, NATO is the largest and most formalised alliance but in the Pacific RN operations will be rooted in a range of smaller alliances such as the new AUKUS, the Five-Power Defence Agreement (FPDA), between the UK, Australia, New Zealand, Singapore and Malaysia, and individual agreements with Japan, India and others. The ability of RN and US Navy units to operate seamlessly together should, therefore, be seen as the 'glue' that helps build more profound relationships.

On 1 October 2021, the RN announced that *Prince of Wales* had been declared fully operational after conclusion of the Joint Warrior/Dynamic Mariner exercises. She had previously commenced F-35B Lightning II flying trials in June, having already been cleared to operate a range of RN, Army and Royal Air Force (RAF) helicopters. On 11 January 2022 she became flagship of the NATO Maritime High-Readiness Force and Rear Admiral Mike Utley, Commander UK Strike Force, became commander of the group, CTG, for a 12-month period starting in March with Exercise Cold

An F-35B Jet from the US Marine Corps' VMFA-211 lands back *on Queen Elizabeth* whilst she conducts a double replenishment with the fleet tanker *Tidespring* and Dutch frigate *Evertsen* in July 2021 in the course of the CSG 21 deployment, which is described in detail in this chapter. The US Navy destroyer *The Sullivans* (DDG-68) can be seen on the far horizon whilst a mixture of USMC and British 617 Squadron F-35Bs, in addition to anti-submarine and airborne early warning Merlin helicopters, are arrayed on the aircraft carrier's flight deck. The demonstrated ability of *Queen Elizabeth* to operate both British and American F-35B jets is viewed as an important element in developing the special relationship that exists between the Royal Navy and its US counterpart. Moreover, the intention that both navies have to introduce unmanned elements into their carrier air wings holds out the prospects of increasing capability whilst reducing costs. *(Crown Copyright 2021)*

Prince of Wales commenced F-35B flying trials in June 2021 and was subsequently declared fully operational at the conclusion of the Joint Warrior/Dynamic Mariner exercises. This picture shows an F-35B from 617 Squadron being manoeuvred in her spacious hangar in September 2021. *(Crown Copyright 2021)*

Queen Elizabeth pictured sailing up Loch Long to berth at the Glen Mallan ammunitioning facility in March 2022. The jetty plays an important logistical support role handling the large quantities of munitions that can be embarked aboard the Royal Navy's two carriers, completing a £67m (c. US$85m) upgrade in 2021. *(Crown Copyright 2022)*

Response in Northern Norway. This was the first time a *Queen Elizabeth* class carrier had operated in the Arctic, where it led a task force of twenty-five ships from eleven nations. Meanwhile, after returning from CSG 21 *Queen Elizabeth* underwent a period of maintenance in Portsmouth before sailing in March 2022 to take on ammunition at Glen Mallan in Loch Long. During 2022 she is scheduled to participate in a series of exercises and sea training evolutions to maintain operational readiness.

In answer to a Parliamentary question in July 2021 Jeremy Quinn, Minister of State at the Ministry of Defence stated that twenty-one F-35Bs had been delivered to the British Joint RN/RAF Force that operates them with a further twenty-seven aircraft in various stages of production and delivery. Of the twenty-one, three were serving with 17 Squadron based permanently at Edwards Air Force Base in the USA and eight with the training unit, 207 Squadron at RAF Marham. A further eight were with 617 Squadron embarked in *Queen Elizabeth* at the time and two were with the maintenance and finishing facility at Marham. A statement in November 2021 confirmed that three further F-35Bs had been delivered in October with a further six scheduled for 2022 and eight in 2023. There has been no mention of 809 Naval Air Squadron beginning to form up with F-35Bs as yet. When asked in April 2022, a Royal Navy Command spokesperson replied that the date of the unit's commissioning as a Lightning II squadron was 'currently under review'.

Whilst the F-35B undoubtedly forms a major part of future Royal Navy aviation, unmanned systems will also play increasingly important roles. Two innovative naval aviation projects stand out. Designated Vampire and Vixen, they recall aircraft with significant places in Fleet Air Arm history. A de Havilland Sea Vampire was the world's first jet aircraft to land on a carrier in 1945. The de Havilland Sea Vixen was the first Fleet Air Arm fighter to have an all-missile armament designed to form part of a comprehensive fleet weapons system, serving for over a decade from 1959. Both projects are managed by the Develop Directorate within Royal Navy Command. A Navy Command source has explained that in the short term the aims of both projects are to demonstrate the potential operational utility and value for money to be gained by developing unmanned air systems (UAS) by 2025. More specifically Vampire involves evaluating the potential for small, relatively inexpensive, high performance fixed-wing UAS to give the RN choices on how best to invest in such systems. Vixen is to explore, with allied and industry partners, the potential development of a carrier-capable, medium-sized UAS able to deliver persistent wide-area surveillance from 2030.

Both projects have longer-term aims. The Navy Command source described Vampire as delivering a strike fighter emulator capable of conducting realistic training whilst at sea and deployed. On a wartime basis it would be expected to deliver a variety of operational effects. Meanwhile, Vixen is to deliver long-range intelligence, surveillance and reconnaissance (ISR) capability to provide force protection for a carrier strike group, including airborne early warning (AEW) missions. Whilst flying an AEW barrier, a UAS could also act as an important data node for a widely dispersed task force and, with spiral development, could be adapted for other roles to give the carrier air wing greater mass at a much-reduced cost per flying hour. UAS only need to fly when operationally necessary, they have no need to maintain aircrew currency and do not need to be disembarked when the carrier is in harbour. In mid-2022 the RN had not decided which air vehicle will fulfil the Vixen requirement. At this stage, the air vehicle itself is less important than the technology involved with enabling the right

level of autonomy and the selection of sensor payloads, in particular their size, weight and power (SWAP) requirements. Other factors requiring resolution are the systems required for maritime operations, including carrier launch and recovery and how they dovetail with the wider combat enterprise, much of which is likely to blend with other defence programmes. Vixen also has to be coherent with the prototype UAV being produced for the RAF's Project Mosquito 'loyal wingman' UAS but the core element of Vixen is its digital connectivity requirement which must be a common system able to dock with the Naval Strike Network. The air vehicle itself, therefore, is unlikely to be the same as Mosquito, although the systems, sensors, payloads and digital architecture are likely to be shared. Asked if Vixen was the reason why catapult and arrester wire applications are being investigated, the Navy Command source replied that it was one of the reasons, adding that 'fitting assisted launch and recovery equipment would give greater flexibility for future initiatives and open up the deck to a wider range of capabilities, including those fielded by our allies'. The Ministry of Defence's 2021 request to industry for information about catapult and arrester wire options stipulated a maximum launch weight of 55,000lbs and arrested landing for aircraft weighing between 11,000lbs and 47,000lbs. Putting these numbers into context, they would allow the launch of a French Navy Rafale fighter at its maximum take-off

weight of 54,000lbs and also its recovery with unused weapons.

The first step towards Vampire was taken in September 2021 when QinetiQ Jet 80+ Banshee UAVs were flown off *Prince of Wales* using a launcher fitted on the flight deck. Although they were recovered ashore by parachute, the demonstration confirmed that the launcher and UAV support equipment can be effectively integrated with other activities on a carrier flight deck. In January 2022 the Ministry of Defence issued an invitation to tender for a suitable air vehicle to meet Phase 1 of Project Vampire, which required six air vehicles painted in RN markings to be delivered between 2023 and 2025 and with an option to purchase up to ten more. It also stipulated one launcher with an option for two more; a ground control station complete with aerials and an option for two more; and operator training and the training of maintenance personnel for first-line servicing. In March 2022 it was announced that a Phase 1 contract – worth £6.7m (c. US$8.5m) – had been awarded to QinetiQ, with the Banshee as the chosen UAV. The first aircraft is to be delivered by October 2023.

The Banshee is powered by two small gas turbine engines that give a maximum speed of 400 knots and it is derived from a series of aerial target designs used since 2010 to test new missile systems. It is capable of operating at up to 25,000ft and has a 220lb payload capacity. This would enable it to be

Two images of QinetiQ Jet 80+ Banshee UAVs during trials from *Prince of Wales* in September 2021. The jet-powered Banshee, which looks like a mini fighter aircraft, can soar to 25,000ft, skim just above the waves, and flies at speeds up to 400 knots. Its initial role will be to simulate attacking missiles and jet aircraft as part of sea training. *(Crown Copyright 2021)*

The US Navy nuclear-powered aircraft carrier *Harry S. Truman* (CVN-75) seen in company with her French counterpart *Charles de Gaulle* in March 2022. A British naval aviator achieved a first when he assisted the cross deck deployment of US Navy aircraft to the French carrier whilst serving as Landing Signal Officer (LSO). *(US Navy)*

fitted with an EO/IR camera or, possibly, a small active phased-array type radar. Banshee is likely to replace some of the threat simulation and aggressor tasks previously carried out by the Hawks of 736 Naval Air Squadron. Commander Rob Taylor RN, Head of RN Air Test and Evaluation, has described it as the first step towards operating UAVs from the *Queen Elizabeth* class carriers. He added that in the short term it can 'replicate a range of threats at low cost and provide a test bed for future payloads'.[2]

On a smaller scale, the AeroVironment RQ-20A Puma UAV continues to be used by 700X Naval Air Squadron with flights capable of embarkation in virtually any RN warship. Another element of 700X trains new operators for the operational flights and teaches a broad range of UK military personnel how to operate quadcopters. It is also tasked with research and the evaluation of the wide range of remotely piloted systems being developed within industry. The RQ-20A was first used by the US Marine Corps in 2008 and achieved IOC with the RN in 2020. It weighs 14lbs, has a wingspan of 9.2ft and is launched by hand. Recovery is achieved by super-stalling the aircraft onto a typical helicopter flight deck. Consequently, virtually any RN or Royal Fleet Auxiliary ship can embark and operate the type. 700X Naval Air Squadron has three flights designated Phantom A, B and C and their primary mission is ISR using a Mantis i45 gimballed EO/IR and low-light camera with a x 50 zoom capability. Images can be data-linked by live-stream video back to the parent ship at ranges of up to 11 nautical miles. Each flight has a single Puma, a detachment commander, maintenance technician and aircraft handler and all three are trained to operate the UAV, controlling it using a keyboard and roller-ball. A Puma can search an area of 270 square miles in a single sortie. It has a maximum speed of 45 knots and can cruise at 26 knots for up to 2.5 hours. Later versions can extend this to 3.5 hours and one of the flight commanders, Lieutenant Ash Loftus RN, recently told media that the Puma 'may look simple but it is a rugged and sophisticated piece of kit and that means that it can be deployed from the stern of any ship with the minimum of effort'.[3]

The withdrawal of most of Britain's Hawk T 1 jet training aircraft as part of the Integrated Review has led to the decommissioning of 736 Naval Air Squadron, which – inter alia – previously performed an important role simulating hostile aircraft in fleet training exercises. *(Crown Copyright 2017)*

The RN continued to embed pilots within the US Navy during 2022 to fly F/A-18E/F Super Hornets with front-line squadrons as part of a specialist skills programme begun in 2010. One of these, Lieutenant Rory Cheyne RN, was serving as a squadron Landing Signal Officer (LSO) embarked in *Harry S. Truman* (CVN-75) for NATO Exercise Neptune Strike in the Mediterranean during February 2022. When *Truman* cross-decked aircraft with the French carrier *Charles de Gaulle*, Cheyne was selected to oversee the evolution. During the subsequent Super Hornet landings he became the first British pilot to carry out LSO duties on a French carrier recovering American aircraft, an example of close allied co-operation. NATO Exercise Dynamic Manta in the waters around Sicily during early 2022 was another example of this collaboration. A single Merlin HM 2 of 814 NAS was joined by two Poseidon MRA 1 maritime patrol aircraft of 120 Squadron RAF, the offshore patrol vessel *Trent* and a number of ships and aircraft from other nations. The Merlin was deployed to Maristaeli Air Base near Catania. The exercise was considered to give invaluable experience of realistic tactical scenarios to newly qualified aircrew in an unfamiliar environment. It also helped to produce a cadre of anti-submarine specialists within the alliance who are used to working closely with each other.

Meanwhile, it was announced in the Integrated Defence Review last year that the BAE Systems Hawk T 1 would be withdrawn from service at the end of March 2022.[4] As a result, 736 Naval Air Squadron has been disbanded. Based at Royal Naval Air Station (RNAS) Culdrose, it had flown Hawks on a variety of fleet requirements and other second-line tasks since 2013 and the aircraft had been used before that by the un-numbered Fleet Requirements and Aircraft Direction Training Unit. 736 NAS also acted as a fast-jet 'pool' for pilots waiting to move on to F-35B training; helped to train airborne surveillance and control specialist observers, fighter controllers and air traffic controllers besides providing targets for radar and systems development work. Much of the Hawks' tasking is likely to be taken over by virtual systems but the emulation of hostile fast jets by Banshees may have a part to play in due course.

The Royal Marines have begun their transition towards the Future Commando Force structure, which is intended to reach IOC in 2023. It is based

A Merlin HC 4 helicopter pictured at Royal Naval Air Station Yeovilton in May 2021. All twenty-five Merlin helicopters within the Command Helicopter Force have now been modified to HC 4 standard and will form an important part of the Littoral Response Group concept. *(Crown Copyright 2021)*

on a new integrated operating concept that requires commando forces to be forward-deployed and be ready both to operate and fight at very short notice. In the new littoral strike concept commando forces, including elements of the Commando Helicopter Force (CHF) and specialised ships, are to offer asymmetric advantage that supports theatre access effort in both 'operate' and 'fight' domains. 'Operate' reflects a change in UK defence policy in so far as it relates to units optimised to compete in the ambiguous grey space of hybrid warfare below the threshold of all-out warfare. 'Fight' requires peer adversaries to be countered above that threshold, delivering multi-domain, hybrid warfare integrated with other allied forces. The Royal Marine Commando force is to deliver two permanent Littoral Response Groups (LRGs), one routinely east of Suez and one west. Each is to comprise ships, aircraft and landing craft with an integrated commando task force headquarters, information warfare team, commando strike teams, fires team,

surface and aviation manoeuvre elements, a logistic team and a medical team fused with partners from other government departments. All twenty-five Merlin helicopters within the CHF have now been modified to HC 4 standard and are operated by 845 and 846 NAS. Detachments will be allocated to the LRGs when required for operations or exercises and – from 2023 – it is possible that unmanned quad-copter drones will be used for ammunition and other logistical activities. RQ-20A Puma drones of 700X NAS are already being used on a regular basis on ISR missions during amphibious exercises.

Both LRGs are expected to be able to operate routinely in high threat land but only medium-to-low threat maritime or air environments. To meet the latter two, the basic LRGs are to be scalable with additional force provided, when necessary, with additional strike companies and maritime effects up to and including a British carrier strike group to produce a UK expeditionary force capable of operating anywhere in the world for extended periods.

They are to be equally capable of operating alongside a NATO force package or a US Marine Corps (USMC) Expeditionary Force if necessary. Capability enhancements include the full force of Merlin HC 4s and Wildcat AH 1s in the CHF and an interesting array of potential drones. Lightweight vehicles capable of being carried inside Merlin HC 4s are to allow movement over significant ranges at speed with minimal signature. New communications and secure data links are to enable widely dispersed operations by small groups, exploiting the abilities of fast jets, naval gunfire and commando artillery batteries to engage an enemy force. The Royal Marines' new LRG structure was evaluated in late 2021 during Exercise Green Dagger at the US Marine Corps' Twentynine Palms range in the Mojave Desert, Southern California. The exercise area comprised 2,000 square miles of desert and mountain terrain and, at first, the USMC 'enemy' controlled 80 percent of it. Lieutenant Colonel

Andy Dow RM who commanded the British force said that the LRG's focus had been on 'integrating the new LRG capabilities … to deliver disproportionate effect in the face of a free-thinking peer adversary'. The LRG dominated the battle space and 'enemy' operations were halted by a long-range commando assault into key areas supported by air attacks. The exercise ended with the British LRG in control of over 65 percent of the exercise area.

CARRIER STRIKE GROUP 2021 DEPLOYMENT

The RN Carrier Strike Group 2021 Deployment, CSG 21, carried out between May and December 2021 and centred on the aircraft carrier *Queen Elizabeth,* proved to be a significant success, interacting with forty-four different countries. The flagship visited twenty-four different ports and the CSG participated in eighteen named exercises in addition to a number of smaller passage exercises. The avia-

tion assets that deployed with the group included eight F-35B Lightning IIs of 617 Squadron (jointly manned and operated by the RAF and RN), ten US Marine Corps F-35Bs of Marine Fighter Attack Squadron 211 (VMFA-211), seven Merlin HM 2s of 820 Naval Air Squadron (three of which were fitted with the Crowsnest airborne surveillance and control system), three Merlin HC 4s of 845 Naval Air Squadron and four Wildcat HMA 2s of 815 Naval Air Squadron.

The embarkation of USMC fighters was, in itself, a major achievement. It was the first time American fighters had deployed operationally aboard a British carrier since 1943, when US Navy Grumman F4F-4 Wildcats embarked in *Victorious* while she was lent to the US Pacific Fleet. The two F-35B squadrons worked interchangeably within a bi-national agreement that allowed the free exchange of data to achieve a common flying programme and joint rules of engagement. No other navies have demonstrated this level of co-operation and both are determined to see it continue. At the end of the deployment, the Ministry of Defence revealed that CSG 21 aircraft

Queen Elizabeth departs Portsmouth Harbour at the start of the CSG 21 deployment in May 2021. Involving interaction with some forty-four countries, the half-year long mission has been seen as a significant success. *(Crown Copyright 2021)*

had flown for 4,723 hours during the deployment with 1,290 of those at night. The F-35Bs flew 1,278 sorties totalling 2,200 hours and conducted 44 combat missions in June 2021 to support UK Operation 'Shader' and US Operation 'Inherent Resolve', counter-ISIS strikes against targets in Iraq and Syria. The strikes were the first from a British aircraft carrier in a decade, demonstrating 'the speed and agility with which a UK-led CSG can inject 5th generation combat power into any operation, anywhere in the world'. The USMC Senior National Representative to the CSG, Colonel Simon Doran USMC, said that the strikes by Marine F-35Bs from *Queen Elizabeth* had 'demonstrated how effectively interoperable our combined naval forces are'.

The re-creation of a British CSG took a quarter of a century from vision statement to the declaration of IOC. Having done so – and assembled the hardware and the dedicated teams needed to operate it – the RN is back in the business of providing a global conventional deterrent force on an enduring basis, although it needs to have larger air wings embarked to achieve maximum effect. It sent the message that the United Kingdom can and will escalate its growing forward-deployed presence with a powerful, conventional strike group to maintain the rule of law at sea. The ability of *Queen Elizabeth* to deploy as part of the 'Global Britain' initiative with embedded allied units, working with other like-minded nations throughout the deployment has emphasised the RN's willingness to enhance relationships across the world. At a strategic level, the deployment demonstrated a welcome return to British policies based on seapower and a recognition of the intimate relationship between the maritime trade upon which the UK depends and the co-operation with other navies that is needed to protect it.

The RN also demonstrated the ability to sustain a major global deployment logistically, a capability few other navies possess. Continuous support was provided by RFA shipping, with underway replenishment undertaken to keep the ships at sea for prolonged periods. They made their own port visits to collect fuel, stores and replacement parts when necessary. The CSG was also able to draw on British facilities around the world at sites including Gibraltar, Oman and Singapore in various ways and at different times. A planned overseas support package for the ships and their combat management systems together with both nations' embarked F-35B aircraft was provided by BAE Systems which –

together with its partners and equipment manufacturers – deployed over 100 engineers and technicians across the world and on board some of the ships to deliver support. In September a team that included RN technicians helped to carry out a self-maintenance period in *Queen Elizabeth* during her visit to the US naval base at Guam, during which scheduled maintenance was carried out on the ship's engines and aircraft lifts. The RAF's transport aircraft carried spare parts, personnel and mail wherever they were needed. A machinery defect suffered in the Mediterranean by the destroyer *Diamond* drew adverse publicity. However, even here there were positives, since she was repaired by a team of thirty BAE Systems personnel that joined the ship in the Mediterranean at short notice so that she didn't have to return to the United Kingdom. The RN's carefully orchestrated global supply chain was a model of its kind that supported the CSG almost without a hitch.

The CSG was not just an exercise in naval deployment; it operated extensively with allied air forces and the presence of the carrier task group encouraged joint exercises, including with British Army units in the Far East and Oman. The presence of a powerful British force unlocked renewed interest in mutual defence collaboration with a number of

friendly nations. The challenge now is to ensure that similar CSG deployments maintain the momentum, drawing in the potential of the Royal Marines' LRGs to demonstrate forward-deployed capability in three dimensions. From an American perspective, the new interoperability was typified in August 2021 when aircraft of Carrier Air Wing 2 (CVW-2) embarked in *Carl Vinson* (CVN-70), flew in exercises with *Queen Elizabeth*'s aircraft in the Philippine Sea. Captain Tommy Locke US Navy, Commander of CVW-2 said that 'in a very short amount of time we were able to seamlessly combine the collective 5th generation capabilities of joint strike fighter aircraft from two services [US Navy and USMC] and a partner nation together with the rest of the advanced capabilities of our entire air wing'. Speaking at the end of the deployment, Major General Bradford Gering USMC, Commanding General Third Marine Aircraft Wing, added that CSG 21 had been a premier opportunity for Marines to train alongside allies and garner valuable lessons from operating in a combined environment across multiple theatres of operation. VMFA-211 had been the first Marine F-35B squadron to deploy as a ten-strong jet unit, the number outlined last year in the USMC Commandant's planning guidance. Other squadrons are to follow its example.

VMFA-211and 617 Squadron F-35B Lightning II strike fighters operating from the deck of *Queen Elizabeth* in June 2021 during the course of CSG 21. The carrier was participating in strikes against ISIS targets in the Middle East at the time. The embarkation of USMC fighters was, in itself, a major achievement, representing the first time American aircraft had deployed aboard a British aircraft carrier since 1943. *(US Navy)*

Japan's 'helicopter carrying destroyer' *Kaga* (DDH-184) and the US carrier *Carl Vinson* (CVN-70) operating with *Queen Elizabeth* in the Bay of Bengal as part of Maritime Partnership Exercise (MPX) in October 2021. CSG 21 provided an excellent opportunity for the Royal Navy to demonstrate its interoperability, not only with the United States but also with other global partners. *(US Navy)*

The aircraft carrier *Gerald R. Ford* (CVN-78) successfully completes the third and final scheduled explosive event of Full Ship Shock Trials in the Atlantic Ocean on 8 August 2021. Reports suggest the ship stood up to the tests – the first carried out on a US Navy carrier since 1987 – better than had been expected. *(US Navy)*

The F-35 Joint Programme Office, JPO, in Washington subsequently evaluated both the *Vinson* and *Queen Elizabeth* deployments to see how F-35s had performed in the largest deployments to date. The Programme Executive Officer, Air Force General Eric Fick, told the US Naval Institute that both afloat spares packages and pre-deployed spares packages were being examined closely to see if the planners had got them right. Both involved large sets of boxes and the Joint Program Office (JPO) wanted to ensure that their dispositions had given the most effective results. Fick was fully briefed on both deployments and had a team working on known F-35 corrosion issues. The JPO found that that the F-35Bs on board *Queen Elizabeth* experienced much less corrosion than had been anticipated but that the F-35Cs in *Vinson* had a surprising number of corrosion issues. Apparently some F-35C seals had not functioned as planned in the sea environment.[5]

CSG 21 ended on 9 December 2021 and was greeted by a message from Her Majesty Queen Elizabeth, who sent her best wishes to the personnel from all over the Commonwealth and the United States who had served in *Queen Elizabeth* and took note of the important work that they had carried out. A single incident had marred the deployment when, on 17 November, an F-35B of 617 Squadron, ZM 152, crashed on take-off in the Eastern Mediterranean and sank in water with an average depth of 1,500m. The US16E ejection seat worked perfectly to save the pilot, with three air bags inflating in a two-stage process to protect the pilot's head and neck from the effect of the heavy helmet filled with image-projecting technology. Apparently the F-35B software incorporates a feature that ejects the pilot automatically if it detects that the lift fan has failed as its loss on leaving the ski-jump would cause the aircraft to pitch nose-down faster that the pilot could react to pull the handle to eject manually. The seat would, therefore, leave the aircraft while it was still sufficiently close enough to the horizontal to ensure safe ejection.

Although the exact point where the aircraft hit the water was known, it might have glided for a considerable distance before arriving at the seabed and there were concerns that Russia might try to salvage the wreck. The British Ministry of Defence's Salvage and Marine Operations team immediately asked for US Navy assistance as it had no assets nearby. This was to prove yet another instance of allied co-operation. The wreck was located and recovered by a

NATO team that included the United Kingdom, the United States and Italy, whilst a Spanish salvage company under contract to the US Navy from Rota is understood to have brought the wreck to the surface by the end of December. It was returned to the United Kingdom for inspection by the British Defence Accident Investigation Branch. A F-35C has also been recovered after going over the side of *Vinson* during a deck landing incident. Speaking of the two incidents, General Fick said that he had not been made aware of any need for fleet-wide notifications as a result of the mishaps.

UNITED STATES NAVY

In February 2022 Huntington Ingalls Industries' Newport News shipyard had more carriers alongside than at any time in the previous three decades. According to a briefing provided to USNI News, these comprised:

- *Enterprise* (CVN-65): In storage prior to final disposal.
- *George Washington* (CVN-73): Undergoing mid-life refuelling and complex overhaul (RCOH).
- *John C. Stennis* (CVN-74): Undergoing RCOH.
- *Gerald R. Ford* (CVN-78): Completing maintenance following 2021 shock trials.
- *John F. Kennedy* (CVN-79): Towards the final stages of construction.

- *Enterprise* (CVN-80): In the early stages of construction.

Ford had achieved IOC in December 2021 and is due to begin its first operational deployment in the autumn of 2022. Rear Admiral James Downey USN, the program executive officer for aircraft carriers, briefed USNI that *Washington* is due to complete its RCOH by 2023, incorporating upgrades that will allow her to operate the F-35C. *Stennis* is expected to complete her RCOH in 2025. Meanwhile, *Kennedy* is due to be delivered in 2024 and *Enterprise* (CVN-80) was said to be about 12 percent complete ahead of her planned delivery in 2028. Newport News is also in the early stages of fabricating *Doris Miller* (CVN-81), for which first steel was cut on 25 August 2021. She is due to be delivered in 2032.

The *Ford* shock trials – encompassing three separate detonations moving progressively closer to the ship between June and August 2021 – were the first to have involved a carrier since *Theodore Roosevelt* (CVN-71) in 1987. The detonation of 40,000lbs of explosive in the water near the hull to test the ship and its systems were carried out without causing any major flooding, fires or injuries. After detailed assessment, the ship required only 20 percent of the work *Roosevelt* had needed to rectify damage and the ship's company had carried out over four-fifths of the work.

In December 2021, *Ford*'s eleventh and last advanced weapons elevator was accepted. The technology behind the design had proved reliable in commercial applications but the need to work within the exact tolerances of interlocks, doors and shafts within a ship's hull that is constantly flexing, albeit by only small amounts, whilst at sea proved extremely difficult to achieve. The advanced weapons elevators are one of a number of systems – also including electromagnetic catapults and advanced arrester gear – that are intended to increase the carrier's sortie generation rate. In mid-2022 *Ford* and her air wing are to carry out a series of exercises that will bring her up to full operational capability prior to a maiden deployment later in the year. This is some four years after her originally intended debut in 2018.[6]

In February 2022 *Carl Vinson* returned to San Diego after a six-month operational deployment to the West Pacific which involved F-35C strike fighters and CMV-22B carrier-on-board delivery (COD) aircraft forming part of an air wing for the first time. The deployment allowed the ship's company and CVW-2 to get used to the new types as well as working up to a high tempo of exercises with both regional and global allies and partners. *Vinson*'s commanding officer, Captain P Scott Miller USN, briefed the press after her return that she had operated with *Queen Elizabeth* and ships of the Japan Maritime Self-Defense Force (JMSDF), as

A F-35C Lightning II, assigned to the 'Argonauts' of Strike Fighter Squadron 147 (VFA-147) and a CMV-22B Osprey, assigned to the 'Titans' of Fleet Logistics Multi-Mission Squadron 30 (VRM-30) pictured operating from *Carl Vinson* (CVN-70). The carrier's six-month deployment between August 2021 and February 2022 was the first time the two new aircraft types had formed part of a deployed carrier air wing. *(US Navy)*

well as with US Navy big-deck amphibious warships and their embarked F-35Bs. Miller said that his ship's operations with the Seventh Fleet in the Western Pacific had represented a pivotal change in how and where US carriers operate, explaining that, since he was a young Lieutenant, carriers had largely carried out close air support missions in the Middle East with complete air supremacy. Now they must counter a near peer competitor who is active in the air, on and under the sea surface and on land with the result that 'you have to shape the air wing … to best handle that activity'.

Vinson's 70 aircraft flew 15,000 hours with approximately 7,700 catapult launches and arrested

recoveries during her deployment. She had embarked two extra EA-18G Growler electronic attack aircraft, making a total of seven, and they operated so well in the region that the air wing wants to increase that number still further. Apparently Growlers proved particularly effective when operating with the F-35Cs, complementing each other in a region where the collection of electronic data has critical importance. CVW-2 also included an extra E-2D Advanced Hawkeye to make a total of five and Miller said that he felt this number was necessary to get the maximum value from the F-35C. The CMV-22B had performed well and its ability to land vertically by day or night on other ships as well as the

carrier had given much greater flexibility than the C-2 Greyhound COD aircraft that it replaced which had to be catapulted and arrested. The US Navy gave up requiring C-2 pilots to qualify for night deck landing some years ago and so the ability to recover CMV-22Bs at night gave more opportunities to receive deliveries without having to close up a large part of the flight deck team. The structure adopted by CVW-2 is widely seen as representing the US Navy air wing of the immediate future.[7]

The F-35C that crashed on the deck of *Vinson* was lost over the edge of the flight deck after a landing mishap on 24 January 2022. There was no damage to the deck but seven sailors, including the pilot who ejected and was recovered from the water by helicopter, were injured. The aircraft sank in 12,400ft of water 170 miles west of the Philippine island of Luzon according to a notice to mariners issued by the Japanese Coast Guard. The US Navy subsequently announced on 3 March 2022 that it had been successfully recovered by the diving support vessel *Picasso* using a CURV-21 remotely-operated vehicle which attached specialised rigging and lift lines to it. The ship's crane hook was then lowered to the seafloor, connected to the rigging before hoisting it to the surface and inboard. The cause of the accident is still under investigation.

In January 2022 *Abraham Lincoln* (CVN-72) sailed from San Diego for a deployment to the Western Pacific with CVW-9 embarked. The air wing included the first USMC squadron to embark with F-35C Lightning II strike fighters, VMFA-314 the 'Black Knights'. The deployment marked another first with Captain Amy Bauernschmidt USN being the first woman to command a nuclear-powered aircraft carrier. Meanwhile, an earlier carrier deployment – by *Ronald Reagan* (CVN-76) – led to some controversy within the House Armed Services Committee (HASC). Representative Elaine Luria, a former US Navy surface warfare officer and current vice chairman of HASC, described the move of the carrier from its forward base in Japan to cover the withdrawal from Afghanistan as a major strategic error. She argued that while China is the Defence Department's top priority, planning and budget appropriations do not show this to be the case and the US Navy needs to have more forward-basing arrangements to improve familiarity with operations in the Pacific.

There are still members of the HASC who criticise the high cost of nuclear-powered aircraft carriers

Table 4.1.1: US NAVY PLANNED AIRCRAFT PROCUREMENT: FY2022–FY2027

TYPE	MISSION	FY2022 Authorised[1]	FY2023 Requested	FY2024 Planned	FY2025 Planned	FY2026 Planned	FY2027 Planned	FYDP[2] Planned
Fixed Wing (Carrier Based)								
F-35B Lightning II JSF	Strike Fighter (STOVL)	17 (17)	15	16	16	16	17	80
F-35C Lightning II JSF	Strike Fighter (CV)	20 (20)	13	19	19	19	18	88
FA-18E/F Super Hornet	Strike Fighter (CV)	12 (0)	0	0	0	0	0	0
E-2D Advanced Hawkeye	Surveillance/Control	5 (5)	5	0	0	0	0	5
Fixed Wing (Land Based)								
KC-130J Hercules	Tanker	6 (6)	5	2	0	0	0	7
T-45 Replacement[3]	Training	0 (0)	0	0	7	12	12	31
T-44 Replacement[4]	Training	0 (0)	10	24	24	0	0	58
Rotary Wing								
CH-53K King Stallion	Heavy-Lift	11 (9)	10	15	21	21	21	88
C/MV-22/B Osprey	Transport	12 (8)	0	0	0	0	0	0
TH-73A[5]	Training	36 (36)	26	0	0	0	0	26
Unmanned Aerial Vehicles								
MQ-25 Stingray	Refuelling	0 (0)	4	4	4	4	4	20
MQ-4C Triton	Maritime Patrol	2 (0)	3	4	0	0	0	7
MQ-9A Reaper	Surveillance/Strike	8 (6)	5	5	0	0	0	10
Totals:		129 (107)	96	89	91	72	72	420

Notes:
1. FY2022 authorised numbers reflect numbers actually funded in the Consolidated Appropriations Act signed into law on 15 March 2022; figures in brackets reflect aircraft numbers set out in the Biden Administration's Presidential Budget Request of 28 May 2021. As is frequently the case, the US Congress added material numbers of aircraft over the original request.
2. FYDP (Future Years Defense Program) for 2021–5 as at time of the FY2023 Presidential Budget Request. No FYDP figures were presented for FY2022.
3. Refers to replacement of the T-45 Goshawk training aircraft. Unlike the current aircraft, the replacement will reportedly only be required to perform touch-and-go landings on the US Navy's aircraft carriers.
4. Refers to replacement of the T-44 Pegasus (Beechcraft King Air series) twin-engine turboprop trainer.
5. Refers to the Leonardo AW119 variant selected to replace the TH-57 Sea Ranger (Bell 206 series) training helicopter.

The US Navy's FY2023 aviation procurement plan includes commencement of production orders for the MQ-25 Stingray refuelling UAV. Meanwhile, during a test flight on 4 June 2021, Boeing's MQ-25 Stingray T1 prototype successfully extended the hose and drogue from its US Navy-issued aerial refuelling store and safely transferred jet fuel to a US Navy F/A-18 Super Hornet, becoming the first unmanned air vehicle to fuel another aircraft. *(Boeing)*

and urge a return to smaller, conventionally-powered hulls. This argument is still a long way from resolution.[8] In the meantime, Jay Stefany – who was performing the duties of Assistant Secretary of the Navy for Research, Development and Acquisition – briefed the press in April 2022 that one short-term option to enlarge the carrier force that might be considered is an extension to the service lives of the early *Nimitz* class carriers. At present *Nimitz* (CVN-68) is scheduled to be de-commissioned in 2025 and *Dwight D Eisenhower* (CVN-69) in 2027, both at their 50-year life point. *Nimitz* is due a maintenance period in 2023 where the necessary work could be done but Vice Admiral Scott Conn, deputy chief of naval operations for warfighting requirements and capabilities, OPNAV N9, said at the same briefing that any such extension was 'pre-decisional'. The work would have to offer a good return on investment and its implementation would depend on the number of other carriers undergoing maintenance.

The usual overview of planned future US Navy aircraft procurement is set out in Table 4.1.1. Although plans to end production of the FA-18E/F Super Hornet were thwarted by Congress with the approval of c. US$1bn of funding for twelve additional aircraft in the FY2022 National Defense Authorization Act, the US Navy continues to envisage closing the production line to new orders. This would free funds for the development of F/A-XX, part of the next generation air dominance (NGAD) programme.

At the heart of the debate between Congress and the US Navy is an ongoing shortfall in the number of fighter aircraft (FA-18E/F Super Hornets and F-35C Lightning IIs) in naval service. The US Navy is required by law to maintain nine carrier air wings – each including 44 fighters – for a total of 396 aircraft. It needs a further 263 for training and development tasks and 126 in long-term mainte-nance, making a total of 785 fighters which does not include any held in reserve against attrition. Whilst a number of initiatives – including reforms intro-duced as part of a revised sustainment system – have reduced the shortfall from sixty-five aircraft in 2018 to around thirty-five aircraft as of 2022, there is continued scepticism over when the gap will be closed. A major issue is the number of variables impacting the calculation, including the number of F-35Cs being procured, the pace and quantity of F/A-18E/F Block II aircraft proceeding through the planned Service Life Modernisation (SLM) programme, and the size and number of embarked F-35C squadrons. However, at the current time, the point at which the required numbers will be achieved seems to be moving backwards. Equally, the US Navy is reluctant to buy an arguably 'legacy' design which – with a potential 30-year fatigue life – might well remain in service in 2055, when the potential threats they might face could be very different from today. Congress is clearly thinking in the short term and does not want a mature produc-tion line closed to fund new and as yet untested technologies but the US Navy has its attention fixed to the medium and longer-term future.

The FY2023 aviation procurement plan request US$16.8bn to buy a total of ninety-six aircraft for the US Navy and USMC. In general terms, this plan – and future planned appropriations – represent a decrease from previous projections. For example, only thirteen F-35Cs (nine for the US Navy; four for the USMC) are requested compared with the twenty seen last year and previous expectations that this procurement rate would continue into the future.[9] The US Navy has justified this by saying that the new total reflects the need to balance aircraft, ship and weapons construction portfolios, although it will hardly help resolve the fighter gap referenced above. The navy is also being criticised for keeping the cost of its NGAD 6th generation fighter programme classified for the third year in a row.

Comparatively little is known about the range of characteristics and capabilities that will be embedded in the design but the new aircraft will need to come on line in the 2030s to replace the earliest F/A-18E/F Super Hornets and EA-18G Growlers as they reach the end of their fatigue lives.

The FY2023 budget request does envisage the start of procurement of production models of the MQ-25 Stingray aerial refuelling drone. The MQ-25 Stingray prototype T1 made history on 4 June 2021 when it refuelled an F/A-18 Super Hornet in flight, demonstrating the Stingray's ability to carry out its primary aerial refuelling mission. The F/A-18 test was followed by similar trials with E-2D and F-35C aircraft, after which the aircraft was modified for deck handling trials on board *George H. W. Bush* (CVN-77) The engineering management and development (EMD) Stingray models, due to be delivered from 2022, will be fully capable of operating from a carrier and are designed to deliver up to 15,000lbs of fuel at a radius of 500 nautical miles, relieving Super Hornets of the burden of carrying out this task and effectively prolonging their service

lives. The first MQ-25 unit, Unmanned Carrier-Launched Multi-Role Squadron 10 (VUQ-10), stood up in October 2021 to become the fleet replacement squadron for the type. It is to be followed by VUQ-11 and VUQ-12, which are to be fully carrier deployable. In April 2022, Vice Admiral Kevin Whitesell, Commander Naval Air Forces, told a panel at the Sea Air Space 2022 Symposium that the US Navy is on track to achieve IOC with the MQ-25A by 2025 and to deploy the first operational unit with an air wing embarked in *Theodore Roosevelt* (CVN-71) by 2026. In December 2020, the US Navy announced a new specialist warrant officer designation – Aerial Vehicle Operator (AVO) – to operate the new aircraft. Whilst the MQ-25 is initially to be focused in the tanker role, it has significant ISR potential and is likely to be subject to spiral development.

Final US Navy E-2D Advanced Hawkeye procurement – under an existing multi-year contract – is due to be authorised in FY2023 but the US Navy is working on improvements intended to keep the airborne early warning aircraft effective into the

late 2040s. Captain Pete Arrobio US Navy, who heads the Airborne Command and Control Systems Program Office (NAVAIR PMA-231), outlined them at the Navy League's annual Sea-Air-Space conference in 2021. They include enhancements to cockpit avionics and mission systems, communications, and cyber security. They are to be implemented through what are known as delta system software configuration (DSSC) upgrades that each take about four years to mature from initiation to deployment. In 2021 the latest was DSSC 3.1, which introduced elements of the Joint Tactical Radio System and Link 16 that allow the E-2D to meet the latest Department of Defense mandated cyber security standards and improve its ability to link, co-ordinate, distribute and assess the effects of targeting information. Further DSSCs are projected including DSSC 4, due in 2023, delivering upgrades to data fusion, GPS and radar performance. As of mid-2022 air test and evaluation squadrons VX-20 and VX-1 are flying with development versions of DSSC 4. Arrobio said that DSSC 5, due in 2025, is projected to upgrade carrier air wing performance against an enemy using anti-access/area denial (A2/AD) systems but its exact nature is highly classified. Beyond that, DSSC 6 is expected to allow interoperability with the Joint All-Domain Command and Control, JADC2, system and improved naval operational architecture.

Surprisingly, Arrobio told his audience that by the latest standards the E-2D's computer architecture is 'antiquated and obsolete', dating back to 2005, and this is challenging because the aircraft is being tasked to do more than it was originally intended to do. The absolute priority, he said, is to harden the mission computer and displays against current and future enemy cyber capabilities. 'There are risks we can no longer accept', he said. Resolving them comes as part of the Hawkeye Cockpit Tech Refresh (HECTR), which brings avionics up to current standards and introduces a head-up display for the pilots. New theatre combat ID and mission computer displays have been designed with an open-systems architecture intended to reduce the time taken to install future software upgrade packages. Arrobio said that this was because the US Navy can no longer afford the time it currently takes to incorporate new software into the E-2D. Although it is not yet a stated requirement, the US Navy is also considering an improved landing mode (ILM) for the E-2D to at least partially automate carrier land-

Production of the E-2D Advanced Hawkeye AEW aircraft is now well advanced, with final authorisations for the type expected in FY2023. In January 2022, manufacturer Northrop Grumman announced that it had delivered the 51st production aircraft – AA-52 – out of the US Navy's planned procurement of seventy-eight aircraft. *(Northrop Grumman)*

ings in line with the 'magic carpet' systems used by the F/A-18E/F and F-35C. This is because aerial refuelling allows E-2Ds to remain airborne for up to nine hours and pilot fatigue could become a factor in deck landing. The E-2D is not a fly-by-wire aircraft and it is less stable on the glide-slope than a fighter and, as longer sorties become more commonplace, Arrobio believes that ILM will become a major priority.[10]

On a smaller scale, the US Navy announced in April 2022 that it intends to embark four small logistic drones, each capable of lifting up to 50lbs, in a carrier by the end of the year. Naval Air Forces Atlantic is seeking a faster way to transfer critical parts from auxiliaries to warships under way and has calculated that 90 percent of critical aircraft mission failures can be repaired with a payload weighing less than 20lbs, well within the capacity of several commercial unmanned systems.

UNITED STATES MARINE CORPS

The US Marine Corps continues to evaluate its longer-term aviation requirements but the thinking behind the air vehicles required to implement them has changed frequently. The latest concepts were articulated in February 2022 by Brigadier General Matt Mowery USMC, Assistant Deputy Commandant for Aviation, who said that the corps was no longer looking at replacing its existing individual platforms on a like-for-like basis. The latest analysis favours a vertical take-off and landing (VTOL) family of systems. The general briefed the National Defence Industrial Association's annual Expeditionary Warfare Conference that the aim is now to create an umbrella programme of VTOL systems for operation beyond 2030. It will include things like a projected large unmanned logistics system – airborne. 'As we look at the distances we've got to cover out in the Pacific', he said, 'something unmanned that can do very repetitive work, riskworthy, but over long distances and at an airspeed that makes a difference on the battlefield, that may be actually a priority … over a UH-1Y Venom replacement.'

The USMC had already decided on a family of systems approach for the much changed MUX goal and has been experimenting with MQ-9A Reaper drones to help develop its specification.[11] The US Navy also wants a family of systems approach for its future vertical lift maritime strike capability and – while the navy and marine requirements are still

The USMC continues to evaluate different aviation concepts for both the short and longer term. Here the new amphibious assault ship *Tripoli* (LHA-7) is pictured with twelve F-35B Lightning II strike fighters on her flight deck whilst docking at Yokosuka June 2022. The previous month had seen her embark as many as twenty jets as part of an evaluation of the 'Lightning carrier' concept. *(US Navy)*

In February 2022, the amphibious assault ships *Essex* (LHD-2) – bottom – and *America* (LHA-6) – top – teamed with the carrier *Abraham Lincoln* (CVN-72) in the Noble Fusion exercise that tested, inter alia, the new Expeditionary Advanced Base Operations (EABO) concept. *(US Navy)*

under discussion – some missions might align together. The US Navy and USMC efforts to develop new rotary-wing capabilities are housed in the same programme office but the requirements may differ significantly; for instance the navy needs helicopters to operate off destroyers and frigates far more than the USMC does. Despite this, the shared programme office does allow synchronisation; whatever shapes the airframes might end up with they are likely to use the same technology, networks and software.

More immediate capability was demonstrated on the new amphibious assault ship *Tripoli* (LHA-7) at the end of March 2022 when she embarked sixteen F-35Bs to undertake the latest test of the 'Lightning carrier' concept. The total embarked had grown to twenty by the end of the ten-day long exercises and included eight aircraft from the 'Wake Island Avengers' of VMFA-211 (fresh from their deployment in *Queen Elizabeth*), eight from the recently re-equipped 'Vikings' of VMFA-225 and four from the 'VMX-1' test and evaluation unit. Both operational squadrons form part of Marine Aircraft Group 13 (MAG-13), 3rd Marine Aircraft Wing, providing the opportunity for a MAG commander to practice large-scale operations from the sea. Like her sister *America* (LHA-6), *Tripoli* has increased aviation fuel and magazine space instead of a well deck, facilitating the sustainment of a larger group of fighters. Whilst a USMC press release suggested the trials had gone well, much remains to be done to bring the concept into routine operations.

Earlier in 2022 US Marines embarked in *Essex* (LHD-2) and *America* took part in Exercise Noble Fusion across hundreds of miles of littoral geography in the islands off south-west Japan to test the Expeditionary Advanced Base Operations Base (EABO) 'island-hopping' concept. The *Abraham Lincoln* (CVN-72) carrier strike group and elements of the US Air Force and Japan Self Defense Forces were amongst other units that took part in operations that were described as demonstrating how forward-deployed US Navy and USMC units 'can rapidly aggregate at sea with other joint force elements and allies in order to conduct lethal sea-denial operations, seize key maritime terrain, guarantee freedom of movement, and create advantage for US, partner and allied forces'. The exercise was the first time since 2018 that two amphibious ready groups had worked together in the Indo-Pacific region, providing an excellent opportunity to put new USMC operating concepts into practice.[12]

A MRH-90 Taipan helicopter prepares to lift off from the Australian amphibious assault ship *Canberra*, which relieved her sister *Adelaide* during the relief efforts that followed the volcanic eruption in Tonga. The Taipan itself is due to be retired early as a result of Australian dissatisfaction with the type's reliability. *(Royal Australian Navy)*

AUSTRALIA

In December 2021, the Australian Government announced the surprise retirement of its entire fleet of MRH-90 Taipan helicopters more than a decade earlier than originally planned. The Taipan is an Australian-specific derivative of the NH Industries NH 90 TTH. The Australian Army Air Corps (AAC) had forty-one in service in early 2022, with a further six allocated to the Royal Australian Navy to equip 808 Naval Air Squadron. All of them are capable of operation from the navy's *Canberra* class amphibious assault ships in the amphibious warfare, humanitarian aid and disaster relief roles. Defence Minister Peter Dutton briefed the press that the Taipan had been a project of concern for a decade with the whole fleet grounded on nine occasions, by generally poor availability, a lack of adequate spares support and configuration management issues. The Taipan's poor availability forced the AAC to hire two Leonardo AW139s during 2021 to maintain army and navy aircrew training on the type while Taipans were grounded. The

MRH 90 was intended to remain in service until 2037 but Dutton said that 'up to 40 new UH-60M Black Hawks are to be procured to replace the Taipan by 2027'. He added that this measure would save Australian taxpayers about AU\$2.5bn (c. US\$1.8bn) because the Black Hawk is considerably cheaper to operate. It has less load-carrying capability than the MRH-90 but the AAC will benefit from operating the same type as the US Army. The Taipan is the second European helicopter capable of embarkation within a joint air wing to be scrapped by the AAC during 2021 after the AH-64E Apache was selected as the armed reconnaissance helicopter to replace the Eurocopter Tiger at the start of the year.[13]

In a separate deal first reported in October 2021, the United States approved a deal for a further batch of twelve MH-60R Sea Hawk helicopters under the FMS regime. They were to augment the twenty-four MH-60Rs then serving in 816 and 725 Naval Air Squadrons. It is not yet known whether the extra aircraft will form a new squadron but they will be operable from destroyers, frigates and auxiliaries as well as the amphibious assault ships. A single MH-60R was lost later in October 2021 while operating from *Brisbane* in the Philippine Sea. Consequently, the firm contract announced in May 2022 increased the purchase to thirteen of the rotorcraft, an investment estimated to cost AU$2.5bn (US$1.7bn)

A Royal Australian Navy task group including *Canberra* carried out the Indo-Pacific Endeavour Deployment 21 (IPE-21). Due to the COVID-19 pandemic, engagements were limited to contactless port visits including a range of virtual workshops and at-sea activities. The deployment included participation in the Five Power Defence Agreement Bersama Gold exercise which marked the 50th anniversary of the group, which includes Australia, Malaysia, New Zealand, Singapore and the UK. The MRH-90 Taipan force was grounded at the time and so 808 Naval Air Squadron, which would normally have embarked in *Canberra* for the deployment, was unable to take part. Royal Australian Navy MH-60R Sea Hawks were embarked in ships of the task group.

Australia was one of a number of nations that provided disaster relief in Tonga after the Hunga Tonga-Hunga Ha'apai underwater volcano exploded in January 2022. *Canberra*'s sister, *Adelaide*, was a key element of the Australian effort and she continued to operate despite suffering a power failure. Back-up power enabled essential systems including sanitation, refrigeration, food supply and air-conditioning to function but a team of civilian specialists had to be deployed to assess the affected machinery. The ship had recorded twenty-three positive COVID-19 cases whilst en route although all were said to be mild or asymptomatic. Because of this a contactless unloading of supplies was carried out.

CHINA
The People's Liberation Army Navy (PLAN) continues to test its expanding naval aviation capabilities. Late in 2021, its *Liaoning* carrier strike group carried out an extended period of sea training, crossing the Yellow Sea and East China Sea before entering the Western Pacific via the Miyako Strait. *Liaoning* had J-15 fighters and Z-9 and Z-18 helicopters embarked, which flew both day and night missions. Exercises began logically with search and rescue drills and replenishment before moving on to air and anti-submarine warfare scenarios and

ended with complicated command and control exercises. Throughout its time at sea the group was monitored by the Japanese 'helicopter-carrying destroyer' *Izumo* (DDH-183) and tracked by US and Japanese maritime patrol aircraft. A similar deployment for what China described as a 'realistic combat training exercise' commenced in May 2022. This also travelled via the Miyako Strait between Miyako and Okinawa islands; increasingly the PLAN's chosen route to access the Pacific. Meanwhile, the first fully indigenous carrier *Shandong* is reportedly undertaking its first major maintenance period since entering service in December 2019.

The PLAN's third aircraft carrier was launched at the Jiangnan Shipyard on Changxing Island close to Shanghai on 17 June 2022. Designated as the Type 003, she is named *Fujian* after the Chinese mainland province nearest Taiwan and carries the No. 18 hull-number. She reportedly has a length of 1,049ft – 320m – and a full-load displacement estimated at more than 80,000 tonnes. Unlike the two previous vessels, the design will use electromagnetic catapults to launch embarked jet aircraft. There have also been reports that China will use similar electromagnetic launch system (EMALS) for a mooted Type 076 amphibious assault ship that is reportedly under development. Progress continues to be made in inducting the current Type 075 (NATO: 'Yushen') class amphibious assault ship class design. The second unit – *Guangxi* – was reportedly commissioned at the end of 2021 and a third ship is in the course of sea trials.

FRANCE
On 1 February 2022 the French Navy's *Charles de Gaulle* carrier group sailed for its Clemenceau 22 deployment in the Mediterranean. Integrating with NATO and US forces, a notable highlight was the performance of tri-carrier operations with the US Navy's *Harry S. Truman* and Italy's *Cavour* in the Ionian Sea in March. *Charles de Gaulle*'s air wing included twenty Rafale F3R omni-role fighters of Flotilles 12F and 17F, two E-2C Hawkeyes of Flotille 4F, a single Dauphin helicopter of Flotille 35F, a single Panther helicopter of Flotille 36F and a single HH 90 Caiman anti-submarine helicopter of Flotille 31F. Her supporting warships included units from Greece, Spain and the United States – as well as a Belgian helicopter – in a further sign of growing allied interoperability.

This theme was reflected in a press briefing given by Admiral Pierre Vandier, Chief of the French Naval Staff, during a visit to the United States that took place shortly before *Charles de Gaulle*'s departure. In addition to stressing the need for allies to become more interoperable, he noted that the French Navy is only now starting to recover from 30 years of deep budget cuts that had stretched its ability to meet an ever-expanding list of missions. Pointing to current French Navy procurement programmes, he noted that a high level of investment is needed to match competitors' technological advances which threaten the freedom of the global seas.

INDIA
The Indian Navy's 45,000-tonne aircraft carrier *Vikrant* began sea trials in August 2021 She was laid down in 2009 and has a ski-jump and arrester wires to allow the short take-off but arrested recovery (STOBAR) operation of Mig-29K strike fighters together with helicopters in an air wing of about thirty aircraft. She had completed three rounds of trials by the start of 2022 and is expected to be commissioned into the Indian Navy during August 2022.

On 1 April 2022 the first Indian Navy pilots and observers completed their ten-month conversion

India's new aircraft carrier *Vikrant* commenced sea trials in August 2021. She has subsequently undertaken a series of separate phases of testing at sea as she works up to formal delivery to the Indian Navy. The carrier – the first to be designed and constructed in India – is scheduled for delivery in August 2022, but it will be later that she becomes fully operational. *(Indian Navy)*

The Italian aircraft carrier *Cavour* pictured alongside the US Navy's *Harry S. Truman* (CVN-75) and Spain's *Juan Carlos I* during the course of the Neptune Shield 2022 exercises. *(Italian Navy)*

History was made on 3 October 2021 when two US Marine Corps F-35B strike fighters landed on the deck of the Japanese helicopter-carrying destroyer *Izumo* (DDH-183), marking the first time a fixed-wing aircraft had landed on a Japanese warship since the end of the Second World War. *(US Navy)*

training courses on the MH-60R Sea Hawk with the US Navy at Naval Air Station North Island, San Diego. Twenty-four MH-60Rs have been procured under a government-to-government deal. They are to be used in a variety of roles including anti-submarine warfare, anti-ship strike, sea control and combat search and rescue. India has, however, reportedly suspended discussions to acquire additional Russian Ka-31 airborne early warning and control aircraft, which are required for the new *Vikrant*.[14]

ITALY

In addition to its operations with French and American carriers, Italy's Naval Aviation has also been collaborating with other NATO partners following the first landing of an Italian Navy F-35B on *Cavour* in July 2021.[15] In November 2021 F-35Bs from the British *Queen Elizabeth* and Italy's *Cavour* carried out cross-deck flying and integration exercises east of Sicily. There were three phases that began with two USMC F-35Bs of VMFA-211 from *Queen Elizabeth* landing on *Cavour*. Next Italian F-35Bs landed on *Queen Elizabeth*, after which aircraft from both carriers flew integrated formation exercises. Commodore Steve Moorhouse RN, commander of CSG 21, said afterwards that the four operators had demonstrated the ability to fly from different decks to offer tactical agility and strategic advantage to NATO. The Italian Navy expects to declare IOC for its F-35Bs in 2024 after further trials and training.

Subsequently, in May 2022, *Cavour* led a small carrier group northwards to participate in the Neptune Shield 2022 exercises in the Baltic. In addition to further interaction with *Harry S. Truman*, the Spanish amphibious assault ship *Juan Carlos I* was one of a number of NATO and partner ships that also participated in these activities.

JAPAN

On 3 October 2021, two F-35Bs from the USMC's VMFA-242 landed on the Japanese helicopter 'destroyer' *Izumo*. As well as marking the completion of the first stage of a two-part modification programme that will enable the ship to operate the type, the event marked the first landing of a fixed-wing aircraft on a Japanese ship since the end of the Second World War. Costing some 3.1Bn yen (c. US$30m), the work included a new heat-resistant flight deck coating and yellow flight deck markings. The second phase of her modification is due to begin in March 2025 and is to include the fitting of a new bow shape forward to widen the forward part of the flight deck to simplify F-35B launches and modifications to the ship's interior. However, interestingly, Japanese reports make no mention of fitting a ski-jump. This phase is expected to be complete by early 2027.

Izumo's sister-ship *Kaga* (DDH-184) began the modification process to allow her to operate F-35Bs in 2022. The first phase includes both the heat-resistant deck coating and markings and also the changed bow. The additional extent of the work is reflected in the higher cost of 20.3bn yen (c. US$160m). Completion is expected in late 2023,

with further modifications to the ship's interior following in March 2027. It has been decided that the Japanese Air Self Defense Force will operate the embarked F-35B force, since it already operates the F-35A. The first six of a planned forty-two F-35Bs are expected to arrive in 2024 and will be shore-based at Nyutabaru when disembarked.

TURKEY

The amphibious assault ship *Anadolu* commenced sea trials in February 2022. A half-sister of the *Spanish Juan Carlos 1* and the Royal Australian Navy's *Canberra* class, it was originally intended that she would operate F-35B Lightning IIs. However, Turkey was expelled from the programme for

acquiring the Russian S-400 air defence system. As a result, local press reports suggest that she will be modified to deploy indigenous Bayraktar TB 3 unmanned combat air vehicles, a navalised variant of the Bayraktar TB 2 that has gained prominence in the Russo-Ukrainian war. A twin-boom, pusher-propeller design with a maximum take-off weight of 700kg and payload of 150kg, the TB 2 has a maximum speed of 120 knots and an endurance in excess of 24 hours. The TB3 could be launched from the ship's ski jump and – given its low speed – potentially carry out an un-arrested landing with the back-up of security netting. Local reports suggest as many as eighty could be embarked aboard the 27,000-tonne ship.

Notes

1. *We're going to need a bigger Navy: Third report of Session 2021-22* (London: House of Commons Defence Committee, 2021).

2. Commander Taylor was quoted in a press release entitled 'Drones launched from HMS *Prince of Wales* during landmark demonstration' posted to the *Royal Navy* website on 29 September 2021.

3. See '700X NAS Drone Training on HMS *Mersey*' posted to the *Royal Navy* website on 16 November 2021.

4. A small number of RAF Hawk T1 aircraft are being maintained in service, principally to support the needs of the Red Arrows display team.

5. See Mallory Shelbourne, 'F-35 JPO Evaluating Spare Parts Following *Vinson, Queen Elizabeth* Deployments' posted to the *USNI News* website – news.usni.org – on 9 March 2022.

6. The *USNI News* update – also provided by Mallory Shelbourne – was posted under the title 'Record Aircraft Carrier Work Underway at Newport News Shipbuilding' on 9 February 2022. According to another article – 'US Navy carrier *Ford* to go on unusual deployment this year' written by Megan Eckstein for the *Defense News* website on 3 February 2022 – *Ford*'s maiden deployment will be atypical in that she will remain under full US Navy operational control rather than fall under the command of a regional combatant commander. This, perhaps, suggests that the navy wants to keep the new ship on a tight leash until its operational durability has been proven.

7. See further a press release entitled '*Carl Vinson* Carrier Strike Group Returns Home From Deployment' released by US Third Fleet Public Affairs and posted to the *US Navy* website – navy.mil – on 14 February 2022.

8. Amongst alternative proposals to the current nuclear-powered carriers is a new conventionally-powered aircraft carrier of approximate *Midway* (CV-41) class size. Its proponents suggest that it would be capable of performing most of the functions of existing carriers and, critically, would break the monopoly on large carrier construction currently held by Huntington Ingalls Industries' Newport News yard. The arguments for this type of ship – and a review of the alternatives – were set out by John F. Lehman (a former Secretary of the Navy at the time of the Reagan administration) with Steven Wills in *Where Are The Carriers? US National Strategy and the Choices Ahead* (Philadelphia PA: Foreign Policy Research Institute, 2021).

9. The previous, FY2022 budget, did not publish Future Years Defense Program (FYDP) projections. However, projections provided in FY2021 suggested a requirement for as many as twenty-six F-35Cs in FY2023 whilst subsequent press reports speculated on a slightly reduced number of twenty.

10. Captain Arrobio's remarks were reported by several outlets, including *Seapower* and *USNI News*. The original program of record for the E-2D Advanced Hawkeye was for seventy-five aircraft. Despite a subsequent uplift in the requirement to eighty-six aircraft, it seems that production for the US Navy will terminate at seventy-eight units when a current multi-year procurement contract ends in FY2023. Of these aircraft, fifty units had been delivered by the end of 2021, nominally providing sufficient aircraft for nine operational squadrons and a single fleet readiness (training) squadron. Some operational squadrons have yet to complete conversion from the older E-2C Hawkeye but these are no longer used for front-line duties and will all be retired by 2026. In addition, Japan has ordered thirteen of the type for land-based use and France concluded a

Foreign Military Sales (FMS) programme to acquire three aircraft in December 2021. Further FMS transactions are being pursued.

11. The Marine Air-Ground Task Force (MAGTF) Unmanned Aerial System (UAS) Expeditionary programme – commonly abbreviated as MUX – was initially launched to procure a large shipboard drone capable of carrying out a wide range of functions that included ISR, command and control, and early warning. The family of systems approach was adopted when it was realised that the range of requirements was too great for one platform. For further analysis on the USMC's future aviation requirements see Mallory Shelbourne's article, 'Marines Want VTOL Family of Systems for Future Vertical Lift' posted to *USNI News* on 9 February 2022.

12. Further details of the forces involved in the exercises are contained in 'Exercise Noble Fusion kicks off with Joint Combined Expeditionary Training in the Philippine Sea' posted to the *US Marine Corps* website – marines.mil – on 4 February 2022.

13. The Royal Australian Navy is not the only fleet to be experiencing problems with NH 90 series helicopters. In June 2022, the Norwegian Ministry of Defence announced that it would terminate its contract to acquire fourteen of the type, returning those delivered, on the basis of their inability to achieve the standard of performance required.

14. See Vivek Raghuvanshi, 'India halts Ka-31 helicopter deal with Russia' posted to the *Defense News* website on 16 May 2022.

15. Previous F-35B qualification trials off the United States east coast earlier in 2021 did not involve Italian Navy aircraft.

Author:
Norman Friedman

4.2 TECHNOLOGICAL REVIEW

HYPERSONIC MISSILES

Some Considerations

Hypersonic missiles are now often in the news. The Russians, who claim to have a great lead in developing them, say that they are the most decisive of all missiles, impossible to intercept. In combat in Ukraine they have not demonstrated any magical capabilities. Limited Ukrainian air defences have struggled to destroy considerably slower weapons. The US Navy has faced Chinese hypersonic anti-ship missiles for some years, in the form of the maneuverable re-entry bodies associated with their semi-ballistic long-range anti-ship missiles. The US Navy sees its SM-6 missile as a viable interceptor. Many countries are currently trying to develop hypersonic missiles; the United States being the leader in the West.

Hypersonic means simply that the missile can fly more than five times the speed of sound within the atmosphere (below about 90km altitude). Hypersonic missiles differ from ballistic missile re-entry vehicles – which fly at similar or greater speeds – because they are intended to fly for extended periods in the atmosphere. That implies a degree of manoeuvrability, which can be translated as unpredictability – ballistic missiles fly trajectories dictated by the laws of mechanics.

Hypersonic flight is hardly new. As long ago as the Second World War, the Germans were interested in boosting vehicles into the upper atmosphere atop missiles; Eugen Sänger suggested an 'orbital bomber' which would achieve intercontinental range by bouncing off the upper atmosphere. Probably all modern missile re-entry vehicles fly through the atmosphere at hypersonic speeds. For example, Minuteman re-entry vehicles (warheads) are generally credited with a speed of Mach 17. They are not considered hypersonic missiles because they spend very little of their time of flight inside the atmosphere. On the other hand, more than 50 years ago the X-15 research aircraft was flying faster than Mach 6, in the atmosphere. The Space Shuttle flew in the atmosphere at much higher speeds and more recently many unmanned space planes, such as the US X-37, have done so.

During the Cold War there was considerable

The development of hypersonic missiles is making a significant impact in the media, although their ability to revolutionise naval warfare is open to scepticism. This is a graphic of a scramjet-powered Hypersonic Attack Cruise Missile (HACM) being developed by Raytheon and Northrop Grumman for the US Defense Advanced Research Projects Agency (DARPA). It reportedly made its first test flight in September 2021. *(Northrop Grumman)*

interest in manoeuvring re-entry vehicles which are, in effect, hypersonic missiles. For example, in the 1980s the United States became interested in a manoeuvring body which could detect targets using an array-type millimetre-wave radar. One application which was discussed was a means of destroying Soviet anti-ship bombers well before they could get anywhere near a fleet. They would be detected and tracked by long-range radars, including the relocatable over-the-horizon radar (ROTHR) which was actually fielded. The re-entry bodies would be carried into space by land-based ballistic missiles. As they curved down towards the earth, their onboard radars would detect and track the enemy bombers, onto which they would home. This idea died with the Cold War. It does not appear that it was ever tested.

HYPERSONIC MISSILES: GENERAL PRINCIPLES

There are three kinds of hypersonic missiles: boost-glide, air-breathing (cruise) and cannon-launched. In each case, the vehicle must be boosted to hypersonic speed. There is no current propulsion system which can bring a missile up to hypersonic speed and then propel it at that speed. A rocket typically carries a boost-glide vehicle to the upper atmosphere, accelerating it to the desired initial speed. It glides down towards its target. The terminal vehicle of the Chinese fractional orbit bombardment system, which was tested last year, may fall into this category. So does the Russian Avangard manoeuvrable re-entry vehicle. An air-breather is like a ramjet, but much faster. It needs a rocket to boost it to the speed at which its supersonic combustion ramjet (scramjet) can ignite, typically about Mach 4 or Mach 5. The air feeding this engine is typically compressed by shock waves created by a specially-shaped nose. A cannon-launched hypersonic vehicle would use a cannon – such as a rail gun – to accelerate it to hypersonic speed. No such devices apparently yet exist.

At hypersonic speeds a body generates shock waves which create lift. Lift is proportional to air density and to the square of speed, so to stay in the air high in the (rarified) atmosphere a vehicle must move very fast. At the same time heat due to air flowing over a moving vehicle is proportional to the square of the speed and also to the square root of air density divided by the nose radius, so that flying higher (less air density) reduces heating. It does not help, however, that hypersonic vehicles have sharp

Hypersonic flight is not new. The North American X-15 experimental hypersonic rocket-powered aircraft programme undertook nearly 200 flights between 1959 and 1968, achieving a maximum speed of 4,520mph (Mach 6.7). *(NASA)*

Rockets are commonly associated with hypersonic weapons, either to carry a boost-glide vehicle to the upper atmosphere or to boost an air-breathing missile to a speed at which its scramjet can ignite. This photo shows the second stage solid rocket motor of the US Navy's planned Conventional Prompt Strike weapon – a hypersonic boost-glide missile – under testing in August 2021. *(US Navy)*

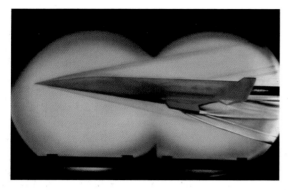

The air feeding the scramjet of an air-breathing hypersonic missile is typically compressed by shock waves created by a specially-shaped nose. This model of a hypersonic vehicle under test in a special wind tunnel in December 2019 shows the shock waves that it generates. *(DARPA)*

creates simply by flying at very high speed will tend to distort its structure.

Heating is more of a problem than with a ballistic missile re-entry vehicle, because it is much more sustained. Sharp leading edges may erode, ablate and oxidise. The airframe is likely to distort under the stresses it encounters. That in turn will complicate flight control. The flight-control system must be able to sense this distortion and correct for it. It appears that developing sufficiently strong structure has been a major problem. For example, some years ago a US test vehicle disintegrated shortly after being launched. The designers of the US Space Shuttle, which certainly was a transonic boost-glide air vehicle while flying in the atmosphere, provided it with a massive structure and large control surfaces, to minimise changes in geometry due to structural bending, minimising the strain on its thermal tiles. The rounded shape of the Shuttle helped limit destructive heating in the atmosphere. The loss of two Shuttles was due to the loss of thermal tiles during take-off. Once a few tiles were gone, the

conventional structure beneath them was subject to the intense thermal stress of hypersonic flight, which it could not withstand. The magnitude of the problem is suggested by the destructive effect of losing just a few tiles.

Missiles are much smaller than the Shuttle, with thinner structures and a necessarily sharper shape much more susceptible to distortion – which the flight-control system must sense and counteract. Hypersonic flight is so stressful that it is not clear to what extent a missile airframe can handle the forces associated with manoeuvres. The need to manoeuvre using control surfaces seems to limit vehicle speed.

A hypersonic vehicle creates a very shallow boundary layer – the layer between the static air immediately around it and the hypersonic flow further out. This layer becomes hot enough to begin to break down air molecules and create a plasma. The plasma in turn may block or distort signals, both to the vehicle (command and navigation [as in GPS]) and from it (data links and radar signals).

It is so difficult to design a viable scramjet that only late in the last decade did any of them produce thrust, even though the principles have been known for decades. Compression, which makes combustion viable, requires that the air flowing into the engine be slowed. Thus a ramjet generally slows air from supersonic to subsonic. A ramjet chokes at very high speed, its air flow ruined by internal shock waves. Hypersonic cruise missiles generally have long specially-shaped noses which create the shock waves which slow down air flowing into an underslung combustion chamber. Burning fuel inside the combustion chamber adds to the structural problems of the missile.

Overall, the difficulty of developing a hypersonic vehicle seems to be proportional to the square of its Mach number.

HYPERSONIC ANTI-SHIP MISSILES

Flight time is very limited; a missile flying 60 miles per minute can cover 300 nautical miles in five minutes. Since a ship does not move very far in five minutes, this kind of speed would seem almost to guarantee hits. That is not quite the case. Hitting requires that the shooter know exactly where it is relative to the target. For example, that may be the case if the shooter uses GPS and the target is located by something (e.g., a drone) also using GPS. Observers of the war in Ukraine have often remarked that Russian long-range missiles rarely hit

noses (i.e., with very small radius). Moreover, although the nose and the wing leading edges may become quite hot, the same does not apply to other surfaces. The strong thermal gradients the vehicle

The US Air Force tested the X-51A Waverider hypersonic missile between 2010 and 2013. It was powered by a scramjet engine. In its tests, the vehicle was carried to altitude under a B-52 and then boosted to Mach 4.8 by the booster of an AGM-140 ATACMS missile. After a successful first flight, it suffered two failures but then it flew for over six minutes in its final flight, attaining a speed of Mach 5.1. Note the long, specially-shaped nose that creates the shock waves which slow down air flowing into an underslung combustion chamber, preventing the scramjet from being choked. *(US Army)*

A computer-generated image of Lockheed Martin's Hypersonic Attack Cruise Missile (HACM), an alternative concept to the missile being developed by Raytheon and Northrop Grumman for the HACM programme. In April 2022, Lockheed Martin announced that the missile had made a successful test flight, reaching speeds in excess of Mach 5. However, even if made to work properly, such missiles need to overcome significant targeting and control challenges to be successful anti-ship weapons. *(Lockheed Martin)*

their targets. That may be an accuracy problem inherent in the missiles. However, it may also be the fault of insufficiently precise knowledge of just where the shooter is at the moment the missile is fired (or, similarly, of how fast it is moving and in exactly what direction). This is a general problem for long-range missiles, apparently insufficiently appreciated by the Russians.

Anti-ship missiles generally depend on their seekers to make up for targeting errors. The faster the missile, the earlier in flight that the seeker must cause it to turn, because the missile structure probably cannot withstand the stress of a high-g turn. All turns stress missile structure, but a hypersonic missile is already badly stressed by its sheer speed, for example as reflected in thermal stresses. It seems unlikely that such a vehicle can make more than shallow turns. Ideally the missile must be launched on a path which will bring it quite close to its target. Anything which limits the range at which the missile can detect the target will make it necessary for the missile to begin its turn closer to the target. The closer the turn, the more gs are involved. In this sense it would seem that a modest degree of anti-radar stealth might turn out to be a useful counter-measure against hypersonic anti-ship missiles.

Alternatively, a missile controller observing the target might be able to command the missile to turn appropriately, even if its onboard seeker could not yet see the target. Whether that would work would depend on how well a guidance link from controller to missile can overcome interference due to the somewhat ionized boundary layer surrounding the missile.

The control problem aside, it might seem that the sheer kinetic energy a hypersonic missile delivers would be devastating. This energy of the missile is half the mass multiplied by the square of the speed, so that greater speed buys a lot more energy hitting the target, even if the missile weighs less. At least in theory, the missile transfers this energy to its target. It is not entirely certain that this is the case. When the French advertised a Mach 3.5 successor to the subsonic Exocet, the main selling points were immunity to defences and the kinetic energy of the missile, which would have been something like twelve times that of the Exocet. Both missiles had similar warheads. The French were unable to convince enough navies to back the supersonic missile project, which was called ANS (*anti-navire supersonique*), to get it started. The targets they had in mind were just not massive enough to need that sort of impact. When heavy armour-piercing shells, which strike at

The kinetic energy produced by a hypersonic missile would be theoretically devastating but a massive target – such as an aircraft carrier – might be needed to take full advantage of this effect. France was unable to garner enough international support to develop a proposed ANS (*anti-navire supersonique*) variant of the existing MM40 Exocet (pictured) because insufficient potential customers needed this capability. *(Brazilian Navy via MBDA)*

high speed, hit unarmoured ships they were often ineffective, passing through thin plating with minimal effect. The Russians and the Chinese may feel otherwise, since they plan to attack massive aircraft carriers, whose structures would presumably stop missile bodies and absorb their energy.

Great kinetic energy buys little unless the missile is likely to hit the target. The Chinese have clearly been somewhat sceptical about the accuracy of their 'carrier-killing' hypersonic weapons. They announced that these missiles would carry a bomblet warhead. At least as advertised, there are enough to cover an area of about a square mile. The bomblets would, for example, sweep aircraft from the deck of a carrier. The Chinese have made much of the claim that the missile carrying the bomblets will follow a deceptive course once it is released into the atmosphere and, hence, will be difficult to intercept.

DEFENCE AGAINST HYPERSONIC MISSILES

Hypersonic missiles are difficult targets. The most important factor is that they offer little warning time and little time exposed to attack. At a speed of 600 knots (about Mach 1), a missile flies 10 nautical miles each minute. A 600-knot sea-skimmer crosses the radar horizon in roughly that time, defining a key requirement in any defensive system. Mach 5 is about 3,000 knots; the missile flies about 50 nautical miles per minute. The missile does, however, have to fly at high altitudes.[1] As a result, a defensive system is likely to spot it much further away, giving itself some reaction time.

Proponents of hypersonic missiles often stress their ability to manoeuvre unpredictably, compared to ballistic missiles. Given sufficient range, a hypersonic missile can put numerous targets at risk. Since the defence has little time in which to react, it may be unable to decide which target is really at risk. Typically there is enough time to mount a point defence – the sort of thing offered by SM-6 or THAAD – but not enough for any sort of area defence. Evolving anti-ballistic missile defences capitalise on the more or less fixed dynamics of the weapon, which requires it to follow a nearly definite path. The sheer speed of a hypersonic missile will limit reaction time, but – as mentioned above – the missile has to fly at high altitude, revealing itself at a considerable distance.

At sea, moreover, there are no area targets, although it is possible that a manoeuvring missile

might be able to hit any one of several point targets. It would have to reveal its target early enough for a point defence to be effective. Evasive or deceptive manoeuvres on the part of the incoming missile are unlikely to protect it from terminal defences.

At very high speed the incoming missile will generate considerable heat, so infra-red sensors should easily pick it up and infra-red homing weapons may well be able to attack it. Note, however, that the body heat of a hypersonic missile is apparently considerably dimmer than the rocket exhaust which, for example, US geostationary satellites usually detect, or the heat visible from a hot body in the coldness of space.

Any attack on a really fast missile presents problems. The explosion of a conventional missile takes time to propagate outward. If the target is fast enough, it may pass the defending missile quickly enough to avoid the explosion. This has been a

Modern air defence missiles such as the US Navy's Standard Missile 6 (SM-6), seen here during a test firing from the destroyer *John Paul Jones* (DDG-53) in June 2014, should have enough time to provide point – but not area – defence against a hypersonic missile. *(US Navy)*

problem for decades; it explains why the US Navy abandoned continuous-rod warheads in favour of blast warheads, the idea being that an explosion would propagate outwards much more rapidly.[2] Even that may not be good enough against a Mach 5 or 6 missile. If the defensive missile flies, for example, at Mach 4, the two will pass at Mach 9 or 10 – say up to 6,000 nautical miles/hour, or 100 nautical miles/minute. In effect the defending missile would get a single shot at the target. Its warhead would have to propagate a killing explosion across a gap of feet and would have much less than seconds to cause catastrophic damage. The warhead can be thought of as a shotgun firing at the passing target, which passes it very rapidly. If the target is 20ft long, it is presented to the defensive missile for no more than 1/500 of a second. The blast (or other effect) of the warhead has to reach the target in that time.

This problem leads defenders to alternatives which can remain focused on the moving target missile: lasers or particle beams, the latter propagating at very high speeds short of the speed of light. Neither would work instantaneously. Instead, each transfers energy to its target as long as it can stay on target. The question is how much energy it takes to wreck the incoming missile. The missile has been built specifically to resist atmospheric heating. Does that mean that a bit more heating, say by a laser, will not really hurt it? Or is it barely able to handle normal heating, necessarily designed to a tight tolerance and very likely to fail if overloaded by a laser beam? How much energy is needed? That decides how long the laser or particle beam must remain on target. Destruction would generally mean destroying enough of the missile's thermal protection that atmospheric heating and stresses would do the rest.

It is sometimes suggested that the current US Navy shift towards much more electric power in ships is inspired mainly by the need to power future electric weapons. These weapons are usually justified on the grounds that a ship's electric power provides, in effect, bottomless magazines. However, if there is a practical limit on the speed of missiles which defensive missiles can destroy, the much more important virtue of an electric weapon is that it can continue to pour energy into a target missile for long enough to destroy it.

Rail guns are sometimes also suggested. However, it seems unlikely that their rather massive structures can manoeuvre quickly enough to track a fast missile.

CURRENT HYPERSONIC WEAPONS

In 2022, the two self-proclaimed leaders in hypersonic missilery are China and Russia, the Russians claiming that they have actually deployed such weapons. There is some reason for scepticism. In recent years the Russians have relied heavily on claims of futuristic super-weapons to show that they should be taken seriously. Combat in Ukraine suggests that many of their weapons are more impressive in the telling than in the reality. It is often suggested that the Russians are happy to proclaim weapons operational at a stage at which the United States would announce early prototype testing. In that case the Russians, and presumably also the Chinese, may be rather less advanced than they claim.

The United States is the most advanced Western country testing hypersonic missiles and it hopes that some will be operational about 2024. Many other countries are pursuing hypersonic research, but none seems likely to field weapons very soon.

Russia: The Russians claim to have fielded three hypersonic weapons. Avangard is a hypersonic maneuvering re-entry vehicle associated with the RS-28 Sarmat (SS-X-30) ICBM and with a modified version of the UR-100N (SS-19). It was tested successfully twice in 2016, failed once in 2017, but then succeeded in December 2018 with a 3,700-mile flight. It is said to incorporate new composite materials to withstand temperatures of up to 2,000° C. The Russians claim that Avangard entered service in December 2019 and that it has reached Mach 20. The Russians describe Avangard and its Sarmat missile as their answer to current US ballistic missile defences. These systems predict the path of an incoming ballistic missile. That is reasonable for an object following a ballistic path. A manoeuvring vehicle is inherently unpredictable, although it is not clear how manoeuvrable Avangard actually is.

The Russians have also displayed the 9-S-7760 Kinzhal missile, carried by a MiG-31 fighter. It was successfully fired by a MiG-31 in July 2018, hitting a target about 500 nautical miles away.[3] This weapon is a modified 9K720 Iskander (SS-26) tactical ballistic missile. When fired by the fighter, presumably it climbs under rocket power, then glides down, accelerating under the force of gravity. The Russians described an analogous version of their Kh-15 (AS-16) short-range air-launched ballistic missile after the collapse of the Soviet Union, when they were hunting foreign partners to pay for the

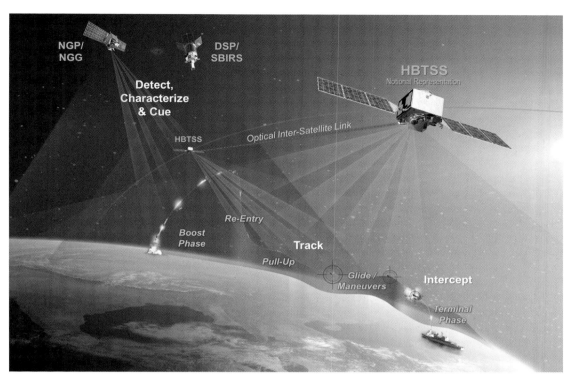

A graphic of the Hypersonic and Ballistic Tracking Space Sensor (HBTSS) that Northrop Grumman is developing for the US Missile Defence Agency. It appears to be designed for use against the boost-glide hypersonic missiles that both China and Russia are known to have developed. The speed of hypersonic missiles makes early detection of their track and likely target significant in mounting an effective defence. *(Northrop Grumman)*

A 9-S-7760 Kinzhal missile carried by a MiG-31 fighter overflies Moscow's 2018 Victory Day Parade. The hypersonic missile – reportedly a modified 9K720 Iskander (SS-26) tactical ballistic missile – is believed to have been used against land-based targets in the course of the current Russo-Ukrainian war. *(Russian Presidential & Information Office: www.kremlin.ru)*

The US Navy and the US Army are working together on a Common Hypersonic Glide Body (C-HGB), which was first successfully tested in March 2020. This photo shows the system's launch from the American Pacific Missile Range Facility, Kauai, Hawaii. *(US Navy)*

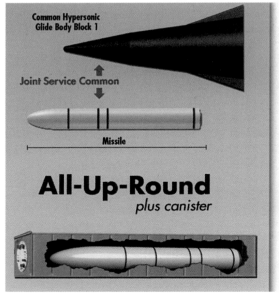

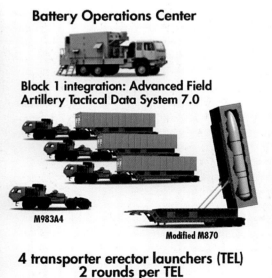

This graphic of the US Army's Dark Eagle – also known as the Long-Range Hypersonic Weapon – gives some idea of the size associated with boost-glide hypersonic weapons systems. The system shares a Common Hypersonic Glide Body (C-HGB) with the US Navy's Conventional Prompt Strike missile, which is to be deployed aboard *Zumwalt* (DDG-1000) class destroyers and later *Virginia* (SSN-774) class submarines. *(US Army)*

development of immature systems. In its anti-ship version, Kh-15 was to have climbed to about 100,000ft and then dived, accelerating to about Mach 5, using a millimetre-wave radar to detect its ship target. Presumably the current aero-ballistic (boost-glide) missile is derived from this project. Kh-15 was deployed as an equivalent to the US SRAM (AGM-69), a bomber penetration aid; it was never deployed in the anti-ship role. The Russians claim that Kinzhal is currently deployed on board MiG-31 and Su-34 fighters and that it will eventually arm medium bombers. Russian media have asserted a speed of Mach 5–10 and a range as great as 1,200 nautical miles when fired by a MiG-31, but some US analysts are sceptical. The missile uses fins to manoeuvre, but its aero-ballistic character probably limits its freedom of manoeuvre. Claimed targets are missile defences and carrier strike groups. Russian reports that an attempt to integrate it with the Tu-160 bomber were encountering problems due to the bomber's low speed are not credible; they would make sense only if the missile needed high air speed to ignite a scramjet engine.

The Russians also claim that they are fielding an air-breathing hypersonic missile, the ship-launched 3M22 Tsirkon (NATO 'Zircon'). Claimed speed is either Mach 5–6 or Mach 6–8; range is 250–600km.[4] The missile can be fired from the new Russian S3-14 Universal UKSK vertical launchers on the nuclear cruisers *Nakhimov* and *Petr Veliky*, the Project 22350 *Admiral Gorshkov* and Project 11356R/M *Admiral Grigorovich* class frigates and the Project 20385 *Gremyashchiy* class corvettes, as well as from Project 885 'Yasen' class submarines. The Russians stated that Tsirkon was successfully launched from a Project 22350 frigate in January and October 2020. As of that time, it was to have entered service in 2023. There have been several subsequent trials.

China: As of 2022, the Chinese are credited with boost-glide vehicles: the anti-ship weapon carried by the DF-21 and -26 'carrier killers' and a longer-range weapon associated with strategic land attack missiles. The Chinese have claimed that their anti-carrier missiles are relatively immune to countermeasures because their re-entry bodies follow unpredictable non-ballistic trajectories once they have been boosted to maximum speed and altitude. It is worth noting that, although the Chinese have built ship-like targets on tracks in the Gobi Desert, they have never demonstrated an attack on a moving ship at sea.

The Chinese have also demonstrated a fractional orbital bombardment weapon; an inertially guided re-entry vehicle which would hit a terrestrial target after making at least a partial earth orbit. In the one known test to date, it missed its target by at least a dozen miles.

United States: There are several US projects, the effort having been inspired by a sense that the Russians and, even more, the Chinese have gained a substantial lead, while the US Defense Department has not bothered to keep pace. Sceptics have suggested that hypersonic weapons do not really add much capability to what already exists. For example, as is well known, current US ballistic missile defences would be ineffective in the face of any substantial Russian or Chinese attack, whilst the distances involved in a strategic attack against the United States suggest that there would be sufficient warning to prompt a devastating reply – which the Russians would be unable to defeat. They ask to what extent is cyber-attack a greater threat? At present the sceptics have failed to make their case. It is not currently clear to what extent announced Russian use of hypersonic weapons in Ukraine will affect this ongoing debate.

The structural and aerodynamic problems seem to have been solved, with attention shifting to the problem of using radar and a data link despite the problems created by a hypersonic plasma. For some years the United States has been interested in prompt strike, meaning very rapid long-range non-nuclear attack against a pop-up target such as a terrorist meeting. To some extent this was a reaction to the failure to hit Osama bin Laden, even when he was definitely located. This project generally involved a non-nuclear munition carried by a strategic missile. One problem was that anyone detecting the flight of such a weapon might mistake it for a nuclear attack and react accordingly. This

The US Navy destroyer *Zumwalt* (DDG-1000) pictured in live fire tests of the SM-2 missile from its Mk 57 launchers. The ship is to be fitted with larger launch cells for hypersonic Conventional Prompt Strike missiles. *(US Navy)*

possibility caused project cancellations, but presumably work done on the projects has left a considerable knowledge base for long-range hypersonic weapon development.

At present the US Navy and the US Army are both working on a Common Hypersonic Glide Body (C-HGB), which was first successfully tested in March 2020. The Air Force dropped out of the project at about that time. The vehicle was adapted from an Army Mach 6 Alternate Re-Entry System tested successfully in 2011 and 2017. The two services expect to use different boost vehicles. The US Navy's Conventional Prompt Strike missile pairs the vehicle with a booster for its Common All-Up Round (AUR). It is to be deployed aboard a *Zumwalt* class destroyer, which has larger-diameter

vertical launch cells, in about 2023. This missile will also go aboard *Virginia* class submarines. Both services are interested in defeating anti-access/area-denial (A2AD); the army sees its missile as a means of suppressing those defences (at ranges up to 1,725 nautical miles) and other long-range enemy fires.

The lead US Air Force project is its air-launched rapid-response weapon (ARRW: AGM-183), which uses a small hypersonic body carried into low earth orbit by a much larger rocket. It glides on top of the atmosphere. It has demonstrated an ability to broadcast radio at hypersonic speeds. AGM-183 leverages DARPA research; it is expected to fly at an average of Mach 6.5 to Mach 8 for about 1,000 nautical miles. Its first free flight – in April 2021 – failed but the programme continues. A B-52 can carry four ARRWs. As of 2022 the US Air Force hoped to integrate the technology incorporated in ARRW with that developed by DARPA for a new Hypersonic Attack Cruise Missile (HACM) programme to produce a smaller, significantly longer-ranged missile. Twenty or more could be carried by a B-52. DARPA has demonstrated sustained powered manoeuvre in the atmosphere in its Hypersonic Air-Breathing Weapon (HAWC) programme. There are probably other US programmes at earlier stages of development.

Notes

1. Hypersonic missiles have to fly high because they would encounter too much resistance in the thicker lower atmosphere, requiring too much power and getting far too hot.

2. Continuous rod warheads used a ring of connected rods – exploding outwards to form a ring pattern – to cut through the intended target. Blast warheads are designed to damage the target primarily through the shock waves caused by the weapon's detonation.

3. Open source reports on the testing and initial use of the Kinzhal missile vary. Operationally, it is believed to have been used in the Syrian Civil War and against targets in Ukraine.

4. The Indian BrahMos II is probably closely related, just as BrahMos I was a version of the Russian P-800 Oniks (SS-N-26) anti-ship missile. The Indians have credited BrahMos II with a speed of Mach 7.

4.3 TECHNOLOGICAL REVIEW

Author:
Richard Scott

THE NAVY AFTER NEXT

How New Technology will Transform the Royal Navy

The United Kingdom government's wide-ranging Integrated Review of Security, Defence, Development and Foreign Policy, published in March 2021, laid out a vision for Britain's role in the world over the next decade. It was followed the same month by a Defence Command Paper, *Defence in a competitive age*, which articulated the contribution of the Ministry of Defence and the armed forces to meeting the objectives of the Integrated Review.[1]

The Integrated Operating Concept, which had first been published the previous year, provided a broad template for the investments outlined in the Defence Command Paper.[2] It set out the continuum between 'operate' and 'warfight', called for greater versatility, flexibility and adaptability in delivering a range of tasks and provided the intellectual basis for a spending review settlement providing an additional £24bn (c. US$30bn) to defence over a four-year period.

Over the next decade, the Royal Navy (RN) budget will increase from £7bn in FY2021–22 to £8.7bn by FY2030–31 to accelerate a drive to be more lethal, more available and more sustainable. Much of this investment will be spent on the modernisation of 'hard power' capabilities in the form of new platforms and weapon systems. For example, the Defence Command Paper laid out an ambitious long-term shipbuilding programme, including new solid support ships, frigates, multi-role support vessels and a multi-role ocean surveillance vessel to protect critical undersea infrastructure. It additionally confirmed plans to radically re-shape the United Kingdom's amphibious forces under the Future Commando Force programme and portended the recapitalisation of RN mine counter-measures (MCM) capability through the introduction of a 'toolbox' of maritime autonomous systems.

But *Defence in a competitive age* also identified the need to invest 'in the agile, interconnected and data-driven capabilities of the future' in order to realise 'generational leaps in capability development' to outpace potential adversaries. 'The pace of technological change,' it added, 'will require us to constantly adapt, experiment and take risks, to preserve strategic advantage.'

NAVY TRANSFORMATION

This conclusion and the greater emphasis placed on the role of science, technology and experimentation as a means to foster innovation and mature game-

The Royal Navy aircraft carrier *Queen Elizabeth* and an *Astute* class attack submarine represent potent symbols of naval power in this July 2021 image. However, the process of constant change is also requiring the navy – alongside other leading fleets across the globe – constantly to experiment with and adapt to new technologies to maintain strategic advantage. *(Crown Copyright 2021)*

The future RN will be less defined by bespoke platforms and more focused on the agile delivery of capability. This is resulting in painful – and potentially risky – decisions to retire legacy systems. This May 2022 photograph shows the minehunter *Shoreham* leaving the Clyde Naval Base for the final time prior to planned decommissioning. *(Crown Copyright 2022)*

changing technologies, was aligned to and coherent with work already underway within the RN. Through its Navy Transformation initiative, the service had previously identified autonomy, Artificial Intelligence (AI)/Machine Learning and digital technologies as critical to an organisation seeking to transition from a force design developed in the industrial age to one that fully exploits the digital revolution of the information age. Attendant to this was the idea of an RN that will be less defined by bespoke platforms and more focused on the agile delivery of capability across a fleet that will be increasingly modular, disaggregated and forward-deployed.

Moreover, Navy Transformation was conceived as a change programme that went far beyond just re-imagining how future ships, submarines and aircraft could operate and interact. Rather, it was about a more fundamental shift in approach to technology, innovation and skills as the RN sought to identify new approaches to problem solving and understand how best to deliver and sustain operational advantage in the decades ahead. Implicit in this was a recognition that the service was confronted with a number of major challenges: a radically changed strategic setting characterised by renewed state-level competition and an increasing focus on operations in a below-conflict threshold 'grey zone'; technological change occurring at a pace that outstripped traditional design cycles and procurement models; and enduring pressures on human and financial resources.

The RN's senior leadership embraced Navy Transformation as a vehicle to promote and embed mind-set change from the top down, taking note of evidence from the private sector that any enterprise change initiative is only as effective as the education and culture that accompanies it. Furthermore, Navy Transformation would consider what sort of people a service increasingly reliant on technology would need, recognising that this would bring substantial changes with regard to knowledge and skillsets; the structures of core professions and specialisations; career management; and the need to increase the flexibility and mobility of personnel so as

to deliver greater ship availability on the front line.

The Navy Transformation narrative underpinned the Royal Navy's submission to the Integrated Review. In its wake, the various tenets of 'transformation' have effectively become enshrined within the RN's 'business process': that is not to say that their importance has diminished, but rather that the core principles of Navy Transformation are now very much ingrained in the way that the service thinks and acts about its development. The accelerated exploitation of innovation and technology are fundamental to this.

THE DEVELOP FUNCTION

The Develop Directorate within Navy Command Headquarters has the responsibility for the development of the RN's future warfighting capability – from both conceptual and operational perspectives – and functions as the through-life sponsor for all navy capabilities. That means it must argue for and implement investment cases to address capability shortfalls; ensure the effective prioritisation of resources to meet the navy's priorities; and make judgements on where to divest of 'legacy' platforms or capacity and/or accept a greater level of operational risk, in order to fund new or higher-priority capabilities.

To deliver its responsibilities, the Develop

Directorate is divided into two parts:

- **Strategic Force Development** is responsible for meeting the changing and future demands of the RN's operational commitments by developing a more agile and adaptable military capability.
- **Capability Sponsorship** delivers the capability portfolio by coordinating and unifying all capability development programme and project activity across Navy Command.

Through the development of future concepts, Develop also leads future thinking beyond these core responsibilities. For example, it leads Navy Command Headquarters' strategic and maritime force development activity, hosts the NavyX team (which serves as an 'accelerator' for innovation across the naval service) and manages collaboration with allies on international capability.

In the last-mentioned case, the Royal Navy has established a partnership with the US Office of Naval Research to establish the UK-based London Tech Bridge (LTB). Opened in June 2022, the LTB is intended to foster dialogue, encourage joint investment and cooperative development between the two navies and explore innovation and technology in key focus areas such as artificial intelligence, autonomous systems, directed energy, green energy and advanced manufacturing.

The Develop Directorate also looks to capture science and technology outputs from the Defence Science and Technology Laboratory's (Dstl's) research programme so as to understand their relevance to solving operational problems and addressing capability shortfalls. Dstl operational analysis also helps the Royal Navy think about the construct of the navy after next and how the service delivers specific capability sets in an operating environment where a number of strategic challenges – including renewed state-level competition, ageing platforms, climate change, technology proliferation, affordability and demographics – are all major drivers for change.

What is emerging from these various strands is a top-level blueprint for a future fleet that will become more distributed in its force structures and operating methods so as to deliver a new Maritime Operating Concept (MarOpC). According to Rear Admiral James Parkin CBE, Director Develop in Navy Command Headquarters, the MarOpC is '… the intellectual framework in which we will define the Royal Navy's part in the Integrated Operating Concept [and] describes how we will operate in the future to meet the challenges of the 21st Century, where we find ourselves operating in a state of constant competition'.

He continued: 'My responsibility as Director Develop is not to look after today's navy, but it is to take account of tomorrow's navy by building the navy after next. This is what the Maritime Operating Concept is designed to lay down the groundwork for: to ensure that whenever we build, whenever we acquire, whenever we purchase, or whenever we operate – the equipment, the platforms or the capabilities that we're proud to fly the White Ensign from – it is all done against a consistent framework. It determines how we use those forces and what we need to think about when we first start running concept and assessment phases.'

The RN's high-level thinking distils into four operating tenets: protect; engage; constrain; and warfighting. These effectively translate into a set of design principles around which future investments will be considered.

At the same time, there is an understanding that the RN will be confronted with some difficult choices as it decides how and where to divest of existing assets to fund new capabilities to ensure the right shape, right size and right balance of maritime forces required for today and tomorrow. 'This will not be easy', said Rear Admiral Parkin. 'We need to repurpose financial and human resource towards future priorities and these priorities …will present uncomfortable choices to the more traditionally minded.'

ROYAL NAVY FORCE DESIGN

The RN's shipbuilding plan out to the early 2030s is now relatively mature. While there is a recognition that un-crewed/autonomous systems will, over time, have a greater role to play, the fleet composition will remain largely platform-focused. However, looking beyond 2035, the Develop Directorate sees the potential for a very different force design. The concept already promulgated to industry at a high level talks of a distributed 'protean' force adopting a 'system of systems' approach.

What does this mean? Distributed, or disaggregated, signals a shift away from a 'platform-centric' fleet to one that will be more widely dispersed and 'network-centric'. And by 'protean', the RN is describing a capability to constantly change and shift form and so be intrinsically adaptable and interchangeable across many different roles. This marks a move from highly bespoke ship classes optimised for a specific role to more modular, utilitarian platforms able to configure according to task.

The 'system of systems' approach seeks to capitalise on this new model. It breaks the link between platforms and capabilities, whilst also increasing the scope for rapid capability development and technology insertion. This means that whereas sensors, deciders, effectors and enablers have all historically been embedded on a single platform, they may now be split across a number of interconnected platforms, either crewed or un-crewed.

A number of advantages are postulated from this approach: increased lethality through the proliferation and disaggregation of sensors and effectors; greater availability, resilience and survivability by reducing single points of vulnerability; and greater utility and increased persistence of effect through a greater mass spread more widely.

The Type 83 Future Air Defence System – projected as the replacement for the Type 45 destroyer and its Sea Viper anti-air guided weapon system from the late 2030s – has been identified as the first major opportunity to realise such an approach. It is therefore possible that this future capability will not be vested in a single large ship, but split across a number of different platforms and sensor nodes. Similarly, the RN's future vision of undersea warfare – given the name Project Atlantis – has conceived of a Maritime Underwater Future Capability that employs a mix of crewed next-generation nuclear-powered submarines and autonomous offboard systems. As such, it is envisaged that

The Develop Directorate within Navy Command Headquarters has the responsibility for the development of the RN's future warfighting capability, represented here by a graphic of the forthcoming Type 26 'City' class frigate. *(BAE Systems)*

autonomous underwater systems will be a key component of future underwater and covert operations. Early work is underway to develop concepts of operation for autonomous underwater vehicles (AUVs) and to further understand how remote and un-crewed underwater systems can interoperate with crewed platforms.

Delivering such a transformative vision hinges on the embrace of innovative thinking and the exploitation of disruptive technologies, such as payload modularity, advanced autonomy and Artificial Intelligence/Machine Learning. Increased digitisation and 'digitalisation' across the force is another critical enabler: a new Naval Strike Network is foreseen as the digital infrastructure within maritime combat systems that will enable maritime forces to 'plug and play' with fully integrated and connected un-crewed force elements.

Making the move to a 'system of systems' will not occur overnight. Moreover, there is no desire to throw away billions of pounds of prior investment in ships and systems. Instead, the RN is adopting a long-term strategy based around what it terms 'wise pivots': that means extracting maximum value from current assets and then making carefully judged investments over time. It also means divesting obsolete capabilities and taking quantified risk.

The Develop Directorate will serve as an arbiter on the balance of investment, identifying where timely investments may unlock downstream savings and/or offer enhanced capability and also judging where other capabilities can be prudently downgraded, gapped or dispensed with altogether. Dstl will provide evidence to inform these recommendations and ensure that choices are made at the right point in the lifecycle of a particular system or capability.

The recapitalisation of the Royal Navy's MCM capability offers an early example of the 'wise pivot' in practice. Over the course of the next decade, the service's existing *Sandown* class and 'Hunt' class MCM vessels will be progressively replaced by a new Mine Hunting Capability (MHC) based on maritime autonomous systems. Although still in its Assessment Phase, the MHC programme has evolved an incremental procurement strategy that breaks the programme into a series of stand-alone capabilities: initial capability insertion/operational exploitation – known as MHC Block 1 – is being delivered in parallel with continuing evaluations of technology and concepts. The remaining *Sandown* class minehunters will be retired by 2025 as deliv-

The Type 45 destroyer *Duncan* pictured escorting shipping in the Gulf in 2019. It is possible that her eventual replacement – the planned Type 83 Future Air Defence System – might adopt a radically different design approach, splitting capability across a number of distributed platforms and sensor nodes. (*Crown Copyright 2019*)

The recapitalisation of the Royal Navy's Mine Hunting Capability (MHC) offers an early example of the move to a 'systems of systems' approach. This graphic shows Atlas Elektronik UK's MHC autonomous underwater vehicle system, which is based on Seacat AUVs fitted with the latest high-resolution Vision Synthetic Aperture Sonar. Three such systems – comprising nine vehicles in total – were contracted in April 2022 as an early component of the MHC Block 1 renewal programme. (*Atlas Elektronik UK*)

eries of MHC Block 1 systems are made. An investment decision point for MHC Block 2 – representing the main part of the MCM recapitalisation – is planned for 2024–5: the intention is that this will allow the remaining six 'Hunt' class vessels to leave service between 2029 and 2031.

ENCOURAGING INNOVATION

Building a future fleet that can meet the ambitions laid out in the MarOpC demands that the RN seizes on opportunities for innovation, as well as nurturing game-changing technologies that will provide the service with a decisive edge in any future crisis or conflict. Part of this is building up closer and more transparent relationships with industry to get early insights on novel concepts and disruptive technologies – not just large prime contractors, but also smaller start-ups, software labs and academia.

Dstl, as an executive agency of the Ministry of Defence, has a critical role to play. As well as developing research and concepts and managing a broad science and technology portfolio, it also brings deep technical expertise to support investment judgements aligned to key themes of lethality, modularity, autonomy and digital.

In parallel, the RN has sought to grow its own maritime innovation 'ecosystem' as a means to catalyse change. Back in 2019 the service initiated an activity known as NEMESIS to bring together a clutch of 'accelerators' charged with focusing on technology and innovation in specific areas. These comprised:

■ **NavyX** as an experimental hub for autonomy.
■ **DARE** as a hub for discovery, assessment and rapid technology exploitation.

■ **MarWorks**, as a technology accelerator focused on agile command-and-control networks.
■ **NELSON**, as an in-house app store/software factory.
■ **The Office of the Chief Technology Officer (OCTO)** to explore and potentially exploit disruptive technologies and approaches.

Over time, the operating model has changed and evolved. NEMESIS has been retired as a name and original 'vision' and NavyX has now been re-launched as the RN's 'innovation engine'. As such, it now embraces the majority of the initial elements of NEMESIS, including DARE (which includes the RN Defence Ideas Platform 'Brainwave' as part of the NavyX Discovery Team). MarWorks and NELSON, meanwhile, have both transitioned to come under the Ministry of Defence's Chief Digital Information Officer organisation. OCTO remains a standalone entity, with a brief to rapidly identify, assess and, where appropriate, adopt disruptive technologies, skillsets, doctrines and working practices.

As the RN's innovation hub, NavyX employs 'agile' enterprise models borrowed from tech start-ups, with multiple concepts and innovations taken forward for rapid experimentation and iteration. The objective is to prove disruptive solutions and then speed up their introduction to the fleet.

EXPLORING TOMORROW'S TECHNOLOGIES

It would be impossible to detail the broad span of technologies being considered by Navy Command for the fleet post-2035, but a number of themes stand out. The first of these is the role that will be increasingly played by autonomy and autonomous systems.

The wider introduction and exploitation of autonomous systems is seen to offer several benefits to the RN front line. For example, autonomous off-board systems may increase the potential of existing platforms by extending specific weapons and sensor capabilities at much lower cost than crewed platforms. Furthermore, the use of un-crewed systems should significantly reduce risks to human life in 'dull, dirty and dangerous' tasks, whilst delivering significant efficiency and affordability gains by increasing mass and extending the navy's range, reach, persistence and depth of effect.

The introduction of autonomous vehicles and technologies is already manifesting in the under-water domain, most notably in the fields of MCM,

'NavyX' has been re-launched as the RN's 'innovation engine', expanding from its original role as an experimental hub for autonomy to prove a broad range of disruptive solutions, and then speed up their introduction to the fleet. One line of work has been examining whether autonomous rigid inflatable boats – a BAE Systems P950 prototype is seen here – can be used to deliver force protection and ISR. *(Crown Copyright 2017)*

hydrography and oceanography. In these cases, the RN has been able to leverage from unmanned underwater vehicle developments in the commercial and scientific domains.

Work is now being taken forward by the Develop Directorate, Dstl and NavyX to understand, mature and demonstrate the applicability of autonomous systems to other more complex and challenging mission areas. These include, amongst others, force protection, logistics resupply, electronic warfare, anti-submarine warfare (ASW) and intelligence, surveillance and reconnaissance (ISR).

In the above-water domain, Dstl's Maritime Autonomy Surface Testbed (MAST) programme has – over the last eight years – sought to explore un-crewed surface vessel (USV) technologies, tactics and applications for the RN. A first tranche of MAST trials and experimentation, using a modified Bladerunner high-speed race boat, sought to de-risk high levels of functional autonomy and safety of navigation in compliance with COLREGs (Convention on the International Regulations for Preventing Collisions at Sea) to investigate the concept of an autonomous high-speed vessel able to safely navigate, in cluttered and crowded waterspace, into close proximity of other high speed surface targets and then execute manoeuvres against these moving targets.

A purpose-built 12.7m aluminium demonstrator vessel, known as MAST-13, was handed over to Dstl in 2019 to support a second tranche of MAST experimentation. Built by L3Harris, MAST-13 serves as an operational demonstrator to enable the RN and Royal Marines to evaluate USV sensors and novel algorithms.

NavyX has subsequently acquired its own surface autonomy testbed, known as MADFOX (Maritime Autonomy Demonstrator For Operational eXperimentation), to support its own test and demonstration cases and concepts of operation. It also provides a platform on which to test new technologies. Built by L3Harris to essentially the same design as MAST-13, the MADFOX craft is being used by NavyX to explore operating and operational issues such as safety, regulatory compliance, mission profiles/payloads and USV integration in the wider fleet.

The NavyX programme has also taken delivery of an Autonomous Pacific 24 (APAC24) rigid inflatable boat from BAE Systems to support operational experimentation. An adaptation of the standard

Autonomous vehicles – on, above and below the water – are seen as being a critical part of the Royal Navy's future. A purpose-built 12.7m aluminium demonstrator vessel, known as MAST-13, was handed over to Dstl in 2019 to support a second tranche of trials into maritime autonomy. NavyX's MADFOX (Maritime Autonomy Demonstrator For Operational eXperimentation) utilises essentially the same design. *(Crown Copyright 2017)*

7.5m Pacific 24 Mk 4 sea boat deployed across the RN surface fleet, the APAC24 is being used to explore how a USV based on a standard sea boat could deliver force protection and ISR.

In the undersea domain, work is proceeding with Plymouth-based MSubs to evaluate the potential for a 'weaponised' extra-large un-crewed underwater vehicle (XLUUV) to function as a low-cost force multiplier that could enhance the reach and range of crewed platforms and support the continued drive to maintain and develop operational advantage in the North Atlantic. The 9m submersible S201 is serving as an XLUUV demonstrator under a Defence and Security Accelerator initiative: trials and experimentation work performed to date has included trials of a thin-line towed array sonar to demonstrate the ability of the XLUUV vehicle to deploy an ASW sensor payload.

Perhaps the most ambitious autonomy initiative being pursued by the RN is the Future Maritime Aviation Force (FMAF), which is exploring the transition of a number of aviation roles – ISR, communications, lift and strike – from crewed to un-crewed air platforms. Being led by the Develop Directorate, FMAF is seen as a means to grow mass, increase persistence, extend range and build in greater flexi-

bility and resilience. Concept development work underpinning FMAF has identified a number of roles where un-crewed aviation could augment or potentially replace crewed aircraft, notably airborne early warning (AEW)/persistent wide-area surveillance; threat simulation and training; and maritime intra-theatre lift. As well as supporting fleet operations, there is a desire that UASs should also serve the Future Commando Force.

A number of capability-based FMAF elements have been scoped. For example, Proteus is considering a medium rotary-wing un-crewed air system (UAS) that can operate from the smaller flight decks of frigates and destroyers; Vixen is focused on larger fixed-wing UAS solutions that could provide AEW/wide-area surveillance and potentially augment strike; while Vampire is exploring lightweight, fixed-wing carrier-borne UAS systems which could potentially support target training among other tasks. Demonstration and experimentation of potential FMAF components is already taking tangible form. For example, QinetiQ was in 2022 awarded a four-year Vampire Phase 1 contract under which it will provide Banshee Jet 80+ targets to help RN aircraft carriers train for real-world scenarios. In addition, the contract will enable the RN to understand and demonstrate the wider concepts of operations for small, attritable UAS to deliver capabilities in areas such as ISR and stand-in jamming.[3]

A QinetiQ Banshee Jet 80+ drone is launched from the deck of *Prince of Wales*. A four-year Vampire Phase 1 contract will provide these un-crewed targets to assist Royal Navy training. More broadly, the Royal Navy is exploring a number of autonomous systems as part of the Future Maritime Aviation Force. *(Crown Copyright 2021)*

Another initiative with potential relevance to FMAF is the Heavy Lift Challenge. A collaboration between OCTO, 700X Naval Air Squadron and Defence Equipment and Support's Future Capability Group, the Heavy Lift Challenge aims to increase the number of un-crewed aircraft systems available on the market, at a rapid pace and so enable the RN to exploit autonomous systems to deliver heavy payloads in a range of environments. Trials have been undertaken using the Malloy Aeronautics T-600 quadcopter and Windracers Autonomous Systems' Ultra drone.

Engineering the integration of autonomous systems within a wider command infrastructure is recognised to be a major challenge: seamless and efficient integration into warship command and control systems is regarded as a prerequisite to the wider employment of autonomous systems on the front line. Dstl's Maritime Autonomous Platform Exploitation (MAPLE) information framework is seen as a key enabler in this regard. Iteratively developed by Dstl and a QinetiQ-led industry team to facilitate the integration of multiple unmanned systems into a single command information environment, MAPLE is planned to be used as the autonomy interface within the Naval Strike Network.

ARTIFICIAL INTELLIGENCE

The RN has also identified the exploitation of AI and wider human-machine teaming, as a key science and technology thrust. This reflects a view that the accelerating pace of warfare and the ever-greater volumes of data available to command teams, threatens to overwhelm the cognitive capacity of human operators and tacticians.

Dstl has been looking at how AI and Machine Learning algorithms can be used to support operators in the maritime environment. Tasks involving repetitive and manually intensive training are seen as priority candidates for automation because algorithms should be more robust and improve faster, than a human. AI also has the advantage that it does not become fatigued or distracted over the course of a watch.

However, it is recognised that the implementation of AI-based techniques brings with it a number of uncertainties and risks, particularly with regard to the role of and interactions with human operators. The organisation and activity occurring within a command environment constitutes a dynamic and highly complex socio-technical system encompassing hierarchical and interacting groups of humans and machines. The big challenge is to demonstrate that AI software running on high-speed computers can deliver the same fidelity of analysis as a human operator in a manner that is explainable and transparent; in essence, there is a need to 'trust' the machine so that the command can be confident that decisions or recommendations comply with prevalent engagement doctrine.

Prototype AI-based tactical decision aids have

The Royal Navy is looking to exploit autonomous systems to deliver heavy payloads in a range of environments. Trials have been undertaken using Malloy Aeronautics' quad copters (pictured here), as well as Windracers Autonomous Systems' Ultra drone, as part of a Heavy Lift Challenge. *(Crown Copyright 2021)*

The operations room aboard *Queen Elizabeth*. Future command decisions will be increasingly assisted by artificial intelligence applications, which have already been the subject of operational experimentation at sea on Royal Navy ships. *(Crown Copyright 2018)*

already been the subject of operational experimentation at sea on RN ships. One example is Roke's STARTLE application, which has been designed to mimic the mammalian-conditioned 'flight or fight' fear response. Embodying fast Machine Learning techniques that trigger the threat analyser agent to investigate potential threats, it is designed to help ease the load on operators monitoring the air picture in the operations room by providing real-time recommendations and alerts. As well as increasing the speed of detection and evaluation of threats, it also presents the operator with the reasoning behind each threat assessment.

Another AI which has been tested at sea is CGI's System Coordinating Integrated Effect Assignment (SYCOIEA) decision aid. SYCOIEA performs automated platform and force threat evaluation and weapon assignment, providing recommendations to the command team to aid the prioritisation and allo-

cation of defensive assets – both hard-kill and soft-kill – and accelerate and optimise the detect-to-engage process. As with STARTLE, all of the decisions made in SYCOIEA are fully explainable which allows operators to build confidence in the system.

Looking to the future and taking a more radical approach to the exploitation of AI, in 2019 Dstl launched the Intelligent Ship project as a first concerted attempt to engineer a 'system of systems', where automation and AI are more closely integrated and teamed with humans to enable more timely and better informed planning and decision-making. Research and experimentation activity led by Dstl in conjunction with partners from industry, small/medium enterprises and academia has

provided early insights into the opportunities arising from improved human machine integration.

The precept of the Intelligent Ship activity has been to demonstrate ways of bringing together multiple AI applications in all key capability areas so as to make collective decisions, with and without human operator judgement. Phase 2 of the project, which completed in March 2022, saw ten different AI applications developed and integrated within a synthetic environment known as the Intelligent Ship Artificial Intelligence Network (ISAIN). Example AIs funded under Phase 2 included an intelligent system for vessel power and propulsion machinery control; a tool to support decision-making in in damage control/firefighting situations; and a prototype AI agent to assist decision-making during pre-mission preparation, mission execution and post-mission analysis.

The selected AI agents were integrated into ISAIN and hosted in Dstl's Command Lab synthetic test environment (emulating a typical warship operations room). Four evaluation events were undertaken, with capability progressively built up. Various operational scenarios – played out in a series of 'vignettes' – were designed to exercise interactions between the different agents.

Intelligent Ship research and experimentation activity completed to date has confirmed the promise of improved human-machine integration in complex command environments. It remains the case, however, that more work is required to mature AI-enabled technologies and techniques, to engineer their transition and implementation to operational settings and to better understand human factor impacts.

MODULARITY

A long-standing concern within the RN has been the time taken to deliver new ships, as well as the costs and constraints attendant to adaptation once in service. Traditional naval architecture and system engineering approaches tend to tightly bind the platform and combat system together, which means that designs are inherently unreceptive to change.

To overcome this tyranny, the RN is studying how it can move towards more capability-agnostic platform designs and at the same time make capability easier to deploy and interchange. Both the Type 26 and Type 31 frigates will deliver a level of modularity, but there is a desire to go further in order to afford commanders a more agile and reconfigurable fleet.

OCTO's concept of a Navy Persistent Operational Deployment System (NavyPODS) is an embodiment of this thinking. Now in the early prototyping stage, the NavyPODS programme aims to develop a range of platform-agnostic, deployable mission modules that are based on an ISO-equivalent shipping container. Each will host a system payload or payload suite that can contribute towards a specific capability. The RN intends that NavyPODS modules should be applicable to platforms across the fleet, as well as Future Commando Force elements ashore. One major advantage claimed for NavyPODS is the avoidance of expensive and time-consuming ship modifications. The decoupling of 'platform' and 'payload' should also facilitate the faster introduction and updating of equipment and enable a new and more efficient way to deliver mission-specific enhancements: for example, it would be possible to pre-position or air freight alternative NavyPODS modules to allow a ship to reconfigure and re-role in-theatre.

OCTO is testing the 'plug and play' NavyPODS concept through the pilot acquisition of a small number of military-specification container modules outfitted with exemplar mission suites/payloads representative of what could be employed in service. These payloads include 'reachback' communications for the control of autonomous systems, a future aviation module and a 'factory in the box' additive manufacturing facility.[4]

LETHALITY

Another key objective regularly articulated by the Naval Staff is to increase the fleet's lethality. This is in part a consequence of a more challenging security environment, but also reflects a long-term under-investment in key offensive capabilities: the imminent retirement of the Harpoon Block 1C surface-to-surface guided weapon without an immediate replacement is a clear case in point.

The Future Cruise/Anti-Surface Weapon (FCASW) programme is intended to deliver a replacement for both Harpoon and the air-launched Storm Shadow deep strike weapon c. 2030. Both supersonic and subsonic missile developments are currently in the frame for FCASW.

Beyond FCASW, consideration is already being given to a follow-on hypersonic (Mach 5+) strike weapon. Hypersonic weapons are particularly hard to defend against because of their high speed and the fact that they can manoeuvre along their trajectory. Also, they operate in a different region of the atmosphere, flying much higher than slower subsonic missiles but far lower than intercontinental ballistic missiles.

While the UK currently has no programme of

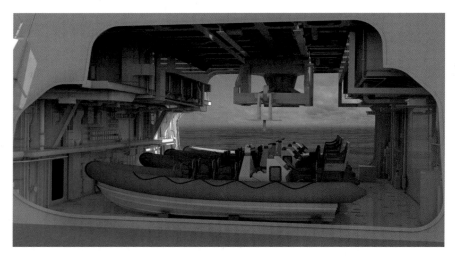

Both the Type 26 (pictured) and Type 31 frigates will deliver a level of modularity through mission bays and other design features. The Royal Navy wants to exploit and expand this capacity through introduction of a Navy Persistent Operational Deployment System (NavyPODS); a range of platform-agnostic, deployable mission modules that are based on an ISO-equivalent shipping container. *(BAE Systems/Crown Copyright)*

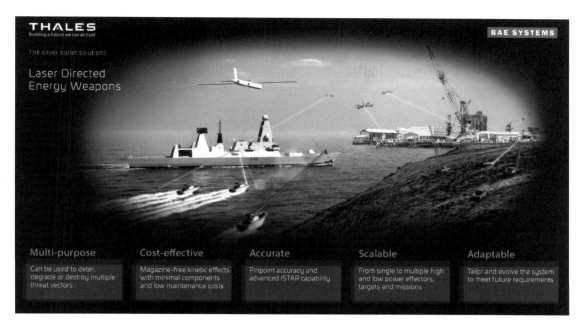

THALES
Building a future we can all trust

The silver bullet solution?

Laser Directed
Energy Weapons

BAE SYSTEMS

Multi-purpose
Can be used to deter, degrade or destroy multiple threat vectors

Cost-effective
Magazine-free kinetic effects with minimal components and low maintenance costs

Accurate
Pinpoint accuracy and advanced ISTAR capability

Scalable
From single to multiple high and low power effectors, targets and missions

Adaptable
Tailor and evolve the system to meet future requirements

A graphic by BAE Systems and Thales outlining some of the advantages of laser directed-energy weapons. An industry team led by Thales had been contracted to develop and deliver a maritime laser directed-energy weapon for at-sea testing on a Royal Navy warship under Project Tracey. *(Thales/BAE Systems)*

record for a hypersonic missile, it is already engaged in work to better understand the capabilities of this class of weapon. One possibility is a co-development programme with Australia and the United States building on research being performed under the umbrella of the tri-nation AUKUS security pact: this research activity is also examining counter-hypersonic technologies that could be applicable to a Future Air Defence System.

The other novel weapon technology attracting keen interest from the RN is directed energy and specifically high-energy lasers. Laser weapons are attractive to navies for a number of reasons; a relatively low cost per shot; the very fast time taken to engage and re-engage; and a large and renewable 'deep' magazine free of the hazards and logistics associated with conventional ordnance. There is also an inherent attraction to a weapon that has the ability to deliver tuneable/scalable effects with high precision, so minimising collateral effects. However, the introduction of such weapons also presents a number of challenges with regard to its operation from and integration in, naval platforms. These include amalgamation with ship power and electrical architectures; the provision of sufficient cooling capacity; system packaging to allow for retrofit within the confines of existing platforms; ruggedisation to deal with the effects of sea spray, humidity, sonic shock and efflux; combat systems integration; and measures to ensure safety/avoid fratricide.

For the time being, the power levels achievable by current-generation laser weapons means that their utility is restricted to short-range engagements against a specific set of targets, such as small boats, UASs and ISR sensors. As such they provide a cost-efficient complement to other self-defence systems, allowing more expensive kinetic effectors to be conserved for use against more stressing air and surface threats.

In September 2021 it was announced that an industry team led by Thales had been contracted to develop and deliver a maritime laser directed-energy weapon for at-sea testing on an RN warship under Project Tracey. The demonstrator system will be integrated into a Type 23 frigate for user experimentation trials starting in 2023, with the system to be integrated into the ship's combat system for the duration of testing. Experiments will explore the full decision-making process for engaging threats and

include detecting, tracking, engaging and countering UAS as well as sea targets: the design requirements are focused on providing user experience and are designed to allow the RN to de-risk operation of high-energy lasers in realistic environments. Parallel work is underway to demonstrate a higher power laser directed-energy weapon under the umbrella of Project Dragonfire. This programme, led by MBDA UK, is exploring innovative high-energy laser technical approaches developed in the UK under MoD and industry funding. Trials and experimentation activity will inform future military requirements and de-risk both technology and capability understanding.

CONCLUSION

Novel thinking and disruptive technology is central to the RN's future vision and meeting the aims laid out in the MarOpC. The challenge for the service – together with other parts of the MoD and the wider maritime enterprise – is to identify, mature and exploit novel systems and techniques such that they can be brought into service in an accelerated timeframe. Achieving this aim requires new commercial and operating models to enable industry to deliver better, faster and cheaper and bridge the so-called 'valley of death' that has in the past stymied the early adoption of innovative systems and concepts. However, it also carries a degree of risk as planners make finely-balanced judgements on what equipment or capabilities should be retired to generate financial 'headroom' for investment in tomorrow's fleet.

Notes

1. See further *Global Britain in a competitive age: The Integrated Review of Security, Defence, Development and Foreign Policy, Cm. 403* and *Defence in a competitive age. Cm. 411,* both (London: HMSO, 2021) and accessible via a simple Internet search.

2. See the *Integrated Operating Concept* (London: Ministry of Defence, 2020). An updated version, dated August 2021, is available by searching the Internet. The Integrated Operating Concept is described as setting out a new

framework approach to the utility of armed force in an era of strategic competition and an evolving character of warfare.

3. See Chapter 4.1 for more details on Projects Vampire and Vixen.

4. The term 'reachback' is used in the US Department of Defense as the process of obtaining products, services, applications, forces, equipment, or material from organisations that are not forward deployed.

Contributors

James Bosbotinis: Dr James Bosbotinis is a freelance specialist in defence and international affairs. He has particular expertise in the study of contemporary maritime strategy, assessing naval and air force developments, geopolitical analysis, and generating understanding of the connections between maritime strategy and national policy. Dr Bosbotinis has extensive experience encompassing academic and policy-relevant research and analysis for a range of customers, including United Kingdom government bodies. He has written widely on issues including the development of British maritime strategy, maritime airpower, Russian maritime doctrine, naval and wider military modernisation, and China's evolving strategy. He is the Book Reviews Editor of *The Naval Review* and an Associate Member of the Corbett Centre for Maritime Policy Studies, King's College London.

Sidney E. Dean: An international affairs specialist by training, Sidney E. Dean is a freelance writer focussing on strategic studies, military technology and military history. He writes extensively for the publications of the Mittler Group and numerous other journals. He is founder and president of Transatlantic-Euro-American Multimedia LLC, and past editor of *Hampton Roads Military History Quarterly* and *Hampton Roads International Security Quarterly*. Having spent considerable time living in Europe and on both coasts of the United States, he currently makes his home in south-eastern Virginia.

Norman Friedman: Norman Friedman is one of the world's best-known naval analysts and historians and author of over forty books. He has written widely on issues of modern military interest, including an award-winning account of the Cold War, and with respect to warship development. Amongst recent works, *Winning a Future War: War Gaming and Victory in the Pacific War* – a description of the way that war gaming at the US Naval War College helped the US Navy prepare for the Pacific War – produced for the Naval History & Heritage Command stands out as a notable contribution to naval history. His latest book, *British Submarines in the Cold War Era*, is the

second part of a two-volume history of Royal Navy submarines that forms part of a wider series on British warship types. In June 2022, he was the recipient of the Anderson Medal for lifetime achievement from the Society for Nautical Research. The holder of a PhD in theoretical physics from Columbia, Dr Friedman is a regular guest commentator on television and lectures widely on professional defence issues. He resides with his wife in New York.

David Hobbs: David Hobbs is an author and naval historian with an international reputation. He has written over twenty books, the latest of which *The Fleet Air Arm and The War in Europe 1939 - 1945* was published by Seaforth in 2022. He has also written for several journals and magazines and in 2005 won the award for the Aerospace Journalist of the Year, Best Defence Submission, in Paris. He also won the essay prize awarded by the Navy League of Australia in 2008. He has lectured on naval subjects worldwide including on cruise ships and has been on radio and TV in several countries. He served in the Royal Navy for 33 years and retired with the rank of Commander. He is qualified as both a fixed and rotary wing pilot and his log book contains 2,300 hours with over 800 carrier deck landings, 150 of which were at night. For 8 years he was the Curator of the Fleet Air Arm Museum at Yeovilton.

Mrityunjoy Mazumdar: Mr Mazumdar, who studied applied physics & mechanical engineering, has been a regular contributor to *Seaforth World Naval Review* since its inception. His interests are the sea services of South and Southeast Asian countries, as well as the lesser known naval and air forces around the world. His words, pictures, and research have appeared in many naval and military aircraft publications including *Jane's Navy International*, IQPC's *Defence Industry Bulletin*, *Shephard Media*, *Ships of the World*, *Warship Technology* and *Air Forces Monthly* as well as the standard naval reference books. Having grown up in India and Nigeria, Mr Mazumdar lives in the 'wine country' north of San Francisco with his wife.

Richard Scott: Richard Scott is a UK-based analyst

and commentator who has specialised in coverage of naval operations and technology for over 25 years, with particular interests in the fields of naval aviation, guided weapons and electronic warfare. He has held a number of editorial positions with Jane's, including the editorship of *Jane's Navy International* magazine, and is currently group Consultant Editor – Naval. Mr Scott is also a regular contributor to other periodicals, including the *AOC Journal of Electromagnetic Dominance* and *Warship World*.

Guy Toremans: Guy Toremans is a Belgian-based, maritime freelance correspondent and a member of the Association of Belgian & Foreign Journalists, an association accredited by NATO and the UN. His reports, ship profiles and interviews are published in the English language naval magazines *Jane's Navy International*, *Naval Forces* and *Warships IFR*, as well as in the French *Marines & Forces Navales* and the Japanese *J-Ships*. Since 1990, he has regularly embarked on NATO, Asian, South African and Pacific-based warships, including aircraft carriers, destroyers, frigates, mine-countermeasures vessels and support ships.

Conrad Waters: A lawyer by training but banker by profession, Conrad Waters was educated at Liverpool University prior to being called to the bar at Gray's Inn in 1989. His interest in maritime affairs was stimulated by a long family history of officers in merchant navy service and he has written on historical and current naval affairs for over 35 years. This included six years producing the 'World Navies in Review' chapter of the influential annual *Warship* before assuming responsibility for *Seaforth World Naval Review* as founding editor. He has also edited *Navies in the 21st Century* – shortlisted for the 2017 Mountbatten Maritime Award – whilst his latest book – *British Town Class Cruisers* – was published at the end of 2019. He is currently close to completing work on a sequel, which will cover the subsequent *Fiji* class cruisers and their derivative designs. Conrad is married to Susan and has three children: Emma, Alexander and Imogen. He lives in Haslemere, Surrey.